From Violence
to Blessing

Dennis & Martha

May your insights
talents and vision
result in many
mimetic structures of
blessing.

Vern Neufeld Redekop

From Violence
to Blessing

How an Understanding
of Deep-Rooted Conflict
Can Open Paths
to Reconciliation

Foreword by Archbishop Desmond Tutu
Winner of the Nobel Peace Prize

NOVALIS

© 2002 Novalis, Saint Paul University, Ottawa, Canada

Cover design and layout: Christiane Lemire and Caroline Gagnon
Cover painting: Ellen Gabriel (detail from "Spirit Guide")

Business Office:
Novalis
49 Front Street East, 2nd Floor
Toronto, Ontario, Canada
M5E 1B3

Phone: 1-800-387-7164 or (416) 363-3303
Fax: 1-800-204-4140 or (416) 363-9409
E-mail: cservice@novalis.ca
www.novalis.ca

National Library of Canada Cataloguing in Publication

Redekop, Vernon Neufeld, 1949-
    From violence to blessing : how an understanding of deep-rooted conflict can open paths to reconciliation / Vern Neufeld Redekop.

Includes bibliographical references.
ISBN 2-89507-309-0

    1. Social conflict. 2. Conflict management. 3. Reconciliation. I. Title.

HM1121.R43 2002   303.6   C2002-904176-7

Printed in Canada.

We acknowledge the financial support of the Government of Canada through the Book Publishing Industry Development Program (BPIDP) for our publishing activities.

10 9 8 7 6 5 4 3 2 1   10 09 08 07 06 05 04 03 02

Contents

Dedicated to Gloria Neufeld Redekop,
my partner in life, who,
by being who she is,
has taught me existentially
what life, love and reconciliation
are all about.

Acknowledgments

This book is the culmination of eleven years of study, training and program development. My doctoral program overlapped with my becoming President of the Canadian Institute for Conflict Resolution (CICR) and later Director, Program Development in Conflict Studies at Saint Paul University, Ottawa. While I was at CICR, hundreds of people participated in over 60 two-day seminars. The seminars, which were interactive and generative, helped to refine many of the ideas presented here. The position at Saint Paul University allowed time for me to complete this work.

Core insights were based on research I did for my doctoral program. Professor John van den Hengel gave excellent counsel for my dissertation and modelled a laudable combination of intellectual depth, respect and enthusiasm for ideas. As a friend and mentor he has contributed significantly to the depth and rigour of my academic work. Likewise, professors Ken Melchin, Jean-Marc Larouche, André Beauregard, Hubert Doucet and Achiel Peelman stimulated my intellectual growth and development. René Girard's work has been pivotal to my own theoretical development, as will become clear in the text; I am indebted to him for both his intellectual contribution and his personal warmth and encouragement.

Those who read portions of the book and made helpful comments include Jean Cormier, Mari-ève Marchand, Brian McQuinn, Mark Williams, Mark Jowett, Derek Simon and Laura Stovel. John van den Hengel made helpful comments on Chapter 9 concerning hermeneutical methodology. Richard Batsinduka, Tag Elkhazin, Abdi Hersi, Vesna Dasović Marković, Wahida Chishti Valiante, and Janet McGrath added anecdotes and observations to the text. Shirley Paré not only reviewed a number of chapters but added a significant reflection on gender issues in the military, in Chapter 7, based on her experience.

To Ellen Gabriel of *Kanehsatà:ke* I am grateful for her review of Chapter 10, on the Oka/*Kanehsatà:ke* Crisis, and for her detailed suggestions. She also agreed to the use of her artwork on the cover. Jessica Hill and Chief Joe Norton of *Kahnawà:ke* also reviewed Chapter 10. Likewise, Padré David Kettle of the Canadian Military reviewed this chapter in the light of his experience and helped me to balance the framing of events. Ian McLeod, a journalist who lived through the Crisis, also read and verified the enclosed account.

Rebecca Adams played a vital role in developing some of the new concepts presented in the book. Her presentation on "loving mimesis" at the Colloquium on Violence and Religion at Loyola University in 1994 was an epiphany for me. Ongoing dialogue with her as a fellow Girardian scholar working on positive and creative dimensions of mimetic theory has helped me discover and clarify such concepts as mimetic structures of violence, entrenchment and blessing. I am grateful that she added a vignette in Chapter 12, telling the story of how she arrived at her original insights.

The staff at Novalis has been truly outstanding. Commissioning Editor Kevin Burns had a knack for providing feedback on what really "worked" in the book. Early on, he caught the vision for what the book was about. Ellen Shenk streamlined the text wonderfully and Managing Editor Anne Louise Mahoney attended to the many details of getting it right. Anne Chevalier and Christiane Lemire attended to the aesthetics of the book.

Christian Bellehumeur and Guillaume Theoret took my rough sketches and turned them into polished graphics.

My parents, Bill and Loreen Redekop, imparted to me a passion for peace as they modelled community action to create what I now call mimetic structures of blessing. They joined my children – Quinn, with his wife Sue, Natasha and Lisa – in enthusiastically cheering me on.

Gloria Neufeld Redekop has continued to share her life with me in a crucible that has allowed me to live the ideas presented. Her honest engagement with me has taken the Self–Other dialogue to incredible depths. She has provided a context in which mimetic desire, human identity needs and other concepts developed below have become part of everyday discourse. Finally, she has allowed me to share specific aspects of our life together in the pages below. For all these reasons I am especially grateful to her.

Foreword

Throughout my life I have come to know violence well. Not only in my native South Africa, where oppressive laws and brutal practices scarred generations, but also in Jerusalem, Addis Ababa, Biafra and Belfast I have felt the imminence of violence in the air. What Vern Neufeld Redekop describes in this book as violence I have known about in all its forms. Now he brings to the table of those wishing to diminish the power of violence in this world a conceptual framework that helps us name with greater precision the dynamics of hurtful actions, policies and impulses.

Nor am I a stranger to blessing as the result of reconciliation processes. "Blessing" as Redekop uses the word has a close family resemblance to the concept of *ubuntu,* which guided many of us through the taxing days of the Truth and Reconciliation Commission. *Ubuntu* speaks of the essence of being human. It includes qualities of generosity, hospitality, friendliness, caring and compassion. It expresses the fact that humanity is shared and that through our human connectedness we find our identities. People with *ubuntu* feel good about the well-being and success of others. There is a reciprocal mimetic quality to *ubuntu* in that the *ubuntu* of one is replicated in another, which in turn adds to the *ubuntu* of the first. There is a communal aspect to *ubuntu* in that it contributes to social good. When Redekop introduces the idea of a "mimetic structure of blessing infusing a relational system," he is in effect talking about the increase of *ubuntu* within a community. All this is to say that good theory helps us better understand and communicate key aspects of our own world view.

Particular aspects of this book resonate with the South African experience and thus help to explain the dynamics of the past. Naming the hegemonic structures, for instance, helps to draw out different dimensions of the apartheid regime. The mimetic and contagious nature of violence is corroborated by the way in which the violence of apartheid contaminated the culture of those systematically victimized, making them more violent. And on the constructive side, the framework for reconciliation gives a name to so many of those elements present within the Truth and Reconciliation Commission and hence provides a framework to make the lessons we learned more readily transferable to other contexts.

Anger, revenge, hatred and aggressive competitiveness can destroy *ubuntu.* These words show the link between emotions and violence. As I chaired the Truth and Reconciliation Commission of South Africa, the most painful and agonizing emotions were powerfully expressed as people talked of the effects of torture, rape and killing. To Redekop's credit, he does not shy away from the emotional dimensions of violence; in fact, the pages that follow help us to see the links at both the biological and experiential levels.

There is also recognition that none of us is immune to the same dynamics and structures that lie behind the worst violence we can imagine. But there is also an invitation to victims and perpetrators to join in the quest for a healing path, and an unfailing passion to search out the human worth of everyone. Anyone who cares about violence in this world should feel that this book is for them.

This book is not only about past and present realities; it also projects a new vision for what is possible in the future. In our troubled world, where deep-rooted conflicts translate into structures of violence in many places, *From Violence to Blessing* stimulates our imagination, so that we can begin to envisage a world in which people desire to free one another physically, intellectually, emotionally and spiritually.

Archbishop Desmond Tutu
Capetown, South Africa
September 2002

Introduction

Deep-rooted conflict has humankind in its grasp. The twentieth century has taught us the vocabulary of genocide, ethnic cleansing, command rape (ordering soldiers to rape women of a particular ethnic group), and nuclear annihilation. We recall images of massacres and refugees desperately seeking safety in the mountains or refugee camps in the next country. Our televisions have shown bombed-out cities, mass graves, funeral processions, and mourning—all with an ethnoconflict theme.

As the twenty-first century begins, September 11, 2001, is etched in our minds as an expression of conflict that touches people at the core of their beings.

However, inter-ethnic conflict and acts of terror are only the tip of the iceberg; identity-based conflict is expressed daily in marital conflict, sibling rivalry, corporate inhumanity, and technological warfare. At a less obvious level are the deep-rooted conflicts we carry in our memories—memories that allow us to depersonalize individuals or groups and wish them personalized "hells on earth." Our longing for our own wholeness makes us question why we have these feelings and what to do about this.

In 1983, pictures of thousands of starving Ethiopians gripped the world. Pop stars donated time and talent in recording "Tears Are Not Enough" to raise money for food aid. "Tears Are Not Enough" T-shirts were sold even in Thompson, Manitoba, north of the 54th parallel.

This was still the Cold War, and an Inter-Church Working Group on Disarmament Issues that I organized sent a goodwill package to Aldan, a Soviet city in Siberia, that included pictures and letters from school-children. The deputy mayor, a former military officer, who participated in this peace effort, spoke about how peaceniks and military folks all wanted peace—we just went about it in different ways.

Henry Rempel, a University of Manitoba economist and guest speaker at one of our peace events, pointed out that behind every mass starvation was a conflict that drove people to use food as a weapon. I decided that I wanted to learn about deep-rooted conflict—to understand the deliberate use of food deprivation to kill thousands of innocent children, women, and men.

I started a doctoral program in 1991 to do my homework and learn about deep-rooted conflict. I wanted to understand identity-based conflict at its core. I didn't anticipate then the events in Rwanda and Bosnia and Herzegovina and that I would develop close relationships with people whose lives were scarred by events in both countries. Nor did I know that I would see this devastation first-hand and train trainers who would work at conflict resolution in such places as Kigali and Butare,

Rwanda, and Mostar and Banya Luka, Bosnia and Herzegovina. Nor did I know that the theories I agonized for years to understand, develop, and present would play such a healing role.

In this book I speak with two voices. In the first voice I am the academic, the conflict and reconciliation theoretician.

In the second voice, set apart by a different typeface, I am simply a human being caught in the realities of conflict, violence, and reconciliation. I offer this second voice because, as I have learned to understand these theories, I have been better able to understand my own story, particularly the emotions I have experienced at different times.

Offering this second voice is important because much of deep-rooted conflict is about what happens within the human person. Each person's interior world, to borrow the concept of interiority from philosopher and Holocaust survivor Emmanuel Levinas, is filled with ideas, memories, passions, desires, and emotions. As political psychologist Demetrios Julius observes, there is a strong illogical side to what people do within conflict situations. As we follow the work of René Girard, we will note likewise that as we imitate desires of others, we are imitating our perceptions of their interiority. This second voice gives a glimpse into my own inner life, *a scary thought*, and also validates the theory, enhances understanding, and, most importantly, emphasizes that this is about real life. This is about responses to the conflicts that could destroy our lives and our worlds, as the lives and worlds of countless others have been destroyed.

I was fortunate to do my theoretical research at the time I was developing a series of two-day interactive seminars on community-based conflict resolution, deep-rooted conflict, reconciliation, and intervention. Hundreds of people from around the world participated in these seminars. The seminars validated the approach that I was developing and helped to generate new understandings that went into the seminars and, ultimately, this book.

Richard Batsinduka and Vesna Dasović Marković have played significant roles in developing and validating the ideas in this book. Richard came to see me in 1996, personally devastated by the loss of his family in the Rwandan genocide. As he took my seminars on deep-rooted conflict and reconciliation he corroborated the ideas in this book, showing their use in understanding the situation and in using that understanding for personal healing and reconciliation. (See Chapter 15 for his personal story of reconciliation with the man who killed his brother.) For Richard to say that the theory I presented helped him to understand and come to terms with that tragedy is a powerful witness to the truth of what I was discovering. Eventually, he worked on a community-based conflict resolution program in Rwanda that sent a group of potential trainers to Canada for training. At the end of the seminar on deep-rooted conflict, they stated that everything I had to say was really about Rwanda.

Vesna initially had no interest in getting involved in her native Bosnia and Herzegovina, where she had been a judge by profession. When the time was right, she initiated a program there and invited me to provide training in deep-rooted conflict and reconciliation. She found that the theories presented here helped her make sense of the ethnic cleansing and mass destruction of her country. This experience encouraged me to develop the ideas in this format.

Other voices will be introduced into the text. These are individuals who have chosen to share how these ideas have touched their own worlds. They are also friends who have read the manuscript in advance and have decided to tell some of their own stories.

I have found that good theory gives us the vocabulary and conceptual framework to understand our experiences. The word "theory" comes from the Greek words *thea* (a sight) and *horan* (to see). Putting these words together gave the Greeks *theoros* (spectator), *theorein* (to consider or look at), and *theoria* (a spectacle, a perception, or a thing perceived). A theory helps us to learn about a phenomenon, providing explanations and generating questions to help us discover new aspects of the phenomenon. For example, Einstein's theory of relativity helped to explain the nature of light and the equivalence of mass and energy. This helped scientists develop nuclear energy because the theory predicted that it should exist. Theory around deep-rooted conflict should help those caught up in conflicts understand their experience and help people longing for peace to discover new possibilities for its actualization.

Theory is good if it enables us to see new aspects of a given reality in a way that leads to insight, wisdom, and practical knowledge. Insight helps us understand why and how something is happening. Wisdom puts insight into perspective. Practical knowledge forms a foundation for action. Ultimately, my hope is that the ideas developed in this book will form the basis for understanding to promote healing and action to open up new possibilities for human relationships. That both Richard and Vesna were empowered to start programs of community-based conflict resolution in countries devastated by destruction resulting from deep-rooted conflict speaks to the possibility of developing new types of relational systems as a result of a process of reconciliation.

"Relational system" is a phrase I coined in response to the question: Where do deep-rooted conflicts take place? To answer this in a general sense, I developed the concept as follows: "relational" speaks of having interaction or mutual impact through time and "system" comes from Greek words meaning, literally, to stand together. A relational system creates a context—such as a family, a workplace, or a region—in which parties have to deal with one another. A relational system may change from being congenial to being contentious or it may begin as conflictual and end as reconciled. It may involve two people or large groups of people, two parties or many parties. A relational system may also be internal, since we may have internal conflicts between ourselves and our conscience, to borrow a concept from philosopher Paul Ricoeur.

In this book I use the terms "deep-rooted conflict" and "identity-based conflict" interchangeably. This comes from the defining work of John W. Burton, who first pointed out that deep-rooted conflict is about a threat to the satisfiers of identity needs. To understand deep-rooted conflict we need to understand identity needs and how we define our satisfiers of these needs.

Identity is very complex. Because we may identify with different groups, sorting out divided loyalties presents many possibilities for deep-rooted inner conflict. I write from experience. Just as we may have trouble as individuals in sorting out the primary groups to which we belong, identity groups struggle over who is in the group and who is not. An identity group is any group with a capacity to impart a sense of identity to its members, even though not all members of the group relate to it in a primary way. We cannot tell by looking at someone what group is primary for their own identity; it may be based on language, religion, gender, ethnicity, profession, sexual orientation, eating restrictions, values, life-styles, skin colour, or geography. Through time, various groups may play different roles in a person's life.

A sound methodology can help break a complex problem into simple, pro-found, and manageable parts. Methodology comes from the Greek words *meta* (after), *hodos* (a road or way), and *logia* (system, word, or speaking). It has the sense of systematically defining the way in which one is proceeding. Methodology is about asking questions in an orderly way.

I have been told repeatedly that individuals had a sense of what I was describing, but the theory I presented gave them words to articulate this hidden knowledge. Knowledge that we cannot quite define has been identified by philosopher Michael Polanyi as tacit knowledge. When knowledge is put into words, it can be shared, interpreted, and, perhaps, reinterpreted. Since our actions are based on our tacit knowledge, articulating the basis of our actions can help us become more deliberate about what we do. For example, when faced with a massacre of innocent non-combatants, many people have a strong urge to retaliate, to bomb the offending party, to impose sanctions, or otherwise harm those held responsible. This powerful urge can be interpreted as imitating scenes where we have seen violence met with violence. It can also be seen as a threat to our need for meaning and justice. Or it can be understood as tapping into a reservoir of emotion based on past victimization. Each of these ways of understanding this urge to kill is based on a theoretical perspective presented in this book.

Part 1 is organized around a certain flow of ideas coming from a series of questions. The first question is: What is deep-rooted conflict and how is it related to violence? Chapter 1 is about the *problématique* of deep-rooted conflict; as the French word indicates, it explores the issues and challenges of a given question and the implications for addressing a problem or issue as well as probing what is at stake in the situation. Chapter 1 also raises another question: How can we define deep-rooted conflict?

This leads to Chapter 2, which deals with human identity needs. This is a logical starting point, since John W. Burton, who first developed the notion of deep-rooted conflict, defined it in terms of a threat or threats to need satisfiers. This chapter asks the question: How do we, individually and collectively, define the satisfiers to our identity needs?

Chapter 3 introduces the concept of mimetic, or imitative, desire as developed by René Girard, a French thinker who has devoted more than 40 years to looking at the origins of violence. This concept shows that we define many aspects of our identity through an imitation of others. Chapter 4 examines other Girardian insights around scapegoating, surrogate victims and the human preoccupation with the creation of difference. This raises the question: How can we understand difference that becomes oppressive when one group dominates the other?

These chapters lay the groundwork for Chapter 5 to illuminate the concept of hegemonic structures in which one group gains the upper hand and dominates the lives of those subjected. Differentiation and the roles of ethnicity, race, and religion are topics discussed in Chapter 6, about ethnonationalism. This chapter looks at political realism, the dominant theoretical framework for understanding such conflicts through most of the last century, and highlights the literature in this field, calling into question some of the basic ideas entrenched in realism. This material on difference suggests that we need to look more deeply at the question: Why do conflicts become so intense?

Chapter 7 deals with the dynamics of the Self–Other relationship, drawing on both philosophical and psychological literature. It introduces the concept of onto-logical rift—a dehumanizing split between people—as a philosophic notion. Gender is also presented as an essential category of analysis. The chapter looks to the literature of political and social psychology for insights into the psychodynamics of victimization.

The final question is: How does all of this fit together? Chapter 8 addresses this with the introduction of the concept of mimetic, or imitative, structures of violence and its defensive side, mimetic structures of entrenchment. These first eight chapters function as a theoretical "dark night of the soul." They are meant to provide insights, concepts, and vocabulary to enter into some of the worst atrocities committed by human beings and to better understand interpersonal conflicts.

Part 2 uses the theory to understand an actual conflict. The conflict in question is the Oka/*Kanehsatà:ke* crisis of 1990, an event that shook Canadian society to its core. There are three steps to this development. The first step, in Chapter 9, shows how to methodologically begin analyzing such a conflict. The second is the narrative of the crisis in Chapter 10. The third step is the theoretical interpretation of the conflict in Chapter 11.

Part 3 introduces the concepts of blessing and reconciliation. Chapter 12 is about mimetic structures of blessing and Chapter 13 provides a framework for understanding the reconciliation of deep-rooted conflict. Chapter 14 places the discourse around deep-rooted conflict and reconciliation into a theological context and Chapter 15 explores some of the processes that can help the transformation from violence to blessing.

After I began writing this book, the world was shocked on September 11, 2001, by the unprecedented act of terrorism against the United States. It has been so significant that I felt compelled to add an epilogue on this attack and its aftermath.

Throughout the book, I will assume an open attitude toward truth and insight, finding it in many quarters. Part 1 has occasional references to biblical texts. From my graduate degree in biblical studies, I often find an interesting link of ideas or an illustration that makes the point and so I refer to these. René Girard, the primary theorist dealt with in Chapters 3 and 4, has also drawn on biblical material in addition to a vast amount of literary, anthropological, and psychological research. It is not until Chapter 14 that I slip into a theological mode. My hope is that I might integrate insights from the social sciences and humanities with theological truths.

Just a note regarding style: since I am committed to inclusive language, I have inserted words or letters in square brackets within quotes to include women as well as men.

Part 1

Violence

Chapter 1

Deep-Rooted Conflict

Deep-rooted conflicts plumb the depths of human emotion and produce incredibly inhumane actions, causing immense human misery. Since the Cold War ended, the world community has seen conflicts between peoples who, having lived side by side for generations, are suddenly participating in unbounded violence. The tools of violence have included burning houses, raping women, destroying historic cities, depriving people of food, "cleansing" regions of ethnocultural groups, and simply killing large numbers of people in a frenzy of mass murder. Helpful intervention is difficult, partly because the complexities of the conflicts make it almost impossible to understand what is really happening. This complexity is evident on the group level, which is the focus of this chapter, but it is also very much a part of interpersonal relationships.

In these conflicts, the distinctive identities of the antagonistic groups are based on kinship, language, race, religion, ethnicity, aboriginality, nationality, political affiliation, or class. Often these identities overlap, as in Northern Ireland, where religiously defined antagonists—"Catholics" and "Protestants"—have historical affiliations with Ireland and Great Britain, respectively, and are separated by class and local geography. They also perceive their kinship differently; various family names are associated with each group. Walker Connor observes that

> [d]espite some intermarriage, the family name remains a relatively reliable index to Irish heritage, as compared to English or Scottish.... One tragic manifestation of this phenomenon has been the tendency of militant Irishmen (described as Catholic) to be particularly aggressive toward Scottish units of the British forces...because of the preponderance of Scottish names among Northern Ireland's non-Irish population.[1]

Class, ethnic, and religious differences reinforce one another. However, as Vamik Volkan observes, minor differences become extremely important in times of stress.[2] Pierre L. van den Berghe asks the question: "How, then, can one establish ethnicity quickly and reliably and also keep cheats under control? What features will be chosen as *ethnic markers*?"[3] His answer illustrates the way groups distinguish between one another:

> First, one can pick a genetically transmitted phenotype, such as skin pigmentation, stature (as with the Tuzi [sic] of Rwanda and Burundi), hair texture, facial feature, or some such 'racial' characteristic.... Second, one can rely on a [hu]man-made ethnic uniform. Members of one's group are

identified by bodily mutilations and/or adornments carried as visible badges of group belonging. Third, the test can be behavioral. Ethnicity is determined by speech, demeanour, manners, esoteric lore, or some other proof of competence in a behavioral repertoire characteristic of the group.[4]

> In some contexts, the expression of these ethnic differences can develop very "violent" attributes towards the Other. In Uganda, Himas perceive themselves as superior to many other ethnic groups, especially the so-called "Bairu." Under normal circumstances, a Hima female cannot show her bare naked body to any Hima male. She cannot get undressed in the presence of a Hima baby boy. *But,* she can enjoy a fresh bath, naked, at a river, in the presence of an adult "Muiru" (singular form of "Bairu") male!!! In her mind, a "Muiru" man is like an "it," like any animal or any other being who cannot have any kind of judgment on her behaviour.
>
> – Richard Batsinduka

The sense of difference is, among other things, a function of history.

Temporality, relating to time, has a significant role in these conflicts, both in relation to the past and ahead to the future. Groups tend to perceive the past in terms of injustice and victimization. In most instances, victims of violence never receive an apology or see any remorse. Stories told to children about the other group's actions keep the collective memory of victimization alive. Serbs and Croats have a memory of the role each group played during World War II that was kept alive until the ethnic cleansing of the 1990s. Compounding the situation in the former Yugoslavia is the memory of Serbs and Croats who changed their religion centuries ago but not their family name: "We remember when you took Islam."[5] Armenians remember the genocide of 1915–16. In addition to stories of hurt and humiliation, groups have stories about their origins that provide a sense of destiny and help to legitimize their cause. Religious Israelis, for example, derive a sense of legitimacy from a promise to Abraham and Sarah four millennia ago.

Imagined future "utopias" are stimulated by memories of the past.[6] Israelis dream of a capacity to absorb any Jews from around the world who wish to immigrate to Israel; this dream is fuelled by the bitter memory of Holocaust persecution when no country offered refuge to Jews who faced certain death. Palestinians dream of a Palestinian state; deeds to confiscated property, held as family heirlooms, keep alive a memory of land they once owned and a hope that someday they can recover lost property.[7] Before the Northern Ireland peace agreement, the Irish Republican Army held dreams of a unified greater Ireland and the Ulster Defense League saw a future in which Northern Ireland would be distinct from Ireland and closely allied with the United Kingdom.

Conflicts are associated with the question of territorial control. Disputes about land and political control become separatist movements in which identity groups seek political control over territory where they are in the majority. Some identity groups—such as the Kurds, who populate sections of Iran, Iraq, and Turkey—wish to become a single state, Kurdestan. Sometimes a relatively small group feels overpowered by a major power and wishes to be independent; examples are the peoples of Chechnya and East Timor relating to Russia and Indonesia, respectively. In Colombia, many of the disputes about land use relate to growth and production of cocaine and control of oil resources.

Underlying many disputes are the internalized beliefs and values linked to group identity. Often they are tacitly accepted prejudices; sometimes they are clearly articulated. Brice R. Wachterhauser talks of a "dialectic of shifting prejudices" involving an interplay between prejudices we are aware of and can articulate and those that operate on a tacit level. We can never catch up with our prejudices, he argues, because "our roots in history go deeper than the eye of reflective consciousness can see" and with our ongoing experience of history "we are constantly forming new prejudices and transforming old ones."[8]

Prejudices are passed to children through countless stories, insinuations, and innuendoes.[9] Many beliefs and values distinguish between the In-group and an Out-group. Some of these beliefs and values are about Self and Other ("We are like this…; They are like that…"), and some are expressed with universal intent ("All people should…").

Raw emotion is common to these conflicts. A visitor to the former Yugoslavia captures it well:

> What strikes one immediately in the Balkan war is the naked hate, a hate without enough decency—or shall we say hypocrisy?—to cover itself up. Not that hate is unique to this conflict. Most wars feed on hate, and the masters of war know how to manufacture it well. It is the proportions of the Balkan hate, and its rawness right there on the fringes of what some thought to be civilized Europe, that stagger us. Think of the stories of soldiers making necklaces out of the fingers of little children! Never mind whether they are true or not—that they are being told and believed suffices. The hate that gives rise to such stories and wants to believe them is the driving force behind the ruthless and relentless pursuit of exclusion known as "ethnic cleansing." This is precisely what hate is: an unflinching will to exclude, a revulsion for the other.[10]

This observation raises several questions: Where do these feelings come from? How can people hate one another with such intensity? What paradigm enables this hate? This strong feeling of revulsion makes possible the inhuman actions that often characterize these conflicts.

Deep-rooted conflicts have the potential for violence. Violence can take different forms, but fundamentally it "is intended to hurt, harm, damage, destroy or to otherwise disempower a person. It is an intrusion on the dignity of another."[11] This disempowerment can rob people of their self-esteem and ability to take action. Whether deep-rooted conflicts actually destroy people, places, or the possibility of action, the effect on humanity is terrifying. I talked with Vesna after she returned from Rwanda and she described the genocide memorial. In one pile she saw the bones of 50,000 people—some were small children. The guide asked if she wanted to see the nine other warehouses; one was enough for her.

Two particular forms of violence are rape and displacement from the land of birth and ancestral connection. I will describe each in greater detail.

Identity-based conflicts are frequently accompanied by rape of women.[12] Ethnic rape may even be an official policy of groups in armed conflict. It is rape under orders, not out of control. It is rape unto death; rape as massacre; rape to kill or make the victims wish they were dead. It is rape as an instrument of forced exile, to make victims leave home, never to return. It is rape to be seen and heard—rape as spectacle. It is rape to shatter a people and drive a wedge through a community. It is the rape of misogyny, liberated by xenophobia, and unleashed by official command.[13] Besides officially sanctioned rape that victimizes some women many times, sacrifice, torture, mutilation, and sexual slavery occur off the record.[14] One result of these actions is that women are displaced from their home communities.

Displaced men and women carry within themselves the effects of deep-rooted conflict. The violence of displacement cuts people off from the land that holds their memories of youth and symbols linking them with their ancestors. A young Bosnian woman in one of my seminars told how painful it was to view her village from a hill and see the house where she grew up now inhabited by other people. Displacement accompanied by ongoing suffering and a hope to return can prompt people to use violent means to address the injustices they feel.

> Internally Displaced Persons who have lived in a camp alien to their habitat for ten years, lose touch with their tools and ability to earn a living in their natural habitat. They become distant from their tribe and clan and start to lose their culture for the new culture of their new community. The longer the conflict persists and the displacement is prolonged, the more problems that the Internally Displaced Persons face when they return home. Their land, their homes, their cattle, sometimes spouses and children would have been taken by others. They go back home from the suffering because of violence, to a desperate situation that may produce a new and different kind of violence.
>
> – Tag Elkhazin

At times the violence around displacement causes such fear that displaced persons feel that they cannot return to their home country. Chuck, originally from Northern Ireland, is one example. After taking my seminars, he had a vision for community-based conflict resolution. However, he was a former police officer in Belfast and had already experienced several attempts on his life. He is not confident that he can ever return to Northern Ireland.

Deep-rooted conflicts between identity groups contain complex characteristics of timing, geography, beliefs, values, history, dreams, power relationships, emotions, violence, rape, and displacement; they can be both protracted and intractable. A theoretical base is needed that guides action to effectively take "steps to remove sources of conflict, and more positively to promote conditions in which collaborative and valued relationships control behaviour"[15] and to *reconcile* these conflicts.

Though the extreme characteristics of deep-rooted conflict are revealed in the highly public conflicts between identity groups, similar conflicts simmer in families, communities, workplaces, and religious groups around the world. In fact, if my own experience of people in many communities is any indication, we are all at some point involved in deep-rooted conflicts.

Deep-Rooted Conflict Defined

In his book *Control: The Basis of Social Order*, published in 1973,[16] Paul Sites argues that effective power can be attributed to "individuals and groups of individuals pursuing their ontological needs. These individuals would use all means at their disposal to pursue certain human needs."[17] When John W. Burton read Sites' work in the late 1970s, it transformed his view of conflict.[18] He came to realize that human needs "reflect universal motivations" and "are an integral part of the human being."[19] In addition to biological needs, there are other "basic human needs that relate to growth and development"[20] in the same way that infants develop separate identities while learning language, behaviour, and values associated with their culture.[21] Burton concluded that when these human identity needs are threatened, people *will* fight.

Deep-rooted conflict is about identity: the beliefs, values, culture, spirituality, meaning systems, relationships, history, imagination, and capacity to act that form the core of an individual or group. Identity can be defined by needs, which are variously described in the literature as human identity needs, ontological needs (needs relating to the nature of being), or simply human needs. The unique and particular satisfiers of human needs make up the unique and particular identity of a given individual or group. Deep-rooted conflict occurs when the most significant human needs satisfiers of a group are taken away or threatened.

> Human needs theory argues…that there are certain ontological and genetic needs that *will* be pursued, and that socialization processes, if not compatible with such human needs, far from socializing, will lead to frustrations, and to disturbed and anti-social personal and group behaviors. Individuals cannot be socialized into behaviors that destroy their identity and other need goals and, therefore, must react against social environments that do this.[22]

Joseph Montville poignantly expresses the effect of these needs not being met:

To measure the importance of these characteristics [needs], one need only consider their opposite—that is, lack of recognition, no status, indifference, degradation. These are attitudes within in-groups that anticipate potential increased dehumanization of, and aggression against, out-groups. In more familiar psychological terms, negative self-esteem results in a growing sense of despair in everyday life. One feels debased, abandoned, denied any supporting love, basically unwanted. The socially dangerous aspect of this state is the potential rage it generates in the individual. Sometimes, the resulting aggression is directed inward, in the form of substance abuse or other self-destructive behaviors. Often, the aggression is directed at an external object.[23]

Needs, then, are inextricably bound to identity and identity formation; a threat to satisfying needs leads to frustration and, potentially, to violence. There is a relationship between human needs and cultural values: "While needs are universal, values form the culturally specific array of needs satisfiers for particular individuals, groups and communities. In other words, they help to give specific definition to identity."[24] Deep-rooted conflict occurs when values linked to the specific identity needs of a group are violated.[25]

We must distinguish between disputes and conflicts. Disputes are "those situations in which the issues are negotiable, in which there can be compromise, and which, therefore, do not involve consideration of altered institutions and structure."[26] Conflict "is the kind of behavior on the part of persons, groups or nations that goes beyond the normal disagreements and confrontations that characterize much of the usual social, economic and competitive life of societies. Overtly it is behavior that is, or has the potential of being, destructive of persons, properties and systems."[27] Conflicts involve "deep-rooted human needs."[28] When considering negotiable dimensions of disputes, one can distinguish between position-based approaches and principle-based approaches that identify the interests of the people involved.[29]

Another distinction is that between deep-rooted conflict and violence. The symptoms of deep-rooted conflict include "hostage taking, illegal strikes, public protest movements, ethnic violence, terrorism, gang warfare, and many other forms of intractable opposition to authorities at one social level or another."[30] Though many of the symptoms could involve violence, Burton is careful not to equate deep-rooted conflict with violence. While "deep-rooted conflict is apt to result in violence ...violence can also result from disputes that are over negotiable interests, and from psychological problems."[31] On the other hand, in some deep-rooted conflicts there is no overt evidence of physical violence, but the negative impact on the emotional and psychological well-being of people indicates the presence of other forms of violence.

A key feature of deep-rooted conflict is the willingness of people to risk both the sense of order that follows compliance with authorities and the sense of security and physical well-being associated with the status quo. In other words, from the perspective of a utilitarian pleasure/pain viewpoint, the symptoms of deep-rooted conflict appear irrational. If, however, humans have dimensions that are more significant than material well-being, the motivation for deep-rooted conflict appears to be quite rational. In the next chapter we will look at these additional needs. Before we examine human needs theory more closely, however, we will explore the question: Why is it so important to examine the theoretical questions raised by deep-rooted conflict?

The Importance of Theoretical Approaches
to Deep-Rooted Conflict

The phenomenon of deep-rooted conflict between identity groups opens up a field of study that can be placed within a number of fields. When these conflicts resemble *war,* they are part of studies of war and peace. Studies of war and peace relate to international law, the just war theories of *jus ad bellum* (which wars are just) and *jus in bello* (how to fight justly), international relations, political philosophy, and the emerging field of ethics of international relations. As they are *conflicts*, they are part of the fields of conflict studies, peace studies, and conflict resolution. The links to themes of *identity* and *violence* raise questions under the scope of cultural anthropology, political psychology, and religious studies. When they are about *inter-group dynamics, relative power,* and *oppression*, they invoke sociology and liberation theology. The *atrocities* of conflicts raise questions of ethics, the structure of human action, and what it means to be human—questions for theology and philosophy.

These overlapping fields draw on a variety of disciplines: political science, psychology, sociology, anthropology, religion, philosophy, and theology. The body of related material is quite large and calls for a balance between a broad inclusiveness that is ponderous and a narrow focus that overlooks significant insights from other disciplines.

Throughout the 1980s and 90s there has been a growing awareness that these conflicts deserve serious study. In 1985, Donald Horowitz claimed that "ethnicity has fought and bled and burned its way into public and scholarly consciousness."[32] By the late 1980s, the reality of conflict between identity groups was more firmly established in world consciousness than ever. Stephen Ryan, in 1990, observed that "ethnic rivalry" even called the U.S. melting pot hypothesis into question.[33] Knowledge of the significance of conflicts between identity groups has come from the increasing number of such conflicts and a greater awareness that these types of conflicts have been present all along.[34]

The area of relationships between humans as individuals and groups has been described by Burton as "the most complex field of study" that could be undertaken.[35] Evidence of this complexity comes from the range of academic disciplines devoted to the study and also from an informed look at any one of the conflicts portrayed on the nightly news. In response to this complexity, Johan Galtung has suggested that we need a number of theories to understand the dynamics.[36]

Burton, describing the evolution of the idea of deep-rooted conflict, speaks of the early stages of the development of his theory when

> the concern was primarily with specific identity-driven conflicts, such as those in multi-ethnic and underdeveloped countries where there was a denial of both identity-related needs and distributive justice. However, *what at first appeared to be unique post-colonial situations of ethnic or cultural conflict, were, in fact, special instances of conditions which are universal, even in small group and face-to-face relationships.* [Italics mine.][37]

Burton's observation raises the stakes for our theoretical understandings. Not only are deep-rooted conflicts evident in high profile, visible, genocidal conflicts, they are present in many situations that appear on the surface to be benign. Whatever the level of intensity, the theoretical challenge is to understand the dynamics so they can be dealt with effectively.

A clearer theoretical understanding of deep-rooted conflict between identity groups is important for several reasons. First, there is a need to take effective action. Since action interventions are based on theory, false theoretical frameworks can lead to disastrous actions. Many initiatives to resolve these conflicts have been largely experimental, but, considering the consequences of such conflicts, there is a need to predict what might happen in various conflicts. Second, many countries, including Canada, are vulnerable to these types of conflicts and will remain vulnerable over the coming years. Third, deep-rooted conflict is pervasive. In many areas of human life, what would otherwise be a positive, creative, and constructive endeavour is transformed negatively by an identity-based conflict into something ineffectual and joyless that produces toxic relationships.

We will now examine each of these reasons in greater detail.

Need for Effective Action

Both the suffering of victims and the relative impotence of the international community to intervene effectively underscore the urgent need for theories to guide intervention strategies. However, many interventions are counterproductive, possibly because the theoretical underpinnings have been wrong. Burton observes that

> an incorrect definition of the cause of a serious conflict leads to the adoption of procedures of management that are inconsistent with the realities of that conflict. The procedures are, therefore, likely to be unsuc-cessful. If a conflict is caused by an unsuppressible need for identity and cultural security, but is defined and treated as one stemming from aggres-siveness, the likely outcome will be protracted and escalating conflict. Equally, if a conflict stems from blatant attempts to pursue ideological or leadership interests, but has been defined and treated as one based on legitimate aspirations, there could be outcomes that would threaten the societies involved as well as the global society. Indeed...all levels of

conflict may be protracted, not necessarily or merely because of their inherent complexities, but *because of the ways in which they have been initially defined*, and because of the means employed to manage them. [Italics mine.][38]

As deep-rooted conflicts have been defined and understood in new ways, new types of intervention have been developed.

Various practitioners have developed programs to address the factors in, and results of, deep-rooted conflicts. Problem-solving workshops,[39] Track II diplomacy,[40] intervention with victims,[41] and Graduated and Reciprocated Initiatives in Tension-reduction (GRIT)[42] have produced good results. Even so, more theory development work needs to be done. As Ronald Fisher points out,

> [d]estructive intergroup and international conflict is the most serious and difficult problem facing humankind. Traditional approaches to conflict management seem to have a limited capacity to deal with protracted conflict, and it is therefore appropriate to search for new analyses and approaches.... The innovative approach of problem-solving workshops is a potentially useful prenegotiation strategy.... Initial theories on its practice are disproportionately based on experimental and pilot work and *there is need for much more research and theory development*. [Italics mine.][43]

As new theoretical work is used in these constructive interventions, the feedback will enhance theory through action research.[44] Furthermore, new and compelling theories will inspire new types of initiatives. In some cases, new approaches to dealing with particular problems have had to wait for theory development.[45] Insights generated through the interplay of theory and action will help in predicting the outbreak of violence resulting from deep-rooted conflict.

As Tag Elkhazin pointed out to me, the challenge to effective action is intensified with the breakdown of respect for traditional leaders, with the increased expectations of people tantalized by global media coverage of what others have achieved, and with the scarcity of resources: water, land, and human services.

Because deep-rooted conflicts have a tendency to escalate, predicting the possibility of a conflict may help in taking preventative action and preparing for contingencies. Burton links predictive capacity to theory, pointing out that

> prediction has two requirements. First it is necessary to have an adequate *explanatory framework in which to predict the probability of a conflict occurring*. Second, it is necessary to have knowledge in advance of the existence of conditions that are likely to lead to a serious conflict.... Prediction as a means of prevention will not be possible until there is a widespread *knowledge of the nature of serious conflict* so that it can be predicted by officials, friends, professional associations, police and decision makers at all social levels. [Italics mine.][46]

The need to predict, prepare for, and, hopefully, prevent violent expression of conflict is more acute with a heightened sense of vulnerability.

Vulnerability

In the 1990s, the sense of vulnerability to deep-rooted conflict increased. Even Canada has been shown to be vulnerable. In the post–Cold War period, the closest Canada came to an armed conflict between identity groups was the Oka/ *Kanesatà:ke* crisis of 1990. For 72 days, the focus of Canadian attention was a conflict that first pitted the Mohawks of *Kanesatà:ke* against the town of Oka, with the backing of the *Sûreté du Québec* (Québec provincial police), and then the Mohawks versus the Government of Canada, with First Nations people across the country prepared to mount aggressive support if the Mohawks suffered any casualties. Like all deep-rooted conflicts, this crisis has its own unique story. Like other such conflicts, though, it shows that a group of people was prepared to fight to the death over something closely linked to its own identity. This conflict will become the focus of analysis in Part 2.

Up until the 1980s, the Soviet Union presented itself as a monolith; its break-up has revealed intense, deep-rooted conflict among the many ethnonational groups within its borders. Bloody warfare between the Azerbaijanis and Armenians and between the Russians and Chechnyans reflect conflicts that already existed. Many countries contain historical identity groups longing to establish a country of their own or immigrant groups that threaten mainstream populations. Ted Robert Gurr observes that

[s]ince the end of the cold war, conflicts between communal groups and states have been recognized as the major challenges to domestic and international security in most parts of the world. Minority peoples also are now the principal victims of gross human rights violations. In 1993 more than 25 million refugees were fleeing from communal conflicts, including 3 per cent of the population of sub-Saharan Africa.... This century's longest conflicts are still being fought over ethnonational issues in the Middle East and Southeast Asia. Communal conflict is also ascendant in the West: ethnic tensions and inequalities drive the most divisive conflicts in the United States in the 1990s, and Quebec is edging toward secession from Canada. Virtually every country in western Europe is beset by growing public antagonism toward immigrant groups of third world origin.[47]

With global networks of expatriates from many countries, there are many identity groups willing to fund and fuel conflicts implicating their people. Because nation-states, regions, and, ultimately, the global community are so vulnerable, it is imperative that every effort be made to understand the genesis and dynamics of such conflicts. This could lead to processes of reconciliation before unfettered violence takes a toll similar to that in Rwanda, Bosnia and Herzegovina.

The Pervasiveness of Deep-Rooted Conflict

In 1992, I studied deep-rooted conflict as a factor in regional economic development. As I reflected on the role of economic activity in the identity formation of people, it became clear that many people find the satisfiers of their identity needs in their economic life. Upon further observation, study, interaction with hundreds of people in my seminars, and reflection, it is clear that the same dynamics that fuel the murderous conflicts of our age are apparent in our day-to-day family, business, and community lives. We can disguise these identity-based conflicts and keep them under cover, as we accommodate the political and social structures that control the ways we show these dynamics. But they still take the joy from our accomplishments and slow the development of new, creative options.

Many deep-rooted conflicts resemble what historian and broadcaster Michael Ignatieff calls "pre-modern jungle-like Hobbesian" situations where warlords rule capriciously and non-members of an ethnocultural group are excluded. These show that the perpetrators of ethnic cleansing and genocide are acting out in mythic proportions the conflicts that seethe beneath the surface in communities around the world. The theory developed in this book will demonstrate this and articulate principles that help to understand how some identity-based conflicts escalate to the point of violent destructiveness.

On a more personal level, when we experience a deep-rooted conflict we are preoccupied with our own pain, victimization, and the injustice perpetrated against us. We need to understand the reasons for our pain and make sense of it. We also need for others to understand and validate our experiences. For reconciliation to occur, we need to enter into the world of the Other and understand how, out of their hurt, they are treating us like this. And we need to have the Other listen to and acknowledge our pain. Likewise, a third party neutral who guides a process of reconciliation needs to understand how there is a coherence, within the world of meaning of each party, to their actions and positions. Understanding deep-rooted conflicts is an important step in reconciliation for the parties and for those playing the role of a bystander or neutral party.

The theoretical perspectives are meant to function as a mirror. As we look into this mirror we begin to see within our external actions and within our interior universes the vulnerabilities of our identities and our own propensities toward violence. They also serve as lenses that help us see key dynamics of conflicts near us and around the world. We turn now to the first of these, human needs theory, which is a field of study in its own right.

Chapter 2

Human Identity Needs

In October 1999, I gave a presentation on deep-rooted conflict to a group of university students in Mostar, Bosnia and Herzegovina. I arrived the day before the presentation and seeing block upon block of shelled-out buildings affected me strongly. I thought about the thousands of people marked by years of fighting and subsequent displacement. In the presentation, I used the need categories of meaning, action, connectedness, security, recognition, and being that are presented in Figure 2-1.

Identity Needs Implicated in Deep-Rooted Conflict

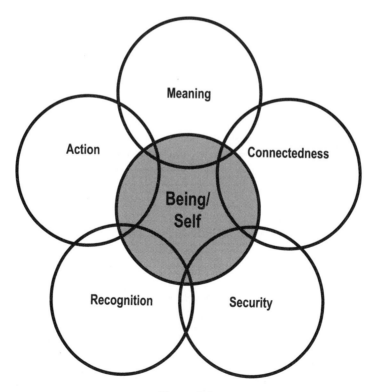

Figure 2-1

When I finished, I took a poll to determine their most significant current need categories. When I got to "security," 95 per cent of the students raised their hands. As I looked into the faces of these students in their early 20s, I realized that most had been teenagers when the fighting and ethnic cleansing took place. I had presented these needs to hundreds of people from many areas of the world, but had never encountered this overwhelming identification with security. In that context, what lay behind the response was incredible pain, fear, and deprivation.

In contrast, during a seminar in Ottawa, a Euro-Canadian male working in the public service challenged me, after I presented these need categories, questioning whether "security" should be included. He had so much security he could not imagine a world without it.

Human needs theory is a powerful tool to understand many of the deep emotions and strong motivations in identity-based conflict. Need categories may be universal, but the satisfiers to those needs depend on culture, values, and experience. In the next chapter I will show that satisfiers to identity needs are formed through mimetic, or imitative, processes; however, we first must know the need categories and their links to emotions and areas of human development. To begin, I will place needs research in its historical context.

Psychologist Abraham Maslow did foundational work on the range of human needs in the 1950s and 60s, and he inspired a whole generation of needs theorists. Current theorists have expanded on many of the needs he identified but have also called into question his "hierarchy of needs."[1] After a 1978 conference in Germany, *Human Needs*, an anthology edited by Katrin Lederer, was published. During the 1980s, John W. Burton used the concept of human needs to define deep-rooted conflict. A second major conference in 1988 brought together sociologists, anthropologists, and political scientists who had been working on human needs with scholars from the field of conflict.[2] These theorists identified the following significant needs: security, safety, connectedness, belongingness, love, self-identity, self-esteem, self-actualization, response, recognition, stimulation, distributive justice, meaning in life, rationality, control of environment, growth, transcendence, welfare, freedom, respect, autonomy, and participation.[3]

Authors such as Katrin (Lederer) Gillwald and William Potapchuk make some significant observations about different types of needs and satisfiers. Gillwald distinguishes between the roles of needs and their satisfiers,[4] arguing that conflicts arise from satisfiers that are temporal (relating to time) and historically determined. This contrasts with needs, which are universal categories that can be satisfied in innumerable ways. Along with Burton, she observes that many *material* satisfiers are exhaustible in principle and "non-material satisfiers are based on human resources that are inexhaustible in principle"; therefore, occasions for conflicts could be reduced "by seeking ways to substitute non-material satisfiers for material ones."[5]

Potapchuk distinguishes between substantive needs, which can be met in the absence of another human (like physical sustenance), and instrumental needs, which can be met only through interaction. The latter include control, identity, recognition, power, and security.[6]

In studying the need categories developed in the literature, I settled on the five primary need categories held together by a need for being, or an integrated sense of Self, that were presented in Figure 2-1. My own theoretical work was inspired by the needs theorists who preceded me. The human needs framework I develop here, however, is a new synthesis and should stand on its own merits, based on its usefulness to people who want to understand their own conflicts and to academics for whom it is a stimulus to make their own discoveries.

Each need functions as a broader category that incorporates a number of the need categories described in the human needs literature.

Meaning

MEANING
- insight
- root metaphors
- justice
- paradigm
- "World"
  of Meaning

For Oscar Nudler, *meaning* is the most significant of human needs. Rooted in this need are the "worlds" we develop, for example, the world of sports, science, art, a religion, or a region. Drawing on psychologist and philosopher William James, Nudler states that "it is our selective attention that makes different 'worlds,' or 'subworlds,' real for us."[7] We can switch from the world of science to the world of myths, but one of these worlds is more significant because it provides the overall perspective from which we value the other worlds. "It has been variously referred to as the life world, the world of everyday life or just World with a capital W."[8] In the words of A. Heelan, a "World then fulfils the most general set of preunderstandings one has about reality."[9] Though an individual's world is "to some extent unique. . . language and culture provide a common framework to which most of the people within its range share a great deal of their worlds."[10] As people find meaning within their context, they transform a living environment into a world in which everything around them has a meaningful place.[11] Within that World of meaning we find answers to questions such as "why we want to get out of bed in the morning" and "why we want to continue to live."[12]

Worlds of meaning are so foundational that deep-rooted conflicts stemming from a clash between completely different ways of perceiving reality are particularly difficult to control.

Now we can see why conflicts between worlds may be so hard to handle: they may imply alternative, competing ways of meeting the need for meaning and, therefore, they may be perceived as putting in danger our own way, a way on which all the rest of what we are depends. Positions in the contest of conflicts implying such a threat may be more emotional and less open to rational bargaining and compromise than in conflicts over scarce material goods. Of course, conflicts which combine both components—as, for example, when class and ethnic cleavages coincide—are among the most difficult to face, particularly when they are approached by ignoring or reducing their complexity.[13]

If the paradigms of one's World of Meaning prove to be wrong, inadequate, or internally contradictory, the result is an identity crisis—an internal, deep-rooted conflict.

In my youth, my World of Meaning was dominated by a Christian fundamentalist perspective. This domination was so strong that during the summer between grades seven and eight I asked my great-grandfather to study the book of Revelation in the Bible with me. Every day we looked at a different chapter and I learned to indwell, or spiritually inhabit, a dispensationalist paradigm of human history. I read books by Erich Sauer, R.A. Torrey, L. Salle-Harrison, and J. Vernon McGee. In addition, missionaries who stayed in our house left books on missions for me to read. I had a mental list of a hundred church leaders and missionaries for whom I prayed regularly. I could not converse with a stranger without feeling the need to pass on something of the Christian message. As I started attending United Nations Seminars, went to university, and made friends with people from around the world, I found it hard to harmonize my World of Meaning with what I was learning from the worlds of international relations, philosophy, and science. At one point I went through an acute identity crisis during which I despaired of ever sorting out the conflicting authorities in my life. It took decades to reconstruct a World of Meaning to replace what had been left behind. With another level of consciousness I can now appreciate the legacy of my childhood and youth.

Nudler points out that different worlds may be founded on root metaphors that "can lead to conflicting interpretations of the same facts and to quite diverse kinds of planning and action courses."[14] To deal with conflicts between different worlds and find a transcendent frame of reference, it is important to engage in what he calls "metaphor dialogue."[15] An integrative understanding of root metaphors, or one's essential understanding of life, occurs through true dialogue with a third party in which parties to a conflict learn to represent the other's root metaphor. Root metaphors play a significant role in determining the categories we use for our different experiences.[16] Our categories, in turn, limit what we can perceive. I remember hearing of an experiment involving cards in which the six of hearts was painted black. Then the card was shown to people who were asked to identify different cards. That card was called either a six of spades (picking up on the colour) or a six of hearts, with no comment that it was black. No one had a category for a black six of hearts, so no one saw it.[17]

At one point in our marriage, my wife and I had conflicts about whether I was doing my share in the household, specifically around kitchen duties. My categories for kitchen work were cooking and cleanup and within my World of Meaning I thought I was holding my own. Yet kitchen work included planning and preparation as well as cooking and cleanup. When I started to understand the amount of effort it took to plan the type of meal, choose a recipe, ensure that all the ingredients were available, and manage the use of available resources, I realized I had been doing half of half the work. My categories had limited my understanding and the subsequent conflict was real. When I understood what was involved, I could change my behaviour (over time). In fact, I can now enjoy doing a greater share of domestic tasks—it will take years until I have balanced out Gloria's accumulated contribution.

Yona Friedman emphasizes the need to know as a key to satisfying other needs. He defines knowledge as the result of the process of "insight" that works with the raw material of information. Knowledge "cannot be manipulated from the outside; it cannot be imposed upon or withheld from the one who looks for it (unlike information). As insight is the key to knowledge and as insight is strictly personal, people try to develop it through training and through persuasion."[18] Justice, logic, and transparency, not implicit in information, are important to our image of the universe. They are "our poetic emotional invention, and they are tightly linked with the process of insight. It is through insight that these justifications of the information received as fundamental facts become our knowledge."[19] For Friedman, this relates to conflict as follows:

> Ideological (religious, scientific or other) conflict is thus the only kind we cannot resolve, and the need of recognition of our insight is a need without any known or acceptable satisfier (as I consider brainwashing or "ideacide" unacceptable). Ideological struggle does not benefit those who participate in it, but they feel that they cannot avoid it: it is part of their very existence. The image of the universe one builds up of oneself (an ideology or a cosmology) is thus a source of intolerance and conflict…. What is nearly impossible to communicate is the personal interpretation that led one to that image and that determines this intellectual adventure: the process of insight.[20]

Where a conflict over Worlds of Meaning is most acute, careful dialogue is needed to develop insights that transcend the boundaries between these worlds. We examine dialogue in Chapter 15.

Included in our World of Meaning are our sense of justice, our understanding of healthy relationships, our sense of fairness, and our sense of reasonable responses by others to our well-intended actions. Any perceived injustice is a threat to the satisfiers of our need for meaning.

Satisfying the need for meaning is complex. It involves interaction with individuals living in a number of worlds and in a context that allows for varying degrees of comparison. We are beginning to see conflict arising from the juxtaposition of an individual's own needs and the satisfiers available to the needs and satisfiers of another.

The next need, connectedness, is inextricably linked to meaning. We generally work out our meaning system within the context of a community of shared values. Shared Worlds of Meaning can be a key factor in bonding individuals.

Connectedness

CONNECTEDNESS
- belonging
- community
- language
- tribe
- land
- nature

Mary Clark critiques Western thought as dominated by a Hobbesian view of humans as self-centred individuals who enter into social contracts "primarily to ensure harmony."[21] This

> offers no way of explaining the existence of family bonds, of lifelong friendships, of the sense of cultural membership afforded by shared language, and a thousand other precious things. Indeed, it totally misses and even denies the deepest requirement that characterizes our species—the need for social identity...humans evolved with a desire to *belong*, not to *compete*.[22]

Hobbes' reading of the problem of unhappy people results from his inability to see that social institutions were not meeting human needs, specifically the need for social bonding that is even evident in primates. Clark points out that connectedness among humans is responsible for passing on the many nuances of culture. Various biological factors are involved. For example, to learn language and culture, larger brains than those of animals are needed. The physical limits to the size of an infant a woman can deliver means that a baby at birth must have a relatively small body.

Thus a human baby takes longer to mature and develop and in the process mother and child are dependent on community support. Larger breasts make possible eye contact during nursing; "the evolution of facial expressions and signals of emotional states conveyed much social information."[23] Weaning at later ages makes possible more individual attention to each child.

The development of the brain also made possible increasingly meaningful social bonding. Quoting neurobiologist J.Z. Young and linguist Noam Chomsky, Clark argues that the human brain must have some "hard-wiring" (inherited organizations of neurons) leading to the ability to form attachments and develop language. With language comes self-consciousness, an ability to discuss the meaning of events, and cultural bonds through self-identity. Out of this comes a further basic need for meaning.[24] She eloquently sums up what is entailed:

> It is not simply language, *per se*, that matters. It is shared goals, values, customs, traditions; it is the shared worldview, the shared jokes, taboos, social niceties, sacred objects and ideas; it is the sense of a people reciprocally sharing a common fate that extends across not just a lifetime but across generations.[25]

Clark considers social bonding an absolute physiological and psychological need; lack of bonding produces separation, alienation, ostracism, and humiliation. Books on primate ethology and biological origins of human behaviour point up the lack of attention to this need:

> there are twenty or thirty times as many entries under "aggression" as under "love" and "altruism." ...Aggression, dominance, hierarchy and appeasement—the skills presumably needed to get along in a competitive and unfriendly world—are tacitly assumed to be the critical traits for survival.... Only recently have we begun to prove "scientifically" what was there to be seen all along: that meaningful social bonds are an absolute need of the human organism, and that rupture of these bonds is—as novelists and playwrights have been telling us for centuries—a tragedy.[26]

Furthermore, Edward Azar observes that conflictual and co-operative events flow together even in the most intense conflicts. Co-operative events are sometimes more numerous than conflictual ones, even during vicious social conflicts. However, conflictual events are clearly more absorbing and have more impact on determining the actions of groups and nations.[27]

Forces running counter to social bonding in the capitalist West are, according to Clark: 1. A decline in "extended social support systems—extended family, lifelong friends and neighbors"; 2. Competition; and 3. The disappearance of shared sacred meaning.[28]

Attachment theory is another body of theoretical literature that reinforces the need for social bonding. It emphasizes young children's needs for strong, stable nurturing individuals so they can develop healthy attachments later in life. Adults need to perceive themselves as having adequate social bonds.[29] Peter Marris says that unique relationships are crucial in establishing a structure of meaning. A structure of meaning enables people to "make sense of experience" by "connecting feeling to action by way of purpose."[30]

Michael Ignatieff associates the need for belonging with a need to be understood:

> As Isaiah Berlin has written in *Two Concepts of Liberty,* when I am among my own people, "they understand me as I understand them; and this understanding creates within me a sense of being somebody in the world." To belong is to understand the tacit codes of the people you live with; it is to know that you will be understood without having to explain yourself. People, in short, "speak your language." This is why, incidentally, the protection and defense of a nation's language is such a deeply emotional nationalist cause, for it is language, more than land and history, that proves the essential form of belonging, which is to be understood.[31]

Conversely, when we talk with people who do not "speak our language," as in understanding where we come from, the issues of our people may seem inconsequential or silly.

For example, I grew up in a church where dancing was considered morally wrong. When my father was organizing a major public celebration, he threatened to resign as chair of the organizing committee on principle if there was a street dance. Years later I shared this story with colleagues at work and they were incredulous; they could hardly believe it could be an issue. I realized that they could not understand where I was coming from, even though by that time dancing was not an issue for me. Others with a similar background know exactly what I am talking about when I share stories of my youth.

Peg Neuhauser uses the word "tribe" to describe what might be thought of as an "identity group" within an organization.[32] Neuhauser describes it as follows:

> Any organization with specialized functions and departments is made up of groups—which I call "tribes"—that look at their work and at the organization in very different ways. Anthropologically, these groups in organizations act very much like "real tribes"; they have their own dialects, values, histories, ways of thinking, and rules of appropriate behavior.[33]

"Tribe" could as effectively describe an identity group within a region. The values of a particular tribe, key for her in defining the identity, can be discerned through storytelling.[34] The rules may operate at a subconscious level[35] to "tell tribal members *how* to accomplish that value."[36]

> Rules of the game are a very powerful and stable tribal characteristic. They evolve over time and are considered the justifiable means to reach the desired end.... Failing to learn and follow the informal tribal rules of the

game will brand a new member as an outsider, or even mark him or her as the enemy.[37]

Burton argues that when fundamental needs are threatened, individuals turn to the groups most likely to preserve them. These may be ethnic or cultural groups or they may be class groups within society.[38] People may belong to different groups concurrently; in addition to class and culture these groups may be based on gender, rank, profession, geography, age, or religion. Which particular identity group is most important at any time could be a function of the needs that are best met by that group or the satisfaction of which needs are most threatened.

Often one identity group takes prominence over others. Terrell Northrup, drawing on the observations of C. Guillaumin, suggests that

> it is primarily adult, white, middle-class males (at least in Western societies) who are members of [a] dominant group and who impose upon other groups their own definition of what is the norm.... [B]eing defined essentially as not possessing the identity of the norm but being devalued for not doing so creates an impossible situation for dominated groups. The contradiction leads to great uncertainty concerning identity.... The result of insecurity is hypothesized to be an energetic search for positive distinctiveness on the part of the dominated group.[39]

This means that dominated groups can be more energetic in defining and struggling for their identity than those who define the norms and take their identity for granted.[40] (Dynamics of domination will be discussed in more detail in Chapter 5 on hegemonic structures.)

Connectedness to land as an historical place and source of interconnectedness to the world is also important. Walter Brueggemann distinguishes between land as space and land as place.[41] For people living in historical communities the tie to a particular geography is extremely important, representing land as place. For newcomers looking for space to live, a given piece of land may be important but it lacks the meaning and connection that it has for those who have lived there a long time. Indigenous people even have a concept of belonging to the land rather than being owners of land. Ties to the land can be spiritual and symbolic; meaning systems are intertwined with references to geography and historical events.

Beyond the attachment to particular geography is the sense of connectedness to nature. Contemporary paradigms of science and spirituality both stress this interconnectivity, using the root metaphor of a web.[42] The concept of being connected to nature through the earth resonates with indigenous references to Mother Earth.

The links from connectedness to security, the next identity need, are clear. Individual security often comes from the group that is bonded together. On the other hand, when the security of the group is at stake, members feel it deeply.

Security

For Ramamshray Roy, human needs are organized around the idea of security, which is ultimately linked to self-identity.

> [T]he concept of security already incorporates the concept of self-identity, because without some notion of one's own identity the individual is unable to define what security means for him [or her]. It does not matter whether he [or she] has a particular identity for life, or for only a part of it. He [or she] must somehow make a connection between his [or her] identity, his [or her] place in society and the capacities and resources necessary to maintain his [or her] identity. For the individual then, self identity and security are not two distinct and distinguishable entities: they presuppose each other. However, it is the notion of self-identity that is primary in lending meaning to the sense of security.[43]

Security, as an identity need, deals with the security of the person and the identity group, in the present and in the future. Security implies physical, emotional, intellectual, and spiritual safety. Physically, the security of the person includes looking after basic needs of food, shelter, and clothing and also security from assault, rape, torture, or murder. The degree of security one needs is a result of fear, which is itself a function of past experiences.

I remember visiting the U.S. apartment of a former Soviet dissident who had spent seven years in a Siberian prison camp. As he and his wife showed us their apartment they drew back the drape, revealing a decal on the window that they hadn't seen before. They immediately recoiled in horror, thinking the place was wired. On examination, they realized it was benign; their first reaction showed the fear bottled up from their past.

When I was executive director of the crime prevention council of Ottawa, I customarily asked people what crimes they most feared. A friend of mine, a Holocaust survivor, responded that she was afraid of war crimes. The year was 1990 and she was in Ottawa. Her response indicated how her experience of 45 years ago was still very present with her.

Emotional security is closely tied to the need for connectedness. Being with people who really understand one's language, experience, and feelings gives a sense of security. Emotional security can be threatened by psychological games, which arouse fears or call feelings into question. Threats, harassment, and expectations built up only to be dashed can all threaten emotional security.

In totalitarian regimes, threats against security resulted in fear and distrust, breaking down connectedness. This was illustrated by a Ukrainian Catholic priest friend, Father Vladimir Olech. In the 1940s a Red Army commander had taken over his house. Over time the officer married and the couple had a child. When the commander's wife left to see her ailing parents, he asked Father Olech to baptize his child on strict condition that his wife not be told. On her return, the husband left for military exercises. During his absence she asked Father Olech to baptize the same child on condition her husband not be told. State threats to security were so successful that distrust was sown in even this intimate relationship.

Economic security is another dimension of the overall need for security. Often satisfiers for other aspects of security come from adequate financial means. This need for economic security may generate an internal conflict over satisfiers of other needs: the need to choose between economic security and personal security is a terrible situation for an individual to face. Many women do not leave abusive relationships, where their personal security is threatened, because they fear they will not have economic security living on their own. Likewise, the loss of a job can be threatening in many ways. In addition to the financial loss, it may also threaten the career World of Meaning. If there had been a strong sense of belonging within the place of work, it would affect connectedness. It could also affect the next need category, action, since many people depend on their work organization to do things that are meaningful to them.

Action

ACTION
- control
  of environment
- power
- autonomy
- agency

Humans have an identity need to take meaningful, significant action. This need points to the self as an actor or an agent and to the action itself. To meet the demands of this identity need, an action must be a matter of choice. And if it is truly a matter of choice, it implies some control over the immediate social and physical environment, an idea developed by Paul Sites.[44]

Paul Ricoeur in *Oneself as Another* offers valuable insights about the Self as an actor or agent of action. He points out that for every action there is an actor who is acting and a "sufferer" who is acted upon. In a mutual relationship there is a balance between acting and suffering. But in an oppressive situation—such as rape, torture, or extortion—the extreme form of action leaves the sufferer no choice.

Emmanuel Levinas sees removing the capacity to act as the worst form of violence.

> Violence does not consist so much in injuring and annihilating persons as in interrupting their continuity, making them play roles in which they no longer recognize themselves, making them betray not only commitments but their own substance, *making them carry out actions that will destroy every possibility for action.* [Italics mine.][45]

In colonial situations, controlling governments systematically removed the possibility of significant action from those who are subjected. Over time, colonial paternalism severely limited capacity to act in a creative and meaningful manner. Likewise, people used to a government doing everything for them find it hard to take initiative when the situation changes.

As a boy, my own need for action was illustrated by my desire to take machines apart. As I grew up, I spent countless hours watching tractor mechanics at work. My passive role, which I internalized, made it extremely difficult for me to plunge into motor mechanics—to take action. I envied my older cousin who could take apart and diagnose the problem of an antique car my father had acquired. In this case, my need for action in this area of life was unsatisfied.

There can be varying degrees of conscious decision around action. In Polanyi's concept of the tacit dimension, many actions are undertaken without a conscious decision. Routine actions fit into this category as do unthinking reactions based on physiological responses to threat that bypass the cortex in the brain, where deliberate thought occurs.

The need for action can be threatened at both the explicit, conscious, and the tacit, unconscious, levels. If someone loses the freedom to act, they can experience strong emotions; a sustained threat to action can lead to depression. Likewise, a circumstance that deprives one of the ability to follow a routine is a threat to this need.

Looking at action from the perspective of agency—the sense that one can imagine an action, decide to take the action, and actually act—shows the importance of self-esteem. Acting consciously shows a sense of self-worth. A diminished capacity for acting also diminishes self-esteem. On the other hand, taking action to regain self-esteem increases the capacity to become a meaningful actor.[46]

One aspect of taking action is to be able to control one's environment. Paul Sites develops the need for control of our physical and social environment, which can be thought of as a fundamental prerequisite for action. He points out that the need for control is reciprocal. We meet some of our needs when we act to affect our environment. On the other hand, permitting others to have an effect on us makes society possible.[47]

Norms, or accepted standards, are used as tools for individuals to gratify needs. Norms provide a context for both control and change. Most people have their needs met by conforming to norms in a context in which they have areas of life they can control. On the other hand, children living in poor ghettos have little control over their lives and, hence, little opportunity for meeting needs such as esteem and security. If they can earn huge sums of money in the drug trade, their ability to satisfy their needs will increase. Broader social norms prohibiting drug use give way to the unwritten norms of the drug world. In other situations, when a child experiences inconsistency in responses from others, the child finds it hard to control a situation and take initiative because constant changes make it impossible to predict or imagine the consequences of an action.[48]

Groups, according to Sites, have a similar need for control. The interplay between control tactics and values is of particular interest:

> If a group's existence is threatened and if control tactics consistent with its values and purposes are not sufficient to maintain the group's existence over time, control tactics inconsistent with its values and purposes will be used in an attempt to insure survival.[49]

An example in the corporate world occurred when the billionaire Reichmanns "opened their books" to bankers as a survival tactic, even though the practice ran counter to their values of strict secrecy about their business dealings. The threat to survival may not be just a threat to physical existence but a threat to survival as an identity group as well.

Taking deliberate action may be seen as an expression of autonomy. Lawrence Haworth values "autonomy" as a descriptive and normal category of human development.[50] For him, autonomy is tied to competence, an ability to act independently with self-control and self-sufficiency. Advanced stages of autonomy involve critical thinking and acting on the knowledge gained through thought.[51] He prefers a community of autonomous individuals who freely share common values to a community of individuals who automatically act in the same way.[52]

The next need category, recognition, has the capacity to enhance all of the others.

Recognition

RECOGNITION
- acknowledgment
- appreciation
- significance
- dignity as Self-worth
- saving face

From its Greek roots, "recognition" means "to know again." It has the sense of acknowledging one's identity and appreciating what we have done, who we are, and how we experience the world.

Francis Fukuyama has analyzed the role that recognition plays as a motivator in human dynamics.[53] Fukuyama begins with Plato's division of the soul into reason, desire, and *thymos*, a Greek word that he associates with the "desire for recognition." This concept plays a role in the philosophies of Machiavelli, Hobbes, Rousseau, Hamilton, Madison, Hegel, and Nietzsche as they refer to concepts of glory, pride, love of fame, ambition, and recognition. These terms refer to that part of the human person

> which feels the need to place value on things—him[or her]self in the first instance, but on the people, actions, or things around him[or her] as well. It is the part of the personality which is the fundamental source of the emotions of pride, anger, and shame, and is not reducible to desire, on the one hand, or reason on the other. The desire for recognition is the most specifically political part of the human personality because it is what drives [people] to want to assert themselves over other [people], and thereby into Kant's condition of "asocial sociability."[54]

Fukuyama argues that the more people value their own worth, the higher the standard by which they achieve appropriate recognition and the greater the propensity to anger if they are unjustly dealt with, receiving less recognition than they deserve. He shows this in the word "indignation," which is derived from "dignity" and "refers to a person's sense of self-worth; 'indignation' arises when something happens to offend that sense of worth."[55] He points out that shame can occur when people realize they are not living up to their own sense of self-esteem; when they are evaluated justly, according to their true worth, they feel pride. Plato's *thymos* is not a desire for any material thing, but a "desire for a desire, that is, a desire that that person who evaluated us too low should change his [or her] opinion and recognizes us according to our own estimate of our worth."[56]

Vesna Dašović Marković told a story that illustrated the importance of recognition as an identity need. On one of her trips back to Bosnia and Herzegovina she met a former colleague who is still working as a judge. He told about the tremendous responsibilities he carried, including the responsibility to sentence people to death. He became conscious of the incongruity of recognition on the day that he sentenced a person to death in the morning but waited in a long line for humanitarian-issued school supplies for his child in the afternoon. He found it very humiliating to be forced to rely on charity when he was responsible for life and death decisions.

The need for recognition begins with the Self, but can be extended to those with whom one identifies or to those perceived as unjustly devalued.

> This occurs most often when an individual is a member of a class of people that perceives itself as being treated unjustly, for example, a feminist on behalf of all women, or a nationalist on behalf of his ethnic group. Indigna-

tion on one's own behalf then extends to the class as a whole and engenders feelings of solidarity. There are also instances of anger on behalf of classes of people to which one does not belong. The just rage of radical white abolitionists against slavery before the American Civil War, or the indignation that people around have felt against the apartheid system in South Africa, are both manifestations of *thymos*. Indignation in these cases arises because the victim of racism is not being treated with the worth that the person feeling indignation believes they are due as human beings, that is, because the victim of racism is not *recognized*.[57]

In the situation of supporting the under-valued, the need for recognition results in a passion for justice. This same need category can also pursue satisfiers that turn the Self into either a narcissist or a selfish individual.

Powerfully motivated people, such as labourers on strike, are driven by a need for recognition. Fukuyama notes:

> The striking worker does not carry a sign saying "I am a greedy person and want all the money I can extract from management".... Rather, the striker says (and thinks to him [or her]self): "I am a good worker; I am worth much more to my employer than I am currently being paid.... I am being unfairly underpaid; indeed, I am being..." at which point the worker would resort to a biological metaphor whose meaning is that his human dignity is being violated.[58]

He notes that Scottish economist Adam Smith asserted that economic life was driven by recognition—the wealthy strive for glory and the poor experience the shame of poverty. Collectively, Fukuyama argues, the same phenomenon occurs as developing countries strive to achieve the status of wealthy nations.

Fukuyama takes the role of recognition even deeper, using the term to blend the variety of identity needs I have described. His arguments underscore how identity needs drive the behaviour of people at a deep level. His understanding of recognition includes recognition of one's ideas (meaning), actions, connections, and sources of security. The need for recognition helps to explain why loss of face is such a powerful drive in some cultures. "Face" is all about *thymos*, or recognition.

Fukuyama gives two variations on the theme of recognition. *Megalothymos* refers to a need to be recognized as superior to others. *Isothymos* refers to the need to be recognized as equal to others. These needs anticipate conflicts related to hegemonic, or dominating, structures, concepts that are developed in Chapter 5. Megalothymos is akin to a prideful narcissus that Roy F. Baumeister links to violence.[59]

These concepts also explain the dynamics of certain leaders who have a desire to be recognized as greater than others. In a closely knit group, followers of these leaders begin to see the leader as representing the whole group, and when the leader receives recognition the need of the group for *megalothymos* is fulfilled by association with the leader.

The need for recognition has been repeatedly corroborated in my own seminars. Two negotiators for the Palestinian National Authority in one of my seminars identified recognition as the key need category for their people with every other need satisfier flowing from recognition.

The poignancy of this need is illustrated by an event in Boston in which Jewish and Palestinian women endeavoured to hold a joint arts and crafts show.[60] As they prepared for the event, they experienced intense conflict over culture recognition. Because Palestinian women did not want to recognize the existence of a Pan-Jewish culture, they would only admit to there being American-Jewish culture, Spanish-Jewish culture, and so forth. They felt, possibly subconsciously, that to recognize Pan-Jewishness would give credibility to the legitimacy of a Jewish state. Jewish women, for their part, would not recognize a distinctive Palestinian culture. They saw only the existence of Arab culture. To admit to a distinct Palestinian culture would, for them, legitimate the need for a separate Palestinian homeland.

Likewise, in discussions with diplomats from Taiwan, it became clear that recognition as a separate state was a key need category for them. They perceived that their other needs could not be satisfied without recognition. Recognition for both Taiwan and Palestine is important for their sense of being and a sense of connectedness. The bonds of connection within each are important to be recognized; at a broader level, formal recognition in the community of nations allows for diplomatic ties and the opportunity to have a voice in the United Nations.

Recognition also means to show appreciation. In this regard it is closely connected to action and meaning. We have a need to be appreciated for what we do. And the degree of appreciation shown should be proportionate to the significance of the action in relation to others.

In some workplaces, senior members and those with the most potential to succeed to the top *must* be the ones who are seen to get credit for good work. One person put it, "… you can really get a lot done around here if you don't mind who gets the credit!" In other words, if one's personal need for recognition can take second place to the recognition of certain others, then one's efforts will have a good chance of being acted upon. Some members must be made to look good and this often happens at the "expense" of recognizing others.

This is illustrated by the story of an awards banquet for a team that had completed a major project. Some of the people receiving the award had poured their heart and soul into the project, working well beyond the call of duty. They were greatly upset when the first in line for the award were those who had put in a few, casual hours of work. This violated the sense of justice within their meaning system.

For most people, external signs are essential to satisfying this need for recognition. However, some very creative people are so secure in their World of Meaning that they do not need external recognition. They know within themselves that what they are creating is significant, even if no one recognizes it, and have an assurance that their contribution will make a difference to the world.[61] Some of these people are only honoured for their accomplishments after they die.

Though all of the need categories discussed so far have an inner and an outer dimension, the focus has been on the outer manifestation—the World of Meaning of oneself in relation to Worlds of Meaning for other selves. The focus has been connection to others, security in the face of others, and action with respect to an exterior environment and recognition, if not by others, at least in relation to others. The human being is always longing to integrate the external within a core inner being. We now turn our attention to this need for being.

Being or "Selfness"

The need for being can be thought of as the need for a kind of "Selfness" that is capable of a relationship with what is "Other." The suffix "ness" means "quality, state, or condition of being." Selfness, then, is the quality, state, or condition of being a Self and having a capacity to act as a Self might act. By introducing "selfness" as a quality we can proceed to think of any Self as being closer to or further from what a full Self would be. This comparison between one's present degree and quality of selfness and the degree and quality of selfness that one imagines that one should have points to a gap. There is always something else we want in order to be complete. Whatever is in this gap becomes the object of intense desire.

"Desire" is derived from Latin roots meaning "from the stars or constellations." Framed in this way, the metaphor of what's in the stars for me points to the sense that there is some ideal selfness to which I have a right. Anything short of achieving this ideal will leave me unhappy. This ideal must be achieved before my full measure of selfness can be a satisfier for any of the human identity needs—meaning, connectedness, action, security, or recognition.

Paul Ricoeur argues that there is an essential dialectical relationship between Self and Other—that we cannot know our Self without some encounter with an Other.[62] There is a constant interplay between Self and Other, modelling what happens within the body where everything that happens is the result of the interaction of internal and external factors.[63] (The theme of Self-Other dynamics will be picked up again in Chapter 7.)

Being as Selfness implies a certain presence. To be present is fundamentally to be—to be conscious of oneself, to exist, and to attend to the Other or the environment. The need to be present anticipates the physiological side of emotions, discussed in the following text. It is to bring the energy of the *mindbody*, both mind and body, into a given situation.

At one of our Muslim–Christian Dialogues, Anne Squire, former Moderator of the United Church of Canada, told about a friend who, in her old age, could not do much any more and lamented her lack of worth as a person. Anne told her that she had done enough in her life and it was enough now just to be. This sense of being present, even when one cannot act overtly, captures the sense of being as an identifiable part of the human person.

Being also speaks to the question of the type of Self who is present. James Gustafson talks about the sort of person we become as having been shaped by countless decisions we have made along the way.[64] These little decisions function like the points on a graph. As they are plotted, a pattern emerges and we can fill in the spaces of what exists and extrapolate where the line will go. In the same way, who I am can be a predictor of what I am likely to do for both my Self and my Other.

One satisfier of the need for *being* is to be fully present, fully attuned to the needs and communication of the Other and conscious of being present in a given situation. I have developed the discipline of making myself 100 per cent present for people at certain times. I am just totally there, attending with my whole being to anything that might emerge from the Other.

When my work involved being totally present with people all day long, I could not sustain this level of being present all the time. So sometimes I was not fully present at home since I was attending, in my mind, to other people and their problems.

The concept of being is akin to the Hebrew concept of heart, which was understood as the integrated centre of thought, volition, and emotion. The concept is that both imagination and action came out of the heart. In this sense, the urges to define and find the satisfiers to other identity needs come from the core of our being. According to Joseph Chilton Pearce, recent neurobiological research has shown that more than 60 per cent of the heart's cells are neural cells similar to those in the brain.[65] These cells are, in turn, connected to the emotional part of the brain and reach out to the major organs. This means that whatever is at the dense centre of many networks of interconnected memories, experiences, knowledge, understandings, and relationships that make us who we are has a strong emotional dimension to it.

We will explore the details of this emotional side shortly. First we need to examine what happens when needs are satisfied and how these needs relate to the temporal dimension of life.

When Identity Needs Are Satisfied

Being is tied through Selfness to the other need categories, particularly when these needs are satisfied. Self within a World of *Meaning* leads to self-recognizance, knowing one's place within the world. Selfness in *action* develops, and is dependent upon, self-esteem. *Action* is dependent upon imagination; when we see ourselves doing something, we do it. Though we do not do all that we imagine, self-esteem allows us to honour our imagination sufficiently to lead to action. To be *connected* with another implies self-respect. To respect the Self of our Other, we must respect our own Self. Selfness with *security* produces self-confidence. Being, itself, implies a self-consciousness, not in the sense of a unitary self but rather an awareness of Self in relation to the Other, to Conscience, and to body.[66] And when our *World of Meaning,* our *actions*, our bonds of *connectedness*, and our *security* needs, are *recognized* appropriately, we experience self-actualization. Self-actualization is not a stable, static condition; rather it reinforces our sense of self-recognizance, self-esteem, self-respect, self-confidence, and self-consciousness, making possible another level of thought, action, relationship, or presence. Fulfilling the need for recognition also leads to latency—the ability to feel satisfaction from a job well done. When this happens, natural serotonin is released in the body providing a feeling of well-being.[67]

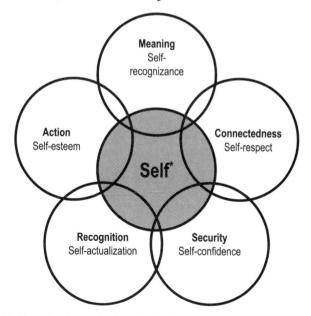

Wellness and Human Identity Satisfaction

* Self-conscious (aware of wellness); self-efficacy (a capacity to move forward)

Figure 2-2

When all these needs are satisfied the Self becomes conscious of its own wellness and efficacy, which can be compared to social capital—an invisible human resource empowering people to creatively take initiative to change the world. Development and fulfilment of need satisfiers happen within an historical context and manifest themselves through a projection into the future. Some additional need categories must be defined in relation to time.

Human Needs Through Time

Paul Ricoeur introduces the concepts of *idem* and *ipse* to represent two dimensions of the Self that are in a dialectical relationship.[68] The *ipse* dimension is temporal and, like a video, the image is constantly changing. If we think of a river, such as the Ottawa River, the *ipse* dimension captures the thought that it is always changing through time—it is not the same today as it was yesterday. Temporality involves looking back to the past and ahead to the future.

Ricoeur's *idem* dimension is atemporal; it does not include the aspect of time. It is like a snapshot at a particular time that shows essential, entrenched, and well-developed characteristics of the Self. For example, the characteristics and identity (width, length, and so forth) of the Ottawa River, as compared with the St. Lawrence River, are clear through time. The satisfiers of the needs for meaning, action, connectedness, recognition, and being are, for any Self, a way of defining the *idem* dimension.

Inspired by the concept of the *ipse* dimension of the Self, I have developed a set of identity needs related to temporality. They can be represented graphically as follows.

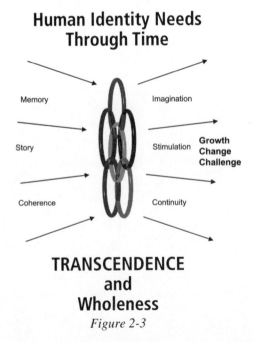

Human Identity Needs Through Time

Memory

Imagination

Story

Stimulation

Growth Change Challenge

Coherence

Continuity

TRANSCENDENCE and Wholeness

Figure 2-3

As we look to the past we have a need for memory, story, and coherence.[69] Memories can be thought of as bits of emotional and cognitive data in which are imbedded temporal and contextual clues. As the memories are linked together in a way that shows one memory causally or temporally linked together, we get stories. The stories are about dynamic interactions of many players, factors, events, and actions. As we reflect on the stories, which become the story of the Self, there is a need for another level of interpretation to give coherence to the story. At this point, theory helps us to see patterns in the stories, making sense of the story. To meet the coherence need, we need to make sense of our emotions. Memories, stories, and coherence may be about any of the *idem* need categories. We can, for example, tell a story of our World of Meaning, a story of our actions, a story about our bonds of connection, a story of our security or lack of security, or a story of our recognition.

Implicit in the *ipse*-past needs of memory, story, and coherence is a need for validation.[70] We need others to accept or corroborate the veracity of our memories and how we interpret them. This is especially important in coming to terms with victimization, as Archbishop Desmond Tutu points out:

> To accept national amnesia...would in effect be to victimize the victims of apartheid a second time around. We would have denied something that contributed to the identity of who they were. Ariel Dorfman, the Chilean playwright, wrote a play entitled *Death and the Maiden*. The maiden's husband has just been appointed to his country's Truth Commission. While she is busy in the kitchen, someone whose car has broken down and who has been helped by her husband enters the house. The woman does not see him but hears him speak, and she recognizes his voice as that of the man who tortured and raped her when she was in detention. She is then shown with the man completely at her mercy, tied up and helpless. She holds a gun to him and is ready to kill him because he denies strenuously that he could have done this and tries to produce an elaborate alibi. Much later, he eventually admits that he was the culprit and, very strangely, she lets him go. His denial hit at the core of her being, at her integrity, at her identity, and these were all tied up intimately with her experiences, with her memory. Denial subverted her personhood.[71]

Looking ahead in time, there is a need for imagination, stimulation, and continuity. Using imagination we can see ourselves being and acting in another place and time. Imagination is linked to our sense of Self; what is imagined is in some way consistent with our identity. Imagination relates to meaning, action, security, connectedness, and recognition.

The need for stimulation implies change, growth, and challenge. People take risks, they break out of an established pattern of behaviour or secure context because of a need for stimulation. This need category is most obvious among young people. As they become accustomed to movies with higher levels of stimulation, they need an increasing number of jolts per minute to hold their attention. Likewise, action-oriented individuals need to take greater risks to get the desired "rush." My daughter Natasha, reflecting on her teenage years, commented on how stupid it had been for her to bungee jump. The particular satisfiers for her stimulation need had clearly changed as she matured, but her ongoing need for stimulation remained.

Different individuals have very different satisfiers for their stimulation need. For example, in my university days I interviewed a scientist who declared that scientists are people who get "turned on by their brains." The need for stimulation may explain why some people are hooked on conflict and violence. Some persons have been tied to an unstimulating life for reasons of security (a job that feeds their family and puts a roof over their heads) or caught in an abusive family situation that failed to provide for many of their personal needs. Their need for stimulation has been repressed by external factors.

Finally, there is a need for continuity. This need is expressed in many ways. It is a need for continued existence as a living being; that is why people fight so desperately to stay alive. It is also a need to be remembered after death, which is why people try to leave a legacy or pass on their story through memoirs. It is also expressed through a desire to continue one's existence after death. Continuity also expresses itself through having children.

The significance of this need was brought home to me in a discussion with Richard Batsinduka about Rwanda. He pointed out that because of the relatively low level of life expectancy, people in their forties are desperate to put in place secure options for their children and anything that might be a legacy by which they could be remembered when they are gone.

Each of the temporal *ipse* needs can be related to the *idem* snapshot needs. For example, we have memories about when and where different aspects of our meaning system came to us, we can tell stories about the evolution of our meaning system, and we can reflect on what gives coherence to the disparate aspect of meaning. Looking ahead in time, we can imagine finding answers to certain questions and can imagine processes for arriving at such answers. We feel a need to be intellectually stimulated and change our ways of thinking. We may also want to preserve aspects of our meaning system. That is why we write books. We can also relate needs for connectedness, action, security, and recognition to the temporal dimension of life as we tell stories in each category and project into the future in each need category.

Human Needs and Emotions

Any observer of deep-rooted conflict will be aware of the intense emotions associated with these conflicts—the anger of the defiant protester, the fear of the refugees, the pain of the injured, the post-traumatic stress disorders that turn the lives of soldiers and victims upside down for a lifetime. We can now make some links between specific identity needs and particular emotions, but first we will look at the relationship between mind and brain.[72]

The mind is made possible through the activity of the brain and the brain is only significant as it does the work of the mind. This dialectic helps us understand the different aspects of emotions. On the one hand, we can approach emotions phenomenologically—reflecting on how we experience our emotions and how we perceive others to experience them. This is the work of the mind. On the other hand, the flow of neurotransmitters and hormones associated with different emotions within the brain and nervous system can now be mapped. This mapping shows the interplay of different parts of the brain, glands, and muscles.

Thinking dialectically in this way is congruent with Ken Wilber's concept of truth as having both an inner dimension and an outer, observable dimension.[73] As we examine both sides of the dialectic we gain new insights. Identity needs theory functions as a bridge between the mind and brain aspects of emotions.

On the brain side of the dialectic, Debra Niehoff points out that many of the physiological processes associated with emotions are governed by the amygdala and limbic system in the brain.[74] The amygdala, an almond-sized part of the brain at the juncture of the spinal cord and brain, is like a command station. It takes in sensory inputs and passes them on to other parts of the brain or turns them into orders to glands and muscles. It is closely connected to the limbic system that surrounds it at the base of the brain. The hypothalamus and other parts of the limbic system add another level of sophistication to the processing of sensory data. They are responsible for much that we experience as emotions. Eventually the information is shared with the cortex where it is processed rationally.

Paul Sites identified different human needs with emotions and their physiological functions.[75] The primary analogies Sites makes are the following: the emotion of *fear* produces a need for *security*; *anger* produces a need for *meaning* (including justice); *depression* is the root of a need for *self-esteem*; *satisfaction* is derived from the need for *latency;* and *boredom* results from a need for *stimulation*. These primary emotion/need pairs interact to produce different secondary emotions with corresponding needs.

On the mind side of the dialectic, emotions do not function independently. Sites points out that they are triggered by how we interpret what goes on around us:

> Indeed, aside from sudden occurrences which may produce such emotions as fear and anger, cognitive appraisal and interpretation are, without doubt, heavily involved in triggering emotional states in humans. How an event is *appraised and interpreted*, correctly or incorrectly, has a great deal to do with emotional states and thus whether or not a person feels a sense of need gratification...the paranoid may *misinterpret* the behavior of others and feel fear when this has no grounds in anyone's reality but her/his own. Or, all of us may, at times, gratify our self-esteem by "kidding ourselves" that others approve of our behavior when this is not called for in more objective terms. In short there is little doubt that *misappraisals and misinterpretations* gratify needs as well as triggering negative emotional states that are not called for from others' points of view. [Italics mine.][76]

What this suggests is that interpretation generally plays a significant role in emotional reactions, and, therefore, action responses to a given situation.

Human Identity Needs and Emotions

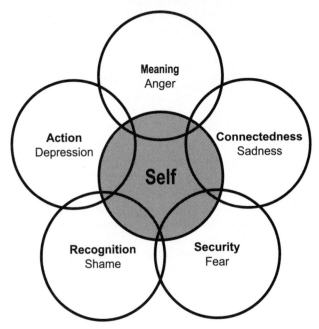

Figure 2-4

As I have worked with Sites' categories I have made some modifications, shown in the above figure. Because of the link between self-esteem and action[77] I have associated depression with a threat to one's ability to take *action*. The fear/*security* and the anger/*meaning* pairs are easily understood emotional couplings. A threat to *recognition*, or a lack of recognition, can lead to a feeling of shame, as Fukuyama has observed. A threat to bonds of *connectedness* is met with an emotion that combines loneliness, alienation, and sadness.[78]

Looking at the *ipse* temporal needs, we note that memory, story, and coherence all beg to be validated, which can provide a sense of fulfillment. Looking to the future oriented needs, satisfiers of the need for stimulation are defined, in part, by the imagination. When these are not met the result is boredom. Satisfiers to the need for continuity are inspired by the imagination; when these are threatened the resulting emotion can be desperation. And imagination itself is inspired by experience of the past. Where the memory of past need satisfaction confronts an imagination of severely lowered expectations, the resulting emotion is frustration. As this frustration produces fear or anger, "actors in society, including the decision makers, may ignore cautions associated with the cerebral cortex and give in to the demand of the limbic system: 'Violence…is produced when certain innate needs or demands are deeply frustrated.'"[79]

A number of composite emotions are very important. Anxiety includes a threat to *security* with an inability to take *action* so it combines fear and depression. The powerful emotions around revenge include anger, sadness, and the desperation that results from a threat to continuity. We can understand the workings of these emotions better as we explore the workings of the brain.

Let us return to the amygdala at the base of the brain. It is the point of entry for data from the sensory nervous system. It can immediately turn the sensing inputs into physiological reactions. The best example is when one touches a very hot object. Without thinking, the hand is quickly withdrawn. The amygdala "tells" the hand to move without "consulting" other parts of the brain. At a secondary level, sensory data are handled by the limbic system, which can quickly activate a host of neurotransmitting molecules and hormones. A physiological control system built into this secondary level of emotional functioning immediately releases neuro-blockers that keep the emotional reaction to a threat from racing totally out of control. For example, the increase in heart rate needs to be controlled. At another level of functioning, the sensory data and the internal emotions are processed by the cerebral cortex. When emotions are totally in control, the cortex—the thinking, reasoning, reflective part of the brain—is largely short-circuited out of the process. But emotions can harness the cortex; this is the case when "terrorists" who are emotionally driven use reasoning to carefully plan acts of violence.

We have already pointed out that sensory data are subject to interpretation. In the case of new data coming in, there may be an immediate cursory interpretation at the level of the limbic system—for example, strange means danger, look out. As more data arrive in the brain, eventually the cortex processes everything and sends signals to the amygdala to notify the appropriate glands to produce certain hormones. The cortex may confirm or deny the original interpretation: for example, strange really does not mean danger.

When the pattern of a complex set of data is repeated, the amygdala takes quick control, especially when a channel for the flow of neurotransmitters has been burned into the nervous system. This is the case when a siren activates an intense physiological reaction in someone who has experienced an air raid siren followed by bombs.

If the threat to human needs is sufficiently intense, the emotional impact reaches the point of trauma. When this happens, the need for security overwhelms the Self and one has limited ability to connect with others. (See Figure 2-5.) In this emotionally vulnerable situation, one becomes unclear about the needs of meaning, action, and recognition. If anything, these are oriented around the pain, fear, and need for security: Why did this happen? How can I get to safety? Would people please recognize my hurt? I will pick up on the theme of trauma in Chapter 8 on mimetic structures of violence.

Trauma and
Human Identity Needs

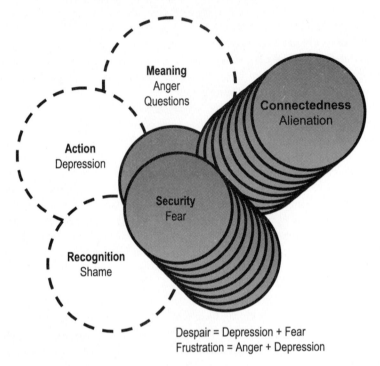

Meaning
Anger
Questions

Connectedness
Alienation

Action
Depression

Security
Fear

Recognition
Shame

Despair = Depression + Fear
Frustration = Anger + Depression

Figure 2-5

Context and Need Satisfiers

Victoria Rader's observations from her experience with the poor in Mexico illustrate how context affects the definition of need satisfiers:

Mexican Indian peoples who continue to live outside the industrial economy, on the other hand, are more materially impoverished than the U.S. homeless; yet their subsistence communities continue to provide some forms of physical security and a strong sense of group identity and autonomy. Indians say that they learn from their elders how to make do with very little without feeling "poor." Communal harmony, economic self-sufficiency, a focus on the spiritual, and local control are values that traditional Mexican communities have not willingly surrendered, even for the promise of advanced levels of material consumption.[80]

Within this context, satisfiers to human needs tend to be derived more from community and connectedness than through acquisition of material goods that, in a consumer society, are the means of satisfying needs for recognition, security, and, perhaps, meaning.

Steven Box speaks of thwarted ambition and wide disparity in living standards between people as contributing factors to crime and, as such, constituting situations in which needs are not being met.[81] Disparity in some circumstances manifests itself as relative deprivation. Former Chief Alice Cook tells how relative harmony in her community in the Inter-Lakes region of Manitoba was disturbed when Manitoba Hydro developed its northern hydro electric dams and a wealthy Caucasian community was established beside her reserve. Where a Cree family had one snowmobile, these new families each had several, as well as other affectations of wealth. After the new community was built, the crime rate in her community increased drastically. In this case, the key point of identification was geographical proximity for what had previously been an isolated, relatively closed social system. This story suggests a link between need satisfiers and conflict, the subject of the next section.

Conflict Creation and Resolution

Theorists William Potapchuk, Ronald Fisher, and Johan Galtung show how the desire to satisfy human needs for self-esteem or wanting satisfiers that are destructive to others may cause conflict. To begin, Potapchuk observes that "one's sources of power will determine how ambitiously one will set the desired level of satisfier. Class, culture, and contextual power issues, among other factors, are likely to have substantial impact on satisfier formation."[82] Thus, for instance, the "satisfiers to instrumental needs in Western culture lead the world toward Western-style representative democracies while the satisfiers to substantive needs lead to increased materialism that surpasses the ability of the earth to meet the demand."[83] He identifies some "potentially fatal obstacles" for people in expressing needs and finding satisfiers:

> First, some groups may pursue satisfiers that will expressly prevent other groups from satisfying their needs. Second, some groups may pursue false satisfiers—changes in the political, social, or economic order that do not truly satisfy the need. Third, and perhaps most damaging, the desire for some satisfiers may never be expressed because the powerful have manipulated the powerless into accepting the status quo.[84]

The latter observation shows a potential interface between needs theory and hegemonic structural analysis, which is developed in Chapter 5.

Fisher shows that the need for self-esteem can create conflict. Observing that "self-esteem is positively related to group identity and cohesion, and negatively related to a perceived threat," he shows how this need can lead to ethnocentric attitudes.

> These considerations lead to a perplexing possibility for Needs Theory in relation to conflict resolution: the need for identity may have a "dark side" which in seeking satisfaction escalates and perpetuates conflict rather than helping to resolve it. According to social identity theory, individuals will strive to enhance their self-esteem and enhance their social identity through

invidious comparisons with other groups, and create negative ethnocentric attitudes. . . . Through a variety of mechanisms, self-esteem and the need for a positive social identity can result in perceptual distortions, emotional hostility and negative comments directed toward outgroups.[85]

One manifestation of this hostility toward outgroups comes from what Galtung describes as the "chosen people phenomenon" in which groups "pursue strategies that they believe will cause others to recognize them as superior to all others."[86] Galtung also makes the point that satisfying the need to belong to a country or group could mean that outdoing "others in wars or economic competition is a satisfier of such needs."[87] These observations suggest that there may be "unjust, illegitimate, or dysfunctional satisfiers of legitimate needs,"[88] or, as Potapchuk argues, that satisfiers may be false.[89]

Richard E. Rubenstein offers several reasons why human needs theory is useful for conflict analysis. Various types of "apparently disparate forms" of conflict can be analyzed using the same analytic tools, especially that of "group identity."[90] Within identity groups, the power and durability of certain needs is evident, since

> in many cases of ethnic, religious, and national violence, needs for security, welfare, and freedom are systematically subordinated to the imperatives of identity, recognition, and belongingness. The peculiar power of this needs cluster in modern world society enables one to predict that, under certain conditions (for example, an attempt by the state to integrate an incompletely developed identity group into the general population), violent conflict will erupt.[91]

Laura Stover points out that the distinction between security and identity is not as clear as Rubenstein suggests since "in times of war, sticking with the identity group is often one's best way of ensuring survival—security, food, and shelter. These are not subordinate but rather driving forces. This is why Bosnians who did not previously strongly identify with their particular ethnic group joined their group in the war. It was the only way to ensure safety."[92] Her comment corroborates the scheme of interlocking circles indicating that security, recognition, meaning, and belonging are interconnected parts of a whole; sometimes satisfiers designed for one category also meet other needs.

The concept of a needs cluster helps connect individual psychology and group behaviour. When seeking solutions to problems that contribute to violence, the structural changes needed to meet identity needs depend on finding ways for each member of the identity group to satisfy needs for security, action, connectedness, meaning, and recognition. Sometimes the same action will satisfy several needs.[93]

For example, granting a people a homeland that they can control can satisfy the need for meaning (an injustice is corrected), a need for action (they can now control their environment), and a need for connectedness. Rubenstein also observes that the need for identity is a need for "multiple identities."[94] This means that in any given situation the identity needs of an individual or group are not immediately apparent.

Needs and Systems

"System" comes from the Greek words *syn*, meaning "together," and *histánai*, meaning "to stand." A relational system demands ongoing interaction between people within a particular context, frequently with some rules of engagement. People often find satisfiers to their needs in the context of a particular type of relational system.

One example is within economic systems. When I researched the role of deep-rooted conflict in regional economic development, it became clear that the identity needs of many people are satisfied through their participation in economic life. This may be linked to an institution, such as a government or business. Many people find meaning, connectedness, security, recognition, and a context for action within the context of their jobs. Many also find their human needs satisfied within religious systems or political systems.

Dynamics of Needs

What helps to determine the relative importance of a particular need at a particular time is the degree to which the satisfiers for that need are threatened or denied. The circles are always growing and contracting. It is also important to note that their relative significance depends on the interaction among the needs. For example, it may be necessary for someone to have an adequate sense of meaning in order to take action. That person may be ready to act but does not know what to do because they are confused. For another person, being able to take an action may be necessary for his or her meaning system. For example, many Muslims feel a lack of completeness until they have made a Haj, a pilgrimage to Mecca.

Figure 2-6 represents an example of someone for whom meaning is particularly important.

Individual
Human Identity Needs

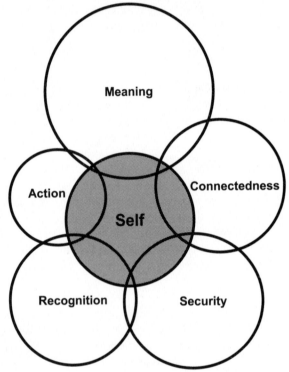

Figure 2-6

Spirituality is a key to understanding the identity of some people and it can play a significant role in meeting human needs. Martyrs, for example, feel secure in the face of death. Their spirituality is central to their World of Meaning, their action is spiritually directed, and their connectedness is with spiritual soulmates. Physicist Fritjof Capra and Benedictine monk David Steindl-Rast see a need for "belonging to the universe" as a universal spiritual need.[95]

Other potential satisfiers that weave their way through the need categories are sex and money. For many, sexuality is very significant in meeting a need for connectedness with their marriage partners; it can also be an important arena for taking action. Many use money as a primary satisfier of a need for recognition; it may also be central to the World of Meaning and the arena of action for materialistic individuals.

Considering the myriad satisfiers people may choose for their identity needs, we need to ask: How does one define and develop specific satisfiers for oneself? To deal with this question, we turn in the next chapter to René Girard and his theory of mimetic desire.

Chapter 3

Imitation and Identity

Chapter 1 showed that deep-rooted conflict drives people to commit the worst of atrocities. This same kind of conflict can play a role in day-to-day human relationships, operating beneath the surface and manifesting itself in ways not overtly violent. Chapter 2 demonstrated that this conflict can be "seen" as a threat to human identity needs, each of which is integrally linked to our emotional make-up. We learned that at the core of our selves is an identity with its own unique set of identity needs satisfiers. The dynamics associated with these satisfiers operate at a tacit, or unconscious, level. People do not say: "I think one of my identity needs is now threatened and that makes me angry!" Rather, the anger points to the fact that one's identity is touched in a way that is interpreted as a threat.

One theme from these initial chapters is that deep-rooted conflict is about emotions. Considering the complexity of humans, it is clear that these emotions are triggered by the way events, actions, and perceptions are interpreted within the individual, particularly at the tacit level, beneath what is consciously articulated.

Deep-rooted conflict is about interiority—the processes and dynamics that occur within a human person. It is difficult to understand these conflicts because no one has access to the interiority of another person; in fact, we are not even conscious of much that happens within ourselves. Other aspects of these conflicts are the words, behaviours, and actions associated with them; there is usually a strong link between what is happening within people and what they do. The links are not straightforward, since people may be deceptive or may do the same things with different motivations.

Interiority is not totally inaccessible to us, however. Novelists explore interiority in a special way, projecting themselves into the interior of each character as they describe what is happening within the characters they develop in their novels. If their descriptions of interior processes are insightful and compelling we say that their work approximates reality.

The challenge to understanding interiority poses a number of questions. How do people develop identity need satisfiers that define the core of their being? How are people drawn into situations where they fight with drive, determination, and unbridled emotion for something that individuals outside the situation would consider trivial? How is something interpreted as a threat? Why does violence escalate when it is introduced into a relational system?

These questions lead us to the work of René Girard. In the 1950s he grappled with the question: What sets masterpiece literature apart from other literature? In our frame of reference, the question becomes: What is distinct about the understanding that authors of masterpiece literature have about the interiority of humans? Girard's answer to his question was that masterpiece authors recognize that we do not arrive at our desires spontaneously, but that we form desires by imitating the desires of others. He calls this mimetic desire. His insight was that the authors of masterpiece literature first identified this phenomenon within themselves and then revealed it through their literary work. With this insight, Girard studied anthropology, psychology, and the Bible, and he made many discoveries about this aspect of interiority. He also found evidence for the scapegoat phenomenon, the focus of Chapter 4.

For me, the first test of the efficacy of Girard's theoretical work was personal. As I reflected on my own experiences, I began to understand them in a new and compelling way. I began to recognize mimetic desire within myself and to gain new understanding of events from the past. I also saw the phenomenon in many situations around me. As I researched deep-rooted conflict, Girard's work opened up new understanding, particularly about the dynamics of human identity needs.

At the core of Girard's work is *mimesis*, a Greek word from which are derived "imitation" and "mime." Using René Girard's scholarship of nearly 50 years, I will argue that we not only imitate the behaviour of others, but we have a deep impulse to copy the interiority of others. Our desires are internal, and these desires are subject to imitation. And what do we desire more than anything? It is the satisfiers to our identity needs, those things which we believe we must have to be whole.

As I reflected on mimetic desire I understood my youth in a new way. I have a cousin a few years older to whom my father, a John Deere dealer and farmer, seemed to give more opportunities to do things at an earlier age than to me. (In later years I talked with my father about this and I understand the reasons why it happened.) This disturbed me since, to establish my identity both as my father's son and as a competent, growing youth, I wanted to do the same things as my cousin. From this passion to approximate my cousin's accomplishments I took some initiatives without proper training, such as the time when I was about 14 that I parked a tractor with a front-end loader. The tractor had been used to unload some heavy pieces of machinery from a semi-trailer and was sitting there idling. I climbed on and drove around the lot filled with tractors to a parking place. The problem was, I didn't have good control of the speed and went six inches too far, puncturing the rear tire of another tractor with the tines of the front-end loader. The briny liquid used as ballast in the tire squirted in all directions. I felt totally crushed. I had failed. I had incurred a cost to a cash-strapped business and had not established my competency in the world of tractors and machinery. Even though I had many other interests, this was significant for me—not because I was drawn to tractors but because I was imitating my cousin, who eventually became an engineer. I had also grown up with stories of how my father had taken on significant responsibilities in the business while in his teens, and I had a mimetic desire to take action in this World of Meaning, the dominant world of my father.

To move logically from human needs theory to mimetic selfness necessitates some conceptual links. First, we see that satisfiers of identity needs are objects of desire. Second, I argue that desires for identity need satisfiers define our sense of selfness. Third, we see that the qualities of selfness at the core of our identity are formed in relation to others, and, finally, I explain that this dynamic is mimetic in nature.

Another section explores Girard's development of mimetic desire. Finally, we will explore the implications for understanding deep-rooted conflict.

Identity Need Satisfiers and Desire

Considering the deep emotions attached to identity needs, individuals have a passion to acquire any particular need satisfier, if it is missing, or to fight to retain it, if it is threatened. This passion is related to desire, defined as "to wish for; or wish strongly for."[1] Its doublet, *desiderate*, comes even closer, meaning "to feel a desire for; long for; feel the want of; want." Both words are from the Latin word *desiderare,* which comes from words meaning literally "from constellation"— meaning "await the fate that the stars bring." The root metaphor relates to identity—a sense that there is something in the works, something coming, or something longed for that is deserved. The allusion to stars implies that there is something unique in store for each person and one cannot be happy or feel complete until this something is acquired or obtained.

Desire and Selfness

In describing the human identity need for being in the last chapter, we examined selfness as a quality of being and acting. Each of us experiences a gap between what we imagine we will become—what's in the stars for us—and what we have become. This gap helps define our most intimate and passionately held desires.

To link to René Girard's ideas, here is part of a Girard interview with James Williams:

> R.G.: ...Part of the problem is with the phrase "mimetic desire." And because of Freud the word "desire" connotes the sexual or erotic. I said recently that we should be able to substitute some other term—I don't know, perhaps "drive," or *élan vital,* or even Sartre's "project." Almost any word that could express the dynamism, the dynamics of the entire personality.

> J.W.: Here you seem to be distinguishing different kinds of mimesis. But you don't want to say that, do you? In other words, mimesis is always along a continuum.

R.G.: That's right. It is something that involves the whole personality. Sartre's idea of the "project" is appropriate in a way, although resorting to Sartre too exclusively would be misleading. Maybe the idea of Kierkegaard, the idea of subjectivity as passionate inwardness and choice, would be helpful.... I don't know; whatever the term, something bigger and other than "desire" should be used. "Desire" has, necessarily, that narrow libidinal connotation.[2]

What I suggest is that "selfness" as developed here could carry this sense of the "dynamics of the entire personality" and "subjectivity as passionate inwardness." In terms of Fukuyama's analysis of Plato's concept of *thymos*, which was distinguished from desire, selfness could include both desire and *thymos*, not to mention reason, Plato's third element of interiority.

Selfness as a Function of the Self-Other Relationship

Paul Ricoeur argues in *Oneself as Another* that the Cartesian *cogito, ergo sum* (I think therefore I am), which forms the basis for much of modern thought, is fundamentally wrong.[3] He believes that there is a relationship between Self and Other to the extent that one cannot define or think of a Self without taking into consideration a relationship with the Other. We form our identities through our relationships with others. The minimum unit of human analysis, in other words, includes Self and Other. Accepting Ricoeur's argument, we take the next step and argue that our sense of selfness is formed in relation to the Other. There are two aspects to this. First, the sense of what we aspire to in terms of selfness is formed in relation to the Other and the appraisal of where we are now in terms of selfness is likewise formed in relation to the Other. The answer to the question of how this might be lies in the concept of mimesis.

Mimetic Nature of Selfness

Using this link between selfness and desire and the evidence[4] of mimetic desire, it is easy to arrive at the mimetic nature of selfness. This means that we form our sense of what we long to become mimetically. We choose Models to imitate. From them we pick up clues about the satisfiers necessary to meet our needs for meaning, action, connectedness, security, and recognition. These Models contribute to the way we frame our stories from the past and how we imagine our future. They set the standards for what we want in terms of growth and continuity.

A woman in one of my seminars lamented that with the concept of mimetic desire she couldn't have had an original thought in her life. Not so. Creativity, as we will suggest later, involves new combinations of what previously existed. Each of us chooses a unique constellation of Models who inspire our sense of selfness. Drawing on concepts from literary criticism, we can suggest two distinct roles for models whom we imitate: flat and round characters. Flat characters are background persons who may have an effect in a collective way, but no one individual stands out. For example, large numbers of people dressed in the latest fashion may influence us to dress in the same way. In fact, all the members of a given culture function collectively as models to one another so that everyone imitates key aspects of that culture. Round models are well-developed characters whom we know as either friends or enemies. We identify with them and get our understanding of selfness from them. Understanding the dynamics of mimetic desire will help us understand this more clearly.

Mimetic Desire

As I have spent the past decade exploring these concepts, my primary laboratory has been myself. Reading the writings of René Girard, I felt that I was exploring the caverns of my psyche with a new torch. In my day-to-day experience, I became conscious of how my own mimetic desire would click in, especially when someone in my league acquired something desirable. At the same time, I became aware of ways the various need categories affected my relationships with people. I have seen the interpretive framework, combining human needs and mimetic theory, corroborated in countless events and relationships.

Girard's choice of the word "mimesis" over "imitation" is deliberate, for mimesis has the added quality of copying interiority. "Imitation" connotes copying what is clearly observable, whereas "mimesis" also includes to copy what is interior and observable only through its effects.[5] While we can never know all that is inside another, we can find what we think is within the other. The clues come from the interaction between knowledge of ourselves and how we act in relation to our desires, and discerning similar patterns with the Other. The clues we use are subject to verification through dialogue and testing. Most of this goes on at the tacit level; we have a feeling that we know what the Other is all about. At times we are right and at other times we are wrong. Whatever the case, we model our desires on what we perceive the desires of the Other to be.

Girard's Development of the Concept

According to Girard, all culture is passed on through mimesis. We learn language, values, and patterns of behaviour by imitating our parents, members of the community, and peers. One characteristic that distinguishes humans from animals is their greater capacity for mimesis. Although mimetic phenomena are evident in animals,[6] the complexity and breadth of culture that must be acquired mimetically to live in a human society takes a substantially greater intellectual capacity.[7] Girard sees the evolution of mimesis as a significant accompaniment to the process of hominization, developing human characteristics. As early humans were developing their mimetic capacity, they began to imitate the desires of others. This phenomenon is close to, but distinct from, two parties desiring the same thing spontaneously, as when food is tossed to birds or animals.[8] With mimetic desire, the value of the object of desire is based primarily on how much the Other values the object.

Imagination plays a role in mimetic desire. After there is a perception that the Other desires an object, the Self imagines having the same object. If there is no point of identification with the Other, it is unlikely that the Self would even be in that position. If there is a significant reason to identify with the Other, it is easy to imagine oneself with that object.

Mimetic Desire

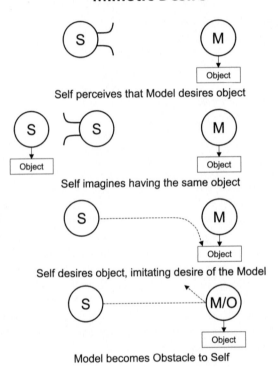

Self perceives that Model desires object

Self imagines having the same object

Self desires object, imitating desire of the Model

Model becomes Obstacle to Self

Figure 3-1

In my childhood and youth, I lived in a culture that valued music. I had a cousin my age who was a good singer and often sang solos. I imagined myself singing solos and was devastated when the choir conductor asked me to mouth the words. In adulthood I learned that I had an ear/voice learning disability. Nonetheless, the mimetic desire for selfness around music and singing continued for years because I could imagine myself doing it; but it never worked out that way.

Girard emphasizes that all people are caught up with mimetic desire.[9] For the Self, the Model is the Other who inspires a desire for something. The desire may be for a physical object, a relationship, prestige, honour, a skill, recognition, status, life conditions, or sex. What is more important than whether the Model actually desires the object is the fact that they are perceived to desire it. In Girard's words, "the mediator's prestige is imparted to the object of desire and confers upon it an illusory value."[10]

The primary characteristic of the Model is that it is a person or group with whom the Self can identify and whom the Self respects or looks up to. In fact, the greater the sense of identification, the more intense the mimetic desire.[11] There is an exponential increase in the potential for mimetic desire as the Self and the Model share the same defining characteristics. These may be class, age, position, vocation, gender, career, origin, or religion—whatever is most important in defining the identity of the Self at that time. Girard describes the distance between mediator or Model and Subject as "primarily spiritual,"[12] suggesting that the degree to which a given Self identifies with a Model may not be readily apparent to an external observer. As the Self identifies with the Model, the Self feels that it has a right to have the object since the Self is as good as the Other. The more intense the perceived desire of the Model, the more intense is the mimetic desire.[13] If the object of desire is a zero-sum commodity—the more one has the less the other has—mimetic desire leads to frustration as the Model becomes the Obstacle to acquiring what is desired. Mimetic desire can lead to mimetic rivalry.

Levels of Mimetic Conflict

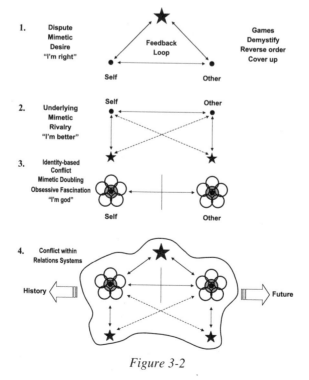

Figure 3-2

Mimetic rivalry begins with mimetic desire, with a Self imitating the desire of a Model. As the Model learns that the Self desires the object, the roles can switch. The initial Self becomes a Model for the initial Model. Switching back and forth can continue, developing into a continuously amplifying feedback loop,[14] intensifying or even initiating a desire that was only perceived before.[15] If a Model realizes that the object is desired by the Self, the Model will desire it even more. This, in turn, will prompt more mimetic desire in the Self, which can lead to reciprocal and mutually intensifying mimetic desire. (See the first part [1] of Figure 3-2.) The Self and the Other become rivals for the object of desire. The intensity of this reciprocal feedback of mimetic desire is described by Girard as follows:

> Once he has entered upon this vicious circle, the subject rapidly begins to credit himself with a radical inadequacy that the model has brought to light, which justifies the model's attitude toward him. The model, being closely identified with the object he jealously keeps for himself, possesses—so it would seem—a self-sufficiency and omniscience that the subject can only dream of acquiring. The object is now more desired than ever. Since the model obstinately bars access to it, the possession of this object must make all the difference between the self-sufficiency of the model and the imitator's lack of sufficiency, the model's fullness of being and the imitator's nothingness.[16]

Girard's description of the feedback loop of mimetic desire shows how an object of desire may gain a significance far out of proportion to what appears reasonable. The difference is that the object becomes a satisfier to *identity* needs—the object must be acquired for one's identity to be complete.

Subsequently, there can be a reversal in which the initial Self may become a Model for the initial Model and may be perceived by the initial Model as greater than the Self perceives itself to be. This is illustrated by Girard in the case of a master-disciple, mentor-student relationship, in which initially the master-mentor is the Model for the disciple-student.[17] If the disciple-student begins to excel, the master-mentor may perceive the disciple-student to be a rival Model and hinder further development, becoming preoccupied with the rival.

Mimetic rivalry is mimetic desire sustained in reciprocal fashion. It takes two forms. First, it may be a rivalry for the same object or cluster of objects. Various pairs of Canadian Prime Minister/Opposition Leader have desired the top job in the country. John Diefenbaker and Lester Pearson were both prime minister at some point in the 1960s and their rivalry was intense. A second form of rivalry involves reciprocal mimetic desires. For example, Pat and Chris (either gender) may begin a rivalry when Pat desires Chris's office. Subsequently, Chris may desire Pat's travel opportunities, and then Pat desires Chris's popularity, etc. (See part 2 of Figure 3-2, above.)

Two things occur as the rivalry progresses. First, the subject "reverses the logical and chronological order of desires to hide his imitation."[18] Second, what-

3: IMITATION AND IDENTITY   69

ever originates with the rival will be belittled while secretly desired.[19] As this preoccupation with the rival intensifies it can evolve to mimetic doubling.

The intensity of mimetic desire increases as rivals become closer to one another. The Model is turned into a "loathed rival."[20] As the rivalry approaches that of mimetic doubles, the initial object is no longer the issue—removing or adding the object would not alter the rivalry. And if the rivalry escalates to the point of mimetic violence, the violence itself displaces any objects as the fuel for increasing violence. The fascination with the Other loses any sense of care for the Other; instead it becomes an obsession with overcoming obstacles to obtaining the desired object. This may even mean destroying the Other, vanquishing the Other, or superseding the Other. The double bind, of course, is that as soon as one succeeds in achieving the object of desire, the focus of identity is gone, since one has become accustomed to defining oneself almost exclusively in relation to the Other. As Girard points out, "the best method of chastising mankind is to give people all that they want on all occasions."[21]

As mimetic rivalry escalates and more feedback loops intensify the reciprocal desires, Self and Other become fascinated with each other to the point of obsession. Their focus is becoming like the Other or becoming the Other. The distinction between their identities blurs. What happens is that the desires related to one's identity no longer come from one's own Self but are based entirely on the perceived desires of the Other. The identity of the Self, then, is not based within the Self or even in a relationship with the Other; it is based on a fascination with the Other. This preoccupation with the Other is a "furious longing to center everything around the self."[22] When the Other has a similar fascination with the Self, the doubles "become entangled in the obligatory reciprocity of the very same game."[23] In other words, identity need satisfiers for Self and Other are obtained almost exclusively from each other. (See part 3 of Figure 3-2.)

This escalation of rivalry can develop to the point that distinctions between the Self and the Model are erased and the two become doubles of one another. Girard gives the clearest definition of the relationship of mimetic doubles in the context of writing about psychopathology:

> Everything that one of the partners to violence experiences, thinks about, or carries into action at a given moment, will sooner or later become observable in the other partner. In the last analysis, there is nothing that can be said of any one partner that must not be said about all partners without exception. There is no longer any way of differentiating the partners from one another. This is what I call the relationship of *doubles*.[24]

This relationship eventually generates "deep-rooted rivalries" in which neutrality is impossible:

> There are only those who dominate and those who are dominated. Since the meaning of the relationship rests neither on brute force nor on any form of external constraint, it can never achieve stability; it is played and replayed in terms of relationships that the onlooker could well believe to be without

any significance. Each time he [or she] dominates or thinks he is dominating his rival, the subject believes himself [or herself] to be at the centre of a perceptual field; when his [or her] rival has the upper hand, the situation reverses. More and more often, and for longer and longer, this rival does or seems to carry the day. So there is an inbuilt tendency for depression increasingly to overtake the initial mimetic euphoria.[25]

In this total obsession with one's double the value of any action or aspect of personality is dependent on the relation to the double. One oscillates between seeing oneself as "the one and only god, who sees everything with the other person, the rival and model for desire."[26]

One of the more famous instances of doubles that Girard analyzes is the relationship between the German philosopher Nietzsche and composer Richard Wagner:

> If we read chronologically, we can see the moment when the "ambivalent" but still "rational" response to the model as obstacle and the obstacle as model gives way to the nightmarish "identity crisis" and "megalomania" that characterize the last stages. . . . [Nietzsche] is dispossessed of his own self and he tries more and more desperately to fill the vacuum not only with the elusive Richard Wagner but with whatever historical or mythological models happen to strike his fancy.... In Nietzsche's last notes, the name of Richard Wagner appears once more in a [triangular] configuration. The other two names are those of Wagner's wife, Cosima, and of Nietzsche himself.... The possession of divinity and the possession of the woman go together.[27]

This reference to divinity coincides with the language of idolatry, which Girard also uses in connection with the relationship of doubles.[28]

In this extreme preoccupation with one's double a subject can feel a "radical inadequacy." The Model, with a jealously guarded object, seems self-sufficient and omniscient. The object becomes more desired than ever. It "appears super abundantly real."[29] Girard uses the philosophical term "metaphysical" to describe this sense of something unreal taking on great significance.

Generating metaphysical desire in the context of doubles is itself a function of interpretation. The specific interpretations, which lead ultimately to psychopathology, begin with "forms of misapprehension generated by mimetic interferences with human needs and appetites."[30] This skewing of perceived needs is then subject to a "process of aggravation and escalation" that leads "toward ever more pathological forms of desire; these forms constitute new interpretations."[31]

What is seen in psychopathology in extreme forms is evident in more subtle and moderate forms within capitalist society where

> [e]verything that brings me up brings down my competitors; everything that brings them up brings me down. In a society where the place of individuals is not determined in advance and hierarchies have been obliterated, people are endlessly preoccupied with making a destiny for them-

selves, with 'imposing' themselves on others, 'distinguishing' themselves from the common herd—in a word, with 'making a career.'[32]

This can democratize and vulgarize "what we call neuroses, which are always linked, in [Girard's] view, to the reinforcement of mimetic competition and the 'metaphysical' aspect of the related tensions."[33]

The situation of doubles is hidden to the protagonists:

This disconcerting return of the identical exactly where each believes he is generating difference defines this relationship of the doubles, and it has nothing to do with the imaginaire. Doubles are the final result and truth of mimetic desire, a truth seeking acknowledgment but repressed by the principal characters because of their mutual antagonism. The doubles themselves interpret the emergence of the doubles as "hallucinatory." [34]

For the doubles, the feelings of hatred are so strong that people would never admit to being "like" their adversary. They cling to their differences and distinct identity when they are actually becoming mirror images of the Other. As they proceed, "the wish to be absorbed into the substance of the Other implies an insuperable revulsion for one's own substance."[35] This cannot help but diminish self-respect since, as Ricoeur observes, to diminish respect for oneself diminishes respect for another.[36]

Girard speaks of external mediation of desire; that is, as the desire comes to us from the Model it is as though it comes from outside our own World of Meaning. If it comes from within our World, desire is mediated internally. External mimetic desire occurs when there is no thought of being or becoming like the Model in an exact sense. One example is when individuals take a great leader or hero as a Model of virtues or characteristics worthy of emulation. It is also seen in the phenomenon of celebrity status in which sports heroes, fashion models, and actors are emulated in some way by fans who know that they will never achieve a similar status. In fact, a key distinguishing factor is that external or distant Models can never be rivals, since they are too far removed.

Girard focuses mainly on internal mediation in most of his work, associating it with envy, jealousy, and fascination, which hold in tension erotic love and visceral hatred.[37] Internal mimetic desire can develop into mimetic rivalry, mimetic doubling, and mimetic violence. These permutations can be understood as a function of the intensity and duration of the mimetic desire. They are distinguished in that the nature of the relationship between Self and Other undergoes a qualitative change from one level of intensity to the other. They are not, however, mutually exclusive. Mimetic phenomena may overlap with one another or there may be a rapid oscillation among them. Mimetic desire can progress from desire for a single object to mimetic rivalry to mimetic doubling; in the process the role of the object of the desire changes. In Figure 3-2, part 4, we see a relational system in which all the levels are present.

What are these objects of mimetic desire? Many times the object of desire is an individual who is an object of sexual desire. In the case of Nietzsche's rivalry with

Wagner, the object of desire was "becoming the cultural hero of the German people";[38] later the object became Wagner's wife, Cosima. For academics, it may be a publication, a prestigious appointment, or some form of recognition. The possibilities for objects of desire range from the material to the ideal, from things to ideas, and from externals to presumed interiority. Sometimes the object is simple, or it may be a whole constellation of things. In the case of wealth, it is not so much the money itself, but the affectations that come from money.[39] It could be a whole life situation or achieving success—or perceived success—over time.[40]

In a mimetic rivalry, an object increases in value "in proportion to the resistance met with in acquiring it."[41] Similarly, the model becomes more prestigious as the value of the object possessed increases: "Even if the model has no particular prestige at the outset, even if all that 'prestige' implies—*praestigia*, spells and phantasmagoria—is quite unknown to the subject, the very rivalry will be quite enough to bring prestige into being."[42] As the prestige of the Other increases three things happen: resentment grows, illusions become more pronounced, and the presumed self-sufficiency of the double is questioned when one is convinced that the Other is not doing as well as they seem.

From Girard's perspective, the role of the object of desire is a function of time. At the beginning, the object is very important. As mimetic rivalry develops the object becomes less important to the point that if it is acquired, it loses its value completely and a new object takes its place. The object of desire plays the greatest role when it seems most inaccessible and before an obsession with the object changes into hatred of or fascination with the Model. This movement can be expressed in Polanyian terms of tacit and explicit knowledge.[43] At the beginning, the object is the focus of desire but the desire is tacitly based on the Model. As the Model becomes the focus of attention, the object is in the tacit dimension of human consciousness. When objects are acquired and certain Models are overcome, the Self may become bored or dissatisfied with the mimetic game and look for bigger challenges.

A Self that has acquired the object of mimetic desire—when the Model/Obstacle is overcome—will find new models with whom to rival until a rival is found that becomes an insurmountable obstacle. This tendency to gravitate toward a Model who will become a greater Obstacle helps to explain the experience of a person moving into another class. When someone moves to a new class they are "above" the rivalry with previous peers.

The notion of Model/Obstacle can become a double bind for both the desiring Subject and the Model. The Subject is attracted (eros) to the Model since the Model is the one significant enough to prompt a mimetic desire. The Model as Obstacle can become the object of hatred. From the Model, the message is "Imitate me, but don't imitate me." That is, "I am flattered by the attention, but if you become as good as me, or perhaps better than me, I will feel threatened." Girard shows how a number of psychological pathologies can be understood in terms of a Self being fascinated by Obstacles.[44] The frustration with Model/Obstacles is frequently at the heart of violence.

Failure to attain an object of mimetic desire may also prompt a frustration that could lead to violence. As the object becomes less accessible, the negative feelings of the subject caught up in metaphysical desire become more intense. Girard describes the experience as a "violent rancour" towards the object. With time, "this most advanced mimetic desire realizes that it is the victim of an illusion. But this will be no more than an intellectual awareness, an abstract form of disillusionment that will not liberate its victims from the traps still being laid by desire the strategist, who exploits every appearance of indifference, whether real or imaginary."[45] This suggests that at an illogical level people can become trapped by their mimetic doubles even if they know at a conscious level that what has drawn them to their object of desire is nothing but vanity.

When mimetic desire intensifies through feedback loops and frustrations over mimetic obstacle or objects increase, the existing tensions may become explosive. Mimetic desire can become violence that escalates from one violent act to widespread violence. First, violence can be introduced in response to frustration. The points of frustration include failure to acquire some object of desire, lack of fulfillment, or the clash resulting from a rush for the same object. Second, considering the mimetic intensity, the initial violence becomes the focus of mimesis and the violence is imitated and returned "with interest."[46] This begins a feedback loop of ever increasing mimetic violence, leading, thirdly, to reciprocal violence that can become an escalating spiral with a capacity to destroy a community. Fourth, as the interdividual[47] distinctions blur and people lose a sense of their own identities, they experience what Girard refers to as undifferentiated violence.[48] It is the violence of sameness, of identity surrender. In Ricoeur's terms, it is the suffering attributed to the person who is always acted upon and cannot take action independently.[49] Fifth, during times of crisis there is a general and widespread violence of undifferentiation, a "reciprocity of insults, blows, revenge and neurotic symptoms,"[50] in which all taboos and moral structures are dissolved. At this point violent contagion can spread quickly throughout a group.

In summary, Girard's understanding of the structure of mimetic desire includes an initial mimesis of the perceived interior desire of another person or group who becomes a Model. This mimetic desire can develop into mimetic rivalry in which the Model becomes an Obstacle to the Self. The initial Self, in turn, becomes a Model to the initial Model. As each party becomes a Model to the Other, a relationship of Doubles ensues. Each party is fascinated with the Other. The intensity of this fascination can become violence in which the identity boundaries of each Self begin to blur. Besides this type of violence, mimetic desire may trigger an act of violence, the imitation of which is known as mimetic violence. Unless the sequence is halted, escalating reciprocal violence can destroy a community. This is the point at which scapegoat theory becomes important, but before exploring this other dimension of Girard's thought, we will look to his work for examples of mimetic phenomena.

Dynamics of Mimetic Desire

The usefulness of the concept of mimetic desire in understanding deep-rooted conflict increases with an understanding of the inner dynamics of mimetic desire. These dynamics include the factors of intensification; the permutations, which show the varied roles of the actors; and the passions, which churn away within those caught up in mimetic desire.

Factors of Intensification

A fleeting desire to have what someone else is enjoying is one thing. It is quite another to be completely obsessed with getting what the next person has and Girard's writings point out the circumstances in which mimetic desire can get out of control. These include a closed relational system; identification of the Self with the Model; the value of the object; the prestige of the Model; deceit around desire; a threat to difference, indifference, and violence. Each of these needs elaboration.

Mimetic Desire Intensifiers

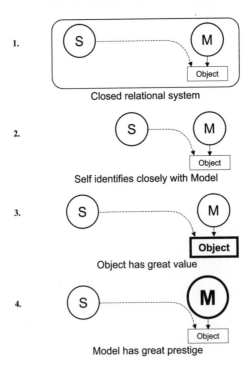

1. Closed relational system

2. Self identifies closely with Model

3. Object has great value

4. Model has great prestige

Figure 3-3

Closed Relational System

A relational system is a set of factors that brings individuals or groups into ongoing contact with one another. An open relational system is one where those involved have significant interaction with a variety of others. In a closed relational system, most significant interaction takes place with the people or organizations within the relational system (see Figure 2-2, part 1). Families may be closed relational systems.

At a larger level, the USSR–USA rivalry was a closed relational system during the Cold War, since they were the only superpowers. A conversation with Stella M. Sabiiti, a Ugandan working for the International Fellowship of Reconciliation, clarified this insight. She pointed out that the relationship between her tribe and a neighbouring tribe was similar to that between Hutus and Tutsis in Rwanda. The reason conflicts were not as intense, she observed, was that there were sixteen tribes in Uganda. In effect, Uganda is a more open relational system than Rwanda.

Girard points out that an open society can tolerate a tremendous amount of mimetic desire both because the number of human endeavours increases and because of the increased capacity for rivalry over symbolized objects "made possible by symbolic institutions."[51] The areas of competition "extend from artistic creation, to scientific research, to economic enterprise."[52] The symbolic institutions make non-lethal rivalries possible. In earlier societies, prohibitions aimed to reduce rivalry but in modern societies rivalries are permitted and encouraged.[53]

As people develop mimetic desire for an object within an open relational system, their attention may soon be diverted to another Model and object either within that relational system or in another relational system. Another way of thinking of this phenomenon is to imagine a person as part of many communities: where they work, where they live, where they join clubs or associations, or where their cultural heritage makes them feel they belong. If each of these brings them into contact with different people, mimetic rivalry or doubling is less likely to happen because there is enough relational change to divert attention from any one Model with whom they might be obsessed. The situation is quite different in closed communities in which people live, work, and worship with the same people.

Identification of the Self with the Model

As has been pointed out, mimetic desire increases exponentially as the Self identifies with the Model (see Figure 2-2, part 2). It is hard to imagine a mimetic rivalry between the mayor of a city and a city road maintenance employee. However, the mayor may have an intense rivalry with a city politician who wants his job or a chief administrative officer who wants control of key functions. The snowplow driver might have intense mimetic desire for the new plow purchased for his peer. Sibling rivalry can be very intense because of this mutual identification.

If the principle of mutual identification is linked to that of a closed relational system, we have a powerful predictor of mimetic rivalry and, potentially, conflict. For example, rivalries between cities work on this basis. Edmonton and Calgary have a strong rivalry. They are part of a closed relational system, Alberta, and are also of a similar size.

The Value of the Object

An interesting aspect of mimetic desire is that value is a function of mimesis. At an auction sale, the value of any object increases as more people imitate the desire for that object. Certain objects take on an accrued value because of their association with certain people or their scarcity (see Figure 2-2, part 3). For example, the wardrobe of a celebrity like Princess Diana or Jackie Kennedy Onassis can bring a premium sum. Likewise, a painting of an artist such as Matisse, Picasso, or Van Gogh takes on additional value because of the high profile of the artist and the scarcity of paintings by that artist. More abstract objects of desire—such as friendship of a certain person, the approval of a parent, the esteem of crowds, or popularity in a public opinion poll—may assume great value between rivals.

The Prestige of the Model

The mimetic effect will be intensified if the Model is very prestigious (see Figure 2-2, part 4). This is true of both external Models, such as popular stars, as well as rivals closer at hand. For example, young people may buy running shoes worn by a popular athlete like Michael Jordan. His prestige imparts value to a given brand. Likewise, former hockey player Wayne Gretzky is paid to advertise any number of items because of his prestige. For the general public there is no thought of rivalry with the "Great One"; however, a budding star hockey player might long to beat Gretzky's scoring record. To match him, considering his prestige, would impart value to the object, the scoring record.

Deceit around Desire

Adults in modern society "have learned to fear and repress rivalry, at least in its crudest, most obvious and most immediately recognizable forms."[54] This does not mean that rivalry is diminished; rather, it is disguised. This contrasts with the behaviour of children, who in a room of toys will quarrel over certain toys.

A key feature of the dynamics of reciprocal mediation is the role of hypocrisy or deceit. In mimetic desire, as in business, which is largely based on mimetic desire, it is important to conceal one's desires so that they are not taken over by the Other. Stendhal demonstrates this within two worlds: the world of the red, that of the soldier, and the world of the black, that of the priest. Within the world of the black, the discipline of self-control makes it much easier to conceal desire. However, the self-control of Stendhal's priest "is as deadly in evil as it can be supreme in good."[55] In particular, Stendhal identified the underground action of the *Congrégation* as a result of internal mediation. For him, "religious hypocrisy conceals double [reciprocal] mediation." However,

[i]n Dostoyevsky's universe deviated transcendency is no longer hidden behind religion. But we must not think that the characters in *The Possessed* are showing us their real faces in becoming atheists. The possessed are no more atheists than Stendhal's devout are believers. The victims of meta-physical desire always choose their political, philosophical, and religious

ideas to fit their hatred; thought is no more than a weapon for an affronted consciousness. Never has it seemed so important, yet in actual fact it no longer has any importance at all. It is completely dominated by metaphysical rivalry.[56]

Concealed mimetic desire has even greater power. The desires of the inner world have a mystique. More desires are projected onto the Model, who becomes hated because the Self cannot be the Other; the Self imagines one scenario after another to get even with the Rival.

A Threat to Difference

Both individuals and groups like to think that they are unique. They have either suffered in unique ways or have made distinct contributions to humankind. When the uniqueness is questioned, they may have increased mimetic desire for defining characteristics of other individuals or groups. Girard's insight on this comes from Stendhal who dealt with the breakdown of differences in the rivalry between the nobility and the bourgeois classes in nineteenth-century France.

Before the French Revolution, French society had a clear sense of hierarchy with people sealed in their own class compartments. The divinely appointed king was at the top and the noble aristocrats were beneath the king. Leading up to the French Revolution of 1789 was the growing power and wealth of the bourgeoisie. Stendhal's work interprets the profound social changes that took place in the decades after the Revolution when aristocrats and bourgeoisie identified with one another and were in mimetic rivalry. Girard explains the process described by Stendhal as follows.

> The transition from external to internal mediation constitutes the supreme phase in the decline of the nobility.... Stendhal clearly understood that the revolution could not destroy the nobility by taking away its privileges. But the nobility could destroy itself by desiring that of which it had been deprived by the bourgeoisie, and by devoting itself to the ignoble sentiments of internal mediation. To realize that the privilege is arbitrary and to still desire it is obviously the height of vanity. The noble thinks he is defending his nobility by fighting for its privileges against the other classes of a nation but he only succeeds in ruining it. He desires to recuperate his wealth as a bourgeois might and the envy of the bourgeoisie stimulates his desire and endows the pettiest of honorary trifles with immense value. Mediated by each other, henceforth the two classes will desire the same thing in the same way.... The nobleman constantly grows nearer the bourgeois, even in the hatred he feels for him. They are all ignoble, Stendhal writes somewhat strongly in his letter to Balzac, *because they prize nobility.*[57]

He points out that aristocrats adopt the same bourgeois values of hard work—going to bed early and economizing—to prove to "Others" that they have earned their privileges. On the other hand, in a symmetrical and inverse move, the bourgeoisie "play at being great lords to impress the aristocrats."[58]

Girard notes that the intense desire that leads to doubling is preoccupied with difference. It "never aims at anything but difference and that difference always fascinates it."[59] This preoccupation leads to the "disintegration of all differences that mimesis brings about."[60] In nineteenth-century France, the differences between aristocracy and bourgeoisie effectively disappeared at the very time each group was trying to distinguish itself from the other. The game of trying to be different—while admiring, imitating, and losing difference—creates the conditions for illusion and delusion.

Indifference

Indifference increases desire. Girard gained this insight through studying Shakespeare, whose plays reveal significant awareness of mimetic phenomena. In a scene from *A Midsummer Night's Dream*, Helena asks for advice on how to woo Demetrios, who loves Hermia. Hermia for her part loves Lysander but is being forced by her father to wed Demetrios. She would rather join a convent than yield her

> virgin patent up
> Unto his lordship, whose unwished yoke
> My soul consents not to give sovereignty.[61]

Lysander and Demetrios are rivals for Hermia's love. Hermia says about Demetrios, "I frown upon him, yet he loves me still."[62] Later, the dialogue continues:

> Hermia: I give him curses, yet he gives me love.
> Helena: Oh, that my prayers would such affection move!(ll. 196-97)[63]

and again

> Hermia: The more I hate, the more he follows me.
> Helena: The more I love, the more he hateth me. (ll. 198-99)[64]

Hermia is a real challenge for Demetrios. She is both Model, along with Lysander, and Object. Her indifference shows that her feelings are the obstacle for him to get his desire. As far as he pins his own sense of self-esteem and recognition among his peers on gaining her affection, her indifference makes him try that much harder to get what he cannot have.

Girard observes, "Every pleasant and willing object is spurned, and every desire that spurns our own desire is passionately embraced; only disdain, hostility, and rejection appear desirable. Mimetic desire efficiently programs its victims for maximum frustration."[65]

These dynamics illustrate that if one really wishes to be the object of desire, when they receive disdain they will try much harder to make themselves appreciated.

Violence

First, regarding the link between mimetic desire and violence, Girard notes that those who imitate one another, continue "each one transforming himself into a simulacrum of the other."[66] When there is violence, the mutual imitation is evident. In blood feuds, vengeance turns the antagonists into doubles.[67] As the rivalry intensifies the rivals forget the objects of desire and become "fascinated with one another."[68] The escalation of mimetic violence continues until the collective murder; this "constitutes at once its paroxysm and its conclusion."[69] This murder is based on conflictual mimesis where a conflict between individuals is subject to contagious imitation and an entire community turns against one individual.[70]

The upward spiral of mimetic desires moves inexorably to violence. As a model desire is turned into one that frustrates the subject, "[b]ecause he [or she] does not understand the automatic character of the rivalry, the imitator soon converts the very fact of being opposed, frustrated and rejected into the major stimulant of his desire. In one way or another, he proceeds to inject more and more violence into his [or her] desire."[71] Girard concludes that, "in the last resort, desire tends towards death, both the death of the model and obstacle (murder) and the death of the subject himself (self-destruction and suicide). This dynamic of mimetic desire does not operate only in those who are 'sick', in those who push the mimetic process too far to be able to function normally; it is also, as Freud acknowledged, a feature of the people we call 'normal.'"[72]

Permutations

Mimetic desire, rivalry, and doubling have different permutations. Each permutation reveals something of the complexity of mimetic phenomena.

Demystification

The task of the desiring subject caught in a doubling relationship is to "convince itself that the other's self sufficiency is just a superficial deception, something that has no right to exist."[73] In popular terms this could be called sour grapes—making the point that what the other has is not so great after all. For the subject, demystifying the Other amounts to "persuading him that he has no reason to believe in his own happiness."[74] Or, in other words, the "other is a victim of mystification and he must be demystified at all costs."[75] The desire to demystify associated with doubling may give rise to revolutionary movements that may become "uniformly oppressive."[76]

Narcissistic Desire

Girard points out that Freud's sense of narcissism is derived primarily from his understanding of women; Freud saw narcissism as a female problem. Girard unmasks the Freudian misconception in several ways. First, he introduces the coquette.

The coquette knows a lot more about desire than Freud does. She knows very well that desire attracts desire. So, in order to be desired, one must convince others that one desires oneself. That is how Freud defines narcissistic desire, as a desire of the self for the self.[77]

The coquette plays a mimetic game and Girard uses the coquette as an example of one who is both the Model and object of desire. This, however, is not the same as a desire of the self for the self. In fact, the appearance by the coquette of desiring herself is but a lure to attract the attention of men. We will return to the coquette phenomenon later.

Narcissism, leadership, adulation, and bondage all can teach someone to make their own selfness an object of mimetic desire. When this happens people project themselves as objects to be admired, obeyed, attached to, or taken advantage of and identity needs are defined in terms of the Other. For the Self to be satisfied, the Self must be desired as an object by others. The Self must be popular, powerful, and the centre of attention. The many acts of either subservience or domination become identity need satisfiers. Attention to the Self becomes important for meaning; connectedness is based on power and authority going either way; security and self-confidence are based on a formal respect; and exaggerated admiration and action involves either dominating or being dominated.

Leaders, artists, and public figures—whose very career and identity depend on public approval—are susceptible to narcissistic desire. The artist who desperately seeks public approval is like the coquette who desperately needs the approval of men. The appearance of self-sufficiency, or having a strong ego, becomes an object in the mimetic game.

Crowds and leaders can act on one another mimetically. As the leader expresses what members of the crowd feel, crowds respond mimetically, expressing the same emotion as the leader. This, in turn, "turns up the heat" for the leader in a feedback loop.[78]

Contrived Mimetic Desire

Girard turns to Shakespeare's *Troilus and Cressida* for examples of how certain words and actions can stir up mimetic desire. The mutual attraction between Troilus and Cressida was nursed by Cressida's uncle Pandarus. He praised Cressida to Troilus, comparing her looks and wit favourably to Helen, the paragon of beauty, and Cassandra, Troilus' sister. Likewise Pandarus, in talking to Cressida, praised Troilus in comparison to other men. When a group of Trojan leaders decides that Cressida should go to the Greeks, whom her father is serving as a priest, Troilus, her beloved, goes along with this decision. When he meets with Cressida she asks,

And is it true that I must go from Troy?[79]

Troilus replies,

A hateful truth.

She asks,

What, and from Troilus too?

Thus she emphasizes that her departure separates them and implies that he could go with her.

He replies simply,
>From Troy and Troilus.
A few minutes later she again asks
> I must then to the Greeks?
Troilus replies simply,
> No remedy.
To this she muses aloud,
> A woeful Cresid'monst the merry Greeks!
> When shall we see again?

This last phrase signals an alarm to Troilus. Let us pick up at this point on Girard's analysis:

> The mere possibility of losing Cressida to the Greeks makes her valuable again in the eyes of Troilus. If we do not attribute this wonderful metamorphosis of Troilus to *mimetic desire*, what shall it be? This incident is the turning point of the whole episode, the rebirth of Troilus's desire; it is supremely relevant to the theme of the present study. Let us be pedantically precise: Troilus's second desire cannot be rooted in Troilus, the subject, since, one minute before, no such desire existed. It cannot be rooted in the object either; his mistress has not changed in any way and, one second before, she did not seem desirable at all. She made herself desirable again by reminding Troilus of the Greeks' erotic reputation. Is it possible to make the secondhand nature of Troilus's desire more explicit than it is here?[80]

Cressida succeeded in arousing mimetic desire in Troilus by construing herself as the object of Greek desire, which he then imitated.

Another example of contrived mimetic desire comes from Mark Twain's story of Tom Sawyer and the fence. Though Tom did not want to paint the fence, he appeared as if he desired the job. This inspired his youthful friends to want to paint and to offer little "treasures" as payment for the opportunity. Wherever markets are open to bargaining, both sides play a game of contrived mimetic desire; the seller tries to make the object appear valuable and the buyer tries to disguise an interest by trying to make the object seem less valuable.

Inverted Mimetic Desire

Avoiding showing mimetic desire is apparent in mimetic inversions. In these cases, there are two levels of meaning. On the surface, one can appear to be giving up something, or having no desire for the obvious object. However, the real object of mimetic rivalry could be at a different level. Examples are the self-effacement of politeness, shown in exaggeration by comedians ("You go first," "No, you…," and so forth). On the surface, it appears that one is renouncing the desire to be first. But the real rivalry is about controlling the situation by holding the door open for the other or appearing to be the more courteous. In some Christian circles there can be competition over who is living the more simple life. Girard also refers to a spirit of renouncing what is fashionable with the new fashion being whatever is unfashionable.[81] It becomes fashionable to be out of fashion—a new fashion. Intellectual life seems endangered as "gurus follow one another more and more rapidly"; fashion accelerates and "fashion itself goes out of fashion."[82]

Changes in Mimetic Relationships

The changes in dynamics are so frequent that Girard uses the metaphor of a kaleidoscope to refer to the varying patterns of mimetic relationships.[83] Sometimes the change is across polarities: "Throughout his entire career, Shakespeare will portray friends and brothers who turn enemies for no reason visible to a non-mimetic observer. The reverse is also true: deadly enemies become intimate friends for no visible reason either."[84] The change may also be one of roles. "For Orsino [*Twelfth Night*] Olivia is simultaneously object, model, obstacle, and rival."[85] Seeming contradictions make sense when one considers the different roles.[86] Even though mimetic desire can be aroused in an instant, and can change frequently, in some cases it takes time to develop.

Passions

Acquisitive mimetic desire is deeply linked to emotions—particularly feelings of envy, hatred, pride, and inferiority. Although mimetic desire and envy are similar, Girard makes a distinction between the two. All envy is a form of mimetic desire, but not all mimetic desire leads to envy. Envy is most intense in mimetic doubling.

Mimetic desire that takes over one's identity and reaches the level of metaphysical desire turns into hatred. Anything can be used to legitimate and camouflage this desire and it becomes more intense as the Model and Self become closer. For this reason, family relationships are particularly susceptible to violence.

Pride associated with mimetic desire is illustrated by Achilles in *Troilus and Cressida*. As Achilles receives ever increasing adulation from his army, he admires himself even more—Girard compares him to a black hole that immediately absorbs everything drawn to it. The hypermimetic world of Achilles is similar to "our own media-crazy world, [where] the value of human beings is measured by something we call their 'visibility'."[87]

Claudio, in *Much Ado about Nothing,* shows the inferiority that can be associated with mimetic desire. Although he loves a woman named Hero, his feelings for her fluctuate, depending on his perception of Don Pedro's interest in her. He almost marries Hero at one point, but is dissuaded by Don Pedro's suggestion that Claudio return Hero to her father. Claudio has such strong feelings of inferiority that he is convinced, says Girard, that if she had a choice, Hero would choose the Other. "Like all hypermimetic people, when Claudio hesitates between several possible interpretations of an event, in the end he always selects the one with the worst implications for himself."[88]

Mimetic Phenomena and Deep-Rooted Conflict

The chapter began with the concept of mimetic selfness. I suggested that this term would both provide a logical link to human identity needs and their satisfiers, which are defined mimetically, and complete the term mimetic desire, used by Girard. I then used the voice and thinking of Girard to provide texture and colour to the concept of mimetic desire by looking at the dynamics that intensify it, permutations of the phenomenon, and passions associated with it. Now I will use the concept of mimetic selfness to advance our understanding of mimetic desire.

Threat to Mimetically Defined Satisfiers

It is possible to have mimetic desire for objects not related to one's identity. It happens often—desire is fleeting and transient. Yet the object that is fleeting for one person may be tied to the identity of the other. It depends on the interpretation. Our identities are built on things that bring together mind, emotions, spirit, and body. If we are strong and autonomous individuals we develop an identity based on self-esteem, self-efficacy, self-cognizance, self-awareness, self-confidence, self-respect and self-actualization. This Self, constructed mimetically with data from many Models, enters into deep, meaningful relationships with Others. However, none of us is this strong Self at all times with everyone. We all get into situations where we feel that those things that contribute to our identity are threatened. This threat may occur when we think our satisfiers are likely to be taken away or are shown as inadequate by some Model with whom we can identify. If they are shown up by someone we feel is inferior to us, the emotional reaction is even stronger.

As president of the Canadian Institute for Conflict Resolution (CICR), I had acted with confidence expediting the establishment of programs, selling the training, empowering people from conflict situations, and developing training programs. Over a period of time, through this position, many of my identity needs were met. In fact, I could hardly talk to a new acquaintance without somehow speaking about CICR. When I left the organization, I lost many of my identity need satisfiers. This made me realize the degree to which I had let my identity become attached to something outside myself.

In the quest to understand the dynamics of deep-rooted conflict, I have shown that human needs theory and mimetic theory can be combined to understand how people feel so passionately about something that they will do anything in their power to acquire it. This often involves violence. There is more. Often whole communities turn on a single victim or one community projects all its violence onto an "enemy." This involves the process of scapegoating, the focus of the next chapter.

Chapter 4

The Scapegoat Function

Consider the following vignettes:

- Paul, an elementary school classmate, was severely intellectually challenged. Having "failed his grade" many times, he was older, bigger, and stronger than the other boys, but still much slower. During recess he was goaded into doing ridiculous things and made the object of ridicule among the boys.

- In a theatre school, Sandra became the object of behind-the-scenes chatter. Everyone knew that she had mood swings and used antidepressants. When she lashed out at the director over what she considered to be an inconsiderate slight, management united against her. She had to go, and appropriate procedures were used to terminate her.

- A televised video of several police beating African-American Rodney King prompted outcries throughout the United States. When the police were found not guilty, riots ensued in Los Angeles. On one occasion, African-American rioters dragged a white truck driver out of his truck and beat him in a manner similar to the Rodney King incident. Rioters also ransacked Korean-American businesses, breaking windows and looting merchandise.

- In April 1994, hundreds of thousands of zealous Hutus, prompted by radio broadcasts, massacred up to a million Tutsis and moderate Hutus over a period of three months. Many were killed by machete.

The common thread in these events is the phenomenon of scapegoating. They are permutations of the scapegoat effect that René Girard describes as

> that strange process through which two or more people are reconciled at the expense of a third party who appears guilty or responsible for whatever ails, disturbs, or frightens the scapegoaters. They feel relieved of their tensions and they coalesce into a more harmonious group. They now have a single purpose, which is to prevent the scapegoat from harming them, by expelling and destroying him.

> Scapegoat effects are not limited to mobs, but they are most conspicuously effective in the case of mobs.[1]

I have experienced many aspects of the scapegoat mechanism. I have been the scapegoat victim; I have been a bystander, watching powerlessly as the scapegoat action ran its course. I have been complicit in scapegoating, taking part in the act of exclusion. The combination of my experience and my deepening awareness of the theory has given me a profound respect for the power of the scapegoat effect and the tremendous challenge to divert or stop it when the scapegoat impulse has taken hold. At another level, Girard's exposé of the scapegoat theme in the Bible has profoundly shaped my own faith.

Whatever the situation, the victims of scapegoating suffer, often for years. Some are killed and leave behind secondary victims who feel their loss. In developing a basic understanding of the scapegoat effect and looking at Girard's development of this concept, we must not lose the human dimension.

The steps along the path linking the vignettes to scapegoat theory are the following: 1. An overview of classical scapegoat theory as Girard has uncovered it; 2. A look at the elements embedded within the structure of scapegoating, making links with human identity needs theory; 3. A mapping of the different types of scapegoating in contexts where deep-rooted conflicts are evident.

The Scapegoat Theory of René Girard

Following is my own reconstruction of Girard's original hypothesis about scapegoating.

When mimetic rivalry, doubling, and violence permeated a community, there was a sense of crisis in the air. There was also a fear that reciprocal, lethal, and mimetic violence could destroy the community from within. At this time of crisis, someone within the community did something to raise the ire of the community. Violence directed toward this individual spread in a contagious instant to all the members of the community. As one, they acted to destroy this individual. All the latent violence, which had been directed toward rivals and doubles, was focused on one person who became the scapegoat victim who was killed by all.

After the first lynching, the immediate feeling in the crowd was one of complete peace and reconciliation. There was a sense of awe at the powerful change in the community. The cadaver left at the end of this generic murder became associated with this good feeling and the awe for the Sacred associated with the change; the victim became deified. There was, however, some ambivalence about the victim. On one hand, the victim was a hero for having saved the community. On the other hand, the hero was a villain and was killed.

The violence had dissipated. A sense of bonding and connectedness returned. The culture of the community started to take shape. With the tacit awareness that the violence resulted from mimetic desire, cultural structures were put in place to prevent another crisis. These structures took the form of myth, ritual, and taboo. The myth was a telling of the story in a way that disguised the scapegoat murder with a careful mix of disclosure and concealment. The mythology alluded to the expulsion or death of a hero while being cryptic about the original faults of the hero/villain and the community's complicity in the murder. The ritual included a re-enactment of certain elements of the myth along with the sacrifice of animals to bring back the sense of reconciliation. Taboos and prohibitions were put in place to prevent the crisis from recurring. Certain things, which were likely to be objects of mimetic desire, were placed out of bounds for community members.

René Girard had his initial insight on the scapegoat phenomenon from reading the story of the death of Jesus. He subsequently found evidence for this phenomenon throughout the Bible; however, his initial writing did not reveal his source. He also examined Greek tragedies and the descriptions of "primitive" cultures in the literature of anthropology and found evidence for his theory linking violence, the Sacred, sacrificial systems, and the development of culture.

Girard argues that there was an original murder at the origin of human culture. For example, the story of Cain and Abel, while written as a myth, must be rooted in an actual prehistoric killing.[2] Furthermore, because of the positive effects of the victimization, the victim is rendered sacred (root meaning of "sacrifice" is to *make sacred*). A mystique is associated with the sacrificed victim so that the origins of culture assume a religious character. The sense of crisis before the sacrificial act may be interpreted as the anger of the god(s).[3] The sacrifice and the sense of peace afterward might be interpreted as an appeasement of the god(s). For Girard, the sense of awe associated with the feelings of peace in the wake of violence introduced the Sacred to humanity.

Because the scapegoat victimization and its specific expression through myth, ritual, and prohibitions are sacred to a given community, these cultural structures become an important part of the identity of the people in a tribal unit. After all, they are rooted in a crisis experience that called into question the very survival of the community. The violation of the prohibitions will jeopardize future survival. Both articulated and tacit prohibitions are woven into the culture in such a way that those living in the culture are unaware of the connection.

Scapegoating "works" for a community in two ways. First, it deals with a crisis of violence, getting rid of the violence by unleashing it onto the surrogate victim. Second, it functions through sacrificial rituals. These rituals are devised to maintain peace within the community through regular acts of sacred violence to a sacrificial victim to purge the community of its violence. (I have argued elsewhere that the criminal justice system functions as a sacrificial system.[4]) When the rituals are no longer effective, a community is again in a sacrificial crisis in which the violence driven by mimetic desire cannot be dissipated and a new form of scapegoating emerges. In any community that experiences mimetic rivalries and the potential for reciprocal violence, a scapegoat mechanism is as likely as a nuclear chain reaction when a critical mass of plutonium is present.

The pattern that has emerged can be considered classical scapegoating. The elements of classical scapegoating include

1. The Crisis
2. Emergence of the Scapegoat
3. Characteristics of the Scapegoat
4. Scapegoat Action
5. A Hidden Process
6. Experience of the Victim
7. The After-Effects

1.   The Crisis

A crisis within a community can occur in two ways. First, it can be the result of many private frustrations caused by people who do not get what they think they need. The sense of "what they need" is established mimetically—they need as much as or more than the next person with whom they identify. People tend to interpret the next person as having more than they do.

A few years ago I worked with a group called Peak Fires, headed by Pamela Pritchard. This group trained dialogue leaders from across Canada and conducted dialogues about the nature and future of Canada in several cities. It was important throughout the bilingual sessions that every word be translated into the other language. A year after the initial training had been given in both languages, the group re-convened and an anglophone and a francophone compared notes on the previous year. The francophone appreciated the experience but lamented that there was more English than French. The anglophone responded, "That's strange; I was convinced and disappointed that more was in French." They mirrored each other in thinking that the Other had it better.

Though this example does not point to a crisis, it illustrates how a crisis begins through perceptions of the Other's presumed favours that become objects of mimetic desire. This can happen individually and collectively. If one group becomes aware of being oppressed, there is a sense that a new category of objects of mimetic desire is available. As they take aggressive steps to achieve equality—act to acquire what the other group has—a crisis can occur.

Second, a crisis can also occur when the society as a whole is challenged in a vital way—high unemployment, reduced living standards, disaster, or uncertainty. The challenge may be caused by humans (high crime rate) or by a natural disaster. Whatever the cause of the crisis, the symptoms and effects are the same. Social structures collapse and individuals feel threatened at the level of each of their identity needs.

Crisis

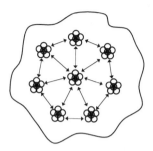

- Everyone against others
- Dissolving of differences
- Feeling of chaos
- Decline and disintegration of community
- Potential for mutual destruction

Figure 4-1

The day after the September 11, 2001, terrorist attack on the United States, Ehud Barak was shown on television calling on democratic countries to band together and use violent means to utterly destroy the groups responsible. He called on them to use intelligence operations, covert operations, and the tools of war. His was a plea to destroy the unknown scapegoat group.

When cultural distinctions are called into question, "order, peace, and fecundity" are at stake. Without proper distinctions there are "fierce rivalries" setting "members of the same family or social group at one another's throats."[5] The loss of differences strips people "of all their distinctive characteristics—of their 'identities.'"[6] One reason that incest is such a strong taboo is that it is about breaking down important distinctions within families, including "that between the mother and her children."[7] In an incestuous climate, family members become objects of sexual desire. Distinctions among people are dissolved and the community, in this case the family, is infused with violence.

Girard describes the sacrificial crisis in terms of the inability of the group to distinguish between impure violence and the purifying violence of sacrificial rites. The result is that "impure, contagious, reciprocal violence spreads throughout the community."[8] The potential of violence threatens the cultural order. "This cultural order is nothing more than a regulated system of distinctions in which the differences among individuals are used to establish their 'identity' and their mutual relationships."[9] At the final stages[10] of the crisis individual lives are put at risk, the religious framework totters, and "the whole cultural foundation of the society is put in jeopardy. The institutions lose their vitality, the protective façade of the society gives way, social values are rapidly eroded, and the whole cultural structure seems on the verge of collapse."[11] In Girard's frame of reference, the cultural structure is based on a sense of the Sacred that is meant to help people deal with uncontrollable threatening forces.

Vengeance is another factor in the pre-scapegoat phase. Girard observes that "[v]engeance professes to be an act of reprisal, and every reprisal calls for another reprisal. The crime to which the act of vengeance addresses itself is almost never an unprecedented offense; in almost every case it has been committed in revenge for some prior crime."[12] Furthermore, "in tragedy each character passionately embraces or rejects vengeance depending on the position he occupies at any given moment in the scheme of the drama."[13] Different cultures handle the vengeance instinct in various ways. These include private vengeance, community councils of elders, ritualized scapegoating, and peaceful transformation of violent energy through spiritual discipline, as happened with Cheyenne peace chiefs who would sit and meditate outside the home of a murderer for four days.

In modern societies, Girard points out, "public vengeance is the exclusive property of well-policed societies, and so our society calls it the judicial system."[14] Looking closely at any situation one can see that the "'reasons' on both sides of a dispute are equally valid—which is to say that *violence operates without reason*."[15] Girard perceives that the tragedians have caught on to this realization that characters are neither exclusively good or bad. By comparison, modern interpreters "have still not extricated [them]selves entirely from the 'Manichean' frame of reference that gained sway in the Romantic era and still exerts its influence,"[16] so that stories in popular culture are framed as good guys versus bad guys.

2.   Emergence of the Scapegoat

Girard argues that "any community that has fallen prey to violence or has been stricken by some overwhelming catastrophe hurls itself blindly into the search for a scapegoat."[17] This statement contributes three truths about the community in this situation: it falls prey to violence, it is stricken by catastrophe, and it searches for a scapegoat. The first raises the question of the nature of violence, the second questions Girard's sense of the sacred, and the third raises the question of why the community looks so passionately for a scapegoat. Girard answers all three in his first stereotype of scapegoating: a generalized loss of differences within the community. The starting point is that cultures like to see themselves as distinct and different:

> No culture exists within which everyone does not feel "different from others" and does not consider such "differences" legitimate and necessary.... there exists in every individual a tendency to think of himself not only as different from others but as extremely different, because every culture entertains this feeling of difference among the individuals who compose it.[18]

Often victims are chosen because they call into question a group's sense of distinctiveness.

Girard's analysis associates the community in crisis with a violence of undifferentiation. In other words, people are lost because their understanding of their distinct identity is questioned, they experience mimetic rivalries and doubling in which their identity is defined in terms of an Other, or there is outright violence.

Anger is another quality associated with violence. Looking at Oedipus's tantrums, Girard muses whether or not they "can be said to perform the differential function upon which the whole concept of 'character' is based?" His answer is that "anger crops up everywhere."[19] Associating anger with a threat to differentiation adds insight to the previous association of anger with a threat to a meaning system, including a sense of justice.

Theologian Raymund Schwager, a primary interpreter of Girard's thought, looks at the role of passionate emotions in generating violence. He asserts that "passion can dupe reason and make it its ally,"[20] indicating that our emotions can take over our cognitive processes. He also points out that at the beginning of a scapegoating process, people think that they are working for justice. "Anger and violence tend to eliminate all differences within a cultural unit and between different cultures,"[21] observes Schwager. He associates violence with deceit, as revealed in the Hebrew Bible,[22] and the crisis feelings before scapegoating with "deadly hatred," "groundless hatred," and "unlimited hatred."[23]

Girard asserts that the "process of finding a surrogate victim constitutes a major means, perhaps the sole means, by which [humans] expel from their consciousness the truth about their violent nature—that knowledge of past violence which, if not shifted to a single 'guilty' figure, would poison both the present and the future."[24] For the surrogate victim to effectively distract individuals and groups from their internal violence, they have to believe fully that the surrogate victim is guilty. This belief is confirmed when peace is restored after the scapegoat event. "The crisis is seen as a mysterious illness introduced into the community by an outsider. The cure lies in ridding the community of the sole malignant element."[25]

Emergence of Scapegoat

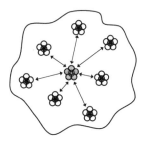

Human Needs of Community

• Threat to security > fear
• Threat to sense of justice > anger
• Threat to connectedness > sadness
• Action is distorted
• Differences not recognized
• Incoherent
• Trajectory imagination of decline
• Continuity is threatened

Figure 4-2

Girard considers anger to be the prominent emotion associated with a threat to meaning. Reflecting on the other identity needs we note that the crisis often severs *connections* among people. Rising distrust curtails people's ability to *act*; social unrest threatens *security*; and the loss of difference erases the significance of traits for which people wish to be *recognized*. The resulting anger and frustration need an outlet—someone to blame. If everyone can blame the same person, that person can be an outlet for everyone.

3.   Characteristics of the Scapegoat

Four qualities distinguish potential scapegoats.[26] Scapegoats must be seen as *different* to be subject to a violence of differentiation. Moreover, they should be *powerful* enough to have an impact on the crisis. They must be *illegitimate* for some reason so that the scapegoat action can be justified. Finally, they must be *vulnerable*, not able to counterattack with enough force to make the scapegoat action ineffective.

Characteristics of the Scapegoat

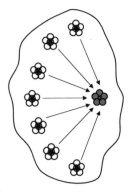

• Illegitimate

• Responsible for threats to human identity needs

• Different

• Powerful

• Vulnerable, no one to seek reprisal

• Tendency to blame someone

Figure 4-3

Many factors make a potential scapegoat different from the community in crisis. They may not be socially integrated. They may be marginalized, lacking the social bonds that most community members enjoy. This may result from ethnocultural grouping, class, or age. The king is a less obvious type of scapegoat. "Is he not at the very heart of the community? Undoubtedly—but it is precisely his position at the center that serves to isolate him from his fellow men, to render him casteless."[27] Likewise, as Vesna Dasović Marković observes, the scapegoat phenomenon helps explain why "the prophet is not accepted in her or his own country." Prophets often emerge at a time of crisis or social decline. Their difference shows in their distinctive message and the different paradigm on which their actions are based. Another difference may be a physical deformity or aberration. The factors setting people apart may be very wide.

If we look at the extremely wide spectrum of human victims sacrificed by various societies, the list seems heterogeneous, to say the least. It includes prisoners of war, slaves, small children, unmarried adolescents, and the handicapped; it ranges from the very dregs of society, such as the Greek *pharmakos*, to the king himself.[28]

The *pharmakoi* to whom Girard refers were individuals in fifth-century BC Greece who were kept at state expense to be sacrificed at certain festivals as well as at a time of potential disaster. In classical Greek the related word, *pharmakon*, means both poison and the antidote for poison. This infers the dual nature of the scapegoat as both the cause and the cure for an ill.

Finally, some scapegoats have traits that set them aside. An example is Julius Caesar, as portrayed by Shakespeare. In the play, Caesar, emperor of the Roman Empire, is killed by men near the centre of power who convince themselves that Caesar must die for the sake of the empire. Cassius is a prime mover in the conspiracy; note the following exchange with Casca. We pick up the speech after Cassius has talked of strange occurrences that add up

> To make them instruments of fear and warning
> Unto some monstrous state.
> Now could I, Casca, name to thee a man
> Most like this dreadful night
> That thunders, lightens, opens graves, and roars
> As doth the lion in the Capitol;
> A man no mightier than thyself or me
> In personal action, yet prodigious grown,
> And fearful, as these strange eruptions are.

Casca: 'Tis Caesar that you mean, is it not, Cassius?[29]

Cassius appears to have strong mimetic rivalry with Caesar, whom he identifies as "a man no mightier than thyself or me." The strange occurrences point to an imminent crisis. Caesar is "set apart" as someone whose death could be curative.

> Everything that Caesar does, everything that we learn about him as a public or a private individual, including the sterility of his wife—which the popular mind readily attributes to a husband's evil eye—makes him look like a man earmarked for victimization. At one point he offers his throat to the crowd in a gesture reminiscent of some sacred king volunteering for the role of sacrificial victim. It is also significant that Caesar would be associated with both the Lupercalia and the Ides of March, two Roman festivals rooted, as all such festivals are, in so-called scapegoat rituals.[30]

Not only must the community view a scapegoat as different, but the scapegoat must be powerful yet vulnerable.

Power is a matter of perception by a community. There are two kinds of power: a positive power to make things happen and a negative power to disrupt. People in society may have little positive power—little money, knowledge, or skill—but a significant power to disrupt. Criminals, often poor and victims of abuse, are perceived as powerful monsters because they take disruptive and hurtful actions. Groups such as the gypsies, stereotyped as disruptive, have become scapegoats on the basis of a perceived power to do harm. In medieval times, Jews were blamed for the Bubonic plague; we now know they had nothing to do with it.[31] Leaders like Julius Caesar are powerful in the positive sense; other scapegoats, such as terrorists, are powerful in a negative sense.

Girard expresses the vulnerability of the scapegoat in terms of immunity from reprisal:

> All our sacrificial victims, whether chosen from one of the human catego-ries enumerated above or, a fortiori, from the animal realm, are invariably distinguishable from the nonsacrificial beings by one essential characteris-tic: between these victims and the community a crucial social link is missing, so they can be exposed to violence without fear of reprisal. Their death does not automatically entail an act of vengeance...sacrifice is primarily an act of violence without risk of vengeance...the desire to commit an act of violence on those near us cannot be suppressed without a conflict; we must divert that impulse, therefore, toward the sacrificial victim, the creature we can strike down without fear of reprisal, since he lacks a champion.[32]

Freedom from the risk of reprisal is paradoxical. The scapegoat action is itself vengeance and sacrificial rites often include references to vengeance, but the capacity of the victim for revenge is ruled out.[33] In a religious context, the surrogate victim appears "as a being who submits to violence without provoking a reprisal; a supernatural being who sows violence to reap peace; a mysterious saviour who visits affliction on mankind in order subsequently to restore it to good health."[34]

Girard highlights a number of ways in which a scapegoat can be considered as illegitimate to justify the scapegoat action.

> Like Oedipus, the victim is considered a polluted object, whose living presence contaminates everything that comes in contact with it and whose death purges the community of its ills—as the subsequent restoration of public tranquillity clearly testifies. That is why the *pharmakos* was paraded about the city. He was used as a kind of sponge to sop up impurities, and afterward he was expelled from the community or killed in a ceremony that involved the entire populace.[35]

Blaming the crisis on the victim casts a sense of illegitimacy on the victim.

> As we have seen, the inquest on Laius's death is in fact an investigation into the general subject of the sacrificial crisis; and it is clearly a matter of

pinning the responsibility for the troubled state of the community on some individual, of framing a reply to the mythical question *par excellence*: "Who initiated the crisis?" Oedipus fails to fix the blame on Creon or Tiresias. Creon and Tiresias are successful in their efforts to fix the blame on him. The entire investigation is a feverish hunt for a scapegoat, which finally turns against the very man who first loosed the hounds.[36]

A scapegoat who has committed a crime may also be considered illegitimate. The word "crime" comes from the Greek *krino*, which deals with judgment about an action or person, and judgment relates to making distinctions. Girard argues that the actions of scapegoating, vengeance, and legal punishment have common factors. "Crimes" are actions that the community believes threaten its distinctiveness. Crimes that "eliminate differences" are of special concern to the scapegoating community. Actions that justify scapegoating strike at the heart of the culture.

> First, there are violent crimes which choose as object those people whom it is most criminal to attack, either in the absolute sense or in reference to the individual committing the act: a king, a father, the symbol of supreme authority, and in biblical modern societies the weakest and most defenceless, especially young children. Then there are sexual crimes: rape, incest, bestiality. The ones most frequently invoked transgress the taboos that are considered the strictest in the society in question. Finally there are religious crimes, such as profanation of the host. Here, too, it is the strictest taboos that are transgressed.[37]

Knowing the cultural taboos is essential in understanding the scapegoat mechanism, because the taboos determine the gravity of what is interpreted as a "crime."

The criminal justice system may be used to exact vengeance even though "it is not self-perpetuating and its decisions discourage reprisals."[38] What separates the scapegoat from those who commit crime is the degree to which the prosecution of the crime is a persecution for being different.

There is also a sense of illegitimacy from violating a taboo. Girard cites examples in which African kingship ceremonies resemble sacrificial rituals where the king commits incest as the grounds for a public humiliation followed by enthronement. In one case, the king's potential partners for incest "are virtually all the women formally forbidden him by matrimonial regulations: mother, sisters, daughters, nieces, cousins, etc."[39] In another instance "the king is required to commit all the forbidden acts that are imaginable and possible for him to commit" to justify a "punishment of the severest sort" whereby "the needful insults and hostilities find their outlet in sacrificial ceremonies in which the king plays the chief role—the role of the original victim."[40]

The illegitimacy in an organization may stem from individual mistakes or taking unnecessary risks. Scapegoat[41] victims can reconcile a community if they are regarded as powerful individuals or groups. This sense of power has two aspects. First, a powerful individual may be the object of mimetic phenomena. Job was first among equals.[42] Caesar was the most powerful in Rome. Kings and the upper class have frequently been scapegoats.[43] Second, the scapegoat must be powerful enough to resolve the crisis. The blood of the victim, either literally or metaphorically, must be able to bring the community to a feeling of reconciliation. The power of the sacrificial victim could reside in the evil the victim can perpetrate or the power or prestige associated with the victim. Both of these were evident in the persecution of the Jews during the Middle Ages. As physicians, Jews were perceived to have power over disease; they were also accused of having an "evil eye" that enabled them to bring about the plague. Those involved in a sacrificial mechanism genuinely believe that the victimization will benefit the group. "In the myth, the fearful transgression of a single individual is substituted for the universal onslaught of reciprocal violence. Oedipus is responsible for the ills that have befallen his people. He has become a prime example of the human scapegoat."[44] The combination of power and vulnerability make it possible for scapegoats to absorb the violence of a community or society.

What emerges is a scapegoat victim who takes on the hatreds and violence generated by the feelings of inadequacy and threats to identity needs resulting from mimetic rivalries. In some way, the victim stands for the whole community. To achieve the desired results, the victim must have some identification with the community, but, to meet the criterion of no reprisals, the victim must be sufficiently dissociated from the community.[45]

Scapegoats may also be venerated, becoming heroes or cult figures. As Girard points out,

> the *pharmakos*, like Oedipus himself, has a dual connotation. On the one hand he is a woebegone figure, an object of scorn who is also weighed down with guilt; a butt for all sorts of gibes, insults, and of course, outbursts of violence. On the other hand, we find him surrounded by a quasi-religious aura of veneration; he has become a sort of cult object. This duality reflects the metamorphosis the ritual victim is designed to effect; the victim draws to itself all the violence infecting the original victim and through its own death transforms this baneful violence into beneficial violence, into harmony and abundance.[46]

This tendency to glorify the scapegoat is expressed in the terrorist world through the concept author Robin Morgan develops as the "demon lover."[47] Women from the groups for which male terrorists fight glorify the violence of individuals who, for everyone else, are scapegoats. A certain romanticism develops around them and they receive rewards.

4.   Scapegoat Action

Scapegoat action is violent and can include killing, physically abusing or torturing, banishing, or emotionally shunning. It is a violence of exclusion— shutting someone out.[48] Sometimes it is a sudden spontaneous action and at other times it is a process that begins with gossiping and accelerates until a common mentality of blame emerges. The structure of scapegoating can be seen in ridicule where individuals laugh at one person saying, in effect, "I'm glad I'm not like *her!*"

I remember a radio interview with a stand-up comic who spoke about the stereotypes in humour. He left the business because of the hateful dimensions of getting people to laugh at the faults, weaknesses and stereotypes of others.

Sometimes a scapegoat action involves a subgroup within a culture. If the bystanders remain passive, the scapegoating happens and the bystanders become voyeurs. Sometimes, bystanders join the scapegoat action and the violence spreads mimetically. A scapegoat action in process is extremely difficult to stop.

Scapegoat Action

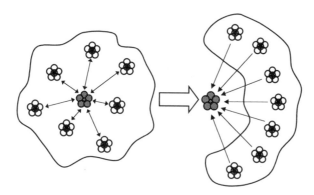

• Unanimity of the crowd – all against one or relative unanimity

• Action of exclusion

Killing	Physical abuse	Physical punishment	Censure
	Beating		Voted out
		Physical banishment	Lose position
	Throwing		Emotional banishment

| Systematic, well planned | Spontaneous |
| Over time | Immediate |

• Emotions captivate mind

Figure 4-4

In a scapegoat action, emotions captivate the mind. These emotions have a physiological dimension to them. The body's neuroconductors engage the whole body for action. The mind is harnessed to determine how to use the built-up energy. The emotions drive the mind rather than the mind driving the emotions. In a crisis, the emotions are violent and directed at the scapegoat. The mind picks up mimetically what everyone else is doing and action serves these structures of violence.

Girard describes violence in terms of root metaphors of seminal fluid, electricity, and microbes. For example, he states that violence has been "transformed into a sort of seminal fluid that impregnates objects on contact."[49] Let us examine the relationship between violence and sexuality and the root metaphor of the microbe.

Regarding the root metaphor of sexuality, Girard makes four very real associations between sexuality and violence.[50] First, sexuality is the basis of jealous rivalries and fighting.[51] Second, sexual desire can be diverted to surrogates if the original object of desire is inaccessible.[52] Third, when repressed energy builds up it can be expressed in a destructive paroxysm.[53] Fourth, sexual arousal and violence share a number of physiological reactions.[54]

Violence is compared to a microbe responsible "for the dread disease of violence."[55] This metaphor leads us to Girard's idea of contagion. Just as contact with the sick poses the risk of illness, so he suggests, "it is wise to steer clear of homicides if one is eager not to be killed." In a society without legal sanctions, Girard suggests, violent contagion could be more important than disease.[56] The awesome power of violence to remain, to grow, and move around creates a sense of awe, a fascination that is associated with the sacred. The potency of violence is seen in both reciprocal violence and the staying power of violence.

Another quality of violence is that people try to counter violence with violence, sometimes to "teach them a lesson." Regardless of the outcome, violence wins. "The mimetic attributes of violence are extraordinary—sometimes direct and positive, at other time indirect and negative."[57] So strong are its effects that the greater the effort to curb violent impulses, "the more these impulses seem to prosper."[58]

The form of violence in a scapegoat action is limited by the tools available. In early societies the means of killing a scapegoat included stoning, burning, drowning, or pushing off a cliff. In fact, the methods of scapegoating eventually became part of the culture; in medieval times the means of killing witches as scapegoats was well established—burning at the stake and drowning were common. Cultures where killing became less accepted used banishment. In nomadic cultures living in the wilderness, banishment was essentially a death sentence. In an office culture, the means of violence can be harassment or subtle, indirect ways of getting rid of someone, like arranging a transfer or using downsizing as an excuse to lay someone off. Although the violence may look benign and be framed in acceptable terms, the emotions and the structure are similar.

Why does everyone get involved in the scapegoat action? Girard's answer lies in mimetic doubling in which people form their identity need satisfiers in response to their double.

> If violence is a great leveller of men and everybody becomes the double, or "twin," of his antagonist, it seems to follow that all the doubles are identical and that any one can at any given moment become the double of all the others; that is, the sole object of universal obsession and hatred.[59]

In this situation,

the slightest hint, the most groundless accusation, can circulate with vertiginous speed and is transformed into irrefutable proof. The corporate sense of conviction snowballs, each member taking confidence from his neighbor by a rapid process of mimesis. The firm conviction of the group is based on no other evidence than the unshakable unanimity of its own illogic.[60]

This violence comes from a spread of doubles that wipes out differences "heightening antagonism but also making them interchangeable. The rebirth of order demands the triumph of disorder."[61]

Girard sees the transformation from disorder to order as almost miraculous.

Here we are in the very midst of the crisis, when all the circumstances seem to militate against any unified course of action. It is impossible to find two [people] who agree on anything, and each member of the community seems intent on transferring the collective burden of responsibility to the shoulders of his enemy brother [or sister]. Chaos reigns. No connecting thread, however tenuous, links the conflicts, antagonisms, and obsessions that beset each individual. . . . Yet it is at this very moment, when all seems lost, when the irrational runs amok amid an infinite diversity of opinions, the resolution of the dilemma is at hand. The whole community now hurls itself into the violent unanimity that is destined to liberate it.[62]

The hatred directed toward the scapegoat unites members of the community. They forget their antagonisms, and the violent emotions that they have had for one another are projected onto the surrogate victim. Everyone becomes united in desiring the same negative—the destruction of the scapegoat.

The range of scapegoating acts has two common elements. First, the scapegoat who was perceived to be different at the onset of the scapegoat action is now viewed as radically different. Second, the person is objectified—the human doesn't really matter. In Buber's terms, the scapegoat becomes an "it." In terms of social psychology, the scapegoat is dehumanized and demonized.

5.   A Hidden Process

The scapegoaters consider the entire process totally legitimate. They see a crisis, believe there is something illegitimate about the one or ones who were "different," and place responsibility for the crisis on those who are different. As feelings rise suddenly a group of people, imitating one another, seize on the victim, others join, and the victim is ejected from the group. The community feels that justice has been done.

No community deliberately sets out to scapegoat someone. Along with the community sense that the process is legitimate is the sense that the scapegoat actually deserves what happens. Girard, throughout his writings, continues to insist that this is essential to the process—it is hidden to the perpetrators.

A Hidden Process

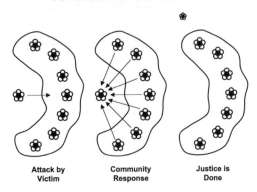

Attack by Victim	**Community Response**	**Justice is Done**

- Process is legitimate
- Victim deserved it
- Victim thought of as impervious to pain – a non-person
- Can't see effects of suffering
- Differentiation
- Not really human
- Better for one to leave than for whole community to suffer

Figure 4-5

Scapegoating is hidden through the language of justice, pragmatism, or fear. The scapegoat has been framed (sometimes literally) as being responsible for a crisis. In response to this mimetically shared "knowledge," which circulates to the point of certainty, is it not just to deal with the problem person? Does the illness not demand a cure? And if the problem is not dealt with there is a risk the situation will get worse.

6.   *Experience of the Victim*

What happens to the victim? Suddenly the whole community turns against the victim with a very real threat of violence. The human identity needs of the victim reveal fear based on the threat to security.

Experience of Victim

Human Identity Needs

- Fear
- Dissociation – hard to connect with others
- Meaning – loss of place, injustice
- Recognition – all good is disregarded
- Powerless

Trauma

- Gripped by fear
- Dissociation
- Inverted meaning – "I must be wrong"

Figure 4-6

In the need for connectedness, the victim is sad at being cut off from former friends. If the attack causes trauma, the victim is alienated and loses the ability to connect with others. The capacity to take action within the community is removed and the victim loses self-esteem.

The threat to meaning raises two possible responses. In the first scenario, the victim accepts the interpretation that he or she has done something wrong and internalizes guilt: "I had this coming to me." In a second scenario, the scapegoat maintains innocence and sees the injustice of the situation. This, in turn, leads to other possible developments. First, the victim may successfully fight back, or at least remove a sense that the process is legitimate, resulting in failed scapegoating. Second, the victim may say, "It is unjust but there is nothing I can do about it." The process would then unfold in an unquestioning way. Third, the victim may unsuccessfully protest or fight back.

7.   The After-Effects

There are two after-effects of the scapegoat action. The first is a sense of peace and an introduction of a new order. The second is the development of myths, prohibitions, and rituals to preserve the community and provide the means to deal with, and prevent, further crises.

After-Effects

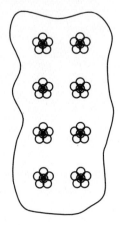

- Order
- Relief
- Togetherness
- Fear of conflict – avoid, put taboos in place
- Nice, nice
- New rituals, practices

Figure 4-7

After the scapegoating, people feel at peace. The community has been united. How could everyone be wrong? There is a sense of togetherness and co-operation. Almost everyone is afraid of violence and another crisis, and individuals go out of their way to co-operate. The absence of the scapegoat creates new possibilities; the vacuum is filled by new positions with new personalities. People know their place within a new order.

According to Girard, after an incident of sacrificial victimization, there will initially be peace, but the community will later confront a new round of mimetic rivalries with the potential of reciprocal violence. To prevent another mimetic crisis, violence within the community can be dealt with through a sacrificial victim. There are two aspects to sacrificial victimage. The first is the act of sacred violence, ritual sacrifices. The second is the aspect of differentiation. Within a culture those with the power to achieve harmony through leadership or victimage are ascribed particular powers (the Sacred). They are in the community, yet somehow differentiated.

Remembering the effect of the sacrificial victimization, the community, in Girard's scheme, develops a sacrificial ritual. The ritual aims to "produce a replica, as faithful as possible in every detail of a previous crisis that was resolved by means of a spontaneously unanimous victimization."[63] This victimization was made possible through eliminating differences in mimetic doubling; it is the interchangeability of doubles "that makes possible the act of sacrificial substitution."[64]

Examples include the founding of Rome through the murder of Remus and the ascendancy of his brother Romulus. Livy says of Remus: *In turba cecidit*—he fell into a mob.[65] Cain, in the biblical account, was the first to build cities; he began after killing Abel. The five Ojibway clans have totems from six "anthropomorphic supernatural beings," one of whom was "caused to return to the bosom of the great water" because his glance was powerful enough to kill people.[66] The staple foods of the Tikopian people were believed dropped from the hands of a foreign being who stole the foods from the table and then was chased away.[67]

Girard sees myth and ritual integrally related.[68] Myth grounds ritual in a meaning system that gives it power and ritual is the means to achieve the positive effects of community reconciliation. Myth and ritual both help to set out the identity of individuals and groups.

The capacity for interchangeable substitution makes sacrificial rituals possible. Different cultures have a variety of substitutions. They include:

1. A human sacrifice can be offered. The classic example of a human sacrifice is the Greek *pharmakos*, discussed earlier, who was honoured for healing powers but was sacrificed or expelled at a time of crisis.[69]

2. A surrogate animal, which resembles the community and is close to the community, can be sacrificed. Quoting the work of Joseph de Maistre, Girard emphasizes that animal victims are the most *human* in nature.[70] For example, among the Nuer and the Dinka of the Upper Nile, society was structured around, and in similar fashion as, cattle. "The cattle are thereby differentiated in such a way as to create a scale of values which approximates human distinctions and represents a virtual duplicate of human society. Among the names bestowed on each man is one that also belongs to the animal whose place in the herd is most similar to the place the man occupies in the tribe."[71] When we understand this phenomenon, the designation of cattle and sheep as "clean"—capable of being sacrificed—by the pastoral ancient Israelites takes on additional meaning.

> In Swaziland, anybody holding a key position in the government or anywhere else is called "Indvuna" which means "The Male." For example Indvuna y'eTemfundvo is "The Male Minister of Education." The king of Swaziland is also called "The Lion of the Swazis" (Ingwenyama Yemaswati). The queen mother is referred to as "The Female Elephant" (Indlovukati) as the most prestigious title.
>
> —Richard Batsinduka

3. The sacrificial ritual can be carried out symbolically on a real person. For example, as noted before, in Swaziland the "king is required to commit an act

of incest, either real or symbolic on certain solemn occasions—notably, at his enthronement or in the course of the periodic rites of renewal" (and during the *Incwala* [harvest] ceremony).[72] The king must commit other transgressions and certain acts of violence associated with evil. He then incarnates impurity. Because of this, he is "subjected to the ritualistic insults and abuse of his people."[73] He is treated as a criminal and the royal army might even stage a mock attack on the king. Eventually he accedes to the throne.

In each of these sacrificial rituals, there is a relationship between the sacrificial victim and the original surrogate victim. The difference is that in "the original event, it is unleashed violence that is checked and at the same time partially appeased; in the ritual reenactment, it is the more or less latent aggressions that are dealt with."[74] Like the original event there is a catharsis. The setting is "so strikingly similar to that of unanimous violence that one can only conclude that it is a deliberate, if not an entirely exact, imitation of unanimous violence."[75] In the ritual, the sacrificial victim is substituted for the surrogate victim of the original event—as opposed to a member of the community or the whole community. "As this [surrogate] victim itself serves as substitute for all the members of the community, the sacrificial substitution does indeed play the role that we have attributed to it, protecting all the members of the community from their respective violence—but always through the intermediary of the surrogate victim."[76] This involves a double substitution, one superimposed on the other: the surrogate victim for the community and the sacrificial victim for the surrogate.

The victims for scapegoating and rituals tend to be different. The initial scapegoat victim comes from inside the community, but the ritual victim comes from outside. This protects the community from another round of feuding and reprisals.[77] Likewise, the function for the two acts is different. The original scapegoating was curative—it dealt with a crisis. Rituals, developed during relative calm, are meant to prevent violent conflicts from erupting by projecting violent impulses onto the sacrificial victim, thus purging the community of violence. In Chinese literature, sacrificial rites are said to "'pacify the country and make the people settled.... It is through the sacrifices that the unity of the people is strengthened' (CH'U YU II, 2). The *Book of Rites* affirms that sacrificial ceremonies, music, punishments, and laws have one and the same end: to unite society and establish order."[78]

Animal sacrifices may receive "scorn, hostility, and cruelty" before slaughter. They take on the "very real (though often hidden) hostilities that *all the members of the community feel for one another*."[79] After death they receive ritualistic veneration.[80]

Common to sacrificial rituals and myths is the theme of unanimity—all against one. The Dinka stampede involves all the young men. If they cannot crush the animal a simulated symbolic stampede is performed before the slaughter. Similarly, in the Arabian camel sacrifice all persons participate in the death.[81]

At a certain point, a sacrificial ritual can lose its effectiveness. This can happen when the sacrificial ritual is exposed as scapegoating. A key point in Girard's theory is that scapegoating must remain hidden to work. In that way it retains a sense of mystery and accomplishes a feeling of community unity, group identity, and reconciliation, which is translated into reconciliation with God. If the sacrificial system is exposed, it loses both its concealment and mystique. It becomes commonplace, losing its sense of being sacred and its power.

In a pluralistic society, where the sense of in-group and community is more diffuse because people participate in many communities, the ritual patterns are more subtle. What figures more prominently in contemporary society is the aspect of social differentiation. As Girard points out,

> [i]f the unanimous victim truly reconciles a community, he[or she] will be turned into a transcendental model of differentiation and the mimetic forces destructive or preventative of symbolicity during the mimetic crisis that triggered the victimage will be rechannelled in differentiated and nonconflictual directions.[82]

When the fundamental rationale for differentiation is discredited as unjust, as when racism and sexism are shown to be wrong, the differentiation turns to mimetic rivalry and a violence of undifferentiation. There is once again a sense of crisis. This crisis is like the crisis precipitated when a sacrificial ritual loses its effect.

A social force in many communities is laughter—often a type of scapegoating. Since laughter is directed at the Other, the one who is different, it reinforces preserving traditional community distinctions. Girard observes that to join the crowd that is laughing, "you must associate with the violence contained in their laughter and not become the underdog. To make other people laugh, you must occupy—voluntarily or involuntarily—the position of the victim."[83]

Girard also sees the criminal justice system playing the same role as a sacrificial ritual, making a link between penal justice and violent retribution. Because it is a public system "an act of vengeance is no longer avenged; the process is terminated, the danger of escalation averted."[84]

After the scapegoating, there occurs what Girard calls a curative process. Harmony is restored to the community, and "the false premises that it maintains acquire, in consequence, an impregnable authority" that "hide[s] from sight the unanimous resolution as well as the sacrificial crisis."[85] The first step to justifying the action is based on the illegitimacy of the victim who has "plunged the community into strife." The second is based on the curative function of the victim who has "banished all trace of violence." This contrasts to the pre-victim state where every act of violence brought more violence. The explanation for the power of the curative transformation "falls to religion."[86]

Another dimension of the scapegoat phenomenon must be mentioned—the connection between scapegoating and the sacred. What is striking about the forces of the sacred is that their dominance over humans seems to increase in proportion to humanity's attempt to master them. Violence outflanks storms, forest fires, and plagues—"violence is the heart and secret soul of the sacred."[87] This can be linked to the human need for security. An overwhelming threat to security through uncontrollable forces produces an incredible fear. This fear calls on the deepest emotions and values and opens one up for the intervention of the sacred.

Sometimes scapegoating does not work as planned.

Permutations of the Scapegoat Mechanism

We have examined Girard's examples of scapegoating and sacrifice to define and illustrate violence that unites a group as it clears away mimetic rivalries that could get out of hand. There are, however, permutations of the scapegoat structure, where many of the conditions of scapegoating are present, but the lack of, or change to, some of the characteristics modifies the phenomenon. First we will examine scapegoating gone wrong—when it degenerates into murder that creates additional violence. Other scapegoating aspects are contrived scapegoating, interiorized scapegoating, complex scapegoat phenomena, and perpetual scapegoating. Examining "failed scapegoating" reveals other aspects of the scapegoat structure.

The sacrifice of Caesar does not work because Brutus cannot unite the people around the action; there is no "mimetic consensus of the entire people."[88] Girard uses the metaphors of hacking and carving to distinguish between two different types of action with similar structures but different motivations. When envy and wrath enter, the victims are mangled through a hacking action. A false differentiation ends up being a violent undifferentiation of the community. On the other hand, in carving "all aspects of culture seem harmoniously blended, the differential and the spiritual, the spatial, the ethical, and the aesthetic. This metaphor illustrates what we may call the 'classical moment' of sacrifice."[89]

> In the primitive ritual view, sacrifice fights violence not with ordinary violence, which would simply cause the crisis to escalate, but with a good violence that seems and therefore is mysteriously different from the bad violence of the crisis, because of its foundation in a unanimity that religion—that which binds men together—tends to perpetuate. If used wisely and piously, this good violence can stop the bad one from spreading whenever the latter reappears, as it necessarily must. Sacrifice is the violence that heals, unites, and reconciles, in opposition to the bad violence that corrupts, divides, disintegrates, undifferentiates.[90]

The effect of classical scapegoating converts the confusion of the mimetic crisis into a "relatively peaceful exchange."[91] The difference between good and bad violence is, in Girard's words, perishable; when it is lost an attempted sacrifice can make the crisis worse. This is what happened with the "sacrifice" of Caesar.[92] Classical scapegoating embodies a sense of solidarity with both ancestors and the whole community; failed scapegoating is contaminated by a mimetic rivalry.[93] Brutus and his co-conspirators made every attempt to appear "noble and disinterested. They must seem truly superhuman or they will not be seen as virtuous men who did what they had to do solely for the love of the Republic."[94]

> Brutus would like his "sacrifice" to be so beautiful that no confusion will be possible; it will be the absolute other of the crisis. The problem, however is that violence has only one absolute other and that is nonviolence, the abstention from all violence. Sacrifice cannot become the perfect other of envy and wrath without renouncing its specific means of action, without denying its own nature. Brutus cannot go the whole way: his real priority remains the murder; he simply wants to make it as effective as possible. He goes as far as he can in the direction of a nonviolence that he cannot embrace.[95]

In this situation we can see an initial scapegoat effect when a group of powerful individuals unite against a victim. Three interrelated things went wrong, from the point of view of scapegoat theory. First, there was insufficient differentiation; rivalry between victim and killers made the motive suspect. Second, killing the victim was not considered legitimate because the charges to justify the killing could not stick and the killing was considered murder. Third, the mob was not persuaded.

Any situation may contain complex scapegoating in which person after person becomes a scapegoat. For example, Shakespeare wrote *Richard III* when his own king was considered oppressive. The play contains many cycles of murder and revenge. All the main characters have benefited from a political murder. But none of the victims was innocent. Richard is presented as a "monstrous villain" with a deformed body mirroring the "self-confessed ugliness of his soul."[96] He is rejected as a scapegoat king in the last act. Throughout the play each character is villain or victim depending on the role played in the War of the Roses at any particular time. "Two images of the same character tend to alternate, one highly differentiated and one undifferentiated."[97] Also the women, Anne and Elizabeth, enter into a rivalry contrived by Richard for power. In structurally similar scenes, they walk over the dead bodies of those close to them to achieve their ends.

> These two women are even more vile than Richard, and the only character who is able to point out this vileness, thus becoming in a sense the only ethical voice in the whole play, is Richard himself, whose role, mutatis mutandis, is comparable to that of Shylock in *The Merchant of Venice*.[98]

According to Girard, Shakespeare makes his spectators uneasy because of the moral ambiguity of the characters. There is no simple answer to the question of who the scapegoat is. Yet the "demand for the expulsion of the scapegoat is paradoxically reinforced by the very factors that make this expulsion arbitrary."[99] Revenge with conviction demands a belief

> in the justice of your own cause. This is what we noted before, and the revenge seeker will not believe in his own cause unless he believes in the

guilt of his intended victim. And the guilt of that intended victim entails in turn the innocence of that victim's victim. If the victim's victim is already a killer and if the revenge seeker reflects a little too much on the circularity of events, his faith in vengeance must collapse.... To seek singularity in revenge is a vain enterprise, but to shrink from revenge in a world that looks upon it as a "sacred duty" is to exclude oneself from society, to become a nonentity once more.[100]

The legitimacy of the scapegoat may be called into question by the guilt of the scapegoaters because they have entered into a structure of mimetic violence. It may clear the air but it does not result in the same type of unity that classic scapegoating produces.

The Gospel story of Jesus and the Gerasene shows an entrenched scapegoat structure. The demoniac is banished to live outside the town in tombs; he has not been killed but is with the dead. The town is united in its sense of being different from this terrifying being.

They cannot do without him or he without them. This conjunction of both ritual and cyclical pathology is not peculiar. As it degenerates ritual loses its precision. The expulsion is not permanent or absolute, and the scapegoat—the possessed—returns to the city between crises. Everything blends, nothing ever ends. The rite tends to relapse into its original state; the relationships of mimetic doubles provoke the crisis of indifferentiation. Physical violence gives way to the violence of psychopathological relationships that is not fatal but is never resolved or ended. The total lack of differentiation is never reached.[101]

The permutations on scapegoating are like the case of Brutus: the scapegoating is neither clean nor decisive. The crisis is not totally resolved. There is a pathological co-dependence between scapegoat and community. They each know their place and play their roles.

The scapegoating is associated with the demonic.

The word *demon* can obviously be a synonym for Satan, but it is mostly applied to inferior forms of the "power of this world," to the degraded manifestations that we would call psychopathological. By the very fact that transcendence appears in multiple and fragmented form, it loses its strength and dissolves into pure mimetic disorder. Thus, unlike Satan, who is seen as principle of both order and disorder, the demonic forces are invoked at times when disorder predominates.[102]

The demoniac embodies the crisis that never goes away and has accepted an identity that mirrors a community.

Jesus commands the demons to leave the man and they enter pigs who run over a cliff into the sea. Jesus alludes to pigs as he warns his hearers not to throw pearls before pigs who would "trample them and then turn on you and tear you to pieces."[103] In the action of the pigs there is another permutation. One way of scapegoating is for a crowd to force the victim to the edge of a cliff and force the victim to fall to a sure death. In this case, the crowd of pigs goes over the cliff.

> What is the force that drives the pigs into the sea of Galilee if not our desire to see them fall or the violence of Jesus himself? What can motivate a whole herd of pigs to destroy themselves without being forced by someone? The answer is obvious. It is the crowd mentality, that which makes the herd precisely a herd—in other words, the irresistible tendency to mimetism. One pig accidentally falling into the sea, or the convulsions provoked by the demonic invasion, is enough to cause a stupid panic in which all the others follow. The frantic following fits well with the proverbial stubbornness of the species. Beyond a certain mimetic threshold, the same that defined possession earlier, the whole herd immediately repeats any conduct that seems out of the ordinary, like fashions in modern society.[104]

After the pig episode the victim is clothed and in his full senses. In this action we see the demoniac first as a perpetual scapegoat, kept outside the community. When the demons leave, the scapegoat phenomenon is transferred to the pigs who imitate a mob in their common action. As they fall over the cliff they mimic what has often happened to real scapegoats. Finally, the former demoniac is rehabilitated. At the turn of events, the crowd from the city is shaken. Their meaning system has been turned around and they ask Jesus to leave.

Girard sees Jesus and Job as "failed scapegoats" who unmask the scapegoat mechanism.[105] The story of Joseph is another biblical scapegoat story—that of a rehabilitated scapegoat. Moses bears many of the stereotypes of scapegoating. Abel has already been discussed. The prophets pointed to the futility of the sacrificial system and some of the Psalms can be read as the voice of the scapegoat victim. The stories of both Job and Jesus point out the innocence of the victim and reveal that the strong forces that attempt to scapegoat Job and succeed in scapegoating Jesus are, in fact, illegitimate even though the scapegoaters have their own rationale at the time. Unlike myths, which camouflage the scapegoat experience, these stories bring the structure of scapegoating into the open.

For Girard, the story of Jesus decisively unmasks the founding mechanism of culture that was hidden since the foundation of the world. This unmasking operates at two levels. First, it exemplifies "failed scapegoating" when the innocence of the victim is apparent. At a deeper level it changes the paradigm by which we view and interpret reality. As we crucify our victims we can no longer plead that "we know not what we do."

Girard describes scapegoating as a violence of differentiation; the scapegoat is thought of as totally different than others in the community.

We turn our attention now to hegemonic structures in which groups of people are systematically treated as "different" over time. This difference manifests itself in one group systematically dominating the other.

Chapter 5

Hegemonic Structures

When I attended a workshop based on the book, *New Vision for the Americas,* held at the American Academy of Religion, a number of the contributing authors were in attendance. George Cummings, an Afro-American liberation theologian, presented his "framework for race and class analysis,"[1] which pointed out that Latin American liberation theologians had analyzed structures of domination based on class, and African-Americans had identified similar structures based on race. Feminist analysts have exposed gender-based power structures and others have analyzed the domination of people based on age or weight. Cummings suggested looking for similar patterns of domination, treating each variant as an example of hegemonic structures.

Components of a Hegemonic Structure

A hegemonic structure is composed of a dominant group and a subjected group. In an ongoing way, the dominant group sets the agenda, makes the rules, and runs the show. The subjected group internalizes a sense of inferiority that keeps it subjected. As we see in Figure 5-1, a hegemonic structure has a number of components—physical, political, economic, discursive (identity and language), and pneumatic (having to do with spirit). Let's look at each of these.

Hegemonic Structures

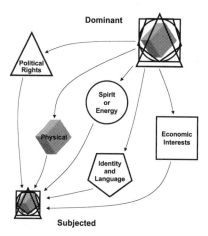

Figure 5-1

First, a hegemonic structure has a physical dimension. This includes using force to either put people in certain places, hurt them enough to force compliance, or confine certain groups to a specific space. To view slavery as a hegemonic structure, note that it began with a defeat of the slave population in a struggle. Then the slaves were chained and forcibly moved. If they did not comply with their masters' commands, they were beaten.

Another example of the physical side of a hegemonic structure is that of Jews in many European cities over the last thousand years. They were frequently forced to live in ghettoes from which it was unlawful for them to move.

The political aspect involves asymmetrical rights—the dominant group have more privileges than the subjected. For years in Canada, women did not have the right to vote. They were considered the property of their husbands. Until the law recognizing them as persons and another law giving them the right to vote, the political hegemonic structure kept them subjected in political processes. In Canada, people of Chinese descent were not allowed to vote for years, nor were Indians under the Indian Act. In South Africa under apartheid, whites, blacks, and coloureds were all named in the legal framework and each was given a different set of rights.

Political power can be formal or informal. Within a democracy, a hegemonic structure ensures that only certain people from the dominant group will be elected to govern. The same structure also ensures that certain dominant interests will have political influence.

Third, the economic interests of the dominant and subjected are differentiated. The rules are such that the wealthy become wealthier and the subjected become relatively poorer. At the extreme end are forms of slavery in which the subjected contribute their energy and those who control them reap the economic benefits. This happened in the British Empire when Africans became the slaves for plantations in the New World. It also occurred in Nazi Europe where subjected people became slave labourers in factories in Germany, Poland, France, and other countries.[2] More subtly, when men make the rules of economic life with their own interests at heart, it becomes difficult for women to enjoy the same level of benefit from the economic system. If, for instance, it is assumed that mothers take the primary role in child rearing, it becomes very difficult for them to compete in demanding careers.

A fourth aspect of hegemonic structures, language and identity, is key to maintaining hegemonic structures. This aspect of hegemonic structures, called discursive by theorist Antonio Gramsci, functions at different levels. At one level, the self-designations of people mean that some are more valued than others. When, during slavery, a grown man of African origin responded when called "Boy," he had internalized a self-designation that diminished his Self.

In the 1980s I came to know Paul Faguy, who had served in the Royal Canadian Air Force during the Second World War. He told of an assembly of soldiers from different parts of the British Empire. The officers commanded all "colonials" to step forward. Soldiers from Australia, New Zealand, and other countries obediently stepped forward. The Canadians stood their ground. All but the Canadians accepted a hegemonic structure that emphasized their inferior position to Great Britain.

Another aspect of language and identity is the pre-eminence of one language. In many places English receives such preferential treatment that one can see a linguistic hegemonic structure in place; access to information is privileged.

In some societies, accent plays a role in determining dominance and subjection. In some Canadian cities, First Nations people know that if they phone an apartment block for an apartment, speaking with an accent that identifies them as being Aboriginal, they will be told it is taken. For someone with a different accent, the apartment will be available.

Fifth, hegemonic structures include a presence or spirit that demands that people be subjected. Dominating people have an "air" that makes it difficult to stand up to them. This presence is expressed physically through a certain posture; it comes through in discourse by a tone that assumes obedience. In many ways it simply emanates from their being.

Discursive Hegemonic Structures

Literature related to hegemonic structures—in both anthropology and liberation theology—refers to Antonio Gramsci. Gramsci was an Italian Marxist who disagreed with Marx in a fundamental way. Marx saw hegemonic structures as basically a matter of class distinction and most significant in their economic and political expressions—what Marx called their superstructures. Not so, said Gramsci. He maintained that the most powerful hegemonic structures were based on language and the use of language and called them discursive hegemonic structures.

Gramsci emphasized that those subjected within hegemonic structures live contradictory lives. On one hand is an implicit consciousness, expressed in word and action, that unites a person with colleagues "in the practical transformation of reality."[3] The other consciousness, accepted uncritically, is a "verbal" conception that

> binds him to a certain social group, influences his moral behaviour and the direction of his will in a more or less powerful way, and it can reach the point where the contradiction of his conscience will not permit any action, any decision, any choice, and produces a state of moral and political passivity. Critical understanding of oneself, therefore, comes through the struggle of political "hegemonies," of opposing directions, first in the field of ethics, then of politics, culminating in a higher elaboration of one's own conception of reality. The awareness of being part of a determined hegemonic force (i.e., political consciousness) is the first step towards a further and progressive self-consciousness in which theory and practice finally unite.[4]

Gramsci's observations suggest that persons caught up in a discursive, or verbal, hegemonic structure are controlled from within. Their interior self-concept limits will and action and there is a tacit intrapersonal conflict between their capabilities inside and outside a particular relational structure. There may be no external boundaries, but the internal boundaries limit actions just as a whale held in captivity, who, when released, swims in circles the size of the former pool.

Discursive structures may be thought of as

the controlling metaphors, notions, categories, and norms that shape the predominant conceptions of truth and knowledge in the modern West...[and] are circumscribed and determined by three major historical processes: the scientific revolution, the Cartesian transformation of philosophy, and the classical revival.... [T]he idea of white supremacy emerges partly because of the powers within the structure of modern discourse—powers to produce and prohibit, develop and delimit, forms of rationality, scientificity, and objectivity which set perimeters and draw boundaries for the intelligibility, availability and legitimacy of certain ideas.[5]

Controlling the root metaphors and the criteria for ideas accepted as legitimate is a tremendous power. Ultimately, this is control of the world of meaning for a civilization, society, community, or tribe. In the previous quote, Cornel West refers to a discursive hegemonic structure in which Western thought shapes the way meaning is produced. Institutions come from meaning. For example, the institution of the United Nations is formed within a discursive structure that gives primacy to a political realism that is itself rooted in the primacy of nation-states.

The ability to establish the language and thought categories enables the dominant to control what happens. This control is so woven into culture that it seems to be common sense. As Linger defines it,

Hegemony is the maintenance of a political structure through the cultural shaping of experience, obviating or lessening reliance on illegitimate force. Although worked-out, explicit symbolic formulations constitute one aspect of hegemony, hegemony is not just ideology. Indeed, ideology is hegemony's weak point. Ideology is vulnerable because it is visible; public statements of belief and justifications of oppression invite contestation. Gramsci's originality lies in his emphasis on hegemony's invisible, insidious, more potent underside: the "practical consciousness" that saturates "the whole process of living...to such a depth that the pressures and limits of...a specific economic, political, and cultural system seem to most of us the pressures and limits of simple experience and common sense."[6]

Discursive hegemonic structures have been woven into the language of Rwanda, as Richard Batsinduka points out.

Tutsis were the dominant group in pre-colonial Rwanda. They then imposed their hegemonic structures on both Hutus and Batwa groups.

Tutsis were referred to as *Imfura,* the kinyarwanda term for "noble." Tutsi and *imfura* became synonyms. *Imfura* means also "first born," and in the Rwandan culture, the first born is the most cherished child by his father, mostly when he happens to be a male. That is why, in the story explaining the mythical origin of the three ethnic groups, Immana (God) had three sons: Ga*tutsi*, the first born, Ga*hutu*, the second born, and Ga*twa*, the last born.

When the first Westerners arrived in Rwanda, they described the Tutsis as cattlemen, Hutus as farmers, and Batwa as hunters.

Having a large number of cows was a good reason to be called a *Tutsi* or an *Imfura*, no matter what ethnic group you belonged to. The richest farmer was just a farmer.

A well-educated child, a child with good manners, had a quality called ikinyabup*fura*—the *imfura* behaviour or the *tutsi* behaviour. It means that it was close to impossible for a Hutu or a Mutwa to be polite. A Tutsi child who showed bad manners was said to be like a Hutu or like a Mutwa!

In brief, whatever was related to excellency was labeled as *tutsi*, and whatever was related to mediocrity was labeled as *hutu* or *twa*.

– Richard Batsinduka

Discursive hegemonic structures can be described as being like water to fish. Fish could not describe water because they do not have any other experience than to live in water. Likewise, those caught in discursive hegemonic structures are not aware of it. They internalize the reality either as controllers, in which case they are accustomed to people accepting their authority, or as people being controlled who feel they have no choice but to comply.

Examples of Hegemonic Structures

Ultimately, hegemonic structures involve a web of physical, economic, political, and discursive factors working together to keep the powerful in their positions and those who are subjected in their places.

In one week I heard speeches from an Israeli, advocating for Palestinians, and from the Israeli ambassador to Canada. Jeff Halpern, an anthropologist from Ben

Gurion University, analyzed the control structures being established by Israel over the West Bank. The elements of control included restrictions on rights of passage (physical), limitations including giving Israel priority in water use (economic), and strategic initiatives involving road construction and settlement placement to ensure control over the lives of Palestinians (political).

Linguistic hegemonic structures are significant in the Israeli-Palestinian conflict. The words used—"Israel" instead of "Palestine" or the "Mosque of Omar" instead of the "Temple Mount"—are examples of language shaping reality. The Israeli ambassador pictured Israel as being vulnerable and under siege—threatened by hostile neighbours and violent groups within the Palestinian population. Considering Israel's importance as a symbol and place for Jews from around the world, the stakes are so high that everything possible must be done to control the situation. What the Israelis consider measures to satisfy their needs for security and continuity is experienced by Palestinians as hegemonic structures. Roads that Israelis consider necessary to "guarantee safe passage between settlements" are seen as physical barriers locking Palestinians into one huge prison with many cells.

South Africa under apartheid exhibited the different aspects of hegemonic structures. Whites had political rights and economic control. The rights were enforced by white police and military officers. English and Afrikaans were dominant languages; discursive structures reinforced the priority of whites. Physically, the races were separated, with certain places off limits to blacks and coloureds. After apartheid was abolished, I met the General Secretary of the Peace and Justice Committee of the South African Conference of Catholic Bishops. He told of dismantling the political hegemonic structures but anticipated that clearing economic hegemonic structures would be more difficult.

Another example of a discursive hegemonic structure is the use of "man" to designate humanity. This, along with male language used when both men and women are involved, serves to underscore the priority of men. In the 1970s, those working on inclusive language were often scorned by men and women alike as being overly sensitive, corroborating the observation that for people who have internalized these structures they are "common sense."[7]

Feminist thinkers consider African-American women caught in a triple matrix of hegemonic structures based on race, class, and gender.[8] The experience within this threefold hegemonic structure is marked by suffering; as one woman said: "Ah done been in sorrow's kitchen and ah licked de pots clean."[9] This suffering can produce passive victims. The challenge for those criticizing these structures is to transform suffering, seen by Emilie Townes as "unscrutinized and unmetabolized pain," into a pain that is "recognized, named and then used for transformation."[10]

Links to Mimetic Theory

Remember that mimetic rivalries between people who identify with one another are most intense? This explains some of the violence patterns of hegemonic structures. Those who dominate identify with others who dominate and tend to become rivals with those groups.

In the early 1990s I met Tissa Balissuria, a theologian from Sri Lanka, who reminded me that during the colonial era the European powers carved the world into empires. Analyzing this observation through the lens of mimetic theory, I realized that the rivalries were not with the subjected people, but among the English, French, Spanish, Portuguese, and Dutch. The objects of mimetic desire were land, gold, and hegemony over peoples who became objectified.

Figure 5-2 illustrates how different relational systems can be understood within the context of hegemonic structures. In the first instance, dominant individuals or groups have mimetic rivalries with those whom they consider at their level. In other words, they imagine themselves in the same situation as their Other. The colonial competition for colonies is one example. In a patriarchal environment, men compete with men in a similar way as in most team sports where only men compete with men.

Mimetic Rivalry and Hegemonic Structures

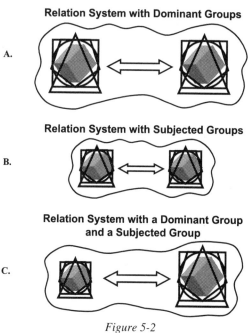

Figure 5-2

The second part of this figure illustrates the competitive relationship among subjected peoples within hegemonic structures. This can take two forms: intra-group rivalries or inter-group rivalries. In an identifiable group that is clearly second class in terms of economics, prestige, position, language, and/or politics, group members tend to vent their frustrations on one another. This is shown in crime statistics. In many United States cities, African-Americans rank high in crime statistics and in the jail population—far out of proportion to their numbers in a given city. Similarly, in Canada the statistics of violence and victimization among First Nations are disproportionately high. These two examples show oppressed people attacking those within their group.

Mimetic structures are most powerful among people who identify with one another. And in a closed relational system, such as a ghetto or a reserve, the potential for violence increases. Oppressed people may also attack other oppressed groups. Gangs, often part of a visible minority, engage in rivalries with gangs from other minorities. During the Rodney King riots in Los Angeles, African-Americans vandalized the shops of Korean merchants, members of another visible minority.

In a third type of relational system, depicted in Figure 5-2C, people who are subjected are in rivalry with people who are powerful. In an entrenched hegemonic structure, the dominant rivalries are at the level of the first two diagrams. When a hegemonic structure begins to break down, and the subjected identify with the dominant, a new type of mimetic rivalry becomes possible. If we consider the race-related hegemonic structures in United States to be in a period of change, we see how the dominant culture has imitated elements of African-American culture and how African-Americans are competing in many worlds of meaning with their Euro-American counterparts.

Change occurs when people who are subjected become aware of their situation and work to change the structures. They begin to imagine themselves in the same position as the dominant. One example is the social change regarding gender roles in North America since the 1960s. Throughout the 1950s, following World War II, women were predominantly cast in domestic roles. As the feminist movement gained ascendancy in the '60s and '70s, women began to see possibilities of work considered men's domain. Previously, their rivalries had been with other women over household and family issues. As the relational system was reframed and women began to identify with men, a new set of mimetic rivalries became possible. For their part, men found this threatening; now someone who did "women's work" was deemed to be at par with them. Some men regarded this as a diminution of their status. Within marriages, where both husband and wife had careers, as well as having greater responsibilities at home (though usually women did much more on the domestic front), new rivalries were possible. The lack of preparation to name and deal with this new rivalry may have contributed to many marriage break-ups.

When Canada was founded, the country was thought to be made up of two equal "founding Nations"—English and French. However, in time the English gained ascendancy and a hegemonic structure evolved with the English dominant. For awhile, the French of Québec were isolated and their rivalries were internal. In the Quiet Revolution of the 1960s, in which this hegemonic structure was identified, sovereignists declared that the way to change this structure was for Québec to become a sovereign nation—establishing hegemony over a particular territory as the English had done. Meanwhile, nationalist sentiment grew among First Nations people, also subjected by English-dominated governments and companies, who felt that their claim to nationhood was more legitimate than the French. They also called into question the "two founding nations" concept.

For decades, Western Canada perceived itself to be dominated by Central Canada and felt that the only way to change this hegemonic structure was through political reform to give the provinces more power. One way this could happen is through an elected Senate with an equal number of senators for each province (as in the United States). This, however, would structurally entrench English hegemony over French, flying in the face of the two founding nations mythology.

Hegemonic Structures and Scapegoating

Scapegoating has been presented by René Girard as a violence of differentiation—the Other becomes so totally other that they are no longer seen as fully human. Within subjected communities, the scapegoat is frequently someone closely tied to the community yet distinguished from the community in some way.

In the early 1990s I presented scapegoat theory to the annual gathering of the Aboriginal Nurses Association. They immediately identified with it because they often worked in communities other than their own. As Aboriginal nurses they were close to the community but could still be singled out. As professionals and outsiders they were different enough to become scapegoats.

Some scapegoats come from within communities and are distinguished by their position within hegemonic structures. Sometimes these are people who excel and are stigmatized as "thinking they are better than others." This happens within both dominant and subjected groups. In a widespread crisis, dominant and subjected groups become scapegoats for one another. A subjected group may blame its problems on the dominant group and a dominant group may feel under grave threat by a subjected group. This especially happens when a hegemonic structure has been exposed and begins to disintegrate. In South Africa, when apartheid was being exposed and challenged, black South Africans united against the dominant whites and many of the whites banded together against the black threat. Now that the apartheid political hegemonic structure has changed, crime rates have risen drastically. White people are increasingly victimized by black people, who are no longer held in check by a hegemonic structure that locked them into identifying only with their own kind.

In other writing I have argued that the criminal justice system can be seen as a scapegoat-sacrificial mechanism in which people on the bottom side of hegemonic structures are expelled from the community through the criminal justice system.[11]

At a broader level, a hegemonic structure can be seen as a permanent, or relatively permanent, and ongoing mimetic structure of violence. The subjected become a perpetual scapegoat class for the dominant.

Hegemonic Structures and the Role of Theory

Hegemonic structures are well hidden, shown only in subtle ways. Uncovering the hegemonic structures is one of the tasks of hermeneutics, or interpretation. George Cummings emphasizes ways in which these structures are particularly evident in discourse, the focus of hermeneutics.[12] Hermann Rebel describes the hermeneutical task more definitively:

The hermeneutical approach calls into question and undermines our confidence in commonsensical interpretative approaches to our own and others' presentations—in speech, texts, rituals, and so on—of living experiences. Secure in the knowledge that no one is able to return to an original "text" of reality, the hermeneuticists' enterprise is essentially subversive, pointing out the self-contradiction and incompleteness of ostensibly integrated and authoritative histories of literature, of history or of the self.[13]

Hermeneutics consciously brings an awareness of theory to the interpretation of reality. In this case, a knowledge of mimetic theory, human needs theory, and theory about hegemonic structures helps us see new dimensions of different conflicts.

Besides helping to analyze several dimensions of the conflict (threat to the need for distributive justice, need for autonomy), this mode of analysis uses a strong ethical dimension when it acknowledges that domination and control are oppressive, hence, morally wrong. This understanding was developed by liberation theologian George Cummings looking for a transcendent category that could show similarities of oppression based on class (classical Latin American liberation theology), race (developed by black liberation theologians), gender (feminist and womanist analysis), sexual orientation, and age. The study of discursive structures of domination helps to explain the subtle and powerful ways used to keep various identity groups in a subordinate position.

Hegemonic structural analysis of deep-rooted conflict exposes hidden patterns that have a strong psychological impact on individuals and groups. These patterns reinforce feelings of shame and entitlement in both "oppressed" and "oppressors." Rafael Moses expresses the relationship this way:

I choose to put shame and entitlement together because I believe that there is a connection between the two. They are connected in that each of them is closely related to the self and to narcissistic proclivities. Even more than that, it seems to me that shame and entitlement are in some ways opposite sides of the same coin. A person who is full of conscious shame will usually not really feel a conscious sense of entitlement. The converse is also true: a person brimming with a conscious sense of entitlement mostly does not consciously feel shame. Nor do shame and a sense of entitlement consciously coexist, either. However, repressed shame, particularly of past suffering perceived as shameful, at times serves as the basis for a sense of excessive entitlement that may be or become conscious. This latter dynamic of repressed shame leading to a strong sense of entitlement helps to explain the powerful emotions behind liberation movements.[14]

Moses' observations show that within subjected groups the consistent lack of recognition produces ongoing shame. The sense of entitlement among the dominant shows that satisfiers for their need for recognition are high—leaving them vulnerable to threat if ever they are not recognized in the way to which they have become accustomed.

As analysts expose these structures, they provide a rationale for significant social change by explaining that many different groups can experience similar patterns of entrenched power relationships. If the structures are based on ethnonationalist groupings, the resulting call for change may lead to open conflict. Where violence is legitimized through the language of liberation, the deep-rooted conflicts that break out may be quite violent.

Hegemonic structural analysis, however, does not answer the question: How do hegemonic structures originate and what might be an ethical foundation in a society without such structures? It also does not account for the significant amount of violence within subcultures, which are themselves dominated by others, nor does it provide an ethical program to be in effect when the "oppressed" come to power.[15] Cummings, citing West, makes the point that "the idea of supremacy in the modern West [cannot] . . . be fully accounted for in terms of the psychological needs of white individuals and groups."[16] This suggests that something in the pattern of relationships acquires a life of its own. This anticipates the concept of mimetic structures of violence developed in Chapter 8.

Chapter 6

Ethnonationalism

Ancestors are a part of us and, hence, a part of our stories, contributing to our identity. Their own stories were passed down to us with our mother's milk and our genetic makeup comes from them. Our forebears gave us culture—a vast array of values, behaviours, gestures, affectations, and markers that tell us when and how to speak, how to respond to provocation, and what to feel bad about. Persons with the same ancestors have the same culture, know the same myths, and can laugh at the same jokes. They are our kin, our people, and we share an ethnocultural group with them.

I grew up with a mixture of ambivalence and ambiguity about my own ethnocultural group. I was raised in the Mennonite Brethren Church—and here begins the ambiguity. The MBs (as they are known within Mennonite circles) originated as a reform movement within the Mennonite colonies in the southern part of the Russian empire (Ukraine) in the early 1860s. My ancestors were part of the Anabaptist movement in sixteenth-century Holland who moved to Prussia in the late 1500s to escape persecution. They lived there as the "Quiet in the Land" until Catherine the Great opened the Ukraine for settlement in 1789. They moved to the southern part of the Russian empire under a special agreement recognizing their pacifist beliefs. Later they moved to Canada with a similar agreement in place.

My great-grandparents Kroeker joined the Mennonite Brethren in Southern Manitoba in the late 1800s and were part of the first MB church in Canada. My family story included grandparents and great-grandparents who had been leaders in the MB church. My "Opa," great-grandfather William Bestvater, who started the first MB institution in Winnipeg in 1905, had lectured on his dispensational Bible chart throughout western Canada and the United States. Grandpa Kroeker was known as "Mr. Sunday School" for having introduced Sunday school curricula into the Canadian MB church in the 1950s. My Grandma Redekop, sharp-witted and strong-willed, challenged the moderator at a Canadian MB Conference about her right to speak up as a woman. I grew up with the missionaries, Bible teachers, and conference leaders who stayed at our house or with my grandparents nearby. Like other "Russian Mennonites," I loved ethnic foods such as rollkuchen, porzelky, perishky, wareneki, and holopse. I knew a smattering of Low German and could sing the old High German religious songs.

So what was my identity group? If it was faith-based, as proclaimed, where was my ethnicity? And if I was Mennonite by birth and ethnicity, what did that say about my relationship to those Mennonite Brethren from other backgrounds who joined the church out of conviction? And the fact that the ethnic foods I grew up with bear strong resemblance to traditional foods of Ukrainians, Germans, and Dutch—reflecting the places my ancestors lived—calls into question my own senses of difference.

It is interesting how religion and ethnicity converged for me, because throughout history many have been gripped by similar convergences.

Before continuing, I must emphasize that self-awareness of being part of an identity group comes about in the presence of one's Other. In many cultures, the word for one's tribe is the word for human being, as if all the humans that were known or recognized belonged to that group. Between training sessions in Taiwan, I talked with the Aboriginal people about the names of their peoples. One young woman pointed out that her tribe's name was the word for human being. In broken English she jokingly stated, "I am human being, you are not human being." As one encounters the Other, various features of identity that were taken for granted as part of the tacit knowledge base become clear and articulated. The next chapter will focus on the dynamics of the Self-Other relationship; ideally, it should be read concurrently with this one because the self realizations in this chapter come through interaction with other identity-groups.

Intertwined Strands of Ethnonationalism

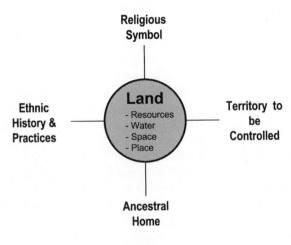

Figure 6-1

From the literature on ethnonationalism, stories I have heard from around the world, and a reflection on my own identity, emerge five strands that can be braided together to form an ethno-identity, a sense of belonging to a people. They are ancestry, ethnicity, religion, land, and politics. For each individual and each group, the relative importance of each strand is different. Each strand has within it key elements with varying degrees of significance.

The following table indicates key elements involved in each of the five strands.

Ancestry	Religion	Ethnicity	Land	Politics
Blood	Ritual	Culture	Space	Leadership
Perception	Tradition	Language	Place	Governance
Story	Transcendence	Values	Symbols	Laws
Family	Spirituality	Chosen trauma	Belonging	Institutions
Clan	Authority	Chosen glory	Territory	Control
DNA	Ultimate values	Collapse of time	Control	Realism
Psychological	Ultimate rewards	Ethno-drama	Purity	Nation-State
DNA	Ultimate punishment	Boundary markers		Entitlement
	Root metaphors	Rules of inclusion		Rights
		and exclusion		Ideology

Before elaborating on these five strands, I must acknowledge that new types of identity groups are forming on the basis of shared values, such as environmentalism or multinational business. Their role in relation to ethnonationalism will be discussed at the end of the chapter.

Helpful tools in understanding these strands are the concepts of enframing (who we are) and emplotting (when we began). Ethnic or religious groups involved in an identity-based conflict enframe who and what belong to their identity group very carefully; sometimes others enframe the identities of people very differently. For instance, Jews in Europe who converted to Christianity enframed themselves within the Christian Church. They were, however, considered Jews by the National Socialists. In one case, the enframing was based on religion; in the second, it was based on "race." Emplotting is critical to group identity. When did the group start and what events were pivotal in its formation? Going back very far, most persons are related and part of the same identity group. If the group definition uses a later start date, the identity group is smaller.

If I start the emplotment of my own religious heritage in 1525, for example, I am locked into the Anabaptist tradition; if I begin at 1536 I am differentiated as a Mennonite. However, if I wish to start in the year 1400, my ancestors were part of the Roman Catholic Church in the Netherlands.

An interesting example of emplotment occurred with the Greeks who had been part of a polyglot cultural group within the Ottoman empire. When modern Greece was established in the 1800s, their history was re-emplotted to connect contemporary Greeks with ancient Greek civilization. People changed their identity and language.

Definitions

Literature in the field helps to define related terms associated with ethnonationalism.

One of the most influential theorists on this topic has been Walker Connor, who first introduced and defined the concept of ethnonationalism.[1] Connor and other theorists help us define ethnonationalism and the related concepts of aboriginality and consociation.

Connor sees ethnonationalism as synonymous with nationalism: "Nation connotes a group of people who believe they are ancestrally related. Nationalism connotes identification with and loyalty to one's nation as just defined. It does *not* refer to loyalty to one's country."[2] Connor stresses that the essence of ethnonationalism is the intangible attitude of a "self-differentiating ethnic group."[3] Vesna Dasović Marković takes the sense of uniqueness a step further in her observation that some groups, like the Serbs, see their people as being "celestial."

However, a "prerequisite of nationhood is a popularly held awareness or belief that one's own group is unique in a most vital sense. In the absence of such a popularly held conviction, there is only an ethnic group."[4] The strong sense of uniqueness comes about through an awareness of others, as Patrick Macklem writes: "The optimistic position fails to consider that, while the idea of being friends presupposes knowledge of each other, so does the idea of being rivals. Indeed, the self-awareness which is the *sine qua non* of the nation requires knowledge of non members."[5] Macklem draws on Max Weber for the idea that the consciousness of being a separate group is "derived from a *myth* of common descent. Members of the nation feel or intuitively sense that they are related to one another."[6] Similar to the myth of descent is what Michael Levin calls an "ethnodrama, a history of denial and victimization…which justifies nationalism and a state as the only means of survival."[7]

Though ethnonational groups may have a number of tangible characteristics, for Connor, "such characteristics are relevant to the notion of the nation only to the degree to which they contribute to the intuitive sense of kinship as well as to the sense of vital uniqueness from non members."[8] This is corroborated by Manning Nash:

> The most common ethnic boundary markers in the ethnographic record and the most pervasive in any system of ethnic differentiation are *kinship*, that is, the presumed biological descent unity of the group implying a stuff or substance continuity each group member has and outsiders do not; *commensality*, the propriety of eating together indicating a kind of equality, peership and the promise of further kinship links…only one step removed

from the intimacy of bedding together; and a *common cult*, implicating a value system beyond time. [They are expressed through a] *single recursive metaphor*—blood, substance and deity.[9]

This vital sense of belonging is summed up in Rupert Emerson's disarming definition of a nation as "the largest community, which when the chips are down, effectively commands [people's] loyalty, overriding the claims both of lesser communities within it and those which cut across it or potentially enfold it within a still greater society."[10] In terms of passion, few expressions come closer than Bismarck's terse call as he was trying to unite Germans: "Think with your blood!"[11]

Some scholars offer other defining characteristics. Gurutz Bereciartu distinguishes among "*ethnic group*: human collectivity established on a determined territory with a community of consent and culture; *nation*: ethnic group endowed with its own political consciousness; and *nation-state*: a concrete form through which the modern nations have been structured juridico-politically."[12] Ted Gurr provides the following definitions:

> *Ethnonationalists*: Large, regionally concentrated peoples with a history of organized political autonomy... *Indigenous peoples*: Conquered descendants of the original inhabitants of a region who typically live in peripheral regions... *Ethnoclasses*: Ethnically or culturally distinct peoples, usually descended from slaves or immigrants, with special economic roles, usually of low status; *Militant sects*: Communal groups whose political status and activities are centered on the defense of their religious beliefs; *Communal contenders*: Culturally distinct peoples, tribes or clans in heterogeneous societies who hold or seek a share in state power.[13]

Michael Levin defines a strong and weak sense of ethnonationalism: "The demand of a state for every people is the strong sense of ethnonationalism, the extreme political expression of cultural identity."[14] The weak sense of ethnonationalism is the right to self-determination. This, however, "leaves unanswered the question of what forms of institutional recognition can meet the aspirations of a 'people' for autonomy.... New political forms which offer autonomy but do not offer sovereignty are difficult to imagine."[15] Regarding the connection between the two, he notes that "some claims to nationhood are expressed in terms of the strong sense of ethnonationalism, but recognize alternative possibilities in their demands for new institutional arrangements. Examples in Canada are the concepts of 'sovereignty-association' for Quebec and 'self-government' for Canadian First Nations peoples."[16] He points out that the "practical impossibility" of a "state for every people" makes "the sense of deprivation in its frustration all the more poignant."[17] However, the "politics of ethnonationalism worldwide draws its importance not from this disproportion of numbers, but from the facts that most states are culturally pluralistic and that more than half the governments of these independent states must deal with political claims made on an ethnic basis where there are few if any workable solutions."[18]

Levin defines aboriginality as a distinct type of ethnonationalism "based on historical experience" emphasizing "status as the original occupants of a place, adding depth to the idea of cultural differences.... As well as a basis for ethnonational claims, it is also a claim against immigrant ethnic groups."[19]

Michael Asch describes consociation as "one of the fundamental ways in which state ideology identifies citizens with respect to ethnonational identity."[20] States with a universalistic ideology, such as the United States, "identify citizens solely as individuals" recognizing "no ethnonational minority communities."[21] States that follow a consociational ideology may do so directly, in which case they refer to ethnonational collectivities in their constitution, or they may do so indirectly as a consequence of other principles, such as forming provinces so that a given ethnonational group is a majority within a given jurisdiction.[22] Stephen Ryan points out some difficulties with consociation theory; namely, "it places too much emphasis on the permanence of ethnic boundaries, exaggerates ethnic cleavages and also undervalues the existence of cross-cutting cleavages."[23]

The concepts of ethnonationalism, aboriginality, and consociation highlight some dynamics of deep-rooted conflict. These are the us-them syndrome, the interplay of similarity and difference, stereotypes, ethnic fusion and fission, the tension between self-determination and sovereignty, and the rights of ethnic groups. I will discuss these as I elaborate on the five contributing strands of ethnonationalism. Note that the relative importance of each of these varies significantly from case to case. They are also so intertwined that it is almost impossible to talk of any one in an exclusive way.

Ancestry

Because of the dynamics of human reproduction, ancestry as a factor in identity group formation and maintenance has a number of ambiguities. Sometimes two groups that are fighting share a common gene pool and biologically have the same ancestors but they frame the group's origin to count the ancestors in a way that sets them apart. Or they may choose to focus on religion or a non-biological factor as a primary identity marker. Another ambiguity arises when parents come from two distinct identity groups, or one parent comes from a clearly defined group and the other from an ambiguous background. Some people's identity may be described as "Heinz 57"—they have so many groups in their ancestry that they cannot be labelled as any traditionally defined group.

Rabbi Irwin Tannenbaum, a guest lecturer in my Hebrew Bible class, told the students that when he performs a circumcision, he has the feeling that Abraham, Sarah, and a long line of ancestors are peering over his shoulder. He places this action in the center of an ancestral path leading to the Father of his people, since Abraham was the first in the tradition to be circumcised.

In 1991, I was an analyst for the Citizens Forum on Canada's Future. Among the thousands of briefs and letters I analyzed were some from Canadians who were proud to be Italian-Canadians, Portuguese-Canadians, and so forth. Some protested the hyphenated Canadian phenomenon, saying that their parents came from many backgrounds and they were just plain Canadian. Some English-Canadians distinguished themselves as being of Loyalist stock and gave the number of generations since their ancestors had come to Canada after the American War of Independence. Likewise, on the French side, some gave the number of generations since their ancestors came as pioneers in the seventeenth century.

In some cases, ancestry in relation to identity is clear.

In my case, all of my ancestors as far back as can be established through genealogies were Russian Mennonites. My name is a common name among such people and it identifies my paternal ancestry as going back to the Netherlands. But maybe not in a strict biological sense. There is some ambiguity about the parents of my great-great-great-grandfather Redekop, and who knows—I may have some German or Polish ancestors from the Prussian period of Mennonite history.

In any case, the designation "Russian Mennonite" is relatively recent since the Mennonites didn't migrate to the Russian Empire until invited by Catherine the Great in 1789. It gained usage as a distinguishing term when Mennonites of different backgrounds began working together. It distinguishes those of this ancestry from "Swiss Mennonites" who came to the United States from Switzerland in the early eighteenth century and to Canada after the American Revolution.

When both parents come from a different background, there are several possibilities. First, one may choose the background of one parent as a primary identity. A friend of mine presents himself as a Scottish Canadian. His identity is rooted in a Canadian Scottish settlement and he knows Scottish history and culture very well. Anyone meeting him would think that he was pure Scot through and through. Only those who learn to know him well discover that one of his grandmothers was not Scottish. It is as though that part of his identity has fallen from his identity consciousness.

Sometimes an ethno or religious tradition has rules of lineage and identity to deal with this situation. Within Judaism, for instance, the mother determines the identity. If your mother is a Jew, you are a Jew. For Muslims, the father determines the identity. The Canadian Indian Act has a number of specific rules to determine who is a status Indian in cases of mixed parentage. In some cases, parents pass on both traditions to the child in a fairly balanced way. The family may also frame their identity according to a new supra-ethnonational designation. In the former Yugoslavia, Yugoslav identity served as a supranational identity within which Muslim Bosnians (known as Bosniacs), Orthodox Serbs, and Catholic Croatians were subsumed. There was much intermarriage and when the country broke up seven million people saw themselves as neither Bosniac, Serb, or Croat—simply Yugoslav.

One of the parents may also adopt the identity group of the other parent. This means that biological ancestry is different from mythological or metaphorical ancestry. This relates to Connor's emphasis that *perceived* common ancestry is what binds people together. The entry into an ancestral story and tradition is the important factor. It is a matter of interpretation.

"Blood" is a key metaphor for expressing the idea that a people have a shared ancestry. It may be a question, "Do you have any Italian blood? Jewish blood? Turkish? Aboriginal?" In the Mohawk quest to assert self-determination and self-governance, one key question has been: Who qualifies as a Mohawk? For a number of years the debate centred on a blood quantum that amounted to a fractional count of how much of the biological heritage was Mohawk.

The metaphor of blood is closely linked to that of race. People of a similar racial background have a sense of a common ancestry since racial characteristics are passed on biologically. In some instances, people of the same race may differentiate themselves as being from a different identity group. This may be based on religion or on starting the ancestry at a fixed point. Suppose all of my ancestors could be traced back to sixteenth-century Holland. Because of their association with the Anabaptist Mennonite movement, there was a new trajectory started so that over time, shared common ancestry with those whose roots predate that time and who did not share this common history becomes less relevant.

I, for example, do not consider myself an "ethnic Dutch or Flemish" person; however, when I walked the streets of Antwerp, I could not help but think that my ancestors could well have visited this city and I could not help but ask the tour guide at the Cathedral about the role of Mennonites in the history of that part of the world.

Race carries with it the ambiguities associated with shared parentage. Thanks to the quirks of genes, people may have racial characteristics that were introduced to the ancestry generations ago.

Even in situations where ancestry is considered pure on the surface, it is possible to discern ambiguities. Mohawks on Turtle Island (the designation of North America) had a practice historically of adopting indigenous peoples whom they conquered. Even a pure Mohawk today could have the "blood" of several tribes brought into the Mohawk people before contact with Europeans.

Shared common ancestry depends on how far back you go. Siblings in a family where the father and mother are the same have a definite shared ancestry. First cousins have a partial shared heritage. Eventually, there are extended families and clans claiming some portion of shared ancestry. These may be linked through race, ethnicity, historical religion, or nationality to others who claim the same forebears. Enframing a present identity group also enframes a particular historical emplotment going back either to the people living in a certain place as long as can be remembered or to a particular time when the ancestral group was set aside.

Shared common ancestry involves shared DNA. With the mapping of the human genome, the analysis of common ancestry can be more precise. It has been determined, for instance, that Northern Europeans can be traced back to a very small group of forebears (fewer than 100) that was nearly extinct. The lack of variation in the genes shows that the original gene pool was very small. By comparison, a country like Nigeria has a much more diverse gene pool.

The role of DNA in the formation of identity is complex. Neurobiologist Debra Niehoff states that within the scientific community the debate between nature and nurture in the development of the individuals has been resolved in favour of a dynamic dialectical relationship between the two. Even at the level of the cell, there is a constant interplay between the internal factors from the genetic code and external messages from neurotransmitters that instruct the cell which aspect of the genetic code to involve in a given response to stimuli.[24]

This constant interplay between genes and enviro-relational factors is related to Vamik Volkan's concept of psychological DNA. Volkan writes that we pick up on many psychologically patterned responses to different types of situations from our mothers, our fathers, and the close circle of family and friends.[25] This psychological DNA comes to us with our mother's milk; in fact, there may be hormones and neurotransmitters that literally are a part of the milk, depending on the emotional state of the mother. Beyond that, consider the hypermimetic characteristics of young children—they pick up voice tones, facial expressions, and other subtle means of communicating psychological states. If each person picks up this psychological DNA from parents, who got it from theirs, and so on, it becomes clear that our ancestors' impact on our identity goes beyond strict biological input. For that reason we must look at many of the factors that relate to identity formation, boundary setting, boundary maintenance, and culture transmission. These all have to do with ethnicity.

Ethnicity

An amazing thing happened when my wife, Gloria, and I travelled from Italy into Austria. We were driving through the beautiful Austrian mountains when Gloria exclaimed, "These are my people! This is my culture! My mother would fit in perfectly here!" Many little details of life in Austria struck a resounding chord with the values and lifestyle with which Gloria had grown up in a way that was not the case in France and Italy. Things like not sleeping between sheets but rather having washable covers on quilts, a sense of order and cleanliness, and continental breakfast that included jam and cheese on rolls made Gloria feel connected, even though she had never lived in Austria.

When I was President of the Canadian Institute for Conflict Resolution, I recruited more than a hundred Aboriginal people to take some Third Party Neutral training. On one occasion we received funding for a course, Third Party Neutral in an Aboriginal Context, specifically for Aboriginal people. On the final day we invited our Aboriginal alumni to a dialogue. One of them told me that she had really enjoyed the training she had taken when she was the lone Aboriginal person in a group of twenty, but that there was something special about a dialogue process "with her own people."

Whether we are talking about tribes, ethnic groups, First Nations, or peoples, we are talking about people who feel that they belong together. A variety of metaphors can be used to describe the cohesiveness around an identity group: web, network, a shared "blueprint for life." Each metaphor emphasizes a different aspect of a shared reality. The sense of ethnic identification sets particular groups aside and provides individual identity. Sometimes there is an overlap of ethnic identities. Sometimes one is nested within another. Sometimes there are ethnic hybrids. What came to Gloria's consciousness in the anecdote was an awareness of shared cultural values; it was a perception of what had been picked up by her ancestors during a 200-year sojourn in Prussia, which had many things in common with Austria. It had been 200 years since that time, and Gloria's mother's ancestors had since lived in the Russian Empire, the United States, and Canada. However, something of the psychological and cultural DNA had been passed on. While Gloria had resonance with some aspects of life, other aspects were very different—aspects picked up in Ukraine and in North America.

An ethnic group has its own culture—patterns of interaction and behaviour that shape life. The visible actions that form a pattern are significant as well as how those actions are interpreted, nuanced, and valued. The minutest detail may figure prominently in the culture, since that detail sets it apart from others. Culture includes the day-to-day activities of eating (what and how you eat), how you work (attention to detail, punctuality, and long or short hours,) how a house is maintained, and patterns of discourse. In some cultures, words are taken literally and something that does not correspond to reality is thought of as a lie. In other cultures, people will be told what they want to hear and there is latitude in discourse to say what will save face even if that does not correspond literally to past events. At another level, culture includes artistic expression such as stories, poems, songs, music, and visual art. Other aspects of culture—mythology and ritual—assume a central place in providing meaning to a people. Language is closely tied to culture.

When our family lived in Québec, we became very attached to the Reesor family, which became like our own family. Pauline, the mother of seven children, died of liver cancer in her forties. In the morning of the day she died, she had held our baby, Lisa, in her arms. At her funeral, there was a time when anyone could speak about Pauline. I got up and started speaking in French, doing just fine emotionally. When I switched to English, I became very emotional and could hardly speak. It was as though my mother tongue was hardwired to my emotions.

Language is closely tied to ethnic identity. In Medieval Europe, Latin united Christendom; it was spoken by the elite and, at least in church, was understood by the masses who spoke in their local vernacular languages. These local dialects blended into one another as one moved from region to region. With the advent of the printing press, language was standardized within nations and literature was developed that helped to forge a common identity within the linguistic group.[26]

When the fine points of language become ethnic cultural markers, the smallest detail of accent, pronunciation, or spelling is considered of supreme importance. After travelling in the former Yugoslavia, Thomas Butler, a Serbian-language specialist, observed that though he was understood by Croatians they often made a distinction in the pronunciation of one syllable. This syllable is pronounced by Croats as *je* or *ije* and the Serbs pronounce it as *e*. Milk for the Croats is *mlijeko* and for the Serbs it is *mleko*.[27]

Among Russian Mennonites, High German was the language of learning and worship, and Low German, which was much more earthy and descriptive of everyday phenomena, was the language used at home. Many within this tradition thought of Low German as a "lower class" language, as something prost (plain, uncultured). It came as a revelation to Gloria and me that before the time of Luther, Low German was the lingua franca of the German-speaking world. One particular Low German-speaking Mennonite realized that Low German was related to Old English when he found he was more comfortable with Chaucerian English than were his peers from an English background. Recognition of this historical reality added a sense of ethnic pride to my identity as a Russian Mennonite.

One way in which a pride of peoplehood was diminished in Canada's First Nations population was when residential schools forbade the use of Native languages. For those First Nations people who have recovered a sense of identity within their own traditions, relearning their language of origin has been an important part of recovering their culture.

In Estonia, language, literature, and literacy were used to establish a separate identity. For the Estonians to be intellectually superior to their occupiers was like a booster for their large-group identity; it was their chosen glory, in place of a military one. By 1897, 96 percent of Estonians could read, and Estonia became the most literate region of the Russian empire.[28] As Estonians re-established a state after the collapse of the Soviet Empire, folk singing became an important part of the struggle to recover a collective identity.

Embedded within cultures are deeply held values; exemplifying positive values is rewarded and prohibitions and taboos are backed by punishment. These values work at both explicit and tacit levels. Some are clearly articulated and may be written down. Others are part of the psychological DNA, and people in a particular culture have a sense that "you just don't do that" within their culture. Bringing a friend into their culture and seeing them transgressing the unwritten rules can be horrifying. As Vesna Dasović Marković observes, in Western Europe people tend to kiss twice, once on each cheek, but in eastern Europe they do it three times.

Gloria and I come from very different family cultures. In her family the pattern of discourse was for people to express themselves openly, often with great passion. In my family, we chose our words carefully in order to be diplomatic. Often there would be long pauses between "speeches." When I brought Gloria home with me during our courtship and early marriage, she would state the obvious as she saw it, very directly. From the perspective of my family culture, she was inadvertently going against the unwritten family rule of carefully and cautiously wording sentences.

According to Vamik Volkan the following key concepts help to understand ethnicity: chosen trauma, chosen glory, and collapse of time.[29] While a given ethnic group may have been traumatized many times in its history, certain traumas are chosen to define group identity. Likewise, some accomplishments make the group special as, for example, Estonians have chosen to glory in educational successes. As these chosen traumas and glories are recounted, time collapses, making it seem as though they happened yesterday—even though they may have occurred centuries ago. Serbs glory in the Battle of Kosovo in 1389. In 1989, to strengthen their identity around this event, the martyred remains of the leader who lost the battle were taken to Serbian villages so that people could pay homage.

Chosen glories and traumas are woven into ethno-dramas that, in schematized fashion, tell the stories of the identity group evolution. Several years ago our family saw an enactment in song and dance of the history of Mexico in Cancun.

Language, values, prohibitions, and symbols from the ethno-dramas of a group combine to form boundary markers. If another identity group is very close in proximity and character, these boundary markers become increasingly detailed. Among North American Swiss Mennonites are the Old Order Mennonites who have as a central value nonconformity to the world. These are the Mennonites who still farm with horses and travel with buggies. Along the way, breakaway groups have started separate churches and denominations. At one time the progression went from buggies to black cars with the chrome painted black, to black cars with chrome bumpers, and, finally, to ordinary coloured cars. This illustration shows visible boundary markers; often, though, boundary markers are subtle or intangible.

Rules of exclusion and inclusion go along with boundary markers. These rules ensure that group members are true to the non-negotiable identity characteristics and quickly identify those not included in the group.

Religion

Religion can motivate people to forfeit their lives for a cause—sometimes out of love and sometimes out of hate, sometimes for the sake of justice and sometimes because of injustice. This is possible because the religion includes spirituality, the sacred, and a relationship with time that includes infinite time before and after this life. It is rooted in stories and teachings that go back centuries and it projects imaginative scenarios about the future. As the root metaphor of religion, "to bind" suggests, religion can bind people together and connect them with the spirits of living beings that may have physical manifestations (like animals) or may be outside the range of the physical senses.

In his overview of population cleansings, Andrew Bell-Fialkoff observes that until the eighteenth century, most population cleansings were based on religion rather than ethnicity.[30] Even today, religion is a significant boundary marker for different groups. India and Pakistan were divided on the basis of religion; Tamils and Singhalese divide on religious lines. The Reverend Ian Paisley has been a visible leader of the Protestants in Northern Ireland; the Serbs identify with Christian Orthodoxy, Croats tend to be Catholic, and Bosniacs are Muslim. In Canada, European hegemony replaced traditional Aboriginal religions with Christianity, even making indigenous rituals illegal.

Where religious lines and ethnic lines have the same boundaries, it is hard to separate religion and culture. Values, language, root metaphors, and the minute details of life forming the culture of a people derive significantly from the historical religion of the group.

The role of religion in deep-rooted conflict is ambiguous. Some of the most helpful insights around reconciliation come from different religious traditions. On the other hand, religion has frequently been used to legitimize violence and the emotion of the religious impulse has been used to stir up hate. There are a number of heuristic tools that can help us to discover different roles of religion in conflict. These are presented as axes in which there is a continuum from one extreme to the other.

LOCUS OF RELIGIOUS EXPERIENCE

Individual	Community	Transcendent	Collectivities

In some contexts, one can experience and talk about spirituality, the divine, the interplay of tradition and contemporary experience, life after death, and so on in a world focused upon the individual. Individuals may have a religious conversion, see a spiritual director, or practice meditation. In another context, people of similar conviction may be linked with a historically rooted religious community and this community takes on significant value—such as English Anglican, Scottish Presbyterian, or "Swiss" Mennonites. Others emphasize a transcendent sense of religious connectedness. One example is the concept of the Islamic global *ummah* in which Muslims of the Middle East, Northern Africa, the Indian subcontinent, Indonesia, and other parts of the world are considered bonded through common religious tradition and belief. Likewise, many Christians consider themselves to be part of one transcendent, invisible "church."

Several other axes help us understand the ambiguous role of religion. These have to do with religious understanding, devotion, and emotional fervour. These determine the degree to which religion helps define the role it plays in personal identity.

Religious people in any religious tradition have wide-ranging differences of understanding about their own tradition. For some, tradition is influential only at the *tacit* level. They could tell you little about their sacred texts or the meaning of the traditions but knowledge still exists at the tacit level through an experience of or exposure to the religion. Then there are religiously illiterate, who know some of the basics and some of the religious markers that set them apart from other groups, but have neither read the texts nor sat at the feet of teachers in the tradition. Religiously illiterate adherents have a religious life based on folk-religion. These people are very susceptible to manipulation by leaders who pick up on a few details about the religion so they can frame a situation religiously in a way that sweeps the illiterate followers into a military crusade. Some persons are visored—they have studied only a narrow aspect of their religion. Some are informed and others have studied the religion in some depth. Those with a profound understanding of a religion can place its development into historical context and can think critically about their religious tradition.

RELIGIOUS UNDERSTANDING

Tacit Only	Illiterate	Visored	Informed	Well-versed	Reflective

The degree of participation in the religious tradition depends on the devotion of the adherent. These range from minimal participation to daily participation in some religious discipline (prayer, meditation) to the point where it becomes totally absorbing. In Judaism and Christianity, some attend synagogue or church only for special religious celebrations—Rosh Hashanah and Yom Kippur for Jews, and Christmas and Easter for Christians. Others attend weekly and some are immersed in the life of the religious community. Islam has the same range—from minimal participants to those who pray five times a day, fast during Ramadan, and make a *haj* to Mecca.

RELIGIOUS DEVOTION

Minimal	Occasional	Disciplined	Daily	Absorbed

There is also a range in religious fervour. Some individuals participate fully in the community, have a profound understanding of the tradition, and have a thoughtful, settled attitude toward their tradition. Others, who may be religiously illiterate, participate minimally in the religious life of the community but are very emotionally fervent about their religious identity. Many other combinations of understanding, devotion, and emotional involvement are possible.

RELIGIOUS FERVOUR

Passive	Thoughtful	Emotional

The world of religion has interesting relationships with temporality. References to eternity transcend conceptions of historical time. Apocalyptic literature in the Jewish and Christian traditions describe cosmic battles that will be resolved by the divine in a definitive way that will last forever. Included in this ahistorical (outside of history) dimension are the Hindu concepts of Nirvana and reincarnation; Muslim and Christian traditions deal with concepts of eternal punishment or eternal reward in the afterlife. Within historical time, significant events from centuries ago are re-enacted through ritual celebrations. Jewish Passover, for example, recreates the night when ancient Hebrews left slavery in Egypt three-and-a-half millennia ago. Christians and Muslims commemorate events in the lives of Jesus and Mohammed, respectively. Different Christian denominations commemorate key events in the genesis of their tradition. Protestants celebrate Reformation Sunday and Catholics commemorate the lives of saints. Both Jews and Christians await the coming of the Messiah, although they disagree on whether it is the first or second time. First Nations people anticipate the coming of a great spiritual teacher. Dispensationalist Christians have clear opinions about what will happen at the end of time.

In contrast to the emphasis on temporal life is that aspect of religious life concerned with spirituality—a desire to tap into an energy unlimited by time or space. Neurobiologists have recently shown that when people of different traditions are in spiritually open states, a certain part of the brain is highly active. The part of the brain where spacial and temporal orientation is sensed pretty much shuts down during the spiritual highs.[31] The world of religion is like a vessel in which the stories of spiritual experience and insight are stored.

Religion also provides many of the root metaphors through which people understand their identities.

Although particular religious traditions still play a major role in many bloody ethnoreligious conflicts throughout the world, some overall religious trends are noteworthy. Bell-Fialkoff points out that religion as a primary factor in population cleansing diminished with the rise of nationalism in the nineteenth century.[32] With nationalism came an intimate relationship with temporality, a sense of historical destiny, and a capacity to link with profound loyalties and emotions.

Samuel Huntington sees the world divided into civilizations that are rooted in different historical religious traditions.[33] On a macro level, he would predict growing antagonisms between civilizations that have a territorial base. On the other hand, there are non-territorial associations of people with deeply held values in worlds of reality similar to religious worlds. Among these are environmentalists, whose care for the earth approaches religious conviction. Other global groups construct their identities around human rights, economic exploitation, and a critique of globalization. While these identity groups are not based in any one territory they are concerned about what happens to the people, land, and water of this earth.

What is clear is that, to a greater or lesser extent, religion plays a key role in deep-rooted conflict. It can be the essential fuel for conflict or it can be the driving force for reconciliation.[34]

Land as a Factor in Ethnoreligious Conflict

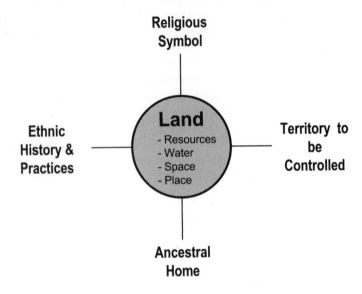

Figure 6-2

Since ethnonationalism is about desiring self-determination, sovereignty over territory, and recognition as a nation-state, land is of critical importance to individual and group identity. We think of land as space—a place to live, move, and act. Its importance increases as land provides resources of use for economic life. Land becomes crucial to identity in the transition from land as space to land as place.[35] Land as place is historically rooted; it is home-land.

As the diagram shows, land interacts with all other categories implicated in ethnonationalism. It can be the home of the ancestors—graves, houses, buildings, and monuments tell the story of the early forebears. Land is also the repository of cultural markers. Geography affects personality and helps to shape culture. Food comes from the land. The food an ethnic group enjoys is tied to the kind of food that was produced as that group evolved. Land holds a special place for religious identity; that is why people make pilgrimages to particular places. Land has a boundary representing where a particular nation is located. In fact, intense fighting takes place over boundaries. When we look at the role of politics in ethnonationalism, we will develop further the importance of territory for nations.

When I was a boy, harvest time was always very special. Throughout my teenage years my job was to drive the grain truck to the combine, which would unload its contents into the box of the truck. When the truck was full of grain I would drive to the granary and unload the grain, which was lifted to the granary by a grain auger. While I waited for the combine hopper to be filled, I would sit in the field, sometimes thinking, sometimes enjoying the sound of the wind, sometimes reading. The land was special to me. The sense of prairie space, seeing great distances, probably helped make me a person of vision.

Farming and work with grain was part of my ancestral heritage; my great-grandfather and his brother had owned a mill in Millerova, a few kilometres east of present day Luhansk, Ukraine. I now have my own little grain grinder that I use to grind Saskatchewan wheat for the bread that I make just as my mother and grandmother made bread by hand. For me, land held overlapping layers of meaning: my ancestors were farmers or in agribusiness for generations, my own culture was formed in relation to land and the cycles of farming, agriculture provided many root metaphors for the religion of my youth (missionaries spoke of the "field white unto harvest," quoting from the New Testament), and my regional secular identity was as a prairie boy and Saskatchewan farmer.

The concept of population "cleansing" is tied to the land—"purifying" the land of people not belonging to the group that wishes to assert hegemony over the territory. Ken Bush told me about visiting Banya Luka in Bosnia-Herzegovina a few years after the civil war where he saw a strange gap in the architecture. In an open space between other buildings grass was growing. In answer to his query, his hosts replied that it was the site of a mosque. This very famous mosque—on the list of UNESCO historical buildings—had not only been destroyed, but every brick and fragment of building materials had been removed. Unless one asked, as Ken did, a stranger would not know what had been there before. It was all part of Serb determination to cleanse the city of any Muslim presence.

Relationship to Land

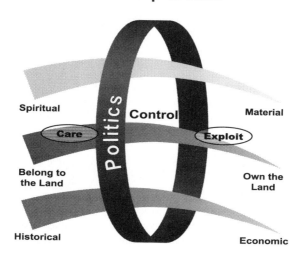

Figure 6-3

In the "troubles" of Northern Ireland, Protestants and Catholics marched along certain routes. The marches signify hegemony over the land—a way of marking territory. They are also re-enactments of past battles, chosen glories, and traumas woven into the ethno-identities of both groups.

One can have different relationships with the land, as can be seen in the preceding figure.

Three spectra pass through the circle of politics. If the political realm determines the rules of land ownership and use, then politics become very important in defining our relationship to the land. Politics, in relation to land, is about identifying territory that might be allocated to a particular ethnonational group. Debates focus on who can be on the land and what they can do with the resources. Currently, a mythology and value system around nation-states, or at least sovereign states, is prominent; this was not always the case. Land in many nation-states is subject to ownership and ownership is documented through land title.

The first spectrum in the figure runs from a spiritual to material view of the land. Land can be perceived as having a certain spirit or land can be viewed as simply a combination of organic and inorganic matter. In his farming days, my father would get up early most mornings of the growing season and walk through the fields. Deer and antelope would often be present and my dad considered these his friends. He did not belong to the land in an Aboriginal sense, but he was attached to the land and cared for it.

When I went for my first sweat lodge ceremony, I spent time with Jim, on whose land the sweat lodge was located. He talked about his journey to find this land. He had looked at other land and had sensed a negative spirit on that land. When he came to this particular property he sensed a good spirit and he bought it.

A second spectrum runs from belonging to the land to owning the land. Traditional Mohawks of *Kanehsatà:ke* refer to themselves as *Kahehsatakero:non*, people of *Kanehsatà:ke* or people belonging to the land of *Kanehsatà:ke*. Valentine Yutzy, a Mennonite farmer in Ohio who has received several awards as a conservationist, explains his farming philosophy this way: "I believe that we are stewards of what God has given us.... If we become possessors of it, we handle things in a much different way than if we are stewards of it, handling it for somebody else. When we are possessors of it, we can be too willing to take a risk, we think too highly of our own abilities, and we want to make a quick dollar. What we really need to do is to handle it and pass it on to the next generation in as good or better shape than it was when we got it."[36]

At the other end of the spectrum is the idea of owning the land, of having title that allows one to use or exploit the land as one wishes. In some places, land title comes with restrictions covered by zoning laws, building codes, or mining regulations that regulate what can be done with the land. Near the left end of the spectrum is a relationship with the land marked by caring for the land.

The third spectrum on the figure passing through the circle of politics goes from historical to economical. One can see land as having a certain history that is worth respecting. Rocks can be thought of as very old. Some land contains fossil records going back millions of years. Land can hold important traces of human history. Land can also be thought of primarily in economic terms. Viewed in this way, it is first and foremost subject to development. I remember Pat Brascoupe, in addressing the analysts of the Citizens Forum on Canada's Future, telling how the First Nations people, who had left the land in pristine condition, were penalized for not having left a "developmental mark." Had they cut down the trees, for example, they would have had greater rights to the land in the eyes of Eurocanadian bureaucrats.

In some cases historical and economical come together in the middle of the spectrum, as is the case when an old castle is made into a tourist attraction and a source of revenue. History becomes an asset.

These days, environmentalists care about not only particular parcels of land but for land as a whole. They see land, water, and air as interconnected and recognize that what is done in one part of the planet has a global effect. An identity based on environmental concerns may be as powerful an emotional driver for people as an ethno-identity tied to a particular piece of territory.

Politics

The political side of ethnonationalism involves both a drive toward nation-statehood and a relationship between leaders and the identity group. To understand the political dynamics facing ethnoreligious groups, it is important to understand political realism as the fundamental paradigm shaping attitudes toward the nature of nations, international relations, and how the world is organized.

Political realism has dominated the approach to international relations during the modern period and particularly since World War II. Its assumptions have been woven into the structure of the United Nations and have been foundational for international law. It is described succinctly as follows:

> The theory propounded by Morgenthau and the "realist" school of political scientists in North America and Western Europe was simple. States are essentially regional actors that can use whatever military, political, and economic power they can generate to advance and defend their interests however they may be defined. War and the threat of war are essential tools of statecraft in the realist school. [37]

The essence of *classical realism*, according to Steven Forde, is a "belief in the primacy of self-interest over moral principle, of necessity and therefore, *as of right*, in international politics," meaning "either that self-interest confers a positive right of some kind, as when the 'national interest' is seen as a moral principle, or that morality is wholly inapplicable to international politics."[38] Hobbes and Rousseau viewed states as being "in a chronic state of opposition or conflict that may break out into battle at any time…. States are left to fend for themselves in an environment that places them all at risk, and that especially jeopardizes those states that allow moral inhibitions to block the pursuit of their own interests."[39] Hobbes believed that nature was essentially competitive, motivating people to enter into contracts with sovereign powers to support their interests; hence, the centrality of the nation-state concept in international affairs. For Hobbes, no nation-state is morally bound to follow the universal code of ethics that he espouses.[40] Spinoza adds the notion of "might is right." Though Rousseau had a more optimistic view of human nature, "he has at least as pessimistic a view of the prospects of justice in the relations of states, once states are formed" since "the well-being of each [is] incompatible with that of the rest."[41]

Twentieth-century realist Hans Morgenthau[42] developed a framework of power politics defending national interests. National power, however, is not unbridled; it is subject to limitations of international morality, world public opinion, and international law.[43] Central to Morgenthau's theory is the sovereignty of nation-states involving supreme judicial, territorial, and legislative authority:

> [T]he sovereignty of the nation as the intended object of a law-enforcing action manifests itself in what is called the impenetrability of the nation. This is another way of saying that on a given territory only one nation can have sovereignty—supreme authority—and that no other state has the right to perform governmental acts on its territory without its consent... War as the extreme form of law enforcement under international law is the only exception to that rule; for it is of the very essence of war to penetrate the territory of the enemy while safeguarding the "impenetrability" of one's own, and international law allows the occupying nation to exercise sovereign rights in the foreign territory occupied by its military force.[44]

The realist emphasis on power and security arises from "an account of human nature that emphasizes self-interest and the egoistic passions and an account of international relations that emphasizes the constraints imposed by international anarchy."[45] Foreign affairs expert and realist Henry Kissinger argued that "a nation's survival is its first and ultimate responsibility; it cannot be put to risk."[46] Considering the value system of a realist, the fact that most deep-rooted conflicts could be construed as threats to the state makes them an "ultimate responsibility" and, hence, demanding of armed intervention. When such conflicts are between relatively small minorities in a sovereign state, they are a matter of internal politics and do not concern the international community. If this conflict challenged the rule of state authorities, it would be legitimate for the state to use all available resources to subdue the internal threat within a realist set of values. If deep-rooted conflicts coincide with state boundaries, then the conflicts are thought of as war and states can do anything they wish to protect their interests.

While realists tend to see the world divided into nation-states, with citizens giving their primary loyalty to the state, in recent years there has been greater awareness of the power of identity groups to hold the allegiance of those who belong to them. In fact, there are persuasive arguments that the nation-state in actuality has existed in only a handful of cases. Connor observes that

[i]f we exclude both the multinational states and those states which, although themselves homogeneous, are characterized by that so-called irredentist situation in which the dominating group extends beyond the state's borders, our only illustrations would be Denmark, Iceland, Japan, Luxembourg, the Netherlands, Norway and Portugal. These states account for less than 4% of the world's population.[47]

Furthermore, culture and religion have been shown to exercise a greater effect on international relations than realism would account for. This is given eloquent expression by R.B.J. Walker:

> The conventional categories of international relations theory seem particularly inappropriate in a world in which the claims of sovereignty co-exist with both complex interpenetrations of cultural identity and plausible scenarios about "interdependence" or an emerging "global civilization." Resolutions of the relationship between universality and particularity at the level of the state alone cannot provide a serious analysis of the patterns of contemporary political community, or claims to authority and legitimacy, or emerging conceptions of human identity or the configurations of economic and military power in the modern world.[48]

Walker's point is exemplified in the aftermath of September 11, 2001, when war was declared on terrorism—not a nation-state—and the prisoners of this "war" were not actual prisoners of war by the United States. Identity-based forces based on culture, religion, ancestry, gender, and primary values around land, economics, and violence are forging new structures of human existence. Yet the mythology around nation-states still hangs on.

When a primary value is to be recognized as a nation-state, ethnoreligious identity groups clamour to establish hegemony over a territory and establish a nation-state. The proto-nations are so numerous that if each one achieved statehood we could be dealing with 10,000 nations.[49] In tension with this trend is a sense of civil statehood where citizenship is based on being born in the state or becoming naturalized as a citizen. Rights are based on individual citizenship, although minority group rights can be a part of the equation.[50]

In a world still largely governed by a realist paradigm, there is tremendous rivalry among ethnonational groups to either gain control of the political system or establish new boundaries so they can control their own destiny.

Dynamics of Ethnonationalism

In his oft-quoted *Ethnic Groups in Conflict,* Donald Horowitz deals with the dynamics of conflict between ethnonational groups. A key idea he develops is the concept of stereotypes.[51] As the "us–them" syndrome develops, the number of stereotypes increases. These may relate to work habits, traits relating to an ability to succeed or fail, patterns of virtue or lack thereof, mental abilities, and ability to have fun. Each stereotype involves a sense of the other as well as what characterizes one's own group. These stereotypes are used to explain disparity in wealth, employment, and opportunity.

Closely related to stereotypes are feelings of jealousy associated with the perceived well-being of another group. Horowitz observes: "I shall simply state my view that this envy, resentment, and fear is to be found, not in the ethnic distribution of opportunities and benefits *per se*, but in what this indicates about relative group capacities and what it portends for group relations across the board."[52]

Horowitz also traces the dynamics of "ethnic fusion and fission."[53] On some occasions, well-defined ethnic groups assimilate and assume a common identity; at other times, there is a process of differentiation whereby a group with a common identity fractures.

Bereciartu argues that the "objective of national claims" should be to gain enough power to

> realize what Breton has qualified as the "decalog of the rights of ethnic groups." These are summarized as the right to life, a collective existence, and an identity; territory; self-determination; language; ethnic culture; natural resources; the benefits of production; work and life in the country; market protection, and a self-centered administrative organization.[54]

Foremost among rights demanded by ethnonational groups is the right of self-determination. This, however, is not necessarily straightforward in its application.[55]

In exercising the right of self-determination, an ethnonational group faces the rights associated with a sovereign state, as described by the dominant theory of political realism. When the state is controlled by a particular ethnonational group, the demand for a right to self-determination by another group invites hostility and inter-group rivalry. As Levin observes, "ethnic identity is the most widely used basis for legitimacy not only for minorities, but also for majority groups sharing a common culture. An ethnic group that is a majority may attempt to imprint its culture on the state."[56]

Stephen Ryan has identified some of the more concrete factors involved in the escalation of hostilities. These include militarization, physical separation, psychological distancing, entrapment (leaders and followers are committed to a course of action that doesn't work but they can't get out of it), and sanctification and demonization. The latter "are terms introduced by Kuper (1989) to describe what happens when a strong religious element is added to inter-group tensions. He argues that religion can do more than just add another layer of differentiation. It can also result in fantasies of 'unspeakable horror or ineffable bliss'.... They draw on deep levels of the unconscious and can result in an interpretation of the conflict in terms of a Holy War between good and bad, God and Satan."[57]

In his study of aboriginality in Canada, Patrick Macklem has analyzed how similarity and difference have been used in subtle ways to benefit the dominant ethnocultural group.

The incontestability of the integrity of Canadian sovereign authority is established and maintained in legal discourse by a rhetoric of similarity and difference. The law has constructed Native people as *different* when to acknowledge their similarities would threaten basic organizing categories of the Anglo-Canadian legal imagination, but it simultaneously has viewed Native people as *similar* to non-Native people when to acknowledge difference would threaten basic legal categories of the Anglo-Canadian legal imagination.[58]

This dynamic is the context for the "drive for self-government, the Native equivalent of an ethnonationalist impulse, [which] is an attempt to seize control from non-Native authorities over the process by which aboriginal identities are constructed."[59]

Leadership

Politicians and other identity group leaders have a complex role in their groups. They are often people with whom others in the group can identify, like Milosevic for Serbs in his day. They appear to transcend what ordinary people experience to project what the identity group could become. If these leaders receive international recognition, the whole group takes vicarious pride. These leaders have significant rhetorical capabilities and use words and symbols in the language of the identity group to evoke deep feeling. They use their knowledge of history to stir up a crowd by evoking chosen glories and chosen traumas.

A sinister side to ethnonationalist conflict has to do with the accumulation of wealth at the expense of the victimized. Ethnic-based conflicts are highly profitable for some people. Money raised for "the cause" may find its way into Swiss bank accounts. The arms trade is a sure source of revenue. Confiscating the property of those killed or "cleansed" lines the pockets of victorious leaders. Drug trafficking and organized crime are added to the mix. In addition, the rules of commerce favour the legitimate businesses owned by people of the preferred group. These factors skew the conflict, which is presented as protecting the honour of the ethnonational group or bringing the other side "to justice." Eventually, seeking material advantage for one's own side assumes a life of its own. The love of money, gained by whatever means, becomes a satisfier for identity needs and is mixed up with chosen traumas and chosen glories.

Terrorism is another sinister side of ethnonationalism. When a group is powerful enough in terms of land base, economic resources, and political recognition, it can use warfare to further its interests. When a group is too weak to realistically fight a war, it resorts to terrorism. Terrorism has two important dimensions. The first is terrorism as a policy option for people in leadership. The second is the action of individual terrorists. Leaders who embrace terrorism provide a framework to legitimate terrorist action. This framework is drawn from all five strands of ethnonationalism:

1. Ancestry—there is a need to protect the threatened interests of those who share a perceived common ancestry; there is a need to uphold the honour of ancestral heroes and right the wrongs suffered by ancestral victims.

2. Ethnicity—the markers of group members and excluded persons are linguistic, cultural, and sometimes racial. These distinctions are portrayed as being threatened in a vital way and important enough to fight for.

3. Religion—religious markers can augment cultural markers; religion, especially if poorly understood, can be used to provide an imperative to fight (God demands it) and rewards for one's efforts through huge memorial funerals or the promise of a reward in afterlife.[60]

4. Land—with all its economical, historical, and symbolic significance, land can serve as a powerful rallying point to inspire terrorism. The land must be reclaimed and "cleansed" for the exclusive use and satisfaction of one's own group.

5. Politics—the fight may be construed as a fight for one's leader, if there is a leader of stature. Or it may be a fight for recognition of one's sovereignty or for political hegemony within the state.

Terrorists themselves are motivated by anger, despair, hatred, frustration, and fear. Joseph Montville notes that they have undoubtedly been severely victimized in their youth or have seen their own people severely victimized.[61] If they identify with members of their identity group who have been victimized, they may also have a sense of vicarious victimization. They believe that this ongoing victimization will continue unless they smash their oppressors. The ethnonationalist agenda may be enhanced with economic interests—promises of benefit to their families or to them if they are successful. At another level, terrorists take on a role of scapegoat, as Roel Kaptein points out:

> Terrorists are murderers, that is clear. They do everything to destroy the ordered community. They do exactly what the scapegoats did in all the myths. At the same time, where culture and structures are fading away, chaos is rising and we need scapegoats desperately. Without knowing it consciously, we are actively seeking them. We, the non-terrorists need and wish them. Terrorists offer their blood to be sacrificed for peace. This longing for peace is our longing too. According to a long Irish tradition, they seek deification by offering themselves, so procuring peace for the world. In a very deep sense, they are doing our business.[62]

Terrorists as scapegoats unite their own people as they become celebrated heroes. They also unite their opponents by becoming "demons" who threaten the identity need satisfiers of security, meaning, action, and connectedness for the opposing ethnonational group.

Chapter 7

Self–Other Dynamics

Implicit in this discussion so far has been a sense that deep-rooted conflicts take place in the context of relationships. Relationships take place within relational systems—a set of factors that bring individuals or groups into significant contact with one another; this is frequently geographical proximity. Within a relational system, there is a Self, the individual or group from whose vantage point the story is told, and there is an Other, to whom the individual or group relates.

Relational System

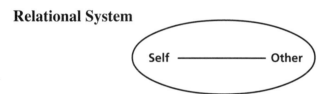

The basis of the relational system may be common interests, common goals, common activities, or common objects of desire. Within a relational system, Self and Other may be friends or enemies. A relational system may be of long duration or it may be short-lived.

Sometimes a relational system is so closed and exclusive that it is virtually the only relationship that matters to the parties involved. It may look like this:

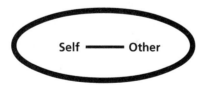

In other instances it may be of less relative importance, and Self and Other may be open to other relationships, like this

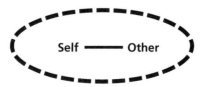

Another feature of the Self-Other relationship is that it does not occur in a vacuum or detached from the rest of life. Self and Other are both part of other relational systems that may be influenced by this relational system. Each relational system is surrounded by bystanders who observe what is going on and may or may not influence the dynamics.

Discourse about Self and Other occurs in both philosophy and political psychology, disciplines that help in understanding the dance between Self and Other in a relational system.

In philosophical terms, both the Self and the Other can be agents of action. Emmanuel Levinas, Janine Chanteur, and Paul Ricoeur have been instrumental in using discourse around Self and Other to describe deep-rooted conflicts.

Levinas: The Face of the Other

Emmanuel Levinas contrasts the concepts of totality and infinity. Totality is an approach to life in which the core of one's being—one's inner life, one's identity—can be grasped and controlled. Within each of us, however, is a vast, infinite universe of thought, feeling, spirit, memory, aspiration, and a host of other factors. The human face is the exterior manifestation of this infinite *interiority*, but it is in the *exteriority* of the face of the Other through which the fullness of humanity is encountered. Communication—using language in face-to-face interaction—is the bridge between Self and Other.

Totality is a violent assault on the infinite as it boxes in what is not meant to be confined. This is not just an occasional event, but it is, for Levinas, a systematic violence that causes a fundamental rift between people. War epitomizes this systematic attack on the Self. It cuts the Self off from its own morality; it tears open the core of one's being, revealing truths previously hidden. The violence of war is a "trial by force" from which there is no escape. This violence

> does not consist so much in injuring and annihilating persons as in interrupting their continuity, making them play roles in which they no longer recognize themselves, making them betray not only commitments but their own substance, making them carry out actions that will destroy every possibility for action. Not only modern war but every war employs arms that turn against those who wield them.... War does not manifest exteriority and the other as other; it destroys the identity of the same. The visage of being that shows itself in war is fixed in the concept of totality, which dominates Western philosophy.[1]

Totality is all about controlling, grasping, and buying into the fiction that all there is to know about the other can be known.[2] It is a power-oriented approach to a basic understanding of who we are as people:

> Ontology as first philosophy is a philosophy of power…which appears in the tyranny of the State…[and is] a philosophy of injustice. Heideggerian ontology, which subordinates the relationship with the Other to the relation

with Being in general, remains under obedience to the anonymous, and leads inevitably to another power, to imperialist domination, to tyranny.[3]

By contrast, the concept of infinity is expressed in the face of the Other. Infinity describes the vast world of interiority of the Other, which for the Self is expressed to the outside world, to the Other, through exteriority. It is possible for us as humans to reveal to one another key aspects of our hearts. The Self perceives its own infinity by looking into the face of the Other and becoming aware of the vast infinity of the Other. This action of looking into the face of the Other for a glimpse into the universe works both at the explicit and tacit levels. We can describe something of what we perceive but much that goes on is beyond what we can put into words. This tacit and explicit knowledge of the Other helps us understand ourselves in two ways: first, it gives us a deeper knowledge of what it means to be a Self, and, second, it makes us more aware of what constitutes our own inner universes. The gaze into the face of the Other needs to be augmented with speech, which is a bridge between the Self and Other. What Levinas describes as speech is akin to the communication that takes place in dialogue.

Peace is produced as this aptitude for speech. The eschatological vision breaks with the totality of wars and empires in which one does not speak. It does not envisage the end of history within being understood as a totality but institutes a relation with the infinity of being which exceeds the totality.[4]

Within deep-rooted conflict, speech breaks down; people do not speak from their hearts, nor do they truly listen. For Levinas, allowing the presence of the face of the Other to enter one's consciousness elicits a moral impulse that gives priority to the Other. Ricoeur's vision of peace (though he does not use the word) is likewise a moral vision expressed in the goal "to aim to live a good life with and for others in just institutions."[5]

Chanteur: Ontological Rift

Totality as a mindset can be linked conceptually to Western thought by the analysis of Janine Chanteur. Chanteur analyzes key Western political thinkers and concludes that among all of them, war is seen to be the normative state of humanity—a position like that of the realists.[6] Even philosophers who advocate peace define peace as of absence of war. Peace is seen as a break between wars— a time to prepare for the next war. Chanteur sees this inclination toward armed conflict as the result of an ontological rift, a dehumanizing gap in consciousness in which the Other becomes radiantly "other," an "it" in Buber's terms, and "violently differentiated" in Girard's.

The pervasiveness of the war mentality corresponds to Levinas' perception of totality as a way of being—a sense that the relationship to an impersonal being is more important than a relationship with the Other.

Gender

For Chanteur the basis of ontological rift is grounded in the rift between the sexes. Chanteur argues that for man, the most "Other" is woman and for woman the most "Other" is man. She uses "man" and "woman" as philosophical notions to argue that at a basic level there is this rift between people based on gender. This is not to say that individual men and women have not had fruitful dialogue. Rather, on the whole, a basic dialogue between men and women has not taken place. This dialogue, Chanteur argues, must take place.

A few years ago, my wife, Gloria, did a research project on women and war. She interviewed older Mennonite women who had gone through the Russian revolution and civil war. The kind of information that came out was categorically different than that described in male-dominated histories. Here is an example:

> There were many orphans. These were often taken into Mennonite homes. One woman recalls a particularly heartbreaking experience that still affects her today:

> There was a Russian orphanage. There was no more food. And then they put them into our villages. Those poor children, they had to stay one week with one family, the next week with another family. Misha came to us, six years old, and we fell in love with him and he fell in love with us. When we had him one week and then he should go to another home, we said, "Mama, we want to keep him." "Yes, we keep Misha." We didn't have a bed for him, it was a very small house, and then we put chairs together, like six little chairs, that's where Misha slept and then when he went to bed, he always said, "Give me a kiss," and we all had to kiss him. And then was the time he should go to the neighbours, the food was getting very, very scarce, then the neighbour said, "If we give you a loaf of bread, will you keep him for us?" "YES, we will." And that wasn't enough for a whole week, just a loaf of bread, so we always had to give him ours, but when we had no more to eat, we said, "No, he has to go to the neighbours, they have to eat, and we haven't, see," and then he was CRYING—"I want to stay home, I want to stay home." And my brother was big and tall and he had to carry him to the neighbour's screaming and crying, and he kissed us all and we all had to kiss him when he went. It was so heartbreaking. And then when we migrated to Canada, that was the most heartbreaking thing ever, we were at the station, and then when the train blew and we had to get in, and we asked, "Where's Misha?" Here he was sitting under the boxcar, crying. "*Eck vell met nu America comen, eck vell met nu America comen.*" (I want to go along to America.) All these seventy years, there's hardly a day where I don't think of Misha and what happened to him. Sometimes when I can't sleep, then I think, "Maybe we should have taken him, maybe we could have hidden him." Even now, you know, I think maybe we didn't do right to leave him there.[7]

The sense of ontological rift between the genders corresponds to Levinas' sense of a failure to appreciate the infinity in the Other. Otherness, as a quality, means to have a sense of alterity. Levinas as a man sees the greatest alterity as the feminine:

The I-Thou in which Buber sees the category of interhuman relationship is the relation not with the interlocutor but with feminine alterity…the discretion of this presence includes all the possibilities of the transcendent relationship with the Other.[8]

This suggests that if we can truly bridge the gender gap—seeing the fullness of humanity each in the other—we can transcend any other differences.

Chanteur identifies the totalizing tendency of men as part of the fundamental problem of ontological rift. Their control of everything has created a profound distance between people. Men have thought that they could represent all that it means to be human.[9] This is similar to Levinas' description of what happens when ontology becomes primary—relationships with others are not necessary to come to terms with the essence of human life. Just as Levinas argues that face-to-face dialogue between Self and Other will lead to a fuller understanding for each, Chanteur points out that neither man nor woman alone can represent humanity. Both must be included for a complete understanding of what it means to be human. The fullness of humanity can be found in a relationship between the two where neither has control or completeness. She concludes that there will be no world peace until there is peace between the sexes. Feminist thinkers who stress the importance of gender as a category of analysis in coming to terms with deep-rooted conflict are consistent with Chanteur's analysis. Some of the dynamics of gender-based conflict are apparent in the following reflection.

> I have been associated with the Canadian Forces, both in and out of uniform, for more than three decades. I had the privilege of observing the integration of women in combat-related employment from the perspective of an officer staffing grievances and human rights complaints for three years. Subsequently, I was Staff Officer to the Minister's Advisory Board on Gender Integration in the Canadian Forces for the next two years, in the early 1990s. The theories of human identity needs, mimetic desire, and scapegoating have provided a certain clarity for me in understanding what happened during the first ten years of gender integration—1985 to 1995.
>
> Until gender integration was imposed by the Human Rights Tribunal in 1984, the Canadian Forces was a male-dominated organization with traditional male values. The few women in the Forces had restricted roles and limited opportunities for promotion, and they did not threaten the dominance of men. Women had little impact on the closed relational system within which the men competed for promotion and recognition.
>
> It seems clear that the Tribunal decision threatened the identity needs of some male members of the Canadian Forces. To be

successful in combat units, women had to be equals and share in ranks and positions. They could not be kept in subordinate positions, nor be sex objects. Was there a hidden fear that some women could perhaps become more successful in the previously male roles? Would they get more of the scarce and coveted *recognition* in terms of promotion? This simply could not be contemplated, although it was openly denied.

Many men stated that the *security* of the combat units was threatened. They didn't believe that a woman could be as capable as a man and thought that using the Forces as a societal "guinea pig" would reduce operational effectiveness. Was their need for *connectedness* threatened? How could men and women work and live together without there being the threat of sexual relations? Some wives resented the presence of women in the field.

Additionally, serving men had a need to take *action*; they needed to do and to be seen to be doing something about this threat to their military identity. How did all of this impact on the *meaning* of life for those men who equated their being with their careers in the Forces?

The Tribunal directive came after a long, drawn-out objection by the Canadian Forces. Trials had been conducted that had "proven" women couldn't do it. In fact the trials were mostly successful—the "failure" was pre-programmed in the minds of many, especially those in combat units.

Not one General publicly supported the Tribunal decision. Many in leadership positions communicated dissatisfaction with the Tribunal decision both overtly and tacitly. There was mimetic consensus among most serving men that the direction of the Tribunal to fully integrate women into combat roles would impact negatively on combat readiness, in spite of the fact that many of the women were combat capable.

Some men sought to "prove" that the societal direction of equality for women just could not be applied to a combat capable military. Other men protected the early pioneers showing favoritism and giving them "extra" help so that they would succeed. Both of these reactions backfired against the women so that true equality was evaded.

Often women were singled out for intense observation. They became the "problem"; they were sometimes held personally responsible for the Tribunal decision.

It seemed that when one unit was "successful" in convincing the few pioneer women that they couldn't or didn't want to be in that unit, other units imitated their strategies hoping also to achieve a woman–free workplace.

The women fit the characteristics of a scapegoat. They were illegitimate, in the traditional combat culture. They were different (women), they were powerful (support of the Human Rights Tribunal and the law), and their small numbers made them vulnerable. In truth, few women wanted these non-traditional roles and fewer still could endure the abuse.

The crisis that precipitated the scapegoating process was the ruling of the Human Rights Tribunal. Both the identity and the cultural order of the combat unit and those in it were threatened by the presence of the women. These women became the target of the anger against the Tribunal ruling, although the perpetrators of this anger likely thought they were working for a just cause, to make sure that women didn't succeed in combat. The anger was disguised and largely below the surface.

What typically happened was that a woman became vulnerable because of poor performance, because she complained about the abuse, or for another reason. Although men could also be singled out for abuse, the men were not subjected to the added force of the repressed anger about the Tribunal ruling. The women returned this anger by a strengthened resolve to succeed in the combat world or by complaining more and more formally. Some eventually went to the media. There was escalating reciprocal violence until the object (the scapegoat) was broken and destroyed. The unit felt that justice was done— "she was not one of us and never would be." The process was hidden to the perpetrators and they felt once again united. Some even spoke about women who remained in the unit as "not like her."

This period in the history of the Canadian Forces was confusing and emotional, as change often is. Much of the emotion was not openly expressed and acknowledged; nonetheless, it had a significant impact on the effectiveness of the integration of women into combat-related employment over the first ten-year

> period. By not speaking out, the senior leaders failed to stop the abuse and, in fact, provided tacit approval for the model all-male unit. Not until 1996 did the Chief of the Defence Staff speak in censure of these discriminatory actions against women.[10]
>
> – Shirley Paré

This analytical reflection brings into sharp relief aspects of gender-based conflict evident in many other contexts.

Ricoeur: An Essential Dialectic

Just as René Girard noted that many novelists believe that our desires arise spontaneously within ourselves, Paul Ricoeur writes that modernity has been caught in the individualistic trap set by René Descartes with his famous dictum: "I think, therefore I am."[11] Ricoeur argues that a dialectic between Self and Other is essential for identity. This means that we work out who we are in relation to others in the same way that Girard argues our desires are formed by imitating those of the Other.

For Ricoeur, violence enters the Self-Other relationship through action. An action involves an actor who acts and a sufferer who is acted upon. In a relationship of mutuality the acting and suffering between Self and Other is balanced. Violence is an imbalance in which one party does all the acting and the other does all the suffering. In a violent relationship the victim is always acted upon. This has the effect of robbing the victim of a capacity to take action.

Ricoeur develops a threefold ontological dialectic of the Self-Other relationship. There is the relationship of the Self to the body, the relationship of the Self to the Other, and the relationship of the Self to the conscience. Furthermore, this Self has two dimensions, both of which must be considered together. The *idem* dimension has to do with comparison and sameness, ascribing truth to the Self. It is atemporal and unchanging. The *ipse* dimension is rooted in temporality, combining both the historical narrative of the Self and future promises. The *ipse* dimension is always changing. In Levinas' terms, inclusion of these two dimensions makes up an infinite interior universe for each person. To concentrate on one to the exclusion of the other dimension would be tantamount to Levinas' sense of totality. It would restrict what there was to the Self to make it controllable.

For Ricoeur, the violence that Levinas associates with totality and Chanteur associates with ontological rift is seen in an analysis of action. These ideas are related to deep-rooted conflict in the following way. In an identity-based conflict there is a failure on the part of each group as a Self to see the infinite humanity of the Other. The desire is to "interrupt the continuity of the Other's existence" through actions designed to lead to control, not understanding. Picking up on the metaphor of the face, the tendency is not to look into the face of the Other, not to ponder what the Other has experienced and is experiencing, and not to use the tools of language to understand the Other. In Chanteur's terms, there is an ontological rift that holds that the Other is so Other as not to constitute a full representation of humanity. Furthermore, it is predominantly men who war with one another, each group of men fighting for control of the Other. Finally, these conflicts can be seen as an attempt by each group to maximize their acting and minimize their suffering, rather than to seek mutuality and balance.

For philosophers of the Self-Other relationship, the result of a foundational belief in the autonomous Self (usually man) summarizes experience in a way that negates an awareness of the infinity of the Other, making the Other into a sufferer.

The Challenge

The urgency of potential conflicts and the endless suffering caused by violence between ethnonational groups cry for the best tools of understanding possible. As Horowitz observes, "[t]he sheer passion expended in pursuing ethnic conflict calls out for an explanation that does justice to the realm of the feelings. It is necessary to account, not merely for ambition, but for antipathy. A bloody phenomenon cannot be explained by a bloodless theory."[12]

We have explored, initially, the role of emotions in relation to human identity needs. It has become clear that attacking, threatening, or removing need satisfiers for meaning, connectedness, action, security, and recognition can result in anger, grief, depression, fear, and shame, respectively. We also saw that people caught in a fierce mimetic rivalry can experience impotent rage, resentment, and hatred. As we look at psychological insights related to Self-Other dynamics, we must consider that these dynamics can involve severe victimization accompanied by strong feelings that produce results such as dehumanization and demonization.

Psychological Approaches to Self-Other Dynamics

Demetrios Julius sums up the distinctive role of psychological methodologies:

In example after example history has shown us that man has formulated rational agenda after rational agenda only to have them change, go astray or be subverted by unseen, unexpected, and often seemingly illogical forces. It is with this irrational aspect of the human condition that psychiatry and psychological theory has always concerned itself.[13]

The "illogical forces" that prompt atrocities—genocide, mass murder, and terrorism—are the focus of much psychological study. In the psychological litera-ture about violence, there is considerable evidence to show that opposite sides of the same phenomena are intertwined: perpetrators of violence were often victims, self-identity develops with enmity, leaders and followers are caught up with one another, and demonization and dehumanization are complementary and reflexive. We will first explore theorists who have combined frameworks of complex inter-acting psychological phenomena that contribute to genocide and mass murder. Second, we will examine the effects of atrocities on victims, tracing the process by which victims become terrorists. Third, we will explore theorists who look at the symptoms of violent conflict between identity groups from the perspective of development, noting parallel mechanisms for both individuals and groups, as they define their own identities and determine their enemies. Finally, we will examine theories of dehumanization and demonization.

Genocide and Murder

In looking at the roots of genocide and murder, a number of theorists have drawn up theoretical schemes. Demetrios A. Julius, discussing what motivates conflict, draws attention to "feelings of anger, rage, hurt, guilt, shame, and mistrust" and the "wish to control and to dominate, the obsession to own, the desire to vanquish, and often the drive to sacrifice the other."[14] Julius provides a framework with three key "intrapsychic processes" that interact to produce the feelings that fuel conflict: *historical enmity*, *dehumanization*, and *victimization*.[15] Memories and feelings of *historical enmity* stimulate the urge to victimize others and *dehumanization* alters perceptions to make it possible. "Victimization is the embodiment of the drive to sacrifice.... [It] represents that tribal ritual that brings about collective cohesion through a sense of collective guilt...[becoming] a defensive process against feelings of overwhelming guilt."[16] These three processes feed each other in cyclical patterns on both sides of a conflict.

A second theorist, John Mack, highlights mechanisms that make members of ethnonational groups sustain "the image of an enemy as an individual or group whom it might be necessary to kill."[17] These include 1. The surrender of responsibility to governing authority; 2. Dehumanization and demonization of the other people and its leaders (to keep control); 3. The externalization of responsibility or blaming the other;[18] and 4. Ideology, mythology, and religion. He stresses that the

> *ideologies of enmity* are psychopolitical thought systems that sustain a nation in its conviction of the worthiness of its purpose and political system when compared to an adversary's.... Ideologies of enmity, which seem to flow like a kind of collective toxin through the bloodstream of a political culture, are the supreme instruments through which a political leader sustains his people's hostile attitudes toward another nation without which a unified war or defence effort is not possible.[19]

Ervin Staub, a third theorist, who turned his attention to understanding the "roots of evil" after a career of research into altruism, sees a continuum of evil. People are not naturally ready to commit atrocities, but various factors contribute to their movement towards evil.[20] Incrementally, people are conditioned to tolerate perpetrating torture and mass murder. Staub has identified five contributing factors to the most horrendous aspects of deep-rooted conflict between identity groups: 1. Difficult life circumstances; 2. A threat to human needs; 3. An ideology of we-they; 4. Compliance of bystanders — those close enough to a situation, in proximity or influence, to influence the dynamics of a conflict even though they are not a party to it; and 5. A tendency to scapegoat.[21] He uses four case studies to demonstrate how the presence of each of these contributes to a movement along the continuum of evil and results in a capacity to perpetrate genocide.

Victims and Terrorists

John Mack and Joseph Montville both recognize the devastating effects of victimization. Mack points out that victims left unattended can lose their ability to feel for others. Montville links victimhood and ethnic-based terrorism.

Mack observes that "national groups have often *formed* out of mythic-histori-cal events of group victimization" creating "victims and deeply hated enemies."[22] These experiences, repeated over the centuries, are passed to children who learn to identify "my people."[23] Cultural symbols—food, geography, and flag—become "all powerful emotional amplifiers. They link affiliation and differentiation at the level of the ethnonationalist group with a reservoir of intense feeling, to which each childhood period of development has made its particular contribution."[24] A result may be *the egoism of victimization* that is

> the incapacity of an ethno-national group, as a direct result of its own historical traumas, to empathize with the suffering of another group. It is analogous to the narcissism or self-centeredness of some individuals who see themselves as having been so hurt or deprived in the past that they can attend only to their own needs, feeling little or no empathy for the hurt they inflict upon others. Similarly, ethno-national groups that have been trauma-tized by repeated suffering at the hands of other groups seem to have little capacity to grieve for the hurts of other peoples, or to take responsibility for the new victims created by their own warlike actions.[25]

In examining the dynamics of terrorism, Montville distinguishes between that which is motivated by ideology and that which is rooted in the victimage experi-ence of identity groups.[26] He shows that victims of violence have specific needs that are almost never attended to. They have a need for mourning, a need for their loss to be acknowledged, and a need for an expression of remorse on behalf of perpetrators.[27] Those who experience profound loss, such as having a home burned or a family member tortured and killed, lose a capacity for trust. When the loss occurs at a formative stage (childhood or youth) and is followed by persecution, harsh treatment, or other injustice, a young person may become desperate to take corrective action. If they associate with terrorist organizations, they are prime candidates to become terrorists. Those who do not become terrorists go through life with very deep fears. According to Montville, terrorists fight because "as individu-als they believe their lives and their identity as a people are mortally threatened not just on one or two occasions, but continuously and into the future."[28] This threat has two aspects to it. One is the sense that it is based solely on being a member of an identity group. Another is that the terrorist has been personally victimized for being a member of a group.[29] This personal dimension can also come about vicariously as people with whom a terrorist personally identifies have been subject to violence.

Montville has been influenced by victimologist Jeanne Knutson, who believed "that what drives the rage of the victimized is the fact that no psychic mechanism or external events can repair the destruction of their central, primitive belief in the safety and meaning of life."[30] Political violence comes from the conviction that further threats can only be reduced by defensive activity. When an act of affirmative violence first takes place, Knutson wrote, "there simultaneously emerges a full, direct emotional awareness of intense rage, as well as unbearable anxiety stemming from the possibility of the loss of even life itself for having dared to defy the aggressor. It is the point of no return for those who engage in continuing campaigns of political violence."[31] She noted, through many interviews, that most "ethnic terrorists had undergone a personal trauma or 'conversion experience', which had brought home to them in a powerful, individual way the victimhood of their ethnic group."[32] The observations about victimization and victimhood for both individuals and groups raise the issue of identity formation.

Identity and Enmity

Both Vamik Volkan and Rita Rogers explore how childhood and adolescent experiences contribute to a sense of self and of the enemy that lays the psychological foundation for deep-rooted conflicts. First, Volkan shows how a sense of identity and enmity is developed through similar mechanisms.[33] As a child begins to differentiate between I and not-I, cultural reservoirs are developed for good and bad. Good reservoirs are externalized cultural symbols associated with well-being and bad reservoirs symbolize the causes for ill.[34] The good reservoirs are

> the building blocks for the children's subsequent structuring of ethnic, cultural, and national identity.... [C]hildren learn to take satisfaction in the properties, both real and intangible, that they share with their own group, and regard what is shared by members of another group as far less desirable—even "bad"—especially if the other ethnic or national group is seen as hostile or is rejected by the adults in their own group.[35]

As children grow up, some of these "bad" symbolic reservoirs become targets of enmity. Shared targets unite a group. The "primitive and unconscious impulses" associated with identity become, in the context of large group interaction, involuntary.[36]

Enemies, then, become a significant part of our own identities, since they "serve as a reservoir for our unwanted selves." Unconsciously, they are somewhat like us, "although on a conscious level they should not seem to be the same as us since they contain our unwanted aspects—those characteristics we vigorously reject."[37]

Second, Rogers gives examples of some ways in which children are given a sense that enemies are dangerous; they may be told that if they are naughty, a ____ [insert name of enemy group] will get them.[38] In adolescence, a young person senses the discrepancy between "the tone of fury when his parents present the fierceness of a perceived enemy...[and] his parents' inner shame and feelings of failure."[39] The parents' excuses fail to justify for the youth, "their own impotence in the face of the cruel oppressor."[40] The youth takes action to "vindicate his elders and gratify their need for revenge, but he also wishes to prove himself stronger than his parents... Indeed, his perception of them as weak inflames his need for action and revenge all the more."[41] The passion and will to violence is expedited by the dehumanization and demonization of the enemy.

Dehumanization and Demonization

Rafael Moses develops the theme of dehumanization and demonization first from the perspective of narcissism. He shows that narcissistic needs and tendencies of leaders and followers can reinforce one another. Moses also develops the idea that dehumanization functions reciprocally between groups.

Moses holds that groups have narcissistic sensitivities that function as their Achilles heels.[42] There is a constant lookout for "narcissistic satisfactions," as when people like and appreciate us, or "narcissistic hurts," as when people dislike and insult us.[43] Conflict between identity groups can be the result of pathological narcissism.

> There is an analogy between normal, i.e., necessary, and pathological narcissism in the individual and a healthy nationalism as opposed to chauvinism for a national group. In both cases, it is not always easy to define the border between the two. Yet, equally, we have absolutely no doubt when we encounter the phenomenon of pathological narcissism—of the individual or the group. Furthermore, there is no doubt about the fact that for the individual, pathological narcissism—i.e., a grandiose self-view accompanied by severe vulnerability to hurts in the areas of the self—is accompanied by and related to its opposite, which is a very low self-esteem. In our psychological processes we often find that two extremes, the opposite sides of a coin, go together: one side may appear in our consciousness; the other, the unconscious, may influence our behavior more markedly.[44]

In particular, during times of hostilities they may contribute to *dehumanization* and *demonization*. "The demonization of the enemy—an extreme form of stereotyping—is functional from the point of view of a society that wants to teach its members to maintain the enemy in his enemy role."[45] These phenomena justify inflicting evil on others in two ways. "First, we are dealing with a demon and with someone less than human. Secondly, this subhuman demon threatens us in such a mortally dangerous way that we must perforce defend ourselves."[46]

Moses also explores the symbiotic relationship between leaders and followers.[47] He points out that leaders need their followers as much as followers need their leaders. Narcissistic, charismatic leaders have special needs that can only be met through the adulation of their followers. They see themselves as protectors of their groups and, as such, may be prone to engage in violence. On the other hand, followers who have experienced victimization and have ill-defined personal identities find many of their identity needs met through identification with a strong leader. Rita Rogers shows how skilled Hitler was at "exploiting adolescent cravings for herd relationships and leadership (security)" to cement a highly cohesive and dedicated following.[48]

Moses comments that there is a temptation to "talk about the dehumanizing behavior of the other side—of anybody but myself and mine" since both sides are "convinced that the adversary is by far the more grievous offender."[49] He describes the relationship between dehumanization and war as follows:

> I believe that in the individual there must be intrapsychic readiness to be dehumanized in order to dehumanize another; this cannot happen, however, unless certain processes in the large group (often a nation) pave the way for it. By and large, these processes are the same ones that help prepare a nation to wage war. The aggressor initiated use of the following collective psychic mechanisms: the demonization of the enemy; projection that ascribes to the antagonist all our evils so that we can view ourselves as good and pure; scapegoating; and polarization that blames the enemy for faults that are our own and paints the world in black and white, with no grey allowed.[50]

Victims of dehumanization become humiliated and degraded. Their helplessness can turn to rage and vengefulness; however, "[s]ometimes—in circumstances we do not yet adequately understand—a strange identification between the victim and his dehumanizer occurs. This has been reported in some hijacking as well as brainwashing experiences, and even in an occasional victim of the Holocaust."[51]

The result of dehumanization is that one feels entirely like an "other." Willard Gaylin captured the feeling well:

> when we are made to feel like the "other"—then we will surely see those privileged and secure representatives of the society and the society itself alien and other to us.... To be totally unaccepted, to be totally unloved, indeed to be almost totally disapproved, either requires the rejection of one's self—an intolerable situation—or a total dissociation with the judging individual...or society...and allegiance to its moral codes.[52]

Gaylin's description makes vivid and concrete the philosophical notions of ontological rift described by philosophers. We turn to mimetic structures of violence with an acute sense of the emotional power unleashed by deep-rooted conflicts.

Chapter 8

Structures of Violence

When I finished analyzing the Oka/*Kanehsatà:ke* crisis, I was overwhelmed by a sense of awe at the power of something bigger than any individual which prompted people to say and do things that went against their own personal values and inclinations. I called this force a mimetic structure of violence. When it was identified and named, its characteristics began to become apparent.

A mimetic structure of violence is a relationship that builds up in such a way that the parties in the relationship say and do things to harm one another. All of the elements of deep-rooted conflict discussed in the first seven chapters come into play within mimetic structures of violence.

We must not lose the human dimension in this analysis. In defining the Rwandan genocide as a mimetic structure of violence, we recoil at the destructive power of actions held together by hateful emotions and distortions of personal interests. We think of a mythology of the past used to legitimize murder, we think of perceptions of historical injustices, and we think of recurring violent episodes of the past. These complex structures have many elements and dimensions. Theories help to understand the complexity and to imagine the many-faceted actions, teachings, and approaches needed to dismantle such structures.

Mimesis works at different levels. Plato used mimesis in reference to ideal types. A chair for instance, imitates an ideal type of chair: it embodies "chairness." In this sense, mimetic structures of violence, in resembling one another, resemble an ideal type of a mimetic structure of violence. If we think of Aristotle's use of mimesis to think of a *mythos*, or plot, of a story imitating the structure of human action, we see how mimetic structures of violence each have their own *mythos*. They develop over time just like the plot of a story.[1] Not only are the structures imitative of one another, the people caught up in these structures are mimetic of one another as René Girard used the term. They are mimetic in relation to desires, satisfiers of identity needs, and other dimensions of interiority. They also imitate each other's violent attitudes, rhetoric, and behaviour.

Various aspects of mimesis are presented in Figure 8-1.

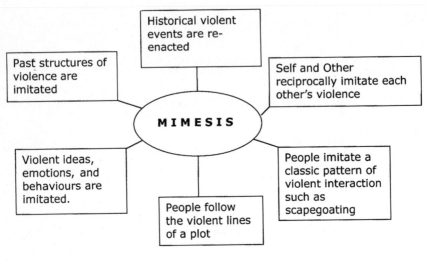

Figure 8-1

At one point in our married life, Gloria and I recognized that sometimes we would get into a recurring pattern of communication that left both of us feeling badly about ourselves. It would start with one criticizing the other; the other would respond defensively. This resulted in both of us feeling bad—one, for having been critical and the other, for the defensive response. We identified this pattern as a mimetic structure of violence in that it was bringing out the worst in both of us and leaving us both in a more miserable condition than when we started. Naming it as such has enabled us to change the pattern of communication (most of the time).

"Structure" is derived from the Latin verb *struere*, which means to pile, arrange, or build. From this root metaphor we have a sense that structures are built up over time with layers of misunderstanding and patterns of behaviour and reaction piled on top of each other in such a way as to reinforce one another. Structure means that a number of interrelated parts are dominated by the whole. In this case, the parts include human identity need satisfiers; feelings of "envy, greed, and impotent hatred" inspired by mimetic desire; and memories of victimization and bystander encouragement—all are dominated by the whole, which is violence. When people in mimetic structures of violence interact with one another they are worse off for the encounter. Sometimes if they "won" in a competitive exchange they might have a fleeting feeling of vindication, pride, or smugness but this is inevitably short-lived. This leads to the question of the meaning of violence.

"Violence," from the Latin *violentia*, has its roots in a word meaning force. It is also related to the word "violate," which has the sense of going against, harming, interfering, or failing to show respect. By violence, we mean that which takes away from the well-being of someone. This can include something that causes death, physical injury, or psychological damage, prompts negative emotion, or results in a wounded spirit. We have to distinguish between violent events that are unplanned and inadvertent, like true accidents, and violent actions intended to do harm. The violence of mimetic structures of violence has within it an intention to harm or get at the other. The different ways of doing violence are pictured in the following graphic.

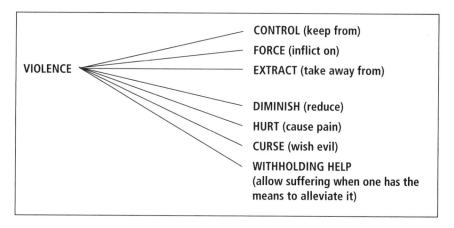

Figure 8-2

Violence, as *control*, keeps people from achieving their ends, holds them back, and puts obstacles in their way.

Violence, as *force*, inflicts goals, actions, or behaviours on people. It makes people subservient, doing what they do not wish to do. It is the work of extortion and brutality. It forces people to choose between two unacceptable options, as when women are forced to choose between unwanted sexual activity or seeing their children hurt.

Violence *extracts* from people what they cherish. It may be the theft of possessions or it may mean extracting information through torture, trickery, or treachery.

Violence *diminishes* people. It makes them lose face, humiliates them, and removes all dignity and self-respect.

Violence *hurts* people. It maims them, burns them, makes them bleed, and kills them. With the physical hurt comes the inner hurt of being deceived or betrayed.

Violence can take place at another level—that of *curse*. Curses involve a desire to see the other harmed. It imagines and desires ill for the Other. Curses have a verbal dimension of demanding that harmful things happen to the object of the curse. They may also have a spiritual dimension where forces are invoked to perpetrate evil against the Other.

Violence can also take the form of *withholding help* from someone who is suffering.

The story is told of a person who went on to the afterlife. They first got a tour of the premises. Hell contained unhappy people looking gaunt to the point of malnutrition. In front of them were tables of food, but their eating instruments were longer than their arms so they couldn't get food into their mouths. In heaven were happy people with the same tables of food and the same long eating utensils. The only difference was that they were feeding each other.

This story illustrates the difference between mimetic structures of violence and mimetic structures of blessing. As we examine this picture of hell as a mimetic structure of violence, we note that people are violent as they refuse to do anything to help the next person. It is mimetic in that all are imitating one another in refusing to help. It is a structure in that it is an ongoing pattern through time. It may be that people fed each other at one time, but at some point one person refused to feed someone who fed her and the hurt feelings and mutual responses to being slighted resulted in a situation where no one fed anyone.

Characteristics of Mimetic Structures of Violence

Mimetic structures of violence are bigger than any individual. They can draw people into a violent situation so that people end up saying and doing things that in isolation or outside of such a structure they would consider completely against their basic beliefs and values. These structures can control the minds and hearts of people to such an extent that they become obsessed with either doing violence to others or preventing their own victimization.

Mimetic structures of violence give a strong interpretive spin to everything that happens. Each gesture on the part of the Other is suspect and interpreted as something intended to do ultimate harm.

I remember when I worked in penitentiaries that some prisoners were unable to accept any loving action. They had experienced so much hate and treachery that they were convinced that anyone who did anything nice for them was trying to con them or get something out of them. They were locked in their own mimetic structures of violence in which the interpretation of actions imitated intentions and structures of actions that they had experienced in the past.

Mimetic structures of violence are closed and confining. People end up having fewer and fewer options. Those caught in them are intensely acquisitive, trying to get as much as possible for themselves. Negative emotions—such as anger, fear, hatred, and resentment—dominate. People are inclined to use the phrase "I had no choice but to…" Ultimately, these structures are oriented toward death and destruction.

Mimetic Structures of Violence and Human Needs Theory

Needs for meaning, connectedness, action, security, and recognition have been shown to be important in developing identity for the human Self. Satisfaction of these needs results in well-being fed by self-recognizance, self-respect, self-esteem, self-confidence, and self-actualization. A threat to satisfiers results in anger, sadness, depression, fear, and shame, respectively.

Persons in a mimetic structure of violence have their identity defined by violence. The satisfiers to each of the identity needs are derived from violence. For example, someone in a motorcycle gang will get meaning out of violence; connectedness is based on being violent with comrades; action undertaken is violent; security comes from a capacity for violence; and recognition comes for violence.

It is interesting to note that individuals whose identity is dominated by having been a victim of violence have identity need satisfiers that are linked to violence. Their sense of meaning and place in the world is as a victim, and connectedness is primarily with other victims of violence. Significant action is around seeking revenge or retribution for the violence. Security is defined as preventing additional violent acts, sometimes leading to obsession with locks, gates, and so forth. The need for recognition is an acknowledgement of the pain and loss of victimization.

When violence is sufficient to cause trauma, the fear and dissociation can immobilize people and lead to an ongoing sense of being caught up with a mimetic structure of violence.

In this situation the link between victimization and participating in terrorism shows the power of a mimetic structure of violence to control identity. The similarity of identity need satisfiers of victims and terrorists is illustrated in the following account of an IRA terrorist called "Eamon" by Jeanne Knutson, who interviewed him. He was from a Republican family and grew up in the 1960s on an integrated street in Belfast, and he talks about a night in the late 1960s.

Quietly, with obvious pain, Eamon tells the story of his own experience with the night of August 14, as follows:

Eamon: Our family was picked out for special treatment at the time...our door was kicked in by members of the RUC (Royal Ulster Constabulary) and the B Specials who were a sacred, again, a paramilitary armed group...

So what they did was they quite roughly dragged us out, all out, you know... and then they proceeded to burn the house down. So they threw petrol bombs and they did this with all the Catholic families down the block. They say there was four hundred houses burned; four hundred families...plus a lot more families who had to leave...because they were afraid of the same thing happening. So we became refugees then, you know...

Knutson: Can you tell me, emotionally, what it felt like?

Eamon: Well...up until then, I—because of my upbringing—violence, I suppose, had been a romantic sort of aspect about it.... It was the first time that I even experienced it...first hand and...the terror I felt, you know, was actually what violence is.... I—I remember at the time that that's what struck me the most... The terror, the fear, physical fear... Just how...helpless you are really...when you are attacked by them and...I suppose that put bigger fear into me, you know—that it would ever happen again...

[Author's note] When asked to talk about the emotional results of taking an active part in a campaign of political violence, he concluded:

... what I felt on that morning our house was burned down and we were abused by these people, I felt that many times after that...the...sheer terror of the violence in action

Knutson: Can you elaborate on that a little?

Eamon: ... I never lost the fear of violence, you know. I never have. But driven on by some force, some greater fear, really, you know—I took part in actions. They were never glorious, you know, and, like you say there's always...a lot of loss for it...you know.[2]

Eamon's story illustrates how a mimetic structure of violence can hold someone in its grip. The terror he felt as a victim is mimetically replicated through his own acts of violence.

For every person the importance of different identity needs varies. This is also true of the way in which violence controls personal identity. For some, it is at the level of meaning and anger around the violence. Others may experience an overwhelming fear and the resulting agoraphobia is so strong that people are afraid to leave their homes and essentially become prisoners.

In July 2001, I made a pilgrimage to Oka/*Kanehsatà:ke* to commemorate the beginning of the Crisis of 1990. There I met Elizabeth Sacca, a friend of the Mohawk people of *Kanehsatà:ke*. She pointed out that since the crisis a number of people suffered from agoraphobia, and the ongoing effects of post-traumatic stress continue to have a negative impact on the community.

Another way in which mimetic structures of violence affect identity is through the temporal dimension of human needs, reflected first in needs for memory, story, and coherence relating to the past. Stories rising out of past victimization define a coherent identity in terms of historic enmity—"we are the ones who suffered." These stories come from clan rivalries, ethnonational differences, or religious conflict, and may go back centuries or may go back only a year. Identity preoccupation is with an enemy; both sides of the victim-perpetrator polarity figure into the equation as one recounts stories of chosen trauma or chosen glory.

For those caught in mimetic structures of violence, the future—as defined by needs for imagination, stimulation, and continuity—is likewise dominated by violence.

The Genesis account of the Flood begins with the observation that people were not only wicked but that their imaginations were filled with violence—an indication of the presence of a mimetic structure of violence. This structure of violence is met with violence; the Flood destroys humankind, except for Noah's family, making the space for a new civilization that would hopefully not get caught up in the same mimetic structures. At the end of the story, God promises never again to wipe out humanity in the same way—in a sense renouncing the violence of the Flood.

Within a mimetic structure of violence, people's minds are filled with fantasies of violence. They are turned on by violence, excited by violence, and wish for violent change. Their own sense of continuity becomes dependent on a violent response to threats.

Mimetic Structures of Violence, and Mimetic Desire and Scapegoating

Though René Girard refers to mimetic desire, mimetic rivalries, and mimetic doubling as structures, he does not use the phrase "mimetic structure of violence." In fact, Girard uses the word "structure" in two different senses. When he analyzes structuralism, he is critical; however, he uses the word positively when referring to mimetic phenomena.

A few years ago I talked with René Girard at Stanford University about his use of the word "structure" and he corroborated my distinction.

What I learned from Girard is that mimetic structures are diachronic and dynamic—as they develop through time they can evolve gradually or change rapidly like a kaleidoscope.

Mimetic desire and scapegoating are implicated in mimetic structures of violence and are key to understanding their dynamics. Mimetic desire can lead directly to violence as Self and Model strive for the same object and may turn to violence to acquire the object. Mimetic desire can lead to mimetic rivalry and doubling, both of which can have violent manifestations. Mimetic selfness can also be patterned on violence such that at the level of identity, one is preoccupied with violence. Violent actions are returned mimetically through escalating cycles of revenge. The differences among these examples of mimetic structures of violence are based on the time element, the complexity, the intensity of the emotional involvement, and the level of violence. Scapegoating is another mimetic structure of violence. In this case, the mimesis involves persons in the crowd imitating one another in a joint violent action against the scapegoat. The action may range in intensity from lethal violence to symbolic violence to shunning, which is itself a form of violence.

A significant insight about mimetic structures of violence comes from Girard's association of mimetic doubling with a violence of undifferentiation and scapegoating with a violence of differentiation. This distinction allows us to categorize mimetic structures of violence into differentiation and undifferentiation.

A violent structure of undifferentiation occurs when those caught in the violence identify closely with one another as rivals or doubles. Their identities are based on one another. There can be profound hatred between them. In mimetic structures of undifferentiation, as the Other is hated to the point of dehumanization, the Self likewise is dehumanized mimetically. There can be rapid oscillation between Self-hatred and Other-hatred.

In structures characterized by differentiation, the Other becomes so totally Other that they become an "it," in Buber's terms. The Other is objectified, dehumanized, and demonized and needs to be removed. Violence is projected onto the scapegoat who is seen as the source of violence.

Mimetic Structures of Violence and Hegemonic Structures

Some mimetic structures of violence become hegemonic structures. Hegemonic structures are generally characterized by a violence of differentiation where the dominant consider the subjected as "less than they are." They are in a subcategory that may translate into being subhuman. Hegemonic structures are often established through physical violence and contain a significant amount of violence. The Subjected are diminished and controlled, with a lifestyle, authority system, and certain values imposed on them. In some cases—such as slavery or extreme patriarchy—slaves and wives are considered property of the "Master."

As hegemonic structures are established, they are interiorized by the Subjected who assume the identity projected onto them by the Dominant. Often the persons subjected imitate the violence of their oppressors on one another or on people or animals that they in turn can subject, developing cascading hegemonic structures that then become mimetic structures of violence.

Hegemonic structures are the same as domination structures. Theologian Walter Wink identifies them with the Powers, described in the New Testament. In a series of books he shows how these structures can assume a life of their own.[3]

Mimetic Structures of Violence and Ethnonationalism

Ethnonationalism takes on a highly mimetic character in two ways. Ethnonationalists want a territorial nation with state status and sovereignty, like every other nation, and they are rivals with other ethnonational groups. When ethnonationalism evolves among people who are part of a state, the ethnonationalist impulse may manifest itself in violence against the state, which may be seen to have an unjust hegemony over the ethnonationalist group. Or it may be directed against people not part of the ethnonationalist group who have territory to which they feel entitled.

The mimetic structures of violence involving ethnonationalist groups can go back for centuries, as in Northern Ireland and the former Yugoslavia. They may go back millennia, as in the Middle East.

Mimetic structures of violence can overtake relational systems. When there are complex interrelationships among relational systems, the mimetic structure of violence can inspire similar structures in some of these relational systems. The image is like that of two tuning forks of the same pitch. If one is tapped and starts vibrating, the other one at the other end of the room will (mimetically) start to vibrate from the strength of the sound waves. The island of Cyprus shows a clear mimetic structure of violence in a relational system where people identity themselves as Turks and Greeks. The violence in Cyprus inspires antagonism between Greece and Turkey.

In another example, Kurds of Iran, Iraq, and Turkey are involved in relational systems with their respective countries that involve mimetic structures of violence. Kurds of all three countries have a vision for a greater Kurdestan to unite them in their own nation-state. Acting on this vision involves violence toward the respective countries and the violence in one area has an impact on structures of violence in the next country. All three countries recognize the threat and are, in turn, violent toward Kurds, thwarting their ambitions and depriving them of the means to offer resistance.

Mimetic structures of violence can also take over economic life as profits are made from instruments of death, extortion, terror, or inflated prices for the necessities of life.

Mimetic Structures of Violence and Self-Other Dynamics

Mimetic structures of violence determine the nature of Self-Other dynamics that, in turn, can intensify or ease the power of these structures. Within mimetic structures of violence, Self-Other dynamics of both sides aim to diminish the well-being of the other with each Self aggrandizing itself at the expense of the Other. Self-Other dynamics are extremely competitive in a malicious way.

In Ricoeur's terms, each Self tries to act on the Other making the Other into a sufferer. This "acting on" is a violent attempt to acquire as much as possible from the Other and diminish the capacity of the Other to take action. Levinas identifies this as the most insidious form of violence.

The psychodynamic factors in Self-Other relationships have the effect of intensifying and entrenching mimetic structures of violence. These include victimizing children and youth, recounting chosen glories associated with violence, and passing on chosen traumas. Political rhetoric is violent, intending to motivate violent behaviour. Bystanders encourage violence and media rewards it by giving it exposure. Violent intentions are projected onto the Other. This can take different forms. For example, a Serb intellectual remarked: "I would not destroy any mosque myself, but I am glad that not one is left in the Republic of Serbska in Bosnia and Herzegovina."[4]

There are certainly degrees to which mimetic structures of violence take over the thoughts, minds, and imaginations of people. These structures work at the emotional level, involving cells throughout the body in preparing for and performing violence. Emotions associated with violence—anger, fear, hatred, resentment, envy, and shame—result from interpreting events in a certain way. That is, we interpret certain signals as threatening some aspect of our identity and this causes an emotional response. The emotions that are aroused influence our interpretation of subsequent experiences and events. The emotional part of the brain cannot differentiate time, so a past emotional memory is reignited, opening up emotional memories that make past events seem as though they happened yesterday.

Within mimetic structures of violence, the emotional part of the mind uses the cognitive mind for its service. People may sometimes appear coolly logical when, in fact, their logic is driven by emotion. Terrorists who plan sophisticated acts of terror use their minds, skills, and organizational abilities to serve their emotions, which have been shaped by violent victimization. They imitate in another form the violence they perceive to have been done to them or their people.

Mimetic structures of violence can have a vicarious dimension. People may take on the victimization of others and identify with it totally. Some activists working for justice for disadvantaged groups can be stronger in their positions than the actual victims.

There are differences in the degree to which a mimetic structure of violence is entrenched within the minds and psyches of people and in the level of violence. When marriages go awry, for example, a well-entrenched mimetic structure of violence may be exhibited in language, attitudes, and actions that are mutually debilitating. However, the level of overt physical violence may be small. On the other hand, there may be a violent flare-up in a bar between people who hardly know each other. The level of physical violence may be high, but it is not entrenched or long-lasting.

Deep-rooted conflict pulls people into mimetic structures of violence, within which they feel that they have no choice but to be violent. Violence shapes identity and tends to escalate. Objects of violence, the ones to whom violence is done, become non-persons. In the process, perpetrators of violence lose their own humanity. The violent Self becomes narcissistic, caught up in a personal woundedness and unable to see things from another perspective. Emotions drive the violence, but they are sometimes camouflaged by cool logic. People's roles are framed as adversaries. Sometimes the urge is to win, sometimes to get even, and sometimes to destroy.

The pressure applied by mimetic structures of violence is so strong that people often feel that they have no choice but to go along with the violence. Sometimes the pressure of these structures comes from outside the Self; at other times the pressure comes from within, from the emotional build-up over an injustice or the pain of humiliation. Breaking free of well-entrenched structures of violence and moving toward structures of blessing opened up by reconciliation takes tremendous strength. To understand certain aspects of mimetic structures of violence, it is helpful to conceptualize mimetic structures of entrenchment that describe the defensive side of violence.

Mimetic Structures of Entrenchment

Chapter 2 showed that severe threats to identity needs traumatize people. When this happens, fear takes over the core of the Self and concern for security becomes paramount. If the threat is sustained or healing does not occur, this need for security has a ripple effect on the other need categories, which become security-oriented. The need for meaning in a context of fear generates satisfiers that are clearly defined and held as absolutes. Those who are "friends" are those who agree with this presentation of truth. The need for connectedness is translated into a good guy–bad guy division of the world in which people who are not connected are perceived as enemies. Action becomes focused on providing long-term security. Recognition becomes defined as that which acknowledges and validates the strictly defined satisfiers. This situation adds up to a mimetic structure of entrenchment. Within these structures there is little room for creativity, tolerance, ambiguity, or growth. In this way, the violence is done to oneself in that one is limiting oneself.

Mimetic Structures of Entrenchment

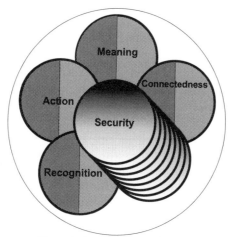

- All needs developed around security
- Self-criticism impossible
- Everything is black and white
- Fundamentalist approach to meaning
- Terminal identity – all that matters is "Are you on our side?"

Figure 8-3

A mimetic structure of entrenchment has several relationships to mimetic structures of violence. It can be seen as the defensive side of violence since it is motivated by fear coming from a threat to security. It provides a rationale, including an emotional rationale, for violence as self-defence. It can be the outcome of a mimetic structure of violence, in that the violence is mutual and hurtful and the violent self can easily reframe its experience as that of a victim.

Those caught up in mimetic structures of entrenchment have the following characteristics. They crave certainty of meaning and tend to formulate truth in fundamentalist-like absolute truths. They are incapable of self-criticism and tend to place the blame for a difficult situation on their Other. They desire one hundred per cent solidarity from their friends; those who do not offer this uncritical solidarity are seen as enemies. They cannot empathetically enter the space of their Other.

In a conversation with Rebecca Adams, with whom I developed this concept, she suggested that often after a period of well-being when someone is victimized there is a mimetic structure of retrenchment in which chosen glories or chosen traumas from the past are relived and form the basis of a repeat "digging of the trenches." The concept of retrenchment shows the dynamic nature of the entrenchment process.

Sometimes, in a deep-rooted conflict, the mimetic structures of violence subside into mimetic structures of entrenchment. People have not reconciled, but for some reason they stop overt violence and settle into entrenched positions, living in a state of passive stalemate.

Leaders can play a key role in developing mimetic structures of entrenchment when victimized people are traumatized with ill-defined identities. Strong leaders with a clear set of well-articulated concepts can frame experience so people know how they have been hurt, who their enemies are, what to believe in, and what to do about the situation.

Some form of mimetic structures of transcendence is needed to release persons from mimetic structures of entrenchment. These involve stepping out from the entrenched position and viewing one's Self and one's Other in a new way. Transcendence allows for self-criticism and openness and provides the basis for mutual understanding. It is the beginning of a process of reconciliation that can lead to mimetic structures of blessing. More on that later; now I will present a case study to illustrate how the theory of mimetic structures of violence can help us to understand an actual conflict.

Part 2

Case Study

Chapter 9

Understanding Through Interpreting

Hermeneutics helps to generate understanding and interpret actions, events, and relationships to give them meaning. Chapter 1 showed that the way in which we interpret deep-rooted conflicts has profound implications for our choices in responding to them. The introduction explained that methodology is, literally, the conscious reflection on the "way in which we proceed." This chapter reflects on the way to proceed in interpreting deep-rooted conflicts through the story of how I interpreted the Oka/*Kanehsatà:ke* Crisis of 1990.

As humans, not content with simple symbols, we use words metaphorically to add layers of meaning. For example we use the word "see" to describe the visual sense of seeing physical things through sensitivity to light, darkness, and colour. We use the same word metaphorically to talk about sensing the significance of actions, for example, "She didn't see what was happening to her." When passions get in the way of noting a certain reality that everyone else is perceiving, we use phrases such as: "Love is blind" or "Blinded by anger, he…" In these phrases, physical blindness is used as a metaphor for failure to see or notice something.

Paul Ricoeur makes the point that as we understand complex actions over time, the plot is the factor that brings together "goals, causes and chance" in a manner similar to the way in which a metaphor brings together two aspects of reality to create meaning.[1] I have adapted Ricoeur's sense of plot and emplotment, as the action of generating a narrative, for use in the hermeneutical, or interpretative, enterprise. Ricoeur develops the idea, building on Aristotle, that a narrative imitates action. He uses the term *mimesis*, the word on which Girard bases the concept of mimetic desire, to show the relationship between narrative and reality. In fact, he develops the idea of *mimesis₁*, *mimesis₂* and *mimesis₃* to show different levels of interpretation.[2] I begin to describe the hermeneutical enterprise with some observations about gathering data, an action Ricoeur associates with *mimesis₁* and then explore the kinds of questions involved in the different levels of interpretation.

Deep-rooted conflict involves data about actions that can be observed and clues about what was going on within individuals and groups to motivate them to act as they did, and it is important that the interpreter listen carefully to all the information available. (Listen is used as a metaphor for attending to data; the Chinese character for "listen" indicates that we listen with our ears, with our eyes, and with an open heart.) In an interview after the September 11, 2001, attack on America, Thich Nhat Hanh spoke about the need for deep listening to the stories of people involved in conflict. He saw this deep compassionate listening as essential for reducing hatred and bitterness. The hermeneutical enterprise is about exactly that, listening care-fully, deeply, and compassionately with a view to understanding. The theoretical framework should help to "hear" at different levels as the story is told.

It is useful at this point to present a framework for looking at different aspects of the truth of a situation.[3] Ken Wilber developed the framework using two axes, which makes four quadrants, to differentiate aspects of reality. On the left is the interior side of reality—how we experience things within ourselves, which in-volves consciousness and subjectivity. On the right is the exterior, which can be observed. Above the horizontal line are individual realities and below are collec-tive realities.

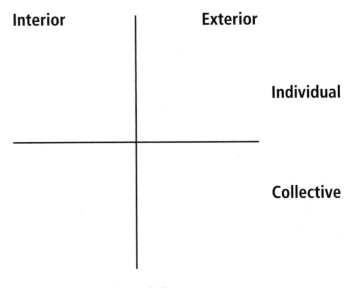

Interior   **Exterior**

Individual

Collective

Figure 9-1

A holistic approach to understanding a conflict involves an integration of all the quadrants. That is why the full range of theories presented so far is important. The different levels of interpretation can work within each quadrant.

The first level of interpretation deals with collecting information about the conflict. The methodological question is this: How does one go about gathering data about a conflict? This includes the questions used to get information as well as the physical process of gathering data. There may be attempts to gather clues about what can be observed as well as clues about how people experienced what happened.

The second level deals with basic relationships among the data. These relation-ships are temporal, so the question becomes: How can the data be linked in a narrative that indicates how events and decisions led one to another? The narrative makes the events intelligible. We think in terms of story; this implies some sense of causality—of how one thing leads to another. The causality may be quite clear that a given decision produced a certain outcome. Or it may be ambiguous if a number of factors appear to contribute to an outcome. The narrative addresses questions about which factors led in a particular way to succeeding events. At this level, the emphasis is on understanding what can be observed, the exterior side of things, at an individual and collective level.

At a third level of interpretation, the questions are: Why and how did things unfold as they did? and How might they likely continue to unfold? Stated another way: What is *really* going on in this conflict? At this level the interior dynamics of groups and individuals become very important. It is for this third level of interpretation that we use the theories developed above. In this chapter, we will develop more fully the hermeneutical methodology at these different levels.

Within the third level of interpretation, deep-rooted conflict can be seen as moving along a continuum toward ever more entrenched mimetic structures of violence with ever increasing violence. Any particular mimetic structure of violence includes a threat to human identity needs, mimetic violence, and a rift between people that results in dehumanization, making people into objects. This rift may be based on some distinction involving ancestry (including race), ethnicity (including language), religion, land, or politics. It may also be based on gender. The rift may also be a result of hegemonic structures that can be a distinct form of a mimetic structure of violence. Each of these points raises questions to be used in interpreting a particular conflict. They help guide us to answers to broader questions such as: 1. What is really happening in this conflict? 2. Why is this conflict so intense? and 3. How did we get into the present state of affairs? We will return to the questions raised by these different theoretical approaches later.

Before Getting Started

Since the stakes of hermeneutics are so high, I would like you to reflect about your role as an interpreter of deep-rooted conflict. This reflection will be based on these interconnected questions:

1. What really *is* at stake in the interpretation of conflict dynamics?
2. What is the agenda of the interpreter?
3. How does personal bias figure into the hermeneutical task?
4. What role do emotions play?

Beginning with question one, let us make a list. First, people decide whether to go to war, on the basis of their interpretations of the actions of the Other. Any kind of violent action, even if it is not war, is based on an interpretation of the actions of other people. Sometimes those actions are interpreted as a threat, demanding a pre-emptive action of self-defence. In other cases, those actions are interpreted as an injustice, demanding retaliation and revenge. Sometimes the actions of others cause separation or death and are interpreted as an evil that needs to be eradicated. Actions of others that prevent us from doing what we wish to do may be interpreted as obstacles to be overcome or as a challenge that demands an aggressive response. If others take action without consultation we might feel slighted or inferior; we interpret those actions as a put down and we respond with vigour so that we might be taken seriously.

My examples have used the human needs of meaning, connectedness, action, security, and recognition as a template. What really makes actions a threat to human need satisfiers is how those actions are interpreted. When people perceive a threat to identity need satisfiers, they take action to either diminish or eliminate the threat. The action needed to diminish the threat is, in turn, an interpretation of the situation.

People imitate stories that operate as dynamic root metaphors to define a response. For example, after September 11, 2001, President Bush created a metaphorical analogy between the attack and a mythology around the taming of the western United States when he said of Bin Laden, "Wanted: Dead or Alive." This metaphor struck a responsive chord with the American public and wanted-posters of Osama bin Laden sold like hotcakes. The "war against terrorism," initially fought primarily within the United States and in Afghanistan, followed on this motif in which the world, like the world of western movies, was divided into Good Guys and Bad Guys. The Good Guys were morally impelled to hunt down the Bad Guys and bring them back dead or alive.

At the personal level, the same dynamic holds. Within a marriage, if a given action is interpreted as being hurtful, the response may be to grossly overplay the sense of victimization or demand a violent reaction.

During our engagement, Gloria and I, with a few friends, took a weekend trip from Saskatoon to Winnipeg. At night, when I went to check out a motel, I came back to the car only to see the car leaving without me, and my friend wrapping his arm around my fiancée. It took only a few minutes for them to circle back and pick me up. It was meant as a joke, but I was devastated and played my victim role to the full. It reminded me of times when I was a child and ridiculed by a crowd of peers. I interpreted it as a much graver offence than was meant.

The second question deals with the agenda of the interpreter, a function of role and values. One can interpret words and actions in a conflict from a role as a party to the conflict, as in the case above, or as a bystander or a neutral intervener. Bystanders or interveners can have values that, like the parties in the conflict, will draw them toward either a violent or peaceful response.

Persons interested in peace-making, reconciliation, or conflict resolution find that their interpretation and careful observation of other's interpretations of what is going on can be critical. It is important to listen deeply and compassionately, in the words of Thich Nhat Hanh, to interpret the situation in a way that honours the subjectivity and humanity of all parties. It is also important to note how the same words and actions are interpreted by the different parties. A key skill of mediators is reframing, basically suggesting an alternative way of interpreting what has happened.

This brings us to the third question dealing with bias. When I organized a case study seminar on the Middle East, I explained to a member of a Jewish organization that we intended to have Arabs (Muslim and Christian) and Jews at the case study along with people who were neutral to the conflicts in the region. He responded that when it comes to the Middle East, no one is neutral; however, he allowed that some might be "balanced."

As Michael Polanyi points out, knowledge is personal and people who wish to rigorously study something to understand it better are driven by intellectual passions.[4] Anyone who wants to do the work necessary to understand a deep-rooted conflict must be highly motivated. This motivation can derive from their own victimization, their passion for peacemaking, or a personal connection to similar conflicts. Miroslav Volf, a theologian who reflected deeply on such conflicts, did so out of a challenge issued at a conference: Could he as a Croatian Bosnian truly embrace a Serb?[5] If hermeneuticists are powerfully driven to do the interpretive work, they will have biases that make them look for certain bits of information and tend to downplay or avoid others.

To answer the fourth question, emotions play a significant role because deep-rooted conflicts touch people so significantly. First, when one is a party to a deep-rooted conflict the perceived threat to identity needs produces an emotional response. This may be fear, anger, depression, sadness, or shame, with any one of these intensified by the presence of the others. If the threat is strong enough, the trauma may include ongoing post-traumatic stress disorders. What we feel as emotions results from a flood of neuroconductors that set in motion the release of hormones and other communicative substances within the body. These all produce physiological responses associated with emotions: increased heart rate, sweaty palms, dry mouth, a "boiling feeling" rising through the chest, and so on. At a highly emotional time, the limbic system, the emotional part of the brain, becomes dominant and harnesses the mind and body to respond to the emotions. The emotions enslave the logical and intellectual skills of the cortex, using them to achieve emotion-driven goals. One can appear totally rational but the direction comes from the emotions. This is the case when someone who has felt victimized debates with someone who understands an event differently. Logic, history, and sophisticated arguments will be used as the debater argues a case that is really driven by emotions.

Enframing and Emplotting

Two ongoing questions that affect interpretation are: 1. Who is involved in this deep-rooted conflict? and 2. When did it start? The first, the "who" question, is about enframing. The second, the "when" question, is about emplotting, which includes the dynamic that has gone on through time and how it is projected into the future along a certain trajectory.

Our goal is to understand a complex, deep-rooted conflict. Emplotment develops a narrative that imitates the conflictual action. As we emplot the conflict, we also enframe, asking who is involved. In answering this question we learn about many subconflicts. So we ask ourselves, Which of these conflicts are we really talking about? The answer changes as various subconflicts take on a greater or lesser role with regard to the actors involved in the conflict. To understand this exercise we need a methodology to help us proceed. Enframing involves working through the question, Who is involved at any particular time? The relational systems must be worked out.[6] For example, one relational system in the 1990 crisis involves the Mohawks of *Kanehsatà:ke* and the municipal council of Oka. Another enframes Aboriginal people and the Government of Canada. Emplotment also involves examining the interrelationships of events. These interrelationships include the parts to the whole: the beginning, the middle, and the end, as well as "pitiable and fearful incidents, sudden reversals, recognitions, and violent effects."[7]

Enframing and emplotment work together dialectically, each as a part of a bigger whole. As we go through time we find the number, roles, and identity of the players changing. Enframing raises questions of emplotting: When did these people get involved? Likewise, emplotting raises questions of enframing: Who are these people now taking action?

Each question plays a big role in the interpretation. When enframing includes naming the parties, it can become a political question. For years, people sympathetic to Israel did not want to admit to a separate Palestinian identity; they thought of Arabs who lived on territory contiguous with Ancient Israel as Arabs who were part of the larger Arab world. To enframe them as a separate identity group called Palestinian would change the interpretation of events.

Likewise, the question of when the conflict started can skew the interpretation and the enframing. When did the Palestinian-Israeli conflict really start? With the partition between Israel and Palestine in 1948 and the subsequent war? With the British white paper on immigration in the 1930s that limited Jewish immigration to Israel just before the Holocaust? With the Balfour Declaration of 1917 that introduced the language of homeland for Jews in Israel into British policy or with Theodore Herzl's writings in the 1800s calling for a Jewish State? Or do the roots of the conflict go back to the formation of Islam? Perhaps the Palestinians represent the Samaritans of the Roman era or the Moabites, Jebusites, Edomites, Canaanites, Philistines, or other peoples who fought against those who established the Ancient State of Israel. Each time frame changes the identity and name of the people involved.

Deep-rooted conflict occurs in the context of a relational system. It carries the sense of a context that brings people together or where they stand together or happen to be. "Relationship" generally has a positive connotation along the lines of friendship; in this case, "relational" is an adjective to emphasize the interrelating of people. Relational system means that for a variety of reasons people are brought into contact with one another—they consider themselves in a similar place either geographically or figuratively. The relational system is made up of a context and people within that context.

Since an individual human is made up of different ontological dialectics, including that between self and conscience,[8] a relational system could be internal to an individual. It may include two people in ongoing contact with one another or it could include groups. One relational system might involve two large groups; each group could have within it a number of relational subsystems.

Enframing is the task of identifying the relational system of a particular conflict. A conflict may be defined broadly, in which case it includes large groups with many subgroups, or it may be defined narrowly with a more circumscribed context and fewer groups. The task of enframing is to determine, for a given moment in time, how large or how small the participation in the conflict is. Enframing may include primary, secondary, and tertiary designations.

In the process of enframing, it is good to be aware of nesting, a concept developed by Gerald Alfred.[9] In his example, the people of *Kahnawà:ke* are nested within the Mohawk people who are nested within the Iroquois Confederacy which is nested within the First Peoples of North America. The concept is similar to Ken Wilber's idea of the holon in which each thing is a part of something bigger and in turn contains its own component parts.[10] In the process of enframing, it is important to determine the nesting level—to decide on the level of inclusion for the sake of analysis. When I applied this concept to the Oka/*Kanehsatà:ke* crisis, as you will see in the next chapters, the natural enframing changed through time. Initially the conflict was between the Mohawks of *Kanehsatà:ke* and the Municipal Council of Oka. Early in the crisis, *Kahnawà:ke* and Châteauguay were implicated as well as the Province of Québec and the Mohawk Nation as a whole. The concept of enframing was very important in clarifying the primary players at any given time.

Enframing is like the zoom lens on a camera; you can decide what is in the picture and what is outside. The closer in you zoom, the more carefully you can see the details of a limited number of players. As you zoom out to wide angle you see the "bigger picture" with an interplay of more players. In a complex conflict that has many subconflicts, enframing helps to break the conflict into its distinct but interrelated parts and each of the subconflicts can be dealt with separately.

When enframing a conflict, it is helpful to note whether the relational system is open or closed. In an open relational system the parties participate significantly in relational systems with other parties. A closed relational system is where the parties interact almost exclusively with one another. Whether a relational system is open or closed may depend on the significance of the action on which the conflict is based. Mimetic desire as a generator of violent conflict is intensified within a closed relational system.

The dynamic nature of deep-rooted conflict demands that we examine the temporal, or time-related, scope of such conflicts including a sense of relational structures—mimetic structure of violence or of blessing—in our analysis. The term "relational structure" follows René Girard's use of the word *structure*: namely, that it is concerned with historical development, relationship-oriented, and hidden yet rooted in human consciousness. The emphasis is on the relationship between deep-rooted conflicts and temporality.

Deep-rooted conflict as a function of time includes three significant factors. The first factor is history as shown in memory. Most deep-rooted conflicts are based in large measure on a memory of victimization. A second factor is change; the specific mimetic structures of violence can change like a kaleidoscope as they interact with one another. A third factor is the promissory dimension of deep-rooted conflict. Most, if not all, deep-rooted conflicts are about imaginations of the future. Various parties either wish to cling to the status quo or radically change it for the future.

The hermeneutical method to establish the relationships between a deep-rooted conflict and the temporal dimension is emplotment. Emplotment unlocks the narrative structure of the conflict, making it intelligible. In doing so, "emplotment brings together factors as heterogeneous as agents, goals, means, interactions, circumstances, and unexpected results."[11] In this second level of emplotment nodes, or intersections, of time emerge. In some instances a decision, event, or action launches the relationship on a significant new trajectory. This may intensify a conflict or qualitatively change the dynamics.

Nodes of decision are times when people have real choices about what to do in a situation. When they act on a decision they begin a trajectory that makes it difficult to return to circumstances at the time of decision. People on a certain trajectory often feel they have no choice but to continue. Mimetic structures of violence are either initiated or take a quantum leap in intensity at these nodes of decision.

The concept of nodes of decision is similar to what Ken Bush refers to as a critical juncture.[12] The difference in nuance is that a critical juncture may affect a change in trajectory simply through a dramatic set of events or circumstances as opposed to a particular decision. A critical juncture brought about by a dramatic set of circumstances invariably prompts a decision to respond in one way or another. Likewise, the decisions of well-placed people sometimes change circumstances, bringing on a critical juncture. Both critical junctures and nodes of decision start people on a new trajectory and it is impossible to return to a previous situation.

One example of a node of decision that launched a trajectory was the decision on the part of the United States administration, with the support of a number of allies, to bomb Serbia after the "cleansing" of ethnic Albanians from Kosovo in the 1990s. When the bombing started, it became impossible to stop until Slobodan Milosevic, the President of Serbia later accused of war crimes, agreed to let the Albanian Kosovars back into the country. There was a sense that Milosevic absolutely could not be allowed to prevail. Had he done so, it would have meant an intolerable loss of face for the Americans, so the bombing simply continued until he caved in.

We now examine how enframing and emplotting assist in the different levels of interpretation, and then discuss in greater detail what is involved at each of the levels.

The first level involves collecting experience bytes. I use the word "bytes" metaphorically to convey the idea that these are bits of significant experiential data. The data involve anything pertaining to the conflict. The first step is an initial enframing to determine which bytes are pertinent to the conflict. This is a dynamic, back and forth, process. In collecting experiential data, more people will be involved and the enframing will change. In the process, the important question will be: How far back do you go? So there will be an initial emplotting.

Once a significant amount of experiential data is collected, interconnections among events and actions will emerge. This will lead to level 2—developing a narrative. The experiential data, which function only as clues about what happened, will begin to suggest how things developed through time—What events lead to the next events? The narrative builds on the emplotting—which elicits the key events, action nodes or critical junctures—by telling the story of the factors leading to these key points and the consequences of various decisions. A key question: When does the narrative about the conflict begin?

Since deep-rooted conflict involves emotions, intrapsychic dynamics, intentions, plans, and actions framed from a particular perspective, merely telling the story does not lead to a full understanding of what happened. The experiential "bytes" offer additional clues to interiority beyond what is expressed in the narrative and these clues need to be interpreted. Looking at the conflict through the lenses of different theoretical perspectives will draw out the feelings, drives, and impulses to present a fuller picture of the real conflict. The perspectives presented in Part 1 contribute to this level of interpretation, but this process does not happen in a clean-cut way. Sometimes, viewing a conflict with a theoretical awareness will show certain dynamics at the beginning. Awareness of what might be driving the conflict is an initial hypothesis that is continuously tested as one collects data, arranges them into a narrative, and interprets the conflict.

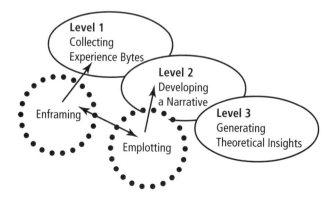

Figure 9-2

In working through the different levels of interpretation, I will show how this played out in my dealing with the Oka/*Kanehsatà:ke* crisis.

Level 1 – Collecting Experience Bytes

The work of collecting experience bytes is like the work of a social historian. It involves tracking down records of who did or said what, when, where, how, and why. At the primary level, one looks for clues at the site, looks for diaries, and talks to the people involved. If literature on the conflict exists, one can build on the work of others who have done the primary historical work.

In the case of the Oka/*Kanehsatà:ke* crisis, I started out by acquiring all the books I could find on the subject. These books functioned as a secondary source of information and provided a good overall perspective. Some of them, like *People of the Pines*, included quotes from the key players. Another information source was a set of press clippings and media interview transcripts collected by the Department of Indian Affairs. This material was primary in that it showed how the event was reported. It was secondary in that it contained quotes from sources such as "Warrior" leaders and academics commenting on historical factors such as the fact that the trees in the Pines were actually planted by Mohawks in the nineteenth century.

I also visited Oka/*Kanehsatà:ke* to locate and visualize where everything had occurred. Initially, I went on my own and looked around. On July 11, 1996, I went back on the anniversary date and participated in a commemorative march. Walking with people who had been part of the crisis gave me a better understanding of what happened. One "Warrior" even took me into the forest and showed me the bunkers dug into the forest floor. I also visited *Kahnawà:ke* to do some training. I spent three days there and was able to visualize the site of that part of the conflict.

A full investigation would include interviews with key protagonists. However, there are limits to every investigation. I realized that with the available time I could not develop an interview methodology and apply it in a balanced way to include representatives of all the stakeholder groups.

Level 2 – Developing a Narrative

After many experience bytes are collected and documented, they will begin reinforcing one another and a series of pictures moving through time begins to come into focus. Looking at the same events from different perspectives creates a three-dimensional view of the dynamics. Over time, the sequence becomes clearer and clearer. Another thing begins to happen. As protagonists begin referring to historical occurrences, the emplotment starting point changes. To understand how the events of the conflict unfolded, it becomes necessary to go further back into history. Knowing that people select their chosen glories and chosen traumas, which have a sense of immediacy through the phenomenon of collapsed time, one realizes that knowing the history of what has happened is important and an appropriate starting point eventually emerges.

As I struggled to develop the narrative of the Oka/*Kanehsatà:ke* crisis, it became clear that since the initial issue was about land rights it was important to study the history of this issue. That meant going back to 1721 when the king of France allotted the land around Oka to the Sulpicians to hold in trust for the Mohawks. Key events around land rights seemed essential to the narrative.

In telling the story I realized that the enframing changed as the crisis intensified. I also saw that in addition to major conflicts between groups, there were significant conflicts within the various groups. I became conscious of secondary enframing to capture these subplots to the story. Eventually, to validate the narrative, I had it reviewed by a number of people who lived through the crisis. In response to their observations, I changed the text so that it would be more finely nuanced.

Level 3 – Generating Theoretical Insights

Remember, the word "theory" comes from a Greek word meaning to see, giving the sense of perceiving a level of reality beyond the physical senses. Eventually, it leads to a narrative presentation of the conflict in terms of universal patterns that resonate with the interpreter's experience.[13] Ricoeur refers to the spiral circle of hermeneutics. In the present situation, I had a sense that mimetic structures were shown as the crisis was unfolding. I could not verify that until I went through the discipline of establishing who was involved and how the events fit together. In effect I went from level 3—generating theoretical insights (Ricoeur's *mimesis$_3$*) to level 1—gathering experience bytes (Ricoeur's *mimesis$_1$*) to level 2—developing a narrative (Ricoeur's *mimesis$_2$*) back to a much more profound understanding at the level of *mimesis$_3$*.

This level of interpretation uses an abductive methodology developed by Pierce and first applied to deep-rooted conflict by theorist John W. Burton, introduced in Chapter 2. An abductive approach starts with a well-developed framework that is applied in an open way to the phenomenon being interpreted. An "open way" means that data are not forced into the framework if they don't fit; rather the theoretical framework is adjusted as anomalies are discovered. This combines deductive and inductive method. The initial application of the framework is deductive; namely, if the theory works we would anticipate certain results. The inductive element involves paying close attention to the details and being open to change the framework to incorporate new insights. After the theoretical interpretation I was left with this sense of awe about something bigger than any of the individuals involved that pressured them to act in a violent way. I called this "something bigger" a *mimetic structure of violence*. This new concept, drawn from my interaction with a particular conflict, became an integrating concept for the theoretical approaches already developed.

Since deep-rooted conflicts involve emotions and what political psychologists call the illogical dimension of life, this level of interpretation seeks to understand these aspects of the conflict. To do this, we assume that there are universal patterns and structures, and knowledge of these will help us understand each individual. We also assume that by "reading" the clues one can glimpse into the interiority of others. Remember I said "glimpse": along with Levinas we must respect the infinite universe within each person. We will never know all that goes on within any other person. We must also qualify this activity by pointing out that the reason to understand the interiority of people is to understand the conflict.

The process of interpretation involves internal dialogues in similar fashion to the way a novelist works with the interiority of the characters in the novel. This entails an acute self-awareness to listen deeply to the other and understand how the other must feel. It involves a sympathetic projection into the life situation of the players, asking, in effect, "How might I feel if I had experienced what they did?" But another level of complexity is involved that includes the frame of reference of the other, which might be radically different than one's own. This is especially important in the dialectic between group and individual identity. In some frames of reference, the experience of the individual matters most; in others, the individuals experience things as a member of a collective, the survival of which might be more important than individual survival.

To do this level of interpretation, the theoretical tools must work in one's own experience. For me, the theories I studied had illuminated various aspects of my own life. For example, I believe mimetic desire to be real because I am aware of it in my own life on a regular basis.

The interpretive process at this level involves a dialogue among Self (the interpreter), theory (illumining experience), and the protagonists in the conflict, based on the experience bytes assembled in the first level. The questions for the dialogue emerge from theory and include: Is there evidence that human identity needs are threatened? If so, what are the satisfiers and what emotions are evident? Are mimetic phenomena present? Do people appear to have models for their behaviour and desires? Do different groups desire the same thing? Is there scapegoating? What are the hegemonic structures? Do groups keep referring to chosen traumas?

The intimate knowledge of the theoretical frameworks, the situation, and an honest self knowledge combine to make the dialogue rich and productive.

The interpretive process can also have a corporate side. People involved in the conflict can be engaged in an interactive process that uses theory to draw out experiences. This way uses hermeneutics as a tool in the process of reconciliation. We look at this in more detail later.

Hermeneutical methodology is the way we interpret a conflict. The concepts of enframing and emplotting are key to determining the players in the conflict and the sequence of events and help in gathering data to develop a narrative that brings together causes, goals, and chance. The narrative, along with other clues about people's emotions, their models and chosen traumas, and other factors form a basis for a theoretical interpretation and reformulation of the narrative.

Chapter 10

The Oka/*Kanehsatà:ke* Crisis of 1990

On July 11, 1990, the Sûreté du Québec (SQ) raided the Pines, a disputed territory claimed by both the Mohawk community of *Kanehsatà:ke*[1] and the Municipality of Oka. In 1989 developers, with the support of the Oka Municipal Council, began planning to cut down the pine trees so they could expand a nine-hole golf course to eighteen holes, build homes around the perimeter, and remove the existing cemetery to expand their parking lot. As it became clear that protests would not deter developers, Mohawks occupied the Pines in March 1990 and remained there into July, ignoring court orders to leave.

In the July 11 attack, Corporal Marcel Lemay of the SQ was shot to death. That day Mohawks blockaded the Mercier Bridge, which runs through the Mohawk reserve of *Kahnawà:ke*, causing great inconvenience to commuters from the South Shore of the St. Lawrence River who worked in Montreal. Passions were ignited to the point of mob action against the Mohawks and Mohawk Warriors prepared to fight to the death to defend their land rights. The standoff in *Kanehsatà:ke* and *Kahnawà:ke* lasted for 78 days and the Canadian military was eventually involved. Mohawks were convinced that there would be significant loss of life in the process.

Present-day Mohawks living near the Lake of Two Mountains think of them-selves as *Kanehsata'keró:non* (people who belong to the land of *Kanehsatà:ke*). This sense of belonging to a particular piece of land is part of their spiritual tradition. Most of the Mohawks living there can trace their ancestry back to those who lived there hundreds of years ago. The people have a collective consciousness of being part of this land and those who join the people adopt that same conscious-ness just as those who convert to Judaism join in a collective sense of being part of the land of Israel as a spiritual place.[2]

We begin with the early history of Oka/*Kanehsatà:ke*. Since the dispute boiled down to who really owned the Pines, we first trace the history of the land ownership issue. The conflict was also about the aspirations of different peoples; hence, we will examine, second, the growth of ethnonationalism among the *Québécois* and Mohawks with some reference to developments at *Kahnawà:ke*, the other key venue for the crisis. Third, we will trace the evolution of the crisis from the original development of the nine-hole golf course and actions taken to expand the golf course. Fourth, we examine key events leading up to the crisis: the occupation of the Pines by the Mohawks and the failure of the Meech Lake Accord in June 1990. Fifth, we explore the beginning of the crisis on July 11, 1990. The sixth step will be an analysis of the dynamics of the crisis as it intensified and new players were involved. The seventh step deals with passions and events of the crisis until it was diffused. Finally, we cover the end of the crisis and its aftermath. The information presented in this chapter will be the foundation for the next chapter in which the events will be interpreted using the mimetic and scapegoat theories presented earlier.

Overview of the Chapter

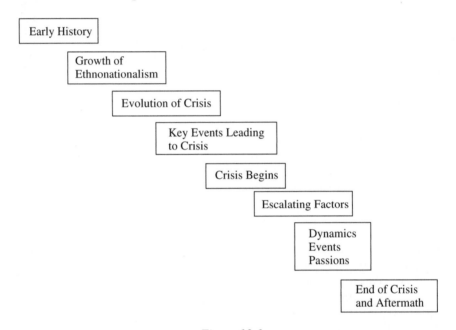

Figure 10-1

In the course of the narrative I will be using the self designations of the First Nations peoples in their own languages, explaining the meaning of the words. One specific designation, the word *Rotisken'raké:ta*, is generally translated as "warrior" but it refers to the men of the community; literally it means "carrier of the burden of peace."[3] The Mohawk concept of peace is more than the absence of war; rather it is the "active striving of humans for the purpose of establishing universal justice" and is "the product of a society which strives to establish concepts which correlate to the English words Power, Reason and Righteousness…. The Power to enact Peace (which required that people cease abusing one another) was conceived to be both spiritual and political. But it was power in all those senses of the word— the power of persuasion and reason, the power of the inherent good will of humans, the power of a dedicated and united people, and when all else failed, the power of force."[4]

Early History

In the 1600s, the French took control of an island in the St. Lawrence River on which there was a settlement of the *Kanien'kehà:ka* (Mohawks, literally People of the Flint) called Hochelaga (now Montreal). At that time, some *Kanien'kehà:ka* moved to a Sulpician (a French religious order) mission at Sault-aux-Recollets and the old Iroquois settlement of *Kanehsatà:ke*. Most of the *Kanien'kehà:ka* population settled at *Kahnawà:ke* on the South Shore of the St. Lawrence. In 1717, the French Crown gave a tract of land (at the present site of Oka) to the Sulpicians to build a mission at the Mohawk outpost of *Kanehsatà:ke*.[5] They were to hold the surrounding territory in trust for the Aboriginal people.

The Euro-centred history of *Kanehsatà:ke* begins with the 1721 move of a group of Christian Mohawks with Sulpician leadership from the area of Montreal to the shores of the Lake of Two Mountains. *Kanehsata'keró:non* affirm that this is one aspect of the reality:

> There is no doubt that in or about 1721, a group of Onkwehón:we [original people], in the company of a priest of the Seminary of St-Sulpice, moved to Kanehsatà:ke. There is no doubt that the Sulpicians founded a mission and that the descendants of this group of Onkwehón:we now live in Kanehsatà:ke.[6]

There is evidence, however, that the history of the *Kanehsata'keró:non* goes back further.

For centuries before contact with Europeans, *Kanehsatà:ke* was a small but significant village among the *Kanien'kehà:ka*. Part of the Turtle clan, it was among the first *Kanien'kehà:ka* settlements to embrace the teachings brought by the Peacemaker;[7] in that regard *Kanehsatà:ke* "is still mentioned in the ancient condolence ceremony of the *Rotinonhseshá:ka* [Iroquois]."[8] It was an important spot for *Kanien'kehà:ka* habitation in connection with hunting and fishing expeditions along what is now known as the Ottawa River. At one point it was a safe haven for women and children during wars with other *Onkwehón:we*.

There is evidence that there was a permanent community of *Kanien'kehà:ka* in *Kanehsatà:ke* before the 1721 arrival of Sulpicians and Mohawks from the Montreal area. There is reference to the presence of people from "Cahghneghsattakegy" at the creation of the Two Row Wampum by the *Rotinonhseshá:ka* and the Dutch in 1613.[9] Several accounts of encounters between Iroquois and the French suggest the existence of a settlement at *Kanehsatà:ke*. The name appears in New York colonial documents with several spellings of a word with the same pronunciation. The earliest reference is in a 1694 message from the governor of Canada in which *Kanehsatà:ke* was called a fort. In the late 1600s, the British referred to the "Canassadagas" as a distinct group, calling them "Praying Indians" because of the French influence.[10] In correspondence written in *Kanien'kehà:ka*, people referred to their home as *Kanehsatà:ke*.[11] By the year 1722 more land was under cultivation than had been the case in the previous settlement at Sault-aux-Recollets, where after 20 years they had cleared 400 *arpents* (acres) of land. It is unlikely that they could have cleared more land than that in only one year.[12] In any case, after the Sulpicians were established in the area, control of the land was transferred to this order by the king of France.

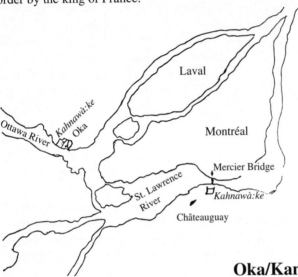

Oka/Kanehsatà:ke

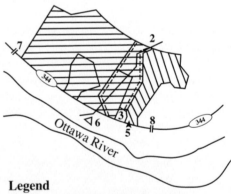

Legend
1. Original Mohawk Roadblock
2. *Kanehsatà:ke* Roadblock and bunker
3. Mohawk Cemetery
4. Oka Golf Clubhouse
5. Main Warrior barricade on Highway 344
6. *Onen'to:kon* Treatment Centre
7. Warrior barricade
8. Army and Sûreté du Québec roadblocks
≡ "The Pines"
\\\ Oka Golf Course
---Proposed golf club expansion lands

In spite of a moratorium on seigniorial concessions in Québec between 1711 and 1732, the French Crown ratified a seigniorial concession of land at Deux Montagnes to the Seminary of St. Sulpice on April 27, 1718.[13] The Sulpicians religious order, founded in France, was interested in missionary activity in the New World. Members of this elite order tended to be sons of judges, officers, surgeons, and small landowners.[14] On September 26, 1733, and again in 1735, Louis XIV deeded more land to the concession. Eventually, the Sulpicians took complete ownership of this land, which, before their arrival, had been Mohawk territory. The Sulpician Order was to be dissolved when the last member of the original order died. However, the British government helped prolong their presumed right to the land from King Louis IV.

The question of rights to the land became ambiguous with the British conquest. In the early years of the Seven Years' War, the *Rotisken'raké:ta* (men of the community, keepers of the burden of peace) of *Kanehsatà:ke* supported the French and had held British prisoners of war. In one encounter with General Montcalm (the French general who lost the battle of the Plains of Abraham that led to British control of Canada), he dismissed the *Rotisken'raké:ta* indignantly. This angry response turned them against the French and on September 20, 1760 they returned the last remaining prisoners of war, unharmed, to the British. An exchange of wampum ratified an agreement between the British and the *Kanehsata'kehró:non*. The people of *Kanehsatà:ke* agreed to be neutral for the rest of the war. British leader Sir William Johnson committed himself to protect the lands, rights, and freedom of the Aboriginal people in Article 49 of the French Capitulation.[15] On June 28, 1761 the agreement with the British was renewed.[16] Johnson later sent word to them through Daniel Clause as follows:

> Brethren, as you are now become one people with us, I chearfully [sic] Join in Strengthening and brightening the Covenant Chain of Peace and friend-ship, and you may depend upon it that no thing on Earth can break it, so long as you all strictly abide thereby, and as you have not the advantage of records like us, I recommend it to you, often to repeat the purport thereof & of all our mutual Engagements, to your young people so as they may never be forgotten.[17]

After the English won the war with France, the British attitude towards the Mohawks became arrogant and the commitment to safeguard their rights and interests declined.

Meanwhile, the Sulpicians were determined to survive in Canada even though Article 35 of Capitulation demanded that they give up their Canadian holdings and leave the country. After the Royal Proclamation of 1763, the Sulpicians swore allegiance to Britain and the land holdings were transferred from France to the Montreal seminary. There was a proviso that no new members from France would be admitted. Had it not been for the French Revolution, the order would have died a natural death by 1796. However, during the French Revolution, some French Sulpicians came to Canada and the British looked aside as they integrated into the Canadian Sulpician community.[18]

To establish control over the land, the Sulpicians exercised *de facto* control while at the same time reinforcing their ties to the British. This two-pronged strategy proved successful. Indicative of their practical ownership of the land, they surveyed the land in the early 1780s and settled on a border with the neighbouring seigneury. As soon as the land was surveyed, they began to grant concessions to settlers. By 1801, 732 settlers had received lots and by 1835 the number reached 1,307[19]. More than six hundred families had moved onto the land by 1847,[20] and it had been subdivided into twelve parishes with the land in eleven already conceded.[21] It should be noted that these settlers bought the land in good faith and passed on title through sale or inheritance to people who did not know that there might be another claim to the land. Their second strategy was to ensure that the British did not act against their claims on the land. In 1789 they swore fealty and homage to the British Crown; they interpreted the acceptance of this oath as recognition of their title to the land.

Nearly half a century later, during the 1837 rebellion, they strategically supported the British. In 1838 the British wished to go to St. Eustache to crush the rebellion. Since they could have been prey to an ambush, the Sulpicians showed Sir John Colborne a map with backwoods trails to get them to St. Eustache safely. Once there, the British set fire to the church and "mercilessly shot down the Patriots as they jumped out the windows to escape the flames."[22]

The Sulpicians were rewarded in the Ordinance of 1840, which confirmed their title to the land. It was passed by a special appointed council that replaced the representative assembly after the rebellion. The Mohawks continued to live on land formally controlled by the priests. Over time, the amount of land open to them diminished as land was sold to settlers.

As the Sulpicians consolidated their control over the land, relations with the people of *Kanehsatà:ke* progressively deteriorated. Some of the Mohawks converted to Methodism and the *Kanehsata'kehró:non* were pressured to move to other lands. They were severely persecuted throughout the last half of the nineteenth century. Persecution involved not allowing them to engage in commercial activity (a canoe built and sold by a Mohawk was taken away from the new owner). They were imprisoned for cutting firewood. As many as four trials for the same event were held in an attempt to convict them; all trials ended in acquittal. There were attempts to evict them from Oka "under the pretense of building or widening streets,"[23] etc. In their own words they

> have been oppressed, culturally suppressed, unjustly charged with crimes, jailed without reasons, relocated against their will, and have their children taken from them. They have been denied the necessities of life and basic human rights. They have suffered attacks on their language, culture and spirituality, and have been subjected to paternalistic assimilationist policies. The people of Kanehsatà:ke have never, not once, been served justice, and in spite of this have not been defeated."[24]

By the late 1800s, much of the land on the escarpment rising from the Lac des deux Montagnes had been cleared and the sandy soil was severely eroded. In 1885, there was a major landslide in the village. The following year, on the suggestion of the Sulpicians, the Mohawks planted thousands of pine trees; these trees today are majestic and make a luscious, thick forest. The Pines is one of the oldest planted forests in Québec.[25]

A trial over land rights began in Montreal in 1909; the government paid the legal expenses for both the *Kanehsata'keró:non* and the Sulpicians. Lawyers for the Mohawks discovered documents in the Paris archives that confirmed "that the lands were granted to the Seminary for the sake of convenience only, and that the grants were made for the benefit of the Kanehsata'kehró:non."[26] However, Judge Hutchinson ruled for the seminary and on appeal Justice Carrol noted that

> [n]either the King of France, nor the King of England intended to confirm rights of property on the Indians. They treated them with tolerance and benevolence for political and humanitarian reasons, but nobody would have given rights of property to these children of the forests who are maintained in a state of tutelage.[27]

The appellate decision was referred to the Privy Council in 1912; it categorically denied Aboriginal title to the land. The Privy Council "reflected the attitude that Aboriginal rights were granted by the Crown and were subject to change at the will of the Crown."[28] The Seminary continued to sell land.

In the 1930s, the Commons and other land used by the people of *Kanehsatà:ke*, was sold to a Belgian company. When this company found out that there might be an Indian claim to this land, they offered to co-operate, but the federal government referred them to the Sulpicians to resolve any questions about legal title. In 1941, the Sulpicians were unable to pay off a million dollar loan from the Province of Québec and they gave one hundred lots to the government; many of these lots were later transferred to the Municipality of Oka for one dollar.[29] In 1945, the remaining Sulpician land was given to the Crown on condition that the Fathers of St-Sulpice were released from any claims the Indians might have against them. Through these transactions, any land to which the *Kanehsata'kehró:non* might have laid claim was transferred to a combination of European private interests and various levels of government. There was a *de facto* attempt to end Aboriginal land rights. These transfers provided a "legal" basis for the development of a golf course in the early 1960s and eventually the attempt to expand the golf course in 1990. The period from 1960 to 1990 was marked by the growth of ethnonationalism among both Quebecers and Mohawks. We will examine that phenomenon and then return to the story of the golf course.

A Backdrop of Mohawk and *Québécois* Ethnonationalism

The conflict over the Pines is also about an expression of ethnonationalism. As André Picard noted, ten days into the crisis,

[i]ronically, the demands of Québec nationalists are very similar to those of Aboriginal nationalists: control over demography, education, the justice system, and freedom to pursue economic development. In fact, as nationhood has become a goal for Québec and the First Nations, there is a realization that the seemingly incompatible quests are inextricably linked.[30]

Visible signs of ethnonationalism, with roots in each group's history, grew among both the *Québécois* and Mohawks in the 30 years before the 1990 crisis. Each has roots in the group's respective history.

Québécois ethnonationalism goes back to the previous century when the negative feelings over English hegemony exploded in the *Québécois* rebellion of the 1830s. The seigneurial system was abolished in the 1850s, making it possible for thousands of farmers to own their own land. The Québec church became more conservative, supporting a position that emphasized loyalty to the pope, over the French Gallican movement, for which the Church of France was more important. In the birth of Canada in 1867 there was a recognition that French Canadians were one of "two founding nations." The first half of the twentieth century was dominated by Maurice Duplessis, who reinforced traditional hegemonic structures within Québec as the people accepted direction from church and political leaders.

In the 1960s, with the election of the Lesage government and the Catholic reforms of Vatican II, came the Quiet Revolution. It involved a blossoming of *Québécois* culture with a concomitant evolution of a political vision summed up by the phrase *Maîtres chez nous* (Masters in our own house). The Quiet Revolution changed the landscape of Québec from a parochial, compliant society to a dynamic, assertive, and nationalistic province. This has had an impact on the whole of Canada. The FLQ Crisis of 1970 exposed a powerful ethnonationalism with territorial interests. This ethnonationalism gained political legitimacy through the election of *Parti Québécois* (PQ) premier René Lévesque in 1976. In 1980, a referendum was held on Québec sovereignty—it was defeated. During their time in office, the PQ established a pro-business environment that spawned a large number of French-speaking, Québec nationalist entrepreneurs.[31] When Liberal premier Robert Bourassa's government succeeded the *Parti Québécois*, he became a strong exponent of nationalist—but not sovereigntist—sentiments through the 1980s.

Mohawk communites also experienced a growth in ethnonationalism in the 30-year period preceding the Oka/*Kanehsatà:ke* crisis. Gerald (Taiaiake) Alfred's concept of nesting helps conceptualize how developments in a broader Aboriginal context affected *Kanehsatà:ke*. Identities are nested within one another, progressing from the local people (*Kahnawa'keró:non* or *Kanehsata'keró:non*) to the Mohawk nation (*Kanien'kehà:ka*) to the Iroquois (*Rotinonhseshá:ka*) to the pan-Native (*Onkwehón:we*).[32] As the Crisis of 1990 unfolded, the nested layers of identity came into play as solidarity was expressed for the *Kanehsata'kehró:non* from ever further distant parts of their identity groups. Most immediate however, was the involvement of people from *Kahnawà:ke* and Akwesasne; considering the close links among these three communities it is helpful to look at developments within and between each.

From the beginning, the *Kahnawà:ke* settlement had positioned itself as an independent linkage community, trading with disparate groups. Many of its members had come from the Mohawk River valley of New York and had brought a memory of close political ties with the Dutch. As British and French gained ascendancy, Mohawks became important traders with links to the French through their Jesuit-inspired Catholicism and links to the British through a history of commerce. They maintained neutrality during the American Revolution but played a key military role backing the British in the War of 1812. Throughout the colonial period, they kept trading and cultural ties with the wider Iroquois population. By 1926, however, the "Mohawks of Kahnawake had been politically distinct from the Iroquois Confederacy for 250 years."[33] That year, Paul Diabo of *Kahnawà:ke* was charged with being an illegal alien in the United States. The show of solidarity by the entire Six Nations Confederacy was a catalyst to the renewal of a traditional political order. Refused the use of the church hall for a meeting of the Grand Council, Mohawks constructed a Longhouse in *Kahnawà:ke,* re-creating ties both with the Confederacy and traditional political structures within the community.[34]

During the 1950s there was a traditionalist revival in *Kahnawà:ke*. Louis Hall, a leader in this revival, and his followers were the more militant among the traditionalists; in contrast, chiefs like Tom Porter emphasized the peace teachings of the Great Law. Hall eventually became the guru for what came to be known as "Warrior Societies." His manifesto advocates violence:

> Now that the Indians have the ability, not only to make peace but also to destroy the white man's peace, it is time to require Canada and the U.S. to render real and true justice to the true owners of this land by restoring some of the stolen lands.[35]

Hall reinterpreted traditional Iroquois teachings in his own way, going so far as to advocate the execution of people who interpret the Great Law in more peaceful ways. He claimed that people like chiefs Tom Porter and Jake Swamp should be executed for treason. Ironically, Hall received the primary inspiration for his conversion to Longhouse religion from a Jewish lawyer and the impetus for his Manifesto from a Nazi who had been a colonel in Hitler's army. Hall recalled the Jewish lawyer saying, "You know a lot of us Jews have no use for any kind of religion, but we are members of our own national religion. We support our religion with money and our presence when needed. It is a force for unity and national survival."[36] His manifesto strongly influenced such people as Akwesasne War Chief Francis Boots and *Kahnawà:ke* warrior Paul Delaronde, both of whom played key roles in the 1990 crisis.[37]

A key event that united the Mohawks was the move by Francis Johnson of Akwesasne to repossess the site of an ancient Mohawk village in New York as a response to the anticipated seizure of lands from *Kahnawà:ke* and Akwesasne to build the St. Lawrence Seaway. It encouraged militancy; it reframed the land issue, showing that land that had been taken could be repossessed; and it stimulated in

Mohawk imagination an even greater sense of being able to stand up to Euro-American government structures.

Gerald Alfred argues that at the heart of Mohawk ethnonationalism are identity, institutions, and interactions with Euro-Canadian society, particularly with the Government of Canada. The interactions with the most devastating effect on relationships with Canada have involved the expropriation of land to build the St. Lawrence Seaway and controversies over membership in the community. The expropriations occurred with no consultation; not only were many community members displaced, but the Seaway denied significant direct access to the river, impacting negatively on community quality of life. This was the most dramatic of a long series of land losses forced upon the community by the government.

The resultant nationalism "at its very core contains an imperative to resist further erosions of the community's national sovereignty"[38] and its ideology "at its core rejects Canada and turns inward toward the traditional ideal."[39] The bitter feelings about the Seaway prompted a traditionalist revival that in the long term generated syncretic institutions: the Mohawk Council of *Kahnawà:ke* has tended to incorporate traditional Mohawk teachings into its structure. From the controversies over membership came a complex approach to identity that laid out boundaries between its members and others based on a combination of "blood quantum," permanency of being Mohawk (if born Mohawk), participation in the life of the community, and knowledge of language and culture.

The interpretation of identity, interactions, and the development of institutions have been shaped by a political ideology that draws on the teachings of the Great Law. The Great Law system has been consolidated into three principles: "the achievement of sovereignty through the implementation of a traditional form of government; the strengthening of an identity of distinct peoplehood through a focus on ancestry; and the redress of historical injustices surrounding the dispossession of Mohawks from their traditional lands."[40] This dispossession was part of the reality in *Kanehsatà:ke* over the 30-year period from 1959 to 1989.

Developments in Oka/*Kanehsatà:ke* from 1959 to 1990

The municipality of Oka and the Mohawk Nation of *Kanehsatà:ke* reflected, on a micro scale, what was happening in the wider communities within which each was nested. The forces of nationalism with an impulse toward economic development, evident in Québec generally, were part of the reality for *Québécois* living at Oka; Mohawk nationalism, a resurgence of traditional teaching and an impulse to redress historic injustices, took on more and more significance during this time.

The *Kanehsata'keró:non* thought of themselves as a separate nation; they were the distant people, separated from the larger Mohawk communities to the southeast and southwest. They had learned their own unique way of surviving without a reserve with clear boundaries. In fact, the land of *Kanehsatà:ke* was a checkerboard of tracts of land within the municipality of Oka. The Commons, or Pines, became a centre for the spread-out community. People came together there for special gatherings and sports events. A lacrosse playing field was established and an open area was used for powwows. Every year a Mohawk community picnic was held on July 1. The cemetery for the *Kanehsata'keró:non* was located in the Commons.

In 1945, the land known as the Commons was purchased by the Crown and in 1947 the land claimed by the Mohawks was sold to the town of Oka. In 1959, the Québec legislature passed a private members' bill giving the municipality of Oka permission to build a golf course on land constituting a portion of the Commons. The bill was sponsored by then Premier Paul Sauvé, the Member of the National Assembly for Oka. The Federal Government had the right to disallow the bill within a one-year period. The *Kanehsata'kehró:non* wrote to one government department after another asking them to disallow the bill but they were simply ignored until the year was up. In March 1961, James Montour and Samuel Nicholas appeared before the Joint Committee of the Senate and House of Commons on Indian Affairs with the following expression of their sentiments:

> We the Six Nations Mohawk of Kanehsatà:ke, Lake of two Mountains, hold the Canadian Government responsible for our plight today.... By remaining criminally silent in the face of injustice, the Government is as legally and morally guilty, as the ones who committed the injustice, though they themselves did not take actual part in the proceedings.... For over a century, the controversy has been waged over this land to our detriment. We have opposed an organization far wealthier, far more influential. Our appeals have been strangled and thwarted in every instance, and our rights have been ignored. Let us this time, reverse the usual order and let Justice have its sway.[41]

These pleas fell on deaf ears and the golf course was built in 1961 beside a Mohawk cemetery. As the trees were falling, "the impoverished Mohawks scraped together $50 and sent [Emile] Colas to Ottawa in an unsuccessful attempt to halt the work."[42]

After the golf course was established, the municipality of Oka continued to grow and many fine homes were built near the golf course. The Mohawks experienced a resurgence of interest in Longhouse traditions and the Mohawk language. During the 1970s, the Mohawks made land claims to the Federal government. Mohawk pride was growing. A drug and alcohol treatment centre was built among the Pines between highway 344 and Lac des deux Montagnes. Euro-Canadians who owned houses in the vicinity had protested the building of the Treatment Centre because they thought it would devalue their homes and create other potential problems.

By the late 1980s, golfers wished to expand the golf course to eighteen holes, making it a full course. Developers prepared plans for the extra nine holes and included in the design 50 to 60 new homes around the outside perimeter. The mayor was a member and shareholder in the club.

In the Spring of 1989, Mayor Ouellette had unveiled plans for the golf course expansion and housing development. The Golf Club was to front the $70,000 to buy eighteen hectares of land for the city from Maurice Maxime (a.k.a. Clovis Arès, who left Canada because he embezzled clients' money) and Jean Michel Rousseau of France; the city in turn would lease the land to the golf course. Over the 30-year term of the lease the city would take in a million dollars. Besides this, there would be tax income from the 10 million dollar housing development planned by Maxime and Rousseau.[43] The plans were released without consulting the *Kanehsata'kehró:non*. A local environmental group, *Regroupement de protection de l'environnement*, collected 1,276 names on a petition against the project.[44] This showed that many *Québécois* were against the plans of the Oka Municipal Council.

The *Kanehsata'keró:non* were determined to prevent golf course expansion. Québec Native affairs minister John Ciaccia had grave concerns about the expanded course. Besides the fact that the Mohawks laid claim to the land, there was a concern for erosion if the trees were removed. There were calls for an environmental study. A number of non-Mohawk citizens of Oka opposed the development.

The Canadian Department of Indian Affairs convened negotiations to try to settle the land claims issue. In September 1989, they made a proposal that would have created a reserve by consolidating some of the land; this would have resolved jurisdictional problems.[45] It was agreed that the Mohawks present would consult with their people about this proposal; when it was presented to a gathering of their people, 201 out of 203 rejected it, with the remaining two abstaining.[46] Nonetheless, as late as July 1990, it was referred to as an "agreement" by the Minister of Indian Affairs.

Despite a series of public meetings and negotiations, the basic issue was non-negotiable on both sides: the Mayor of Oka, Jean Ouellette, and the developers were determined to build the golf course, and the *Kanehsata'kehró:non* were determined that the pines not be cut down. Meanwhile, there was an internal dispute over leadership of the *Kanehsatà:ke* Band. In January 1990, a group of clan mothers[47] removed Grand Chief Clarence Simon and replaced him with George Martin; the resulting feud was only one of several internal conflicts. The nine chiefs on the Band Council were appointed by clan mothers from the Turtle, Bear, and Wolf clans, but the Council needed approval from the Department of Indian Affairs to make any decisions. The *Kanehsata'kehró:non* League for Democracy and the Group for Change wanted to return to band elections, as had previously been the case under the Indian Act. On the other end of the spectrum was the small but outspoken Longhouse, which refused any jurisdiction of the Indian Act.[48] In addition to these rifts, there were cleavages based on religion.

Events Leading up to the Crisis

Despite a call by the Mohawks not to build the golf course until land claims were settled, the town and golf club were determined to proceed. On March 9, 1990, there was a board meeting at the golf club. A group of Mohawks prepared a statement for this meeting with groups inside the community putting aside their differences for the sake of the land. A delegation of five people including a youth,

Ellen Gabriel, and Allen Gabriel went to the municipal meeting where Allen read a petition to members of the board in the presence of a group that had gathered to protest. It seemed to no avail. Ellen recalls that "The French people started calling us names including savages!"

A group of Longhouse members met in the kitchen of the home of Walter David, Jr., to plan a strategy. Convinced that the trees could be cut at any time, they determined to set up an early warning system. The next day, they used John Cree's tractor to pull a fishing shack into the clearing at the Pines; the occupation had begun. When the people of *Kanehsatà:ke* heard that a camp was set up, many of them came to visit.[49]

With the issue of the golf course unresolved, a number of Mohawks decided that they could not trust the federal government, the courts, or any other Canadian institution to look after their interests. They were afraid that the developers would simply move in and start cutting down trees. The only way they could prevent this was to maintain a twenty-four-hour presence in the Pines.

Men and women brought food and drinks to the people occupying the Pines. During the early days, older women came daily with food and coffee. Some teenage girls also tried to help:

> Sixteen-year-old Myrna Gabriel and her two girlfriends became regulars, showing up at the fishing shack by five o'clock in the afternoon, and staying until after it got dark…. Myrna keeps a calendar marking all the important events in her day-to-day life, and March 31 is blocked off in bold red ink: the first time she slept overnight in the Pines. "It hit me, there were no other girls my age involved. We were there defending our land, while all these other teenagers were out partying it up. It made me proud."[50]

Susan Oke went on night patrols with other women with "ugly sticks" for protection. For her, time spent around the sacred fire was part of rediscovering her Mohawk roots including the role of women in caring for the land. When the question of weapons came up,

> [t]he armed men in the Pines asked the women to decide if the weapons should stay. As the traditional caretakers of the land, the women had the responsibility of dealing with this issue, but the decision was not one they wanted to make…. There were strong arguments for and against being armed.
>
> Linda Cree had been an avowed anti-warrior, but the events that took place in the Pines changed her attitude. She was aware of the hazards but was equally afraid of the consequences of a police attack if the Mohawks were unarmed. Denise David-Tolley put it this way, "What choice did we have by then? We said, 'Bury them, hide them, keep them away. Only if they come in to harm us do you bring them out—only then'." After a pause she continued, "They came in to harm us."[51]

During this time, three men had been asked by the chief to represent the Mohawks. In a letter dated June 14, several women, who had played key roles, severed ties with other Longhouse negotiators, feeling that they had been left out. In their argument, they referred to the Great Law of Peace that states: "Women shall be considered the progenitors of the Nation. They shall own the land and the soil." *Kanehsatà:ke* Longhouse women in the Pines held daily women's meetings to keep their spirits up and discuss strategy.[52] They determined to be the front line of defence and invited women from other reserves to join them in the protest camp.

An injunction against the barricade was granted by the Québec Superior Court on April 26. On May 1, the *Kanehsata'kehró:non* gathered in the Pines, coming from the various factions. They were joined by people from *Kahnawà:ke*.[53] Later in May, Akwesasne war chief Francis Boots made two visits to the Pines and the Warriors supplied a Chevy Blazer patrol truck, two-way radios, food, tents, and other supplies. Some of the men in the Pines acquired weapons; others disapproved of the presence of arms. People were asked to come in as Mohawk people not affiliated with any particular group such as the Warriors.

A meeting between Mohawks and Indian Affairs minister Tom Siddon was set for June 21. Preparations for that meeting brought out tensions within the Mohawk community. The Longhouse people were critical of the band council's lawyer, Jacques Lacaille. June of 1990 was also a tense time for Canadians generally and the *Québécois* in particular; it was the deadline for the ratification of the Meech Lake Accord.

Three years before this, Prime Minister Brian Mulroney and ten premiers had made an agreement on constitutional changes that would have paved the way for the Province of Québec to agree to the Canadian Constitution. The agreement stated that the Meech Lake Accord, as it was called, was to be approved by the ten legislatures and the Canadian parliament within three years. The deadline was June 23, 1990.

As the deadline approached, neither Manitoba nor Newfoundland had passed the Accord. Premier Clyde Wells of Newfoundland raised many questions about it, prompting concerned Canadians across the country to write him. His position was that he would support the Accord only if every other province passed it.

One reality of the Accord was that both its process and content excluded First Nations peoples. Assembly of First Nations (AFN) National Chief Georges Erasmus spoke out publicly against it. Aboriginal people were convinced that if the Accord passed, they would be shut out of constitutional recognition for many years to come.

One of the rules of procedure in the Manitoba legislature was that unanimous consent was necessary to move the vote on the Accord ahead in time to pass it by the deadline. Cree member of the Legislative Assembly, Elijah Harper, held an eagle feather as every day he refused to give consent to a motion that would have made it possible to pass the Meech Lake Accord. He was assisted in this strategy by Ovide Mercredi, a constitutional lawyer who was then Vice-Chief of the AFN. The Mulroney government was so intent on getting Harper's co-operation, they sent a high-powered team led by Senator Lowell Murray and that included Stanley Hartt, the prime minister's chief of staff; Paul Tellier, clerk of the Privy Council; and Norman Spector, secretary to the cabinet for Federal-Provincial Relations to try to win Harper's co-operation. He and his colleagues rejected the six-point offer as "trinkets."[54] When it became clear that Manitoba would not pass the Accord, Newfoundland also refused to pass it and it died on June 23.

During the period leading up to the deadline, Prime Minister Mulroney told the people of Québec and Canada that the failure of Meech would mean the rejection of Québec and could tear up the country. Around that time some anti-French actions in Canada were broadcast repeatedly on Québec television. The failure of Meech resulted in a tremendous letdown within Québec and within the Conservative Government of the time. Prime Minister Brian Mulroney and Québec Premier Robert Bourassa had both staked their political futures and place in history on the passing of the Accord. It was to reconcile French and English. When the Accord was defeated in June, Mulroney disappeared from public view for most of the following summer and Bourassa and his *Parti Québécois* opponent Jacques Parizeau were united in their belief that Québec would have to take charge of its own destiny.

On June 29, the lawyer for the Municipality of Oka sought a third injunction to have roadblocks removed from the Pines. Judge Anthime Bergeron granted the injunction and gave the Mohawks ten days to leave. Every day there were new ultimatums from the Oka municipal council as tensions increased. Sam Elkas, Québec Public Security Minister, "announced that the Mohawks must clear the barricades within four days or else the government would take action. He did not specify what kind of action the Mohawks should expect, but the threat of police intervention was implicit."[55] Allen Gabriel urged that the barricades be dismantled and left the Pines with his two allies. Ellen Gabriel and John Cree became the key spokespersons for the Mohawks. The Québec Human Rights Commission proposed an independent committee to sort out land rights. Their telegram to Tom Siddon received no response until four months later but Québec Native Affairs Minister John Ciaccia affirmed his support the same day.[56] Police increased their patrols and were put on standby.

On July 9, John Ciaccia wrote Mayor Ouellette urging him not to call in the police or act quickly on the golf course expansion. He argued that the situation went beyond strict legality. Here is an excerpt from his letter:

> These issues go beyond the strict legality of the situation as interpreted by our tribunals, which base themselves on laws put into place by our society, laws which do not necessarily answer to the claims of Native people.

> We are often accused by Native people of not taking into account their claims and of reneging on our commitments.

> The situation at Oka gives credibility to these accusations...

> I am aware that our laws are on your side in the case of the injunction, but I believe that the present situation goes beyond strict legality. As premier

René Lévesque said during a debate in the National Assembly, concerning the application of a certain law, sometimes "the law is an ass." And if that is the case, those who are elected should not hide behind the laws, but rather act in a generous and responsible manner.[57]

The next day, Jean Ouellette accused Ciaccia of not understanding native issues and requested the Sûreté du Québec "to clear the barricades and stop the 'criminal acts' in the Pines. 'We are counting on you to settle this problem without any further delays or requests on our part', Ouellette told the police in a letter."[58] John Cree, Mohawk spokesperson at *Kanehsatà:ke*, voiced their determination to do "whatever is necessary to defend" the land. When asked about guns he said, "Whatever the police do, we will match. That's up to them... but this is not a joking matter."[59] Warriors continued to strengthen their positions by digging foxholes, stringing fish lines with noisemakers and hooks, and setting "booby traps." Two days after the deadline expired, the morning of July 11, police cruisers raced through the town. Denise David-Tolley, asleep in the Pines, tossed restlessly dreaming about an attack. In her dream, someone died.[60]

The SQ Raid

Early on the morning of July 11, 1990, a hundred members of the Sûreté du Québec SWAT team, including some army personnel and Montreal police, drove west along highway 344 to the area where the barricade had been erected within the Pines. In the clearing around the barricade, a number of women were having their early morning ceremonies around the fire, and John Cree was burning tobacco for the whole group. The SQ officers came in along two lines, one along highway 344 on the southern edge of the land under dispute. The other was along a side road on the eastern edge of the Pines. They had come prepared with body bags for casualties. For over two hours they held their positions. They brought in a loader to clear away the barricade.

The Mohawk people had positioned themselves in the Pines on the north and west sides of the clearing; the women were in the clearing just behind the barricade. The police shot canisters of gas toward the women but the winds from the North sent the gas toward the police. At about 8:30 a.m., one of the Mohawk men ran into the Pines. Three officers ran after him in the direction of the lacrosse box. Shooting started and it came rapidly from both sides for 23 seconds. When it was over, Corporal Lemay had been shot. The SQ seemed unprepared for the strength of the armed resistance. They immediately got into their cars and left the area. Corporal Lemay was rushed to a hospital in an ambulance. He died in less than an hour.

Because of the hasty departure, keys were left in the cars as well as in the loader. As soon as the police left, the Mohawks moved some of the police cruisers across the road to block highway 344 and smashed them with the loader. In all six police vehicles were damaged:[61]

Francis Boots looked on in horror as the vehicles were demolished. "No, no, don't destroy those damned things," he pleaded. "We can use them. We can use the radios."

But it was too late. The Mohawks—including many people who had never set foot in the Pines to help the protesters during the early days of the roadblock—were united in an orgy of destruction, a collective venting of anger.[62]

As soon as the SQ began moving on the barricade in the Pines, the people of *Kahnawà:ke* learned of the situation by radio. Word spread quickly through the community. A dozen Mohawk men, acting on their own, quickly blocked the Mercier Bridge, a bridge joining the South Shore of the St. Lawrence River to Montreal. Their experience as steel builders made it easy for them to move on the girders of the bridge. They tied flares resembling dynamite together and fastened them to some bridge supports and threatened to blow up the bridge if they were attacked. As the conflict became more intense and polarized, the people of *Kahnawà:ke* felt they had no choice but to support the blockade.

A second attack on the Pines was being planned by the SQ. The Mohawks made two parallel but uncoordinated efforts to prevent it. In Montreal, *Kanehsatà:ke* lawyer Jacques Lacaille made 45 phone calls to Québec government officials who did not take the situation seriously. After a warning of a second attack from the SQ, he got through to Premier Bourassa and told him that one officer was dead. Meanwhile Ellen Gabriel, spokesperson for the *Kanehsata'kehró:non,* announced that if any Mohawks were hurt, Mercier Bridge would fall. The second attack did not materialize.[63]

Within hours after the initial raid, the police set up their own barricades on highway 344 opposite the Mohawk barricades. These barricades controlled access to the Pines, initially blocking all food, medicine, diapers, clothing, and family members. Some officers within the SQ had a history of bad relationships with Mohawks; there were also a number of officers with a good bit of sympathy for Mohawk grievances.

The Mohawks made good use of the loader. Besides building up the barricades, they brought it into the Pines to dig bunkers at various strategic locations. These bunkers would become home for the warriors for the next two months. They commandeered golf carts and established positions through the Pines and the golf course. Additional Aboriginal people found their way into the Pines to help.

With the events at *Kanehsatà:ke* and *Kahnawà:ke,* the entire Mohawk nation became implicated in the struggle that now involved the government of the Province of Québec. Primary negotiations during this time period were with members of the provincial cabinet, especially John Ciaccia, Minister for Indian Affairs.

On July 16, a funeral was held near Québec City for Corporal Lemay. Nearly a thousand attended to hear him eulogized by Robert Lavigne, the director of the

Québec Police who had ordered the attack. At the Pines, the Mohawks flew their flag at half mast since they "consider all life as precious as the Earth itself."[64]

The Crisis Intensifies

Within days, the crisis intensified, igniting passions throughout Canada and turning world attention to Oka, *Québec*. Some fourteen factors helped escalate the conflict and we look at each:

1. Reinforcements brought in on both sides and perceptions of greater strength
2. Hardships experienced by people in Oka and Châteauguay
3. Mob action
4. Festering resentment over the killing of Corporal Lemay
5. Protests against government action
6. Actions of local politicians
7. Blocking of food supplies
8. Growing support of Mohawks by other First Nations
9. Harassment of a number of groups involved
10. Vandalism of *Québécois* property
11. Attention of international community and institutions
12. Controversy over negotiations
13. Inflammatory treatment of symbols
14. Entrenchment of positions

First, both police and the Mohawk community got reinforcements and there was a mutual perception that strength on the other side was stronger than it actually was. By July 13, additional police reinforcements brought their number to a thousand.[65] On Thursday, July 12, the SQ asked the military base at Val-Cartier for an inventory of soldiers and equipment. Though soldiers and military equipment had been in the area on July 9, by July 16 there was a movement from Val-Cartier near Québec City to Longue Pointe garrison in east-end Montreal.[66] One Warrior boasted that the Mohawks had mortars, land mines, and grenades in addition to a wide assortment of guns.[67] In Montreal, the threat to blow up the bridge was given credibility by France Goupil, president of *Géophysique GPR International Incorporated,* a firm in the business of demolishing buildings who said it would take only two to three hours to install the explosives.[68]

Second, the blockades caused hardships for the citizens of Oka and Châteauguay, and they called for strong action to rectify the situation. The blockade made the commute to Montreal from Châteauguay at least an hour-and-a-half-longer. When the crisis began, many Châteauguay residents had supported the Aboriginal cause, but the stress caused by long commuting times eventually led to feelings of frustration that exacerbated tensions. Anger was directed at both the Government, which should do something about it, and the Mohawks for barricading the bridge.

The SQ sealed off the roads going into *Kahnawà:ke*.[69] Some businesses in Oka experienced a drop in business.[70] Residents had difficulty getting to their homes.

Third, the frustration in Châteauguay brought out mob action that was mainly directed towards anyone who looked like a Mohawk but eventually turned on the police. Mobs burned Mohawks in effigy, sometimes yelling repeatedly, "Burn the savages." On July 13, grandmother Betty Coles was angry at the Mohawks over the bridge closing. After watching a mob besieging a Mohawk woman in the grocery store, she was so disgusted with the mob action that she called the *Kahnawà:ke* radio station to ask how she could help supply food to them.[71] As she put her efforts into helping the Mohawks, the scene of the barricades turned into a daily "hatefest."[72]

Many who participated in the mob action came from outside Châteauguay. The mobs did not represent the attitudes and positions of the entire community and took on a life of their own.

On July 15, the burning of the warrior in effigy was accompanied by a thousand people howling mocking war whoops.[73] They painted a red target on the effigy's chest, stuffed a cigarette pack in its pocket and placed a noose around its neck. The crowd chanted "F— the Warriors! the damned savages."[74] Sylvain Leblanc, of Châteauguay, who was responsible for one of the effigies, stated, "I have nothing against the Indians. I am angry at the gun-toting Warriors who are the equivalent of the Indian Mafia."[75] Sharon Fournier found the burning "disgusting," and pointed out that many "don't understand the Indians' plight."[76]

Bourassa was also burned in effigy because he did not act more quickly to call in the army.

On July 18, three hundred RCMP came to aid the SQ in controlling the crowds in Châteauguay.[77] Local roads were clogged. It was reported that one man lost his job because of the bridge closing.[78]

Fourth, within the Government of Québec and the SQ there was hurt and anger over the killing of Corporal Lemay and a concomitant desire to lay blame. Even Premier Bourassa was said to be very angry. Both the Government and the SQ lost face over their failure to achieve their goals and the ignominy with which the police left the scene. All government ministers who might have been responsible at the time (many were on vacation so responsibility was passed on to others) denied having given approval for the raid. Indian Affairs Minister John Ciaccia even went on record saying that he had told Mayor Ouellette not to call in the SQ.[79]

Fifth, there were numerous protests about the attack and government action. Much of the rhetoric of protest was very graphic, using metaphors that strongly denounced both police and government. As tension mounted in *Kahnawà:ke* over the closing of Mercier bridge, Goldie Hershon of the Canadian Jewish Congress sent a letter to the Mayor of Châteauguay suggesting "that the daily burning of effigies and the expressions of racism have contributed to a deterioration of the climate for negotiation."[80] Jean Dorion of the St. Jean Baptiste Society pointed out that native rights had been denied for hundreds of years and "their grievances must be considered in this context and not treated in narrow legalistic terms."[81] Michelle

Falardeau-Ramsay, deputy chief commissioner of the Canadian Human Rights Commission, criticized Indian Affairs Minister Tom Siddon for inaction, claiming that Canada's international image had been tarnished: "Imagine what would be our reaction if it was in another country," she said. "We would say: Isn't that awful that they use such tactics. They are not allowing the Red Cross vehicles to bring food. They don't allow a supply of drugs to come in."[82] The Human Rights Institute of Canada referred to the raid as "insane."[83] Three Québec bishops called for negotiations instead of force.[84]

Sixth, local politicians spoke up against Mohawk actions. The Mayor of Châteauguay, Jean-Bosco Bourcier, threatened to launch a class action suit against the Province for the losses of south shore residents who had trouble getting to work. In defence of his community, he insisted that those making racist remarks were not from Châteauguay: "Rather," he said, "there is a small group of about 200 young people, mostly from Montreal, who try to provoke police because they have been beaten by other police forces in the past."[85] He reportedly stated a preference that "residents vent their frustration by burning Mohawks in effigy" rather than "disrupt life in the community."[86] Furthermore he charged that his people are "innocent victims in a larger dispute over native land claims."[87] Both mayors and crowds blamed provincial and federal governments for not taking appropriate action. Châteauguay MP Ricardo Lopez asked Brian Mulroney to send in the army.[88]

In Oka, Mayor Ouellette left for a few days because of reported death threats but continued to stand by his decision to call in the SQ. A group of mayors from the surrounding area met to declare their support for Ouellette. They began to point out that there was more at stake, since a huge portion of Québec was subject to Indian land claims. Deputy Mayor Gilles Landreville replied in the affirmative when asked about taking the barricades by force.[89] Guy Dubé, from an Oka citizens' group favourable to the mayor, "blamed the dispute on a group of radical Mohawks, 'prone to terrorism and blackmail'."[90] And on July 15, Gilles Landreville, then acting mayor of Oka, criticized the government "for holding talks with 'armed criminals.'"[91]

On July 23, Harry Swain, deputy minister of Indian Affairs, claimed that the Mohawk Warriors were a "criminal organization" who had hijacked Kahnawà:ke and Kanehsatà:ke. Theirs was a "potent combination of cash, guns, and ideology," he said, describing the crisis as an "insurrection" by an "armed gang."[92]

A seventh evidence of conflict intensification occurred when food supplies to both Kahnawà:ke and Kanehsatà:ke were blocked, in effect using food as a weapon. In some cases, residents couldn't get through to their homes and relatives. In one case a 69-year-old woman was denied access to food. The police were afraid that some food would get to Mohawks behind the barricades.

Angry store owners in Châteauguay refused to sell food to Mohawks. Many Mohawks would not venture into the city anyway because they had been "yelled and jeered at and even pelted with stones."[93] Jocelyne Desrosiers, a store owner in Châteauguay open to Mohawk business, was asked by vigilantes to close her store, with the threat that the window might have an "accident" if she didn't. Police told her they couldn't guarantee a rapid response to a distress call.[94] At the same time, thirty sympathetic whites formed a food pipeline to get food into *Kahnawà:ke*.[95] The Federation of Chinese Students and Visiting Scholars in Canada and Montreal's Chinese community donated food to the Mohawks of *Kanehsatà:ke* and *Kahnawà:ke*.

On July 13, an SQ official told a member of the Québec Human Rights Commission that "there was no question of [allowing] 'individuals of native origin' to cross the police barricades with provisions."[96] Contrary to Québec's Charter of Rights and Freedoms, no Commission representative was allowed access to investigate.[97] On July 21, Québec Cabinet minister Claude Ryan said that "the refusal to allow food into Mohawk communities was official government policy, not police vindictiveness."[98] A few days later Ciaccia told reporters, "There was never any question of depriving them of food."[99]

Commenting on the tactic of blocking food, Frank Chalk, a Concordia University historian and genocide expert, commented that "deprivation of food as a pressure tactic should not be permitted in a democratic society under any circumstances."[100] Red Cross doctors and nurses checked the situation and determined that there was no food crisis. Some native groups responded to the food crisis by organizing a food bank and delivering food by boat. Some Mohawks, though, smuggled food into the reserve and charged three times what perishables would normally cost.[101]

An Aboriginal woman named Claudette Commenda-Cote put the food issue into historical perspective: "One hundred years ago the governments starved our people into signing treaties. It is 1990 and the methods are the same. We demand that the police action must be stopped."[102]

Eighth, within a day or two of the raid, other First Nations began supporting the Mohawks of *Kanehsatà:ke*. Initial support came from Matthew Coon Come of the Northern Cree and then Conrad Sioui, Vice-Chief of the AFN for Québec and head of the Québec chiefs, joined. Ovide Mercredi, then AFN Vice-President for Manitoba, collected food and financial support for the Mohawks, only weeks after he had discussed scuttling the Meech Lake Accord with Elijah Harper. These leaders argued that the structure of the conflict and oppression resembled the situation faced by other First Nations, emphasizing that 85 per cent of the territory of Québec was under dispute. They pointed out that Mohawks had endured some of the longest oppression (350 years) of any First Nations in Canada.

On July 17, in a march on Parliament Hill "speaker after speaker condemned [Indian Affairs Minister Tom] Siddon and Prime Minister Brian Mulroney for not intervening in the dispute."[103]

More than one hundred chiefs from across the country went to *Kahnawà:ke* for an emergency meeting. They were challenged to form "a country wide network of warrior societies, likened to a standing army, to defend native lands" and to set up road barriers.[104] Their nine-point resolution included a promise to take appropriate action in support of Mohawks. They also passed a resolution expressing condolences to the family and friends of Marcel Lemay.[105]

At their gathering, Conrad Sioui, Québec chief of the Family of First Nations, stated that "there is a direct link between (the current crisis) and Meech Lake."[106] He accused Mulroney and Bourassa of being in collusion and blamed both for this situation. Other chiefs joined in blaming Bourassa and the "Conservative government and its separatist buddies"[107] for the crisis.

Gerard Guay, a lawyer for the Algonquin Indians of Barrier Lake, warned on July 14 that this could spark "Indian warfare" across the county. Russell Diabo, a Mohawk working with the Algonquins, called the crisis a tinder-box situation resulting from "centuries of frustration across the country." He reported that "Indians in Quebec will be backing up the Mohawks—this isn't just a Mohawk situation like the press have painted it."[108]

There were many other signs of support: Micmac children in Nova Scotia went on a hunger strike; Indians of Baie Comeau threatened to block the provincial highway; Lillooet and Chilcotin Indians blocked roads in British Columbia; and young Saulteaux Indians blocked a road in Manitoba against the wishes of their leaders.[109] In addition, residents of the Roseau River reserve in Manitoba blocked a secondary highway.[110] Micmacs of Restigouche slowed traffic on an interprovincial bridge and Algonquins of Barrier Lake slowed campers in their area.[111] Residents of the Grand Rapids Reserve closed one of the major highways to northern Manitoba; Ojibways blocked one lane of traffic on the Trans-Canada highway near Georgian Bay and distributed pamphlets to motorists. In Alberta, chiefs threatened blockades and power transmission line destruction. Enoch Cree Nation Chief Jerome Morin stated that the province could be shut down.[112] Sixty natives marched on the Québec legislature to support the Mohawks because "their action…affects all natives in Canada," according to Ghislain Picard, vice-president of the Attikamek-Montagnais council.[113]

On July 18, one week after the raid, Chief Billy Two Rivers of *Kahnawà:ke* said on CTV's *Canada AM,* "I'm sure that our people will defend to the end. But that is not the way. If they want to wipe out the Indian people and commit genocide, then call the army in because we will fight to the last man and woman and children."[114]

Besides the actions of support, a new attitude was evident among Aboriginal peoples. Native leaders mentioned that Aboriginal people no longer blamed themselves for their problems. Georges Erasmus stated that Canada's political leaders "are the clearly defined enemy, not the Canadian people." Phil Fontaine of the Assembly of Manitoba Chiefs said, "For years, our suicide rate shows our frustrations have historically been turned inward. Now the frustration appears to be turned outward. Our people have been sensitized. We no long blame ourselves."[115]

At a Manitoba conference of three hundred native leaders, Peguis Chief Louis Stevenson called for a violent response if the police or army attacked the Mohawks. Blackfoot Chief Strater Crowfoot said, "Throughout history, whenever there were confrontations, it was always the Indians who laid down their arms first, and we know what happened to them. So this time, we are saying no." Saul Terry, president of the Union of British Columbia Indian Chiefs, said to the Warriors,

"You have successfully protected your territory and citizens. In doing this, you have forcefully asserted the Mohawk Nation's sovereign right of self-defence in the face of government propaganda, deception, manipulation and military power. You have shown First Nation citizens throughout Canada that direct action can speak louder than words, and that sometimes this is the only way our peoples' voice can be heard."[116]

Liberal MP Ethel Blondin said she could never denounce the Warriors since they symbolized the struggle "to defend our land and our rights." Alanis Obomsawin, an Abenaki Indian film-maker who hated violence, pointed out that Aboriginal people were ignored until they picked up weapons.[117]

In addition to the high profile support, hundreds of Canadian Aboriginal people came to help. For example, on July 15 nine Micmacs arrived at *Kahnawà:ke* and on July 16 four of them made it to *Kanehsatà:ke*. They were motivated in part by the wrongful imprisonment of cousin Donald Marshall for a murder he didn't commit.[118] Others who came to help were a "hundred Oneidas from New York, Wisconsin, and southwestern Ontario; an Algonquin from northwestern Quebec; and Indian women from several regions of British Columbia and the Yukon."[119]

Ninth, the Mohawks were harassed by police and residents, and residents by Mohawks. One Mohawk man who claimed to be unarmed during the police raid was detained and roughed up after the police retreat. That convinced him to join in the fighting: "Now it doesn't matter whether I stay at home or come out here with my gun. Any time I take a step off this territory, they'll be all over me. They know who I am, and it's not going to end. After all of this has blown over, the harassment is going to continue, and even worse."[120]

In Oka, in addition to the death threats to Mayor Jean Ouellette, members of a community association that supported the Mayor were threatened and feared reprisals if the police left.[121] In Châteauguay, Aboriginal people were threatened on the street; some were too afraid to take the bus to work.[122]

Tenth, a group of Mohawks, including non-Natives who were coming over by boat, vandalized property in the vicinity of the Pines. One of the first to be vandalized was the clubhouse of the Oka Golf Club. When the Mohawks occupied it, it was reported that the kitchen and bar were littered with smashed beer bottles, rotting food, and broken club trophies that had been ripped from glass showcases. Files, papers, and membership lists covered the office floor.[123] In addition, the glass door was smashed, lockers were broken open, and telephone lines were cut.

Eleventh, the international community began to pay attention to the conflict. Protests were made to the United Nations and there were calls for international observers. Kenneth Deer of the Longhouse went to Geneva on July 20 to visit embassies and a UN human rights organization; he subsequently reported to an Aboriginal conference.[124] At the *Kahnawà:ke* meeting of chiefs, Joe Norton suggested economic sanctions against Canada similar to those invoked against South Africa for apartheid. He stated that the Canadian government treats natives in a similar manner to the way in which the South African government treats blacks.

Leader of the Opposition, Jean Chrétien, said at the same meeting that the crisis has "escalated to the point that it is an issue in Europe today."[125]

On July 20, a *Kanehsatà:ke* negotiator pointed out that the barricades would be removed in short order if the matter were referred to the World Court at the Hague.[126] The group of chiefs also advocated a United Nations commission to investigate the "abuses and violations of the civil, political, human and constitutional rights of the Kanehsatà:ke and Kahnawà:ke Mohawks."[127]

Twelfth, over the first days and weeks of the crisis, Québec Native Affairs Minister John Ciaccia carried on negotiations in *Kanehsatà:ke*. These negotiations provided some hope but also occasioned criticism about who was involved in the negotiations and whether they were carried on in good faith. Some Mohawks did not think it appropriate to negotiate with a province; they wanted to negotiate with Canada on a nation-to-nation basis. Within the federal government, Indian Affairs Minister Tom Siddon believed that it was inappropriate to negotiate with an armed group:

> ...I think all Canadians will want to ask themselves the question should their government, any government, be held hostage to the demands of the group which does not have an elected or democratic mandate to speak for the majority of the people of that community, to be held hostage in the face of armed intimidation in this way. And then to ask where these powerful automatic weapons are coming from, AK-47s, and even more powerful assault equipment, some of which was used against most of the folks of Akwesasne only two months ago. How is that kind of armament being used within this democratic county of ours to create a state of insurrection and place demands on governments in this way.[128]

Though the negotiations and requests for negotiations were meant to move the conflict toward resolution they also introduced other secondary conflicts.

Thirteenth, a variety of symbols provoked strong feelings. On July 14, four anglophones carried a Canadian flag into the crowd at Châteauguay. They were surrounded by francophones, some carrying Québec flags. Police escorted one to safety as two hundred people chanted, *"Québec, Québec."*[129] Later that night between six and seven hundred people, led by youths carrying *fleurs-de-lys*, rushed the barricades. The crowd grew to a thousand and "roared its approval" as some tried to burn a Canadian flag. When it didn't burn it was ripped in shreds, people stomped on it and chanted, *"Le Québec aux Québécois"* and *"Vive le Québec libre."*[130] Teenagers on top of a Châteauguay bus stop displayed sheets reading "American Mohawks go home" and, in French, "Mohawks are filthy savages."[131] On the other side of the barricade, Mohawks chanted and drummed, taunted the crowds, pointed weapons at the crowds, and burned a Québec *fleur-de-lys*.[132]

On July 15, Irene O'Brien Neal, a Châteauguay woman wearing a Canadian flag on her sweatshirt, was jumped from behind by two women who punched and gouged her face as they tried to tear off an Indian necklace. Police stood by; eventually they intervened, asking the woman to leave and telling her that her sweater was provocative.[133] One of the women who attacked her called the maple leaf "an insult to all Quebeckers."[134] Neal, for her part, didn't want to cause problems. "I just came here to support the natives," she said.[135]

Fourteenth, entrenched positions generated their own dynamics. Two American lawyers came to help the Mohawks present their case: Stanley Cohen, a New York lawyer passionately committed to their cause, followed by civil rights lawyer William Kunstler, who had defended some members of the American Indian Movement after the Wounded Knee stand-off. Kunstler was in *Kanehsatà:ké* for a day and in the area for only a short while. Cohen eventually became the more dominant influence:

> Around July 21, [Owen] Young arrived in Kanesatake by motorboat to meet Cohen, but he never made it off the beach. After a brief conversation with the New York lawyer, it was obvious to Young that Cohen's radical fervour would pose serious problems. In Young's view, Cohen was interested less in helping the Mohawks negotiate an end to the dispute than in encouraging them to take no-win positions. He jumped back in the motorboat and left in disgust.[136]

Within the Québec government, a crisis committee was set up, led by Claude Ryan. This reduced the maneuverability of John Ciaccia, who declared that the Mohawk demands were out of his jurisdiction. Premier Bourassa "was emphatic that there would be no negotiations on the question of possible criminal charges arising from the crisis."[137] On the federal side, Tom Siddon kept repeating that there could be no negotiations with guns and barricades in the picture.

In a matter of a few days, this local conflict had escalated to an event pitting First Nations of Québec and other parts of Canada against the Government of Québec and the SQ, and Mohawks throughout Québec against citizens, local government, and the Québec government. Social justice groups joined in solidarity with the Mohawk cause.

As the conflict escalated, the Mohawks of *Kanehsatà:ke*, *Kahnawà:ke*, and Akwesasne united as they had not done for a long time. The various factions of *Kanehsatà:ke* began working together. In *Kahnawà:ke*, the small group that had acted on its own was supported by the entire Warrior Society and then, reluctantly at first but with increasing resolve, the elected band council supported their action.

Over the next months, the escalation in these fourteen areas continued. As tension was increasing, residents from the Onen'tó:kon Treatment Centre, across highway 344 from the disputed land, were sent elsewhere.[138] Eventually the Centre would become the last holdout for the Mohawks. Meanwhile in Québec City, after the first week of the crisis, Bourassa stated that he had no intention of requesting intervention from the Canadian Army. He also voiced regret that there had not been better coordination between the SQ and politicians before the raid.[139]

A Mixture of Passions

Within the first ten days after the attack the crisis intensified significantly. A number of passions emerged within Canada. Over the next 30 days, many deep, contradictory passions would churn; the whole nation would be affected. There were resolves to "not give in" on many sides of issues and fears of violence and significant loss of life. A passion to find a peaceful settlement also existed, in part for reasons of Canadian identity and, in the case of politicians, for their place in history. There were intense negotiations on the one hand and rioting on the other.

Within Châteauguay, the mob action became better organized. Yvon Poitra, a retired SQ officer and an aspirant to the Mayor's office, organized *Solidarité Châteauguay* to demand military intervention. On August 1, they led a march of 10,000 people.[140] Gilles Proulx of Montreal's CJMS gave the group media support: "Proulx was loved by thousands of South Shore listeners because he professed to understand the frustrations of the Châteauguay mobs and was not afraid to verbally pummel and abuse the Mohawk warriors on the air."[141] The protest also attracted fringe groups like white supremacist members of the Aryan Nation and Longitude 74, a branch of the Ku Klux Klan.[142]

From the beginning, there were strong opposing factions within the Québec government. On July 14, Native Affairs Minister John Ciaccia had negotiated an agreement to open Mercier Bridge; no one in *Kahnawà:ke* would be prosecuted over the blockade, *Kanehsatà:ke* Mohawks would co-operate with a police investigation, and many police would be withdrawn. Hawks in the cabinet balked at the agreement. One official stated that "you can't make an omelette without breaking eggs." Instead of withdrawing, the police dug in even more and the deal fell through.[143] According to Ellen Gabriel, the agreement failed because it was made with individuals who did not inform all the people.

In the town of Oka passions on both sides of the issue were strong. One antique dealer who called for reconciliation with the Mohawks had a rock thrown through his window. Petitions were circulated on both sides of the issue: one side calling for the mayor's resignation, the other supporting his stand.[144]

When Ovide Mercredi and other representatives of the Assembly of First Nations arrived on August 4, there was a significant conflict between different factions within the *Kanehsatà:ke* group. Those who were with the Longhouse accused the AFN representatives of being government agents since they recognized the Indian Act. The split, which broke out more openly on August 5, was based in part on a sense of cliquishness perceived on the part of the negotiating team.[145] On that day, Premier Bourassa gave a 48-hour ultimatum to the Mohawks to take down the barricades. That ultimatum united the Mohawks and precipitated an exodus of non-natives and about a third of the Mohawk community from *Kanehsatà:ke*. Peter Diome, a warrior spokesperson stated, "We are one people, one nation, and we will not be brought to our knees before anyone."[146] When the deadline expired in the afternoon of August 8, Bourassa invoked the National Defence Act and called on the Canadian Forces to replace the SQ.

Within the Oka council, there were strong feelings about selling the disputed land to the federal government. There was thunderous applause in the council chambers as an angry taxpayer said, "I'm insulted, I tell you, I'm insulted to think that you would sell these lands to the federal government."[147] On August 8, after a threat of expropriation, the council regretfully accepted a deal giving them $3.84 million for the land that they had bought from the developer for $70,000.[148]

Some of the deepest passions were ignited by symbolic acts. On August 12 a deal was signed in the open space of the Pines with Tom Siddon representing Canada. The late Walter David, Sr., signed on behalf of the people since he was secretary of the Longhouse at the time. At the last minute, unknown to the people of *Kanehsatà:ké,* a warrior with his face covered, codenamed "4-20," signed for the Mohawks of Akwesasne. After it was over, he presented a Warrior Society flag to mediator Alan Gold. The signing ceremony was met with fury among Quebecers.[149]

While the signing was taking place in the Pines, *Solidarité Châteauguay* focused on the St. Louis de Gonzage Bridge that crossed the St. Lawrence Seaway. They planned to use their cars to thwart the revolving segment of the bridge, blocking the Seaway. Eighty officers tried to control the crowd. One had his helmet torn off and was beaten. Seven people, including Yvon Poitras, were arrested. When the crowd tried to free the seven, the police locked themselves in the detachment offices. The crowd moved on to the Mercier barricades for the worst rioting since the crisis began:[150]

> This time, the Mohawks were all but forgotten by the mob. After the confrontation on the St. Louis de Gonzage Bridge, the police were now the enemy, and the crowd's fury was directed at them. By 9:30 p.m. the mob had swelled to several thousand. Once again, it was a family affair. More than one man arrived with a baseball bat in one hand and a child gripping the other. Someone climbed onto a police cruiser and smashed its dome light and its windshield. With that act of vandalism, a collective roar went up in the crowd. Young men advanced menacingly towards the line of officers, waving baseball bats and tire-irons, rattling the metal gate that separated the police from the mob…. Protesters peeled chunks of pavement off the roadside curbs, heaving them and anything else they could lay their hands on—eggs, bricks, rocks—at the police. RCMP officers, called in to reinforce the Sûreté du Québec, stood shoulder to shoulder on the front line, protecting the SQ officers behind them…. One middle-aged police-man was struck in the chest with a flying brick and collapsed on the ground.[151]

When the mob lit fires, opened a fire hydrant, and smashed police vehicles, the police used tear gas and then charged:

> Once again, journalists were a target for the mob's rage. About thirty angry men surrounded a radio reporter, wrestling with her, trying to tear away the purse where she had hidden her recording equipment. "If you stay here one

more second you won't have a face!" one man screamed at her. Two or three men pursued her down the street until she got to her car and drove away.[152]

When the riot was over, 35 people had been taken to the hospital. Ten of these were RCMP officers. A number of RCMP resented that they had been placed between the SQ and the crowd, taking the brunt of the mob anger directed toward the SQ. In the following days, the SQ changed tactics and started to mingle with the crowds; this significantly reduced violence.[153]

Overall, the SQ suffered greatly through the crisis. They were humiliated by their initial pull-back on July 11, and they lost one of their officers. They were supplanted by the RCMP and eventually the army. They became the butt of jokes. There was a loss of face.

After the reactions to the signing ceremony and the Châteauguay riots, pressure on the Québec government to bring in the army increased. The 48-hour deadline had expired. The crisis committee of cabinet was divided. John Ciaccia was convinced that a military solution would sow the seeds of future violence with Aboriginal people. Premier Bourassa and Claude Ryan were cautious, and the rest of cabinet hawkish. In the end, Lieutenant-General Foster convinced the provincial government that a military assault would not resolve the crisis. Ciaccia describes him this way.

> The general, even with an army under his command, was a peaceful man, looking for a peaceful solution. He would rather restrain the force that was available to him rather than unleash it, as he could have, against the recalcitrant Warriors who were bottling up an entire region. I remember after a particularly difficult meeting when he resisted the demands of the hardliners to take more forceful measures, calling me the next morning to thank me for having supported his position.[154]

In this approach, Foster had the support of Prime Minister Brian Mulroney who did not want to be remembered historically as "the butcher of Oka."[155]

Though he did not plan a military assault, on August 13 Premier Bourassa asked the troops to move in closer. By August 16, they were in place. On August 17 Bourassa asked the army to take over from the SQ and on August 20 they took over the barricades on Mercier Bridge and in Oka. As members of the SQ left the barricades near *Kahnawà:ke* they exchanged taunts with the Mohawks.[156]

The Canadian Army

When the army arrived at Mercier Bridge, they started unravelling razor wire. Lieutenant-Colonel Robin Gagnon walked into the no-man's land separating the two barricades and met and shook hands with some Warriors who walked in from the other side. This began respectful relations between the two groups at *Kahnawà:ke*-Châteauguay. Many of the Mohawk warriors were veterans of the American military and the Canadian army treated them as adversarial colleagues.

A "hotline" was established between the two groups and they kept each other informed of activities to avoid an outbreak of violence. The Mohawks of *Kahnawà:ke* had a clear command structure and were prepared to "deal with the army on a 'soldier to soldier' basis."[157]

In contrast, no Mohawk people agreed to meet Colonel Pierre Daigle, commanding officer of the army contingent sent to *Kanehsatà:ke*. Instead, some community volunteers met with him. When the army rolled its razor wire much closer to Mohawk positions than the Mohawks felt tolerable, the Mohawks informed Prime Minister Mulroney and Premier Bourassa that they would not talk until they were assured that the army would not advance any further. Part of the reason they were so adamant was that they feared if the army came too close they would realize how few warriors were in the Pines.[158]

The *Kanehsatà:ke* group was a distillation of the most "fervent of the Mohawk idealists and militants."[159] They were not going to give up until their sovereignty was recognized. They had no formal command structure and they were not inclined to co-operate with Lieutenant-Colonel Daigle.

On August 27, Bourassa asked the army to dismantle the barricades. This set in motion a new chain of events. In *Kanehsatà:ke* the people behind the barricades went on red alert. The next day civil protection authorities advised Oka residents to evacuate their homes while the Red Cross brought in stretchers and body bags.[160]

In *Kahnawà:ke*, elderly people, women, and children were evacuated on August 28 by a 75-car convoy. As they left, demonstrators stoned the cars and the police made no attempt to restrain or arrest the stone throwers. The father of Joan Lacroix, a 76-year-old French Canadian, was hit on the chest by a rock the size of a football and 71-year-old Joe Armstrong died a week later of a heart attack.[161]

The mobs of Châteauguay and LaSalle also made life difficult for the international observers. On August 24, they attacked a car of international observers whom they saw as Mohawk sympathizers. They found other ways of blocking transportation and inspiring fear. Finn Lynghjem, a Norwegian judge, remarked, "The only persons who have treated me in a civilized way in this matter here in Canada are the Mohawks. The army and the police do nothing. It's very degrading...to us, and perhaps more degrading to the government who can't give us access."[162] On August 27, Bourassa asked the observers to leave.

On August 28 two intense sets of negotiations were occurring in the Dorval Hilton. In one room a group of Mohawks from *Kanehsatà:ke* and *Kahnawà:ke,* including Grand Chief Joe Norton, met with John Ciaccia for a last ditch negotiation to end the crisis. The other negotiation involved military leaders and *Kahnawà:ke* warriors. Proposals from the first negotiation were taken to a crisis cabinet committee meeting that night. Ciaccia had only one supporter in the room, which had turned hawkish. The other negotiations ended with an unwritten gentleman's agreement that warriors and soldiers would dismantle the Mercier barricades together. This was done on August 29.

The Mohawk people and their allies at *Kanehsatà:ke* were disheartened watching the Mercier bridge barricades being dismantled. Many did not learn about the deal until they saw it happening on television. Stonecarver, a pacifist until the July 11 raid, went to say his last goodbye to his mother. He was convinced he would die in the army raid.[163]

During this time, there were reports of police detaining Mohawks from *Kanehsatà:ke* and beating them to try to learn who had killed Corporal Lemay. On August 26, Angus Jacobs was taken to a barn, where he was choked and kicked by police. This is his account:

> We stopped at a building in the woods that I think was their headquarters. They showed me a photo of a masked man in the pine woods holding a gun. I think it was taken on July 11. They said they knew it was me. I denied it. They called me a dirty Indian bastard. They put a shotgun in my ear and made me crawl on the floor and called me a dog and said that they were going to kill me like a dog if I didn't make a confession. For the next two-and-a-half hours they took turns beating me. They split up in teams of two or three. They took off their heavy shoes and put on sneakers so the marks wouldn't show as bad. They punched and kicked every part of my body.... One of them grabbed me by the balls and twisted and then I almost passed out.... My kidneys and stomach hurt real bad and my private parts were painful too. They kept saying I had to sign this confession they put in front of me. Finally I signed it just so they would stop. I didn't even look at what I signed.[164]

Daniel Nicholas was taken to the detachment at St. Eustache where he was kicked and burned with a cigarette on the stomach. He was detained for several days so the swelling would go down before he appeared in court.[165]

In the coming days the focus of action was to narrow considerably.

Confinement to the Treatment Centre

After the Mercier Bridge was re-opened, military forces around the *Kanehsata'kehró:non* began to tighten the boundaries. A group of women, Warriors, children, and journalists were confined to the Treatment Centre and the surrounding woods. Tensions increased. Two events stand out as symptoms and symbols of that tension: the face-to-face stare of Private Patrick Cloutier and Warrior Brad Larocque, code-named Freddy Krueger, and the beating of Randy Horne, code-named Spudwrench. In the last days of August there was a chain of violence that increased the internal tensions among the *Kanehsata'keró:non*.

Dr. Réjean and Andrea Mongeon, who had a farm and veterinary clinic near the Pines, had left their property in the hands of one of the Mohawks for a few days. They had, over the years, cultivated friendly relations with the *Kanehsata'keró:non*. When they returned on August 31, they found their house vandalized. They were furious. Mohawk ambulance driver Ronnie Bonspille offered to help them but they refused. It was believed that Lasagna, Noriega, and friends had vandalized because this gang also went into the food bank and threatened *Kanehsata:ke* community members with their automatic weapons. They were afraid that Bonspille would "rat" on them. Francis and Cory Jacobs (his son) were on security patrol when the Lasagna gang searched for Bonspille. As the gang approached, Bonspille fled to the military position and Francis and Cory were badly beaten by Lasagna and company. Then the gang went to Ronnie Bonspille's house where they smashed two ambulances and the house windows. The gang was only disarmed the following day, in a move initiated by the women of *Kanehsatà:ké* and some warriors, and held in a house. Lasagna escaped and went to the community centre, where he shouted, yelled, and pounded his baseball bat; the people listened, afraid he might pull out his pistol and start shooting.[166] From Lasagna's perspective, Francis Jacobs and Ronnie Bonspille were traitors "who gave his name and picture to the SQ after having left the Oka area to collaborate with the police."[167]

On September 1, as the *Kanehsata'kehró:non* were dealing with the aftermath of the Lasagna episode, the army mobilized and moved forward in the early afternoon. They took over all the Pines north of highway 344 and encircled the Mohawks on the grounds of the Treatment Centre. As the army advanced, the Warriors offered resistance. One Warrior screamed and lunged at the soldiers but was restrained by a Mohawk woman. Mad Jap kept telling the Warriors to hold their fire. Micmac Tom Paul was angry and wanted to shoot; he was just waiting for the first shot. On the army side, Major Alain Tremblay, the officer in charge of the operation, yelled "*Restez calme!*" On both sides the adrenalin was flowing. Traditional native healers warned that their protective medicine would not work if the Mohawks fired a single shot. During this time of mounting tension the famous staredown between Brad Larocque and Patrick Cloutier occurred.

The army had been moving its barbed wire closer to the Treatment Centre and mutual exchanges of insults were common. In the midst of this, a Warrior thrust his face inches away from the soldier and yelled "Boo!" then called him a "Motherf—er." That image with those words was captured on film and videotape and was shown around the world. The soldier just stared impassively into the face of the warrior, showing no reaction. The soldier was Patrick Cloutier from Gaspé who had been called from vacation with his parents to join in the action at Oka. His previous experience included Red Guard sentry duty at the Citadel where he was accustomed to keeping a straight face when tourists (especially women) would try to disturb his stare. Before he left home, his mother pointed out that the Mohawks had a lot of good demands; she told him, "Patrick, you're going to Oka, you're going to do a job, but do it with love in your heart, not hate."[168] He later told his mother that at the time of the staring his heart was racing but he wasn't scared.

The warrior was Brad Larocque from Saskatchewan. He was an Ojibway from Poor Man's reserve north of Regina. As a toddler he had been taken from his family and adopted by white parents in Weyburn. As he reached adulthood, he rediscovered his Aboriginal past and met his biological siblings. He attended the Indian Federated College and became an activist working for Aboriginal rights through non-violent protests. Until the crisis he had not approved of warrior activity. After the July 11 raid he was approached by the Canadian Federation of Students to travel to Ottawa to work with fifteen others on a position paper on the crisis. As part of the research they took a boat from Montreal to *Kahnawà:ke* where he witnessed the mob action of Châteauguay from the Mohawk side; all of a sudden the position paper seemed trivial.

When the call for reinforcements came from *Kanehsatà:ke,* he signed up. When he arrived by boat, he was given "camouflage gear, an AK-47 rifle, and a codename—Freddy Krueger. He had become a warrior."[169] All of a sudden, the peaceful protests out West seemed futile: now he was with people who were taking action. The staredown ended when two Mohawk women arrived at the front lines with pizza. When the crisis was over, Cloutier was promoted and Larocque quietly went back to university in Regina.

In the evening, the army captured the last bunker in the Pines. They allowed the warriors to remove their possessions, which they did in a wheelbarrow. By September 3, the Mohawks were limited to territory bounded by highway 344 to the north, the Lake of Two Mountains to the south, and gullies to the east and west of the Treatment Centre.[170]

Meanwhile on September 3 in *Kahnawà:ke,* a number of warriors regained control of Mercier Bridge, which was being repaired. The army moved in to recapture the bridge. The warriors went with their weapons to the Longhouse. Because an army helicopter had observed their route, a raid on the Longhouse resulted, with physical fighting between troops and Mohawk women who were protecting what to them was a sacred space.[171]

At the Treatment Centre, psychological warfare became the order of the day. The army shone bright lights on the Mohawk position. Mohawks answered with mirrors from the treatment centre, reflecting the glare to the soldiers. Flares and low-flying aircraft intensified the pressure. Faced with the pressure and with a determination to fire if there was an attack, more than half of the Warriors made their wills and burial arrangements.[172] By September 6, verbal abuse between Mohawks and soldiers intensified and eventually they threw stones at one another. The next day, all younger Warriors were ordered away from the front lines.

Randy Horne, an older Warrior, was posted at night in a fox hole near the front line. At about 4:00 a.m. he woke up

> to see a soldier stepping over him. When he brought his arms out of his sleeping bag to defend himself, he was immediately grabbed by two other soldiers on either side of the foxhole. He tried to call for help, but the soldier began beating him on the head with clubs. Spudwrench pulled out a small knife and slashed at the soldiers, injuring them slightly, but the soldiers kept clubbing him furiously. He put up his hand to protect himself, but they kept swinging away, inflicting deep gashes on his skull and face. He lost consciousness as the soldiers dragged him away.[173]

Splinter, the warrior in the neighbouring bunker, heard the noise and shone a light on the soldiers, who ran away. He took Spudwrench to the Treatment Centre.

Because Spudwrench was in critical condition he was moved to Montreal General Hospital. Despite military promises that he would be returned to the Treatment Centre, he was arrested by the SQ on September 12.

By mid-September it started to get colder; pressure increased on those inside the Treatment Centre as cellular phones of journalists were made non-functional by a court order initiated by the SQ. Wilfried Telkamper, vice-president of the European parliament, wrote to Prime Minister Mulroney protesting cutting off the treatment centre phone line.[174] Joe Deom "said the army had refused to allow in blankets and heavy clothing, despite temperatures that were to dip to near zero overnight.... [He] said the army was using the cold as a weapon."[175]

On September 17, the Bear Island Chief was reported saying, "Many native groups across the country will be taking action as a result of the Oka situation,"[176] and Cree Chief Bill Diamond claimed that young people advocated taking arms but have been looking for leadership to take the initiative. He went on to say that the "Mohawk Warriors have proved that leadership and the young people are really looking up to them. It's like hero worship."[177]

In *Kahnawà:ke* there was mob action against soldiers who were conducting raids to search for weapons. On September 18, they searched Tekakwitha Island and one soldier was dragged into the crowd, punched, kicked, and choked with a binocular strap. Another soldier almost had an ear ripped off.[178] Twenty soldiers were injured (two with concussions) and seventy-five Mohawks needed medical attention. Among them was fifteen-year-old Kelly Ann Meloche, who claimed that they would never forgive or forget; she thanked the army "for making us stronger, for making us unite stronger."[179]

On September 16, there were negotiations in Toronto between members of the Iroquois confederacy and John Ciaccia, who had done what he could to find a peaceful end. The Government of Québec refused to accept terms Ciaccia had negotiated and the initiative only deepened a rift between the Warriors and members of the Confederacy.

On September 19, the Canadian Police Association placed an ad in eighteen papers across the country associating the actions of the Warriors with terrorism. In the ad they stated that during the July 11 raid, the "Sûreté never returned any gunfire!!!"[180] a statement disputed by media reports.[181] *The Globe and Mail* refused to print the ad, calling it "indefensible" and "provocative."[182] The tensions between the SQ and Mohawks intensified as allegations of police torture were revealed. These tensions took on a French-English spin as the *Montreal Gazette* "ran a cartoon that portrayed a provincial police officer as a mutt in aviator glasses. On the mutt-officer's cap, the force's crest was rendered with the words 'Chien Chaud' [Hot Dog] below."[183] SQ Director-General Robert Lavigne accused the "the anglophone media of taking the natives' side in vengeance for the failure of the Meech Lake Accord."[184] This sense of a linguistic war came through in a piece by John Yorkton of the *Montreal Gazette* in response to an editorial by Alain Dubuc of *La Presse*:

"What is worrying is that the native issue is degenerating into a linguistic war," Dubuc said. "And that is not the fault of the Quebec media. Elsewhere in Canada, especially in Ontario, there is a widespread movement in support of the Mohawks, without a basic distinction between the demand of the Mohawks and the warrior guerrillas.".... Dubuc said the movement had reached a climax with the publication in the Toronto Globe and Mail of a full-page advertisement denouncing the government's use of force. It was signed by unions, Protestant churches, civil rights groups and many individuals. He mentioned writers Margaret Atwood and Pierre Berton.[185]

Back at the Treatment Centre, accusations of provocation came from both sides. Both the military and Mohawks cited instances in which someone from the other side fired an unloaded weapon at the other side.[186]

On September 23, Warrior Dennis "Psycho" Nicholas married Cathy Sky in a traditional Mohawk ceremony at the Treatment Centre that was led by faithkeepers Loran Thompson and Bruce Elijah. In the following days, tensions among the people at the Treatment Center intensified. Cigarette rations were significantly reduced. The provincial government was not willing to consider appointing an independent prosecutor, so there seemed no hope of successful negotiations to disengage. Most of the people agreed to disengage within 48 hours, but a few like Lasagna and Noriega wanted to hold out to the end. Stonecarver observed, "We're beginning to eat ourselves. It seems like we're turning against ourselves now. It's like an animal that's beginning to gnaw on its own stomach because it's so hungry."[187] The end of the crisis was approaching.

The End of the Crisis

September 26 was the day of decision. A message was sent through a secret communications system, using the local radio station, from the negotiating team in Pointe Claire congratulating the Warriors for holding on and suggesting they had accomplished as much as they could. Earlier in the day, Prime Minister Mulroney had promised a new Aboriginal agenda in the House of Commons. They had achieved the goal of hanging on until parliament resumed. In separate clan meetings lasting until about 3:30 p.m. consensus to leave the Treatment Centre was achieved.

A bonfire was set outside the Treatment Center where any incriminating evidence and weapons were burned. The *Kanehsata'kehró:non* had decided to walk home. They would not surrender or give up. By 5:52 p.m. everyone was in camouflage gear and they had a final tobacco-burning ceremony that included Lasagna, the last to decide to leave with the group.

At 6:50 p.m., they began marching toward the front line. They put stretchers over the razor wire and scrambled across; then continued along highway 344 toward Oka. The soldiers were caught by surprise. They ordered the Mohawks to stop but the orders were ignored. The first five Mohawks (Loran Thompson, Vicky

Diabo with her infant daughter, Noriega, and Cathy Sky) walked through the military lines into the town where they were surrounded by supporters.

At the top of the hill, soldiers struggled with the Mohawks, some wrestling and scrapping. Some of the Mohawks were clubbed with rifle butts. Fourteen-year-old Waneek Horn-Miller was stabbed in the chest by a bayonet. By 7:10 p.m., the soldiers had the group corralled into a small section and handcuffed the Warriors. At 7:50 they were loaded into buses and driven away. Within two hours Lasagna was being interrogated and beaten by police at Parthenais detention centre.[188]

Aftermath

Roughly a month after the crisis ended, a seminar to promote healing at Oka was held. Robert "Mad Jap" Skidder told the group that the resistance was worth it because "it has led to new unity among natives. I am proud to be a part of this history."[189] At the same meeting, Tona Maon of the national Canadian Alliance in Solidarity with Native Peoples, said: "There needs to be a braiding of hair of the nations to bring them together in one spirit, one body, one mind."[190] The issue of unity was also a theme as Ron "Lasagna" Cross reflected on events:

> But when the people do come together, like in 1990 with all the trouble we had, no matter what you were—a Catholic or a Protestant or from one of the two Longhouses or a Band Councillor—everybody came together as one to defend the Territory and the people. I mean, I was right next to a guy who was Band Councillor and the guy on the other side of me was a priest and we all worked together to defend the Territory, thinking as one. That's why we were so strong in 1990. The governments made a mistake by doing what they did because when all the people come together as one, that's the strongest you can make the Indian people.[191]

Cross attributed the feeling of unity to the religious ceremonies.

> The ceremonies that our people did at that time to help us get out of that situation were very powerful. We were protected very well because every-body was together as one mind: There was no bickering amongst each other, there was no hatred, there was no anger it was all together as one, as brother and sister. So it made us very strong in 1990. Spiritually, the odds were totally against Canada and any forces that came against us. It's like getting a religion you believe in a hundred per cent: You have faith in it; it's there for you when you need it, as long as you don't abuse it. That was the spiritual situation in 1990.[192]

The unity was a dynamic unity since, as has been noted, there were conflicts among the *Kanehsata'kehró:non* over strategy, tactics, and feelings of betrayal. Although the traditional divisions were overcome, "once 1990 was over and things started to get back to normal, the factions came back into place, and people started pointing fingers at each other and blaming each other, so it pulled our people apart again."[193]

Well after the crisis was over, Hélène Sévigny, a Québécoise journalist, decided to write a book on Ronald Cross, code-named Lasagna. In it she describes her initial fears at being in a room alone with this notorious "terrorist." While the book is a story of his life, it is also a story of Sévigny's change in consciousness and awareness. Another level of insight comes from *Lasagna*, the book. In the English-language edition, Sévigny talks about the reaction to her original French-language edition. On live radio, Gilles Proulx screamed that she went to bed with terrorists and read a letter saying she was a prostitute to Warriors. Though the author of several other books, she sensed a kind of ostracism by her peers after the publication of *Lasagna*:

> Despite the strident opposition to the book from some sectors of the media, what surprised me most is the position of silent "neutrality" that many of my fellow journalists, colleagues and even my friends have adopted since I published this biography. I began to realize, over the past year, that the negative public reaction to this book in Québec had to be based on something more than a simple attempt by the francophone media to cover up its misrepresentation of the events at Oka in 1990. The larger dimension of my increasing alienation from my former colleagues in journalism, the legal community, the conference circuit and even my social circle, began to give me pause for considerable thought. I began to realize that the overwhelming majority of people who had criticized the book had not even bothered to read it. Indeed, the most common reaction from people I spoke to, both publicly and privately, as soon as they heard I had written a book like this, but before they had read it, was to accuse me of "being on the side of the Mohawks," of "justifying their violence" and of "having no sympathy for White Quebeckers." No statement brings this into sharper focus than the first question I was asked by the journalist covering my launch of the book in Trois-Rivières: "Do you know that Quebeckers see you as a traitor to your own race?"[194]

Others besides Hélène Sévigny felt victimized in the wake of the 1990 crisis. Even before the crisis was over, André Picard quoted Alain Dubuc of *La Presse* as saying that anti-francophones were painting Quebec as "intolerant and repressive."[195] This sense of anglophones picking on Québec was developed in greater depth by Robin Philpot in *Oka: dernier alibi du Canada anglais* in which he comments on English press comparisons of Québec to the Mississippi oppression of Afro-Americans as well as many other allusions to the racism of Quebeckers.[196] He argues that what is overlooked is the anti-Aboriginal racism throughout English Canada and the positive side of Québec–Native relations.

Meanwhile, as of the writing of this book, land claims and other issues involving the peoples of Oka/*Kanehsatà:ke* were still unresolved.

* * * * *

This analytic narrative of the Crisis of 1990 forms a foundation for an interpretation of the major and some of the minor conflicts that took place throughout, using the framework of mimetic structures of violence. By attending to the early history and the growth of ethnonationalism in this chapter, I laid a foundation for showing that mimetic phenomena may have a long and protracted development. Focusing on both the broad developments, as well as some of the interpersonal dynamics of the key players, provides opportunity to examine the interplay of mimetic and scapegoat phenomena on different scales. The allusion to what happened in newspapers articles and books published after the crisis shows the significance of interpretation of events and that even at that level of action there is opportunity for mimetic desire and scapegoating.

Chapter 11

Interpreting the Oka/*Kanehsatà:ké* Crisis

Waneskewin is a buffalo jump on the banks of the South Saskatchewan River just north of Saskatoon. For 6,000 years indigenous peoples used the jump to hunt the buffalo they needed for food, shelter, and clothing. Hunters dressed as buffalo—"fake buffalo"—would start a herd of buffalo moving toward the jump. When the buffalo were all headed in the right direction, other hunters would get behind them making a noise to frighten them. The buffalo would start running in the direction of the jump. Piles of rocks would funnel the herd toward a well-defined, abrupt steep hill leading down to the river. They would be running so fast and so close together that by the time the animals in front would see the cliff it would be impossible to stop the momentum built up behind them. They would tumble down the cliff only to be slaughtered by waiting hunters.

Waneskewin, from a buffalo's perspective, becomes a metaphor for a mimetic structure of violence. There is a movement in the direction of violence; events stir up emotions, such as fear, that intensify the phenomenon. At a certain point the structure takes on a life of its own with its own momentum, and it is virtually impossible to stop or turn things around. Furthermore, those who, like the "fake buffalo," were there to deceive may have set the action structure in motion. The remarkable thing about the Oka/*Kanehsatà:ke* Crisis is that the buffalo slowed down and turned around before falling over the cliff; the crisis ended without widespread destruction and death.

As I have talked about the crisis with people who were there and reflect on the data, I have the distinct impression that Canada came close to the kind of bloodbath that would have changed its history for the worse. For this reason, it is extremely important to understand how we got ourselves into this type of situation—to understand the intertwined mesh of deep-rooted conflicts involved there.

The crisis was a complex phenomenon with many dynamics and sub-dynamics. In the analysis that follows, I methodically enframe a number of relational systems and use the theories that give definition to mimetic structures of violence to discover the inner dynamics of the operative structures. The overall picture that emerges is one of many highly conflicted relational systems that are interconnected—what happens in one has an impact on the others. The interconnections are of three kinds: first, some of the same players participate in more than one relational system; second, there is a direct impact in that a decision made in one relational system has a direct bearing on the other—blocking the Mercier Bridge at *Kahnawa:ke* had a direct impact on Oka/*Kanehsatá:ke*; and, third, there is a mimetic impact as structures are imitated from one relational system to another: for example, it became clear to First Nations across Canada that the structural components of what was happening at Oka/*Kanehsatá:ke* resembled structures of violence that they had experienced. They responded by imposing blockades and threatening to blow up strategic targets, mimetically joining in solidarity with their Aboriginal sisters and brothers.

Referring back to Ken Wilber's quadrants as depicted in Chapter 9, there is a need to understand observable external dynamics as well as internal dynamics. In Chapters 2 to 8, I developed a number of theoretical perspectives that I argued would help us understand the internal emotions, drives and motivators within people participating in mimetic structures of violence. In Chapter 10, I presented an analytical narrative that presented the external dynamics—what was presented is empirically verifiable in that the data can be traced to the sources. I am now going to take the interpretation to another level—one that looks at internal structures. Based on the evidence of what happened and on statements of what people said at the time, we will examine the conflict using the theoretical constructs we have developed in Chapters 2 to 8.

The first level of verification comes from the readers: Do you think you might have felt and acted as the protagonists did if you had been in their situation, based on the theories and context presented? The second level of verification will come when people caught up in real conflicts say, "The theories of deep-rooted conflict and mimetic structures of violence help me understand why I feel like I do, why I am drawn to violence, and what is going on around me." The third level of verification will come when people use this awareness to respond to conflict in new ways, based on the theories presented, with good results.

This chapter is not simply about the Crisis of 1990; it is about mimetic structures of violence around the world. However, dealing with a specific conflict helps us see the theory in action as opposed to speaking in the abstract. The analysis will deal mainly with what happens within groups of people; this is, of course, closely related to what goes on within individuals. The spirit of the inquiry is not one of judgment, but about self-understanding—one's self and another's.

To begin, I will briefly review Chapters 2 to 8 so that there is clarity about the theoretical concepts used for the interpretation. I will then interpret thirteen different relational systems evident during the conflict using the components of mimetic structures of violence. Seven of these will be inter-group relational systems and six will be intragroup. Looking at these component parts will enable us to make some observations about the conflict as a whole. I will then provide a second narrative, much more condensed than the first, that will tell what happened during the crisis using the language and concepts of deep-rooted conflict. Note that by doing this I am integrating an atemporal analysis—looking at the relational systems apart from time—with an interpretation that emphasizes change through time—as a I present a second narrative.

Mimetic structures of violence have a number of component parts that I will review in a schematic, condensed, and un-nuanced way. Invariably, there is a threat to identity need satisfiers of meaning, connectedness, action, security, recognition, and selfness as having particular integrated qualities of being. This threat produces an emotional response with some combination of anger, fear, sadness, depression, and shame. If the threat is powerful or prolonged enough, it produces trauma and fear and the desire for security takes over the core of one's being. In time, if there is not sufficient healing, the trauma leads to a defensive mimetic structure of entrenchment in which identity needs are defined in terms of security. Hence, meaning systems are expressed in terms of narrowly defined beliefs, people are divided into friends and enemies, and action is defined in terms of security.

The aggressive side of a mimetic structure of violence is shown when people develop violent satisfiers for their identity needs—their beings are oriented toward violence. Mimetic theory is used in tandem with human needs theories. As René Girard developed it, mimetic desire is an imitation of the desires of another for an object.

Mimetic desire can lead to mimetic rivalry, in which two parties each desire what the other has or desires. Mimetic rivalry can intensify to the point that the parties become mirror images of one another. Eventually, one's "selfness" is defined mimetically. The link with human needs theory is that the satisfiers to identity needs are developed along the lines of mimetic desire and rivalry. In other words, identity is always worked out in relation to one's Other. Mimetic conflicts can generate crises that lead to scapegoating in which the violence of a community is projected onto a scapegoat. There is temporary unity as people unite around the same "enemy."

The dynamics of mimetic rivalries and the particular satisfiers to identity needs that result can develop into hegemonic structures in which certain groups emerge as systematically dominating other groups. In a stable hegemonic structure, mimetic rivalries take place between people at the top and between people at the bottom. When people at the bottom start to change these structures, conflictual rivalries break out between the people at the top and those at the bottom. All of these dynamics may involve people identified with ethnonationalist groups that combine perceived common ancestry, ethnicity, religion, land, and politics in the definition of identity groups. They develop an ethno-identity with stories of chosen traumas and chosen glories that are ever present through collapsed time.

Mimetic structures of violence can be thought of as an ontological rift—a dehumanizing chasm of separation—between Self and Other. One such rift is based on gender in which there are hegemonic structures, mimetic rivalries, and the framing of identity need satisfiers so that women can become sex objects for men and violent men may become hero-power-objects to be manipulated by women. Violence may be intensified through bystander compliance or encouragement, rhetoric, victimization of youth, narcissistic wounding and loss of face. These aspects of mimetic structures of violence may be present in differing degrees in various conflict situations.

Mimetic Structures of Violence in Specific Relational Systems

I will begin by interpreting the following inter-group relational systems that I have enframed.

1. *Kanehsata'kehró:non* and the Oka Council
2. Warriors and the SQ
3. *Kahnawà:ke* and Châteauguay
4. *Kanien'kehà:ka* (Mohawks) and *Québécois*
5. First Nations and the Government of Canada
6. Warriors and the Army
7. French and English.

Second will be an interpretation of intragroup conflicts within six different groups involved in the crisis; each makes up its own relational system:

1. *Kanehsata'kehró:non* (people of *Kanehsatà:ke*)
2. The Municipality of Oka
3. *Kanien'kehà:ka* (Mohawks)
4. The First Nations
5. The South Shore Residents
6. The Province of Québec.

Kanehsata'kehró:non and the Oka Council

I use mimetic, hegemonic, ethnonational, and identity needs theories to analyze the mimetic structure of violence that gripped this relational system. In the pre-crisis stage, the land called the Pines was the object of mimetic desire. Legally, the land belonged to developers in Europe who planned to sell enough of it so the city could build a golf course. The Pines were *de facto* in the hands of the Mohawks who used the Commons for their public events and solitary retreats. Members of the golf course desired the Pines for their expansion, mimicking other golf courses with eighteen holes and other housing developments based on proximity to a golf course. As they showed their desire for the Pines a series of feedback loops strengthened the desire of both groups for control over the Pines. With the golf course expansion plans, the Mohawks valued the Pines even more. As they protested the golf course expansion, the resolve of the golfers to acquire the Pines, with the support of the Mayor, increased.

This set of reciprocal actions to gain hegemony over the Pines developed into a mimetic rivalry and eventually into mimetic doubling. The Mohawks in the Pines were prepared to put their lives on the line to protect the land and Mayor Ouellette was prepared to risk loss of life to acquire the Pines. He even took action against the wishes of Québec Minister John Ciaccia. After the raid, he had to leave home because of a death threat; yet he still defended his action.

When it became clear that the legal system would allow the development, the *Kanehsata'kehró:non* decided to physically occupy the Pines. They became an obstacle to the golfers who asked the courts for an injunction. When that did not secure the land the Mayor asked the police to forcibly take the land. In their decision to try to settle the issue *physically*, they became doubles of the Mohawks who had previously determined that they would *physically* stand in the way of development of the Pines. The golfers used the SQ to help them, just as the Mohawks used additional warrior forces from outside their community.

The Pines became a satisfier of a number of needs related to the identity of both groups. The needs for meaning and recognition included the rule of law, history, land rights, and values, and needs for connectedness involved community viability. The need for action included a vision for the future on which they wished to act and in relation to the Pines. Finally, control of the Pines had implications for the need for security. Let's look at each of these.

The first satisfier of the identity needs for *meaning* and *recognition* was the rule of law; there was mimetic doubling involving foundational principles of law. Mohawks agreed that the government had done things "by the book" but immediately stated it was a bad book. James O'Reilly, a lawyer who had represented native people but was not a part of the Oka/*Kanehsatà:ke* crisis, likewise commented that the law taken as a precedent was "bad law."[1] (See John Ciaccia's letter referred to in Chapter 10.) For the *Kanehsata'kehró:non* to accept the legitimacy of the legal and justice framework within Canada meant to accept a system in which all the cards were stacked against them. (See Chapter 8.)

The political and legal systems they faced constituted a hegemonic structure in which the Québec and Canadian governments dominated: that's why a golf course was there in the first place. Now the *Kanehsata'keró:non* wanted out of the control structure and were prepared to stand their ground against the powers that be. Hence, there was a mimetic rivalry over the legitimacy of the whole legal framework for land ownership. The Mohawks went back to the Two-Row Wampum treaty and the concept of inherent indigenous land rights. On the other side, the various levels of government respected a history of legal decisions that granted the land to the Sulpicians to sell or transfer as they wished. Lacking agreement on a legal and justice framework within which disputes could be settled in a fair way parties resorted to a raw show of force.

Second, in relation to *meaning*, there was a rivalry over interpretations of history. From the Mohawk perspective, the land had belonged to their ancestors for hundreds of years (one element of ethnonationalism); their ancestors were the first people to inhabit it. Later, from their perspective, the king of France had allotted it to the Sulpicians to hold in trust for them. They did not respect the right of the king of France to the land, since it was already the focus of their activity. They did not believe that land could be owned; rather, they were owned by the land. Through the years, as they tried to use the land for their own sustenance, they were limited by the Sulpicians and by various forms of government. They, in turn, tried to block encroachments on the land by such things as railroads.

From the point of view of Euro-Canadians living in Oka, the history of Oka began with the movement of the Sulpicians and a group of Aboriginal people, mainly Mohawks, from Sault-aux-Recollets to the Lake of Two Mountains in 1721. Their ancestors were allotted land by the Sulpicians, the seigneurial custodians of the land (note a parallel element of ethnonationalism). When the seigneurial system was abolished in the 1850s, their ancestors gained clear title to the land according to laws in place at the time. They believed that the land was theirs to do with as they liked, as long as it was within the law as set out by the different levels of government.

Third, related to *recognition*, the dispute over the Pines came at the end of two centuries of struggle over control of the land. The Mohawks lost as the Sulpicians gained the support, first of the government of France and then of Britain. In the late 1800s there had been a campaign to get the Mohawks to relocate—that would have removed any future Indian claim to the land. Their tenacity kept alive a hope that one day their land rights would be recognized. For the Pines to be developed would have meant one more irreversible step in extinguishing Mohawk land claims in the area.

A fourth layer of *meaning* concerned a conflict of primary values. For the *Kanehsata'keró:non*, the land had value in its pristine condition. It offered peaceful solace to people who wandered among the trees. It meant that a portion of Mother Earth lay relatively unmolested; it provided a quiet burial place for ancestors. In addition, their forebears had planted the trees to avoid erosion. For the Mayor and his community, the land only had value if it was developed. It could generate revenue for the municipal council and an increase in tourism could bring in additional spin-off businesses. For them, the value of the land was its capacity to generate economic activity. For both groups it was a venue for sports: lacrosse and golf.

Fifth, the Pines played a role in the growth, sustenance, and viability of each community with the potential to contribute to the *security* and *connectedness* of each. Since the *Kanehsata'kehró:non* did not have a reserve *per se*, every bit of land contributed to a sense of place. The Pines was a central meeting place for special events. Their lacrosse box was there. The area was across the highway from the Treatment Centre. Because the community was spread out checkerboard style, a central common space was important to preserve a sense of peoplehood and a variety of institutions, and to sustain the culture. Besides, it represented a primary value in and of itself—it was a sacred space in the same way as a church, synagogue, or mosque are for others.

For the golf club members, expanding into the Pines made their sport more viable. A number of people had built homes near the golf club. With the planned development they would have new neighbours and the golfing community would be strengthened. These people had objected to the Native Treatment Centre since they thought it would reduce property values and cause problems. The golf course project would move the Mohawk presence farther from them and the expanded golf course would increase property values. The Pines represented the entrenchment and expansion of an institution that would be a focal point for a particular community.

Sixth, each group felt powerless to *act* in the face of the other. The Mohawks felt powerless to assert their land rights to the government and judicial institutions that were foreign to them. The municipality of Oka felt powerless to carry out its decisions on land that they believed belonged to them. They wished to develop the land but the Mohawk occupation prevented them from doing so.

Seventh, both groups had a concern for *security*. The Mohawks in the Pines on a 24-hour basis were concerned about personal safety, particularly after the July 11 raid and subsequent apprehension of Mohawks by police. Individuals in the municipality had a sense that the safety of anyone who started cutting down trees for the golf course was questionable. In this context of intense rivalry, people on both sides were threatened with death or violence. Over the longer term, gaining control of the Pines could make the winning group feel more secure.

Each of these layers of need satisfiers functioned as a feedback loop, reinforcing the desire of each group for the Pines. In true mimetic fashion they became doubles of one another in their resolve to gain or keep control of the land. In the end, the rivalry for the land and what it represented evolved to the point where the identity of both groups, their sense of being, was wrapped up in the rivalry over the Pines.

In *Kanehsatà:ke* there was a nascent traditional longhouse community made up of a minority of the community. These people had begun to reclaim their language, culture, and sense of being Mohawk in a long unbroken line of descent. For these people their very sense of being Mohawk was at stake in the preservation of the Pines.

For the Mayor and the investor-developers involved in the golf course endeavour, the situation revolved around what for them was a primary preoccupation and dream. The more the Mohawks became an obstacle for their plans, the more they wanted that golf course. It appears to have become an obsession, so much so that the Mayor made a request to the province to have the SQ enforce the court order.

It becomes clear that mimetic desire led to a mimetic rivalry and a mimetic doubling. Both sides became mirror images of one another in the intensity of feeling they had about the other. In this highly charged environment, when violence was introduced, the tensions reached a new level and the groups played a scapegoat role for one another. The *Kanehsata'kehró:non*, previously divided, became more united than ever in their support of the occupation of the Pines. Other mayors united in solidarity around the Mayor of Oka. The part of the Oka community supporting the expansion was united and eventually passionate about a position that precluded ever giving up the Pines. So strong was their feeling that only the threat of expropriation convinced them to sell the land to the federal government. Some scapegoat effects in this frame were overshadowed by other powerful mimetic and scapegoat structures, such as those between the Mohawks and SQ, the next enframing.

Warriors and the SQ

With the attack on the Pines, the mimetic rivalry between the Mohawk warriors and the SQ became more acute. There had been bad blood between the two through a series of events over the previous decades. After the attack, each group now hated the other with a greater passion. Mohawks hated the SQ for the harassment, the beatings, and the raid on the Pines. The SQ hated the Mohawks for showing them up and for, as the police believed, killing one of their own.

Just before the SQ raid, John Cree had pointed out the mimetic relationship when he said "Whatever the police do, we will match." After the July 11 raid, when the Mohawks barricaded Highway 344, the police set up their own barricades opposite the Mohawk barricades.

After the SQ raid on July 11, the six police vehicles left behind were destroyed as the people "united in an orgy of destruction, a collective venting of anger." There clearly was a scapegoat effect involving mob action—contagious collective violence—that came at a time of crisis. The SQ became symbolic victims; the police cruisers represented the police; and damage to them was symbolic and materially hurt the SQ. It was one unique point of vulnerability on the part of the police since they had left some of the vehicles when they fled after Corporal Lemay had been killed.

On July 11, the perceived stakes of the conflict and the types of force and violence both escalated. The SQ started with a show of force, hoping to intimidate the Mohawks into surrendering the land. The two sides were so much doubles of one another that they used the same ammunition making it impossible to determine whether Corporal Lemay was killed by a police or Mohawk bullet. Immediately after the shooting, the SQ moved a thousand officers to Oka; numerous Aboriginal people from across the country came to help the *Kanehsata'kehró:non*. The *Kahnawà:ke* blockage of the Mercier Bridge was a show of force to intimidate the government-sponsored forces. Furthermore, the Mohawks tricked the outside world into thinking that they had more warriors in the Pines and more high-powered weaponry than was, in fact, the case. The preoccupation of warriors and SQ with one another, even after the army moved in, brought the rivalry to the point of mimetic doubling. Within this concept of inter-group mimetic doubling, each group played a scapegoat role for the other. This was evident in the anger and hatred expressed toward the other, the relative unity within the groups, and the examples of selective scapegoating when individual Mohawks fell into the hands of the police.

Three scapegoats for the SQ were Angus Jacobs, Daniel Nicholas, and Ron Cross, code-named Lasagna. Remember that on August 26, Angus Jacobs was taken to a barn where police choked and kicked him. He said that he was called a "dirty Indian bastard," beaten, and kicked with sneakers. Daniel Nicholas was kicked and burned on the stomach with a cigarette at the detachment at St. Eustache. The name-calling, degrading behaviour, and beating resembled scapegoat actions.

Jacobs bore all the marks of the scapegoat; as a Mohawk he was different and as a perceived warrior even more different. When apprehended he was vulnerable; as a warrior he was strong. The SQ had a sense of crisis over having lost a member and having lost face. His identification with the Mohawks clearly made him illegitimate in the eyes of the police. The scapegoat action was justified on the grounds that it was an interrogation meant to elicit a confession. The same points could be made regarding Daniel Nicholas and, with even greater emphasis, Lasagna.

Lasagna epitomized for them what it meant to be a warrior and he had been particularly defiant. When he was captured at the end of the crisis, he had the marks of a scapegoat victim: he was powerful yet vulnerable; he was clearly illegitimate; his status as an armed person, like the police, called essential differences into question; and he appeared during a crisis. These intensified the police feeling that they had lost face in this situation. Through his notoriety, press exposure, taunts, and threats he had become the top SQ prey. When he walked out of the Treatment Centre he was immediately turned over to the SQ, unlike the others who were taken to a military base.

Kahnawá:ke and Châteauguay

The Mercier Bridge was closed within hours of the raid on the Pines. The Bridge became the object of mimetic desire for Mohawks and citizens of Châteauguay. The mimetic dimension is not immediately apparent since it could be argued that the people of the south shore simply desired the use of the bridge. Evidence of a mimetic desire comes from the rhetoric and action that took place. If the bridge had been closed for renovation or due to a natural disaster, there would not have been mob action or calls for the military. The fact that the *Mohawks* had control of the bridge is what prompted such deep reactions. The Mohawks were a thorn in the side of the people living on the south shore. Why did they have to be different (distinct)? Why couldn't they obey Québec and Canadian laws like everyone else? Why couldn't they respect public ownership of something like the bridge, which was built for the common good? Why did they have to be that way?

The intense reaction to anyone appearing native, the harassment of stores that did business with the Mohawks, the burning of Mohawks in effigy, the passion to stop food shipments—all showed almost an obsessive rage towards the Mohawks. The politicians and spokespersons called for draconian measures to open the bridge. They wanted the army called in. They wanted governments to act. They wanted the government to take control of the bridge.

The passion of citizens was so strong that they burned the premier in effigy for his inaction. Clearly, the traffic disruption created a sense of crisis and intensified the feeling. That is the point of Girardian theory. In a crisis, when things are not working well, contagious mimesis is shown in its full force. There was violence in the air among the mobs. The impact on government consciousness was so great that it took the military leaders to talk the politicians out of forceful action.

Within this crisis context, there were many examples of scapegoating. It was almost like lightning looking for a lightning rod. The violence had to find a place to go. At one point, the police even had to lock themselves inside the police station. At another point, journalists were subject to a menacing mob. At yet another, it was a woman wearing a Canadian flag. The burning of effigies was structured along scapegoat lines. When elderly Mohawks were driven out of *Kahnawà:ke* they were stoned. In the mob at each point was a sense of unity that combined solidarity around concern for the bridge with *Québécois* nationalist expressions. At various points they shouted: "*Qué-bec, Qué-bec*." All of these exemplify the various stereotypes and characteristics of scapegoating.

The characteristics of scapegoats are that they are different, powerful, vulnerable, and illegitimate. All of the scapegoats listed above were subject to acts of violence.

In addition, the police were available as scapegoats because they were close at hand. They challenged the distinctions of being *Québécois* and at the same time different because of their uniforms. The mob viewed them as illegitimate because they were preventing the mob action, protecting the Mohawks, and thwarting the plan to block the St. Lawrence Seaway. The mob thought of itself as different from the "criminal" Mohawks; for the police to intervene against them made the police "criminal" like the Mohawks, who were supposed to be different. The police were vulnerable because of their smaller numbers, yet they had sufficient power to make them worthy scapegoats.

The woman who wore a Canadian flag was, likewise, a stereotypic scapegoat. Her symbol was powerful—it was Canada, which had just rejected Québec through the failure of the Meech Lake Accord. She was obviously vulnerable. Even the police saw intuitively that she was a natural scapegoat and warned her to leave; they in effect blamed her for the problem. Her *Canadian* identification clearly made her illegitimate; the fact that she was a neighbour and was "like them" in one way but different in another way challenged distinctions. The Mohawks in the cars likewise bore the marks of the scapegoat. They were from the hated group, making them illegitimate. The fact that they were Mohawks made them powerful symbols. Being in cars at close range made them vulnerable. At the same time, driving in cars and looking much like the mob called into question the sense of difference; one of the elderly people hurt by a rock was actually French Canadian.

While much of the violence projected by the mobs onto the scapegoats was immediately inspired by frustration over the bridge, there was clearly more to it than that. Meech Lake had been defeated by Elijah Harper, a First Nations person. First Nations people were blockading the bridge. Canada had rejected Québec. Québec had to take control of its own destiny and it now appeared that Québec could not even control of its own bridge. The incident symbolized something bigger.

The Mohawks of *Kahnawà:ke* were similarly motivated through the whole crisis. One can perceive signs of mimetic desire and scapegoating on their part. What helped to fuel their passion to take the bridge was the fact that so much of their meagre land had been confiscated for the sake of Euro-Canadians. Most prominent among the examples was shoreline land taken for the St. Lawrence Seaway. It did not end there. The land to build the Mercier Bridge in the first place had been taken from them and the bridge went right through their reserve. They had been so permanently inconvenienced by control of their land for the benefit of the people on the south shore that it did not seem so consequential to them that people on the south shore were inconvenienced for a few months. Shutting down the bridge was a scapegoat action for the Mohawks. At first there was disagreement but eventually the whole community united around the occupation of the bridge and the forces wanting the bridge to be opened became the scapegoats. What generated the passion was a remembrance of past injustices. The Pines symbolized another land grab by Euro-Canadian governments that they were determined to stop.

Kanien'kehà:ka (Mohawks) and Québécois

During the three decades before the crisis, ethnonationalism increased among the *Québécois* and the Mohawks. This manifested itself in a racial awareness and a drive for political control of their own territory and institutions. First, in both cases, there was a sense of racial distinctiveness. The *Québécois* had a concept of *pure laine,* referring to those who were fully *Québécois* in an ethnocultural sense, and the Mohawks paid keen attention to defining who was a member of their community, for a time including a criterion of blood quantum. Second, tensions between them occurred against a backdrop in which both Québec and Aboriginal people sought special status within the Canadian constitution. A mimetic rivalry over ethnonational discourse had gone on since the 1960s. Both Québec and the First Nations wanted to be recognized as "founding nations." Both used the language of sovereignty and wanted self-government. Aboriginal leaders gained an increased profile through a series of First Ministers' Conferences in the 1980s where they had a voice. These conferences did not produce the anticipated results for Aboriginal people, and, under the Meech Lake Accord, they were left out of constitutional reform. The Meech Lake Accord, however, had been very promising for Québec; included within it were the five key demands Premier Bourassa had made, including recognition as a distinct society.

The failure of the Meech Lake Accord created a sense of crisis in Québec. Québec felt once again "slapped in the face" and rejected. Scapegoating conditions were perfect. At the beginning of the crisis, there was every reason to make scapegoats of the Mohawks. They were different, yet they called into question the difference of the *Québécois* by arguing that they had the greater claim to sovereignty. They were perceived as powerful enough to arouse strong emotions, having been rivals since they had sided with the English in the 1700s. Now the mystique of heavily armed warriors made them seem more potent. They were illegitimate— defying Québec law, keeping the SQ out of *Kahnawà:ke*. They were Aboriginals, like Elijah Harper who had scuttled the Accord. Given their small numbers, they seemed vulnerable. Furthermore, in *Kanehsatà:ke* they were not respecting the rule of law and were accused of shooting a *Québécois* police officer. They were branded terrorists, and, in *Kahnawa:ke*, they had shut down a major bridge across the St. Lawrence River.

When the SQ invaded the Pines, the rivalry between *Kanehsatà:ke* and Oka rapidly became a rivalry between the Government of Québec and the Mohawks. The death of Corporal Lemay played a scapegoat function, even though many of the classic signs of scapegoating were not present. An actual victim served to polarize the two armed groups and, in the polarization, unify each group and strengthen their resolve. At the time of Lemay's funeral, Mohawks flew their flag at half mast; they wished to honour the life of the one who had fallen. The SQ was united at the funeral.

While there was a common lament over this death, superimposed structures of differentiation and undifferentiation followed. The funeral served to cement in the minds of the SQ and many *Québécois* that the Mohawks were the enemy; they were held responsible for Lemay's death. Mohawks remained more determined than ever to protect their land rights and stand up for their claims to sovereignty. The sense of us versus them—putting people into categories—represented a post-scapegoat differentiation. The violence of differentiation became manifest as they intensified their feelings of the other as Other.

Superimposed on the structure of differentiation was a structure of undifferentiation, as the Mohawks and *Québécois* became doubles of one another in their determination to have their claims to sovereignty recognized. The Mohawks were both double and scapegoat, either oscillating between the two or playing both simultaneously. There were many expressions of mutual hate.

When violence was introduced, the mimetic show of force took on a life of its own as the conflict escalated exponentially. It is interesting that right after the raid of July 11, the nature of the conflict changed. The conflict was no longer just about the Pines; it was about First Nations' right to land everywhere in Canada, as evidenced by statements made by First Nations leaders. But it was also clear in what Québec politicians said, most markedly the mayors from the districts surrounding Oka. They recognized that 85 per cent of Québec was under dispute. The double contagion so soon after the attack was striking.

As soon as the Mercier Bridge was blocked, the circumstances were ripe for the Mohawks to become a collective scapegoat for the more nationalistic Quebeckers. They bore all the marks of the scapegoat. There was a general sense of crisis after the failure of the Meech Lake Accord. This crisis was about difference, the distinctiveness of *Québécois* within Canada. Meech Lake's failure had prompted significant hatred toward Elijah Harper and ill will toward Aboriginal people. More acutely, there was a traffic crisis on the south shore. The mobs of Châteauguay acted vicariously for many of the people of Québec who were angry at both the English and Natives. So powerfully had the failure of Meech galvanized the *Québécois* that traditional rivals Bourassa and Parizeau were united in their resolve to strengthen the nationalist agenda in Québec.

There was a sense that the actions of the Mohawks were illegitimate. They were considered lawbreakers and accused of being terrorists. The sense of illegitimacy was heightened by allegations that many of the warriors were from the United States and that they had criminal records, both turning out to be, for the most part, untrue. They were powerful enough to be good scapegoat medicine to resolve a national crisis. The Mohawks were vulnerable. They were a tiny and different group. The Mohawks were Aboriginal people—First Nations. Furthermore, they were distinguished from other Québec Aboriginal groups by their sense of independence, their preference for the English, and their militancy and tenacity.

Kahnawà:ke was probably the only reserve in Canada into which Euro-Canadian police would not enter. It was easy to believe that they were "lawless savages."

Mohawks threatened the sense of difference by which the *Québécois* distinguished themselves from the rest of Canada. This sense of difference came from being one of two founding nations. That was called into question by Aboriginal people generally and the Mohawks most forcefully. The territorial integrity of the Province of Québec was called into question. The Mohawks were a distinct society with a claim to peoplehood and a right to self-determination.

Throughout the crisis the scapegoat phenomenon intensified. Broadcaster Gilles Proulx used his radio station to whip up fury against the Mohawks. The symbolism of a warrior in battle regalia signing the August 12 agreement with Tom Siddon and presenting mediator Alan Gold with a Warrior Society flag intensified the anger in the *Québécois* population and helped pressure Bourassa to call in the army. The deployment of the army made the situation graver. On August 28, as elderly people, women, and children were evacuated, the demonstrators stoning the cars, showed, at a primal level, what many thought ought to happen through a military assault on the barricades.

First Nations and the Government of Canada

As the crisis evolved, the primary relational system grew to include all of the First Nations of Canada, the Government of Canada, and, ultimately, the entire country. Within days of the July 11 raid, other First Nations in Québec and across Canada joined in acts of support and solidarity. This took place on an individual and official level—chiefs and vice-national provincial chiefs. The acts of solidarity included going to *Kanehsatà:ke* and *Kahnawà:ke* to help; raising money and food, and transporting these to the people behind barricades; making public statements of support; and mimetically setting up barricades on roads and threatening to blow up the infrastructure. These acts of solidarity sent a powerful message to the governments of Québec and Canada that if there were an all-out attack involving bloodshed the consequences would be enormous.

The federal government was at first very detached from the situation. It left all negotiations and strategizing to the Government of Québec. When it got involved, it showed a determination to close in on the Mohawks until they surrendered. Undoubtedly, the prime minister and many cabinet members were still reeling over the defeat of the Meech Lake Accord. When, in August, the government attention shifted from Québec to Ottawa, attitudes were very confrontational.

The people of Canada were horrified to have a military operation taking place on their soil. Many were unaware of what Aboriginal people had endured in Canada and the key First Nations spokespersons who appeared on the nightly news helped raise consciousness of this issue. This became evident in the Spicer Commission set up in January 1991; a trend was that Canadians were convinced that Aboriginal justice issues needed to be addressed.

Within this frame of reference, it is clear that there was mutual scapegoating and that the two sides became mimetic doubles of one another. We look first at ways the government played a scapegoat for the First Nations and, second, the way in which Aboriginal people were the scapegoats of the government.

Key to a scapegoat effect is the sense of all united against one. In this case, all (or at least most) First Nations united in their opposition to the government action against *Kanehsatà:ke*. This was largely due to their recognition that the structure of government action in the case of *Kanehsatà:ke* was, in many ways, quite similar to historical and current actions taken against First Nations generally. The structural components of the action included land appropriation, breaches of treaty, using the law and legal systems to legitimize the taking of land, and exercising superior force. The end use of the appropriated land in *Kanehsatà:ke*, as in virtually every other case across the country, was to benefit Euro-Canadians. This structural resonance called for support and suggested that mimetic responses were in order, that is, imitating the resistance of the Mohawks.

The solidarity came from a kinship among the original inhabitants of North America. This feeling of kinship among peoples who often experience considerable internal conflict exemplified a scapegoat effect. The common enemy was the combined forces of the governments of Québec and Canada as represented by the SQ and the army. On July 17, at a Parliament Hill march, pro-Aboriginal speaker after speaker condemned Indian Affairs Minister Tom Siddon and Prime Minister Brian Mulroney for not intervening. A few days later, at a gathering of chiefs, a number of them blamed Québec Premier Bourassa and Mulroney's Conservative government with its "separatist buddies" for the crisis (note: Prime Minister Mulroney had recruited a number of Québec nationalists, including Lucien Bouchard, to be part of his government). Georges Erasmus stated that Canada's political leaders were the clearly defined enemy. Many First Nations threatened violence if the Mohawks were attacked.

The Government of Canada bore many of the marks of a scapegoat. From the perspective of the First Nations, the government was powerful, yet vulnerable (to blowing up or blocking infrastructure) and totally illegitimate. As a scapegoat, the government was potent medicine for unifying the First Nations. This unity occurred up the nesting chain—from Mohawks of *Kanehsatà:ke* and *Kahnawà:ke* to the wider Mohawk community to the Iroquois Confederacy and Québec Indians to First Peoples across Canada to American Aboriginal people. There was a paradox of difference from the perspective of the Aboriginal people. On the one hand they were considered citizens of Canada; this was their government that ran the Department of Indian Affairs and provided many social benefits. On the other hand, this was the government of the newcomers, the ones who had come and imposed their will on the Aboriginal people. In the end, the paradox became a heightened sense of alienation and differentiation from the Euro-Canadian–dominated government. Some of the rhetoric of Aboriginal people stated that their struggle was with the Government of Canada, not the people.

On the other side of the ledger, the Mohawks became the scapegoats for the government of Canada following the demise of the Meech Lake Accord. In this context, there was a crisis within the government. The Accord, which was to have brought about national reconciliation, had blown up due to the stand taken by an Aboriginal member of the Manitoba legislature. Rather than reconciliation, the rift between Québec and the rest of Canada was greater than before and the Aboriginal agenda had been a key factor. The actions of the Mohawks were cast as being illegal, even terrorist, by both the prime minister and by the deputy minister of Indian Affairs; they were illegitimate. The Mohawks and Aboriginal people were powerful in that they could attack the infrastructure of Canada. They were clearly different from other Canadians in the demands they were making and the world view they espoused. Yet, there was a paradox in that they were also Canadian; in a sense, more Canadian than anyone else because of their historical ties to the land. And they were vulnerable to military force.

There was a sense that somehow the challenge to the authority of the government had to be suppressed. For a long time the minister of Indian Affairs refused to negotiate with the Mohawks. The refusal to negotiate with people with arms and the characterization of the Mohawks as criminals played a role in the scapegoat process. Yet the Aboriginal people were not entirely vulnerable; hence, the scapegoat process did not work out as it might have. What made them less vulnerable was the concern expressed by the international community, the threat to infrastructure posed by Aboriginal people across the country, media coverage, and growing public support of Aboriginal people. Even though there is evidence that the structure of scapegoating was present, it did not result in the kind of unity that might have occurred had there been an attack on "terrorist" Mohawks.

Reflecting on what happened, York and Pindera observed that Brian Mulroney's application of the Mohawk right to self-determination was inconsistent with standards he had applied to other similar situations in other countries:

> While denying the Mohawks the right to self-determination, Mulroney has accepted the moral authority of other populations to chart their own destiny. For example, he has argued that the Baltic republics in the Soviet Union have the right to self-determination, and he has never questioned Quebec's right to choose its own future. Constitutional experts have called attention to the strong parallels between the sovereignty claims of Quebec and those of the Iroquois. It is ironic that Quebec should be free to determine its own destiny, while Quebec's aboriginal people—with a longer history of sovereignty—should be denied that same freedom.[2]

This observation corroborates the idea that the Mohawks were a scapegoat for the federal government in general and the prime minister in particular. The government had just made an offer of an Aboriginal royal commission and a promise of a faster track on land claims to Elijah Harper in June as a trade-off for his support of the Meech Lake Accord.

What upped the ante for the government was the loss of face Canada suffered internationally. Canada, the country that spoke up for human rights and sent peacekeepers to hot spots around the world, was shown to have the potential for both human rights abuses and lethal conflict. The government desperately wanted the situation settled. They realized that if the Mohawks were killed, there would be massive uprisings by First Nations people across the country. They spent significant amounts of money to discredit the Mohawks.

In the final analysis, this scapegoating failed because the Mohawks were shown to have a legitimate historical grievance and the background of those involved was significantly less "criminal" than had been presented. In the end, few criminal charges stuck. After the crisis, the Canadian public had general sympathy for Aboriginal people and politicians were held in ill-repute.

Warriors and the Army

As soon as the Canadian Forces moved in, structures between the Government of Canada and the First Nations were established that were similar to those between the *Québécois* and the Mohawks. Again, the prime minister accused the Mohawks of illegal action, casting them as criminals.

Mimetic rivalry took different forms in each crisis location. In *Kahnawà:ke*, there was mutual respect between warriors and soldiers. Some of the warriors had seen combat experience in Viet Nam; others were veterans of the Canadian army. They knew military protocol and culture and the Canadian Army respected them as peers. This sense of doubling was expressed in the joint dismantling of the barriers: allowing both sides to be actors made it possible for both to save face. At Oka/ *Kanehsatà:ke* the mutual mimesis took a different form. The two sides engaged in harassment, threats, cat-calls, and psychological warfare; the Canadian Army shone spotlights on the Mohawks who used mirrors to direct the light back at the soldiers.

Mimetic rivalry and doubling were shown in the famous staredown between a warrior and a soldier. Patrick Cloutier and Brad Larocque became representatives of their respective groups. Both were both roughly the same age. Both stood out as mavericks in their communities of origin. Both of them were totally committed to their groups. Both had a natural personal tendency to deal with issues peacefully. During the staredown they both held their ground unflinchingly. The one difference in their actions was that Larocque was verbal whereas Cloutier just stared ahead impassively. As they each held their ground, their faces inches apart, the tension rose, replicating a mimetic crisis. What broke the tension was the announcement that pizza had arrived.

Mimetic doubling took place on a wider scale when tensions escalated to the breaking point as the army tightened its noose around the Treatment Centre. Mohawk women and Mad Jap moved around warriors calming them down. On the army side, Major Tremblay yelled, *"Restez calme!"* Both sides had individuals who were tempted to shoot and others who realized that the conflict would become more serious if there was gunfire, which would have been returned with interest. Mimetic violence would have claimed many casualties and inflicted deeper emotional wounds.

The beating of Randy Horne showed scapegoat action. The beating was severe enough to question whether he would live. As in the cases where the SQ beat Jacobs, Nicholas, and Cross, the victim bore the marks of a scapegoat.

When the army arrived at *Kahnawà:ke* to check Tekawitha Island for weapons on September 18, the Mohawk mob attacked the soldiers as scapegoats. The army was powerful, yet vulnerable because of smaller numbers; it was clearly illegitimate in the eyes of the Mohawks. At the end, teenager Kelly Ann Meloche thanked the army for the sense of unity they had inspired. Her observation indicates that the mob action played a unifying role as scapegoating invariably does.

French and English

Near the end of the crisis, the *Québécois* became the scapegoats for the rest of Canada. Articles and columns appeared in the English press comparing Québec to Mississippi of the '60s. The allegations of racism in Québec and the groundswell of support for First Nations people across the country helped to isolate Québec even more from the rest of Canada. Anger and resentment felt toward Québec hardened many Canadians against any peaceful constitutional concessions.

This scapegoating stands at the end of a long history of rivalry between French and English in Canada—a rivalry thrown into relief through the prism of Oka/*Kanehsatà:ke*. The rivalry between French and English was for control of the land and institutions of Québec, both a part of Canada and the province of Québec. Power in the hands of the Government of Québec meant that French *Québécois* had greater control over their own territory and institutions. Powers exercised by the federal government could be controlled by the English majority. Hence, the rivalry over relative powers of the federal and provincial governments was a rivalry between French and English hegemony in the province.

The rivalry also translated into who controlled the different levels of government. The demise of the Meech Lake Accord brought the rivalry to a new intensity. The Mohawks were scapegoated by each level of government. For the two governments involved, the crisis brought collaboration: the RCMP worked with the SQ and the decision to bring in the military was a joint decision by both levels of government.

The reasons the scapegoating failed were, first, that the support of the rest of the First Nations made the Mohawks not totally *vulnerable*. Second, the growing recognition that land claims had an historical basis called into question allegations that the First Nations actions were *illegitimate*. Their position was vindicated further when the federal government bought their land. In their *difference* as First Nations and as an Aboriginal group vociferously claiming sovereignty, the Mohawks were not different enough to unite *Québécois* and other Canadians. In any case, the Mohawks as scapegoats failed to unite Canada, even though they served to unite Quebeckers as a group and, to an extent, certain elements of other parts of Canada who tended to look disparagingly upon Aboriginal peoples.

The intensity of the crisis occasioned by the failure of Meech and the Oka/*Kanehsatà:ke* stand-off only temporarily distracted the historical rivalry—the crisis needed a scapegoat victim powerful enough to provide a unifying catharsis. Much of the energy within Québec was driven into a fierce ethnonationalism that eventually saw the *Parti Québécois* return to power and the formation of the *Bloc*

Québécois to bring an unambiguous pro-Québec voice into the House of Commons.

Just as the Oka/*Kanehsatà:ke* crisis became a pretext for some Canadians to make Québec a scapegoat for the problems facing Canadians, the rest of Canada became the scapegoat for the *Québécois*. It was the English who thwarted their plans. As the huge mimetic rivalry and scapegoat structures moved back into position after the 1990 crisis, the Mohawks with their claims and pains were forgotten.

Throughout the crisis, there were rivalries *within* the protagonist groups. These rivalries were affected by, and in turn had an effect on, the conflict as a whole. In many cases, these were hidden from members of other groups and from the public at large. The major protagonist group was the *Kanehsata'kehró:non*, since they were literally at the centre of the crisis and interacted directly with representatives of the other key groups. Other key groups included the Municipality of Oka, the Mohawks, the First Nations, the South Shore Residents, and the Province of Québec.

As we enframe each of these relational systems and note the intragroup dynamics, we note kaleidoscopic changes in structure; changes that occur more frequently because of the crisis. The intensity magnifies the various phenomena. With the complexity of identity bases, communities do not act unanimously, as is the case in classic scapegoating. At one point it was a subidentity group that acted unanimously—the case with the Longhouse traditionalists who initially led the occupation of the Pines. At other times, the logical enframing of a community changed so that a new group emerged that acted with unanimity—the case when the pro-golfing and pro-development groups joined surrounding mayors supporting the mayor and council of Oka.

Sometimes a person who is a part of one identity group, involved in one side of a conflict, goes through a personal transformation resulting in a feeling of solidarity with another group. An example is the south shore *Québécoise* who, after seeing a Mohawk woman denied food, joined with those who were trying to get food to *Kahnawà:ke*. At the beginning, her identity was with her fellow *Québécois(es)*, the frustrated commuters; later, perhaps because of her identity as a woman, it shifted to the food providers who showed solidarity with the Mohawks. This shows the constant changes in intragroup rivalries and scapegoating of groups in terms of their relevant subgroups and group identities.

In terms of the overall schema, we will now look at intragroup dynamics as giving definition to the relational systems within which mimetic phenomena are evident.

Kanehsata'kehró:non

Among the people of *Kanehsatà:ke* there were a series of rivalries before and during the crisis. These involved leadership, cliques, clans, and action groups.

Just before the occupation of the Pines there was a rivalry between Clarence Simon and George Martin. Simon had been Grand Chief until January 1990 when clan mothers replaced him with Martin. Each had their own following within the community, resulting in a rivalry over the basic political organization. In addition, there were rivalries over leadership and political organization. The system of having clan mothers appoint the chief and band council combined the traditional role of clan mothers in selecting leaders with a set of powers defined by the Indian Act. The Longhouse wanted to ignore the Indian Act altogether, but the League for Democracy and the Group for Change argued for a return to band council elections.[3]

In early July, when Public Security Minister Sam Elkas threatened government action against those barricading in the Pines, the debate between those who wanted to comply and those who wanted to stay was intense. This revealed a rivalry within the Longhouse group of the *Kanehsata'kehró:non* over primary values and leadership: Was it more important to hold on to the land at all costs? or, was it more important to settle things non-violently and avoid loss of life at all cost? In the end, Allen Gabriel and his friends left the Pines. Ellen Gabriel and John Cree then took on key leadership roles.

Gender-based conflict was partly based on a desire to recover the traditional leadership role of Mohawk women as guardians of the land. We note that on the morning of July 11, the women were at the front lines, resolute in their determination to stay in the Pines. After the police arrived, some of the men urged them to leave but they remained part of the occupation throughout the crisis. They had a voice both in the negotiations and in interpreting the crisis to the outside world.

On August 4, another factious conflict was precipitated by the arrival of Ovide Mercredi of the Assembly of First Nations. Longhouse people thought the AFN was made up of government agents, since it recognized the Indian Act. There was also an accusation of cliquishness since the negotiating team appeared to favour particular clans. That changed at one point when Bourassa's 48-hour ultimatum united Mohawks against the government. Once again, it became a case of violence of undifferentiation as representatives of the different factions became rivals; they were brought together by a scapegoat effect with Bourassa and the government as the differentiated Other.

Another intragroup rivalry in the *Kanehsatà:ke* camp involved the lawyers who desired to be the primary advisers to the *Kanehsata'kehró:non*: Cohen and Kunstler were high profile lawyers from the United States. In the end Cohen's advice was taken more seriously and Kunstler left.

Finally, there was a rivalry between Ron Cross (Lasagna) and cohorts against Ronnie Bonspille and Francis and Cory Jacobs. Cross was convinced that Bonspille and Jacobs had told the police about his identity. This made them illegitimate to Cross and company, who beat Francis and Cory Jacobs as Ronny Bonspille got away. They also smashed Bonspille's ambulance; this gratuitous violence to get at Bonspille was further evidence of a scapegoat effect. In addition to being illegitimate, the Bonspille group was powerful enough so that any information passed to the police would be destructive, yet they were vulnerable. As Mohawks they brought out the paradox of difference by allegedly working with the police. The scapegoating fury did not abate immediately. Cross went to the community centre where he yelled and pounded his baseball bat. Later, he and his collaborators were confined and almost banished, made scapegoats by their own action.

The Municipality of Oka

Among the residents of Oka there were two clear camps. On one side was the mayor, the council, and the pro-golf faction. These were opposed by many citizens who were against the golf course expansion. The second group was motivated by both a concern for the environment and a desire for peace with Mohawks. In some of the public meetings, strong feelings on both sides were expressed. Each faction circulated a petition, one supporting and one opposing the mayor.

Mohawks

The Mohawks had a number of key internal rivalries. One of the most significant related to interpretations of the Law of Peace. One group, including elders Tom Porter and Jake Swamp, interpreted the Law of Peace as emphasizing a peaceful approach to life. The other perspective, represented by Louis Hall, called for violence to strengthen the Mohawk presence. (Hall had the Jewish people and Israel as mimetic models for his perspective.) Hall became the inspiration for the Warrior Societies. This foundational rivalry had an impact on internal conflicts in Akwesasne, *Kahnawà:ke*, and *Kanehsatà:ke*. In Akwesasne, lines split between pro- and anti-gambling factions, with the Warrior Society supporting the gambling effort. In Akwesasne and *Kahnawà:ke*, the issue of cigarette smuggling was significant and divisions were along the same lines. In the *Kanehsatà:ke* crisis, there was conflict over strategy and tactics. In all of these instances, one object of mimetic desire was to be the authoritative interpreter of the Great Law, another was to have control over what was happening.

As the crisis escalated, the various factions of *Kanehsatà:ke*, *Kahnawà:ke*, and Akwesasne united in a way they had not for a long time. The dominant structure was the unity of a common threat, although various rivalries did emerge from time to time. For example, when the warriors of *Kahnawà:ke* reached an agreement with the military and began dismantling the barricades on the Mercier Bridge, the people at the Treatment Centre at *Kanehsatà:ke* felt betrayed. At other times, people of *Kanehsatà:ke* thought there was too much outside influence from the people of *Kahnawà:ke* and Akwesasne.

The First Nations

A number of mimetic phenomena were evident among the First Nations. The Aboriginal victory in defeating the Meech Lake Accord through the efforts of Elijah Harper increased the First Nations' confidence to take action.[4] The Mohawk Warriors became, in Girard's terms, external models for other Aboriginal people, especially the youth. Across the country, roads were barricaded following the example of Mercier Bridge. Cree leaders of Northern Québec have always maintained that they do not support violence, but they have also warned that they cannot control the younger, militant band members who are strongly opposed to the hydro project. These younger Crees were keeping a close watch on the tactics of the Mohawk warriors in the summer of 1990. "There is no doubt that what the warriors have done will inspire the youth to possibly resort to violence," said Grand Chief Matthew Coon Come,[5] a point reinforced by Cree Chief Bill Diamond. What becomes clear is that the Mohawk warriors became external mimetic Models for Aboriginal youth across the country.

South Shore Residents

On the south shore, there were numerous examples of scapegoat action taken by *Québécois(es)* against other *Québécois(es)*. There obviously was a sense of crisis in each situation. The various cases show other characteristics of the scapegoat. First, Jocelyne Desrosiers, who opened her store to Mohawk business, was told by vigilantes that there might be an "accident" if she didn't close her store. She introduced the paradox of difference in that she was both *Québécoise* and in solidarity with the Mohawks. As a store owner she was significantly visible (powerful) and very vulnerable.

When *Solidarité Châteauguay* tried to block the St. Lawrence Seaway, in mimesis of the Mohawks who had blocked Mercier Bridge, the police arrested some of their leaders. A mob of several thousand turned on the police smashing a cruiser (as the Mohawks had done); waving baseball bats and tire-irons; and throwing eggs, bricks, and rocks at the police as in a stoning. The police locked themselves in the detachment, thwarting the scapegoat action. At that time the crowd also turned on journalists in classic scapegoat style, forcing one woman to flee for her own safety. The police showed a paradox of difference by being both *Québécois* and a force against the mob action. Their smaller numbers made them vulnerable even though individually they were powerful.

On July 14, four anglophones carrying a Canadian flag were surrounded by a crowd and needed police help to escape. The crowd tried to burn a Canadian flag. The next day, a woman with a Canadian flag on her sweatshirt was attacked by two women. These examples introduced the paradox of difference: neighbours were the same in that they were neighbours, yet different as they were Canadian, as opposed to Québec, nationalists. Their symbols were powerful in the context since they went against the mainstream, standing for the Canada that was perceived to have rejected Québec. As a minority in the crowd, they were vulnerable.

Throughout, the mob action united a number of Euro-Canadian groups. Besides the angry commuters, fringe groups associated with white supremacist groups got involved.

The Government of Québec

Within the Québec government there was a rivalry over the approach to take in dealing with the crisis. Throughout, John Ciaccia wished to be conciliatory. Public Security Minister Sam Elkas threatened that the barricades must be dismantled or the government would take action. At various points, there was tension between

Ciaccia and more hawkish cabinet ministers. In mid-July, as Ciaccia negotiated an agreement that would have withdrawn many police, cabinet refused to back the agreement; hawks referred to the need to "break eggs to make an omelette" (quoting Lenin). The police ended up digging in more deeply. On the issue of food deprivation, there was a similar rivalry. On July 21, Claude Ryan said that this policy was government policy but Ciaccia pointed out that there never was a question of depriving them of food. Finally, on September 16, the government refused to accept an agreement that Ciaccia had negotiated.

When the question of military intervention was raised in the Québec cabinet in early August, there were three positions. Ciaccia was against military action, the hawks wanted a military solution, and Bourassa and Ryan were cautious. It took a military officer to convince the cabinet to avoid a military assault. In the end the military was called in but was not ordered to attack Mohawk positions. Later in August, Ciaccia tried to negotiate an end to the crisis but he had only one supporter in the cabinet committee. It is interesting to note that Ciaccia, the conciliator, was himself a Canadian of Italian background. Hence, his own identity would not have had as much at stake as that of the *pure laine Québécois* whose national honour was at stake and for whom there was an ethnonational mimetic rivalry with the *Onkwehón:we*.

Within the protagonist groups there were examples of the whole range of mimetic and scapegoat phenomena. Various cases showed a number of the key principles unearthed by Girard.

An Interpretative Narrative of the Crisis

I will now tell the story of the Oka/*Kanehsatà:ke* crisis of 1990 using the interpretative categories in the various forms of mimetic structures of violence. The story begins with 1721 with the arrival of the Sulpicians to *Kanehsatà:ke* and concludes with the Mohawks leaving the Treatment Centre in September 1990 and the immediate aftermath. Of necessity, the narration of the early periods will be telescoped; however, an overview of the structural developments before 1989 establishes the context—mimetic structures of violence are always rooted in previous structures.

The Colonial Period: 1721 to 1959

The arrival of the Sulpicians in 1721 to land granted by the king of France marked the beginning of the objectification of the *Kanehsata'kehró:non*. In the colonial rivalries of North America the British and French were rivals in a relational system. Among the French, the Jesuits and Sulpicians were rivals for hegemony over the religious affiliations of the First Nations.

After the British conquered New France, the *Kanehsata'kehró:non* and the land to which they belonged were the objects of mimetic desire for the Sulpicians and the British. A bigger prize for the British, after the American Revolution, was retention of "British" North America, which at that time was largely French. The

Sulpicians swore allegiance to the British, aiding the British in their rivalry with the United States and in the French 1830s rebellion. They kept *Kanehsatà:ke*. Thereafter, there was common cause between the English and the Sulpicians, as though they were united, with the *Kanehsata'kehró:non* as perpetual scapegoats. The structure of a violence of differentiation was entrenched with the Privy Council ruling of 1912 reaffirming the right of the Sulpicians to the land.

That this structure was still intact in 1959 is shown by the fact that despite the protests of the Mohawks, nothing was done to stop building the original golf course.

Regaining a Capacity to Act: 1959 to 1989

As long as they were acted upon, Aboriginal people were sufficiently removed from the dominant groups in society that no true mimetic rivalry was possible between First Nations and Euro-Canadians. Between 1959 and 1989 Aboriginal people developed a voice. Mimetically, they were inspired by the events of Wounded Knee in the United States. It was also a time when the language of self-determination and liberation from colonialism was in the air. Many new countries were formed from the ashes of the British Empire. Strong Aboriginal leaders, with no hesitancy in standing up to the "First Ministers" of Canada, began to emerge. The Indian Brotherhood became the Assembly of First Nations. Other Aboriginal peoples developed national organizations with leaders who could represent them at meetings of prime minister and premiers. What had been external mediation—having a distant mimetic model—now became internal mediation—having a model who could be a rival. Aboriginal people began to develop rivalries with dominant societies over land and jurisdiction.

Meanwhile, new dynamics were emerging in the Canadian political relational system. Before this time, all but the French elite were so spiritually distant (in Girard's phrase) from English Canada that they could not see themselves as political or economic rivals. That changed with the 1960s Quiet Revolution in which *Québécois* began to frame the relationship with Canada as colonial. They wanted full equality as a people, which, for many of them, meant sovereignty. A mimetic crisis over difference was developing. When Canada was formed, Québec was one of two founding peoples. Canada was meant to be a French-English partnership. Through language laws outside of Québec and waves of English-speaking immigrants, the relative power of English Canada had increased considerably. Some voices within Canada, particularly in the West, began to frame the country as consisting of ten provinces, rather than two founding peoples. The French fought for, and got, some concessions, but sovereignty was the goal. The defeat of the 1980 referendum was a setback, but many *Québécois* were determined to get what the English had—control over their own country.

There was a significant rivalry between Québec and the rest of Canada. The rivalry was over difference—Québec wanted to be recognized as a "distinct society." Meanwhile the *Québécois* were losing difference—evident in changes such as the shift to becoming secular entrepreneurs (like the English). Although significant differences in orientation between Québec and the rest of Canada remain, traditional marks of differentiation, such as Québec being Roman Catholic and less entrepreneurial, are being eroded.

In the relational system of Aboriginal people and Quebeckers there was a rivalry over who had the stronger claims to self-determination. Québec argued that they had a viable political territory—Québec—and that, as a nation, they could determine for themselves to become a sovereign country. Premiers of Québec were welcomed as heads of state in Paris. Mohawks argued that they had never given up their sovereignty, and asserted it by using passports issued in Onondaga by the Iroquois Confederacy and seeking recognition in Europe.

The Decision to Build a Golf Course

The most significant relational system for the *Kanehsata'keró:non* in 1989 included the municipality of Oka. The decision to build a golf course and develop housing in the Pines made the Pines an object of mimetic desire, as previously discussed. The establishment of a Longhouse group at *Kanehsatà:ke* meant that Mohawks were rediscovering their language and ties to the land. Recovery of their sense of identity switched the framing of the satisfiers for their identity needs. From being overtaken by a victim mentality they developed a sense of being an historical people with pre-contact ties to the land, and the land had become a non-negotiable satisfier of identity needs. As it became more significant to them, the municipality of Oka became more determined to go ahead with plans to build the golf course. The decision to build the golf course set in motion a new relational trajectory that eventually led to the crisis.

The Decision to Occupy the Pines

The decision by three Mohawks to occupy the Pines likewise set in motion developments that would lead to the crisis. Had there been no occupation there would have been no crisis. The decision to stand up to the hegemonic structures of Canadian and Québec government, law, and police was mimetically inspired by other Mohawk actions at *Kahnawà:ke* and Akwesasne. The decision to defend the Pines physically was later mimed by the Oka municipality through the SQ.

The Defeat of the Meech Lake Accord

When the Meech Lake Accord failed, there was a crisis of difference within Québec. For example, the idea of special recognition as a distinct society prompted other provinces—Newfoundland and British Columbia—to mimetically assert that they were also distinct. In fact, one of the arguments against the Meech Lake Accord was that Québec was not the only distinct province. The pressures from Western Canada for Senate reform—advocating that every province elect the same number of senators—likewise tore at Québec's sense of difference.

Within the relational system of Canada there was a sense of crisis at the defeat of the Meech Lake Accord. Quebeckers became united in their hurt, anger, and determination to take control of their own destiny. The government of Brian

Mulroney was devastated; Mulroney had staked his place in history on a national reconciliation brought about by the Meech Lake Accord. The sense of crisis made Canada ripe for the scapegoat mechanism.

The SQ Attack

The SQ attack on July 11, 1990, caused an almost instantaneous change in relational structures in Canada. The media focus shifted from post-mortems on the demise of the Meech Lake Accord to what became known as the Oka crisis. With the closing of Mercier Bridge, the Mohawks became scapegoats for many Quebeckers. Any anger and frustration that they had toward Canada, which was invulnerable, they could take out on Mohawks who were much more vulnerable. In particular, Ron Cross, a.k.a. Lasagna, became the warrior whom they loved to hate. Had many Quebeckers had their way, the army would have used force to bring the Mohawks to their knees.

The Escalation of Violence

As support for the Mohawks by Aboriginal people built up, the crisis quickly took on national proportions. As never before, the Aboriginal people had recovered a capacity to act and to act together in solidarity. For them, Bourassa, Mulroney, Siddon, the SQ, and the local politicians supporting the anti-Mohawk action played a scapegoat role. There was a nearly unanimous feeling among Aboriginal people that this group, who together controlled the forces oppressing the Mohawks, were *illegitimate*, *powerful*, and *different* and their interests, at least, were *vulnerable*.

Within the relational systems of Mohawks versus the SQ, the people of *Kahnawà:ke* versus Châteauguay, and the *Kanehsata'kehró:non* versus Oka, violence and tensions were increasing. Structures of mimetic doubling multiplied as Mohawk warriors and the SQ—Québec "warriors"—squared off against one another. The burning of effigies in Châteauguay and the mob action against various individual scapegoats intensified the sense of urgency.

The Deployment of the Canadian Forces

With the deployment of the Canadian Forces, the Mohawks became the scapegoats of the Government of Canada. Enormous resources were used to surround, control, and harass the *Kanehsata'kehró:non*. The rhetoric of the prime minister and the deputy minister of Indian Affairs, referring to the warriors as terrorists, was meant to cast the Mohawk resistance as totally *illegitimate*. Ultimately, the scapegoating structures turned into failed scapegoating since the cause of the Mohawks gained legitimacy through public opinion, international support and the purchase of the land for them by the federal government.

The End of the Crisis

As the people holed up in the Treatment Centre left, there was again a change of structure. In large measure, the Mohawks were vindicated for the stand they took. Canadian consciousness concerning the injustice perpetrated against the Aboriginal people had been raised, and there was widespread support for initiatives that would contribute to a better sense of justice for Aboriginal people. Insofar as there was scapegoat action against them by the government during the crisis, Canadians held a positive image of Aboriginal people after the crisis.

Attitudes of many English Canadians turned against Québec in a scapegoating backlash after the crisis. Before the crisis, many English Canadians thought in terms of keeping Québec in Canada at all costs, but now many wondered aloud if Québec wasn't the cause of many of Canada's problems. A vindictive spirit was kept alive for some time. Some articles in the Canadian press have made Québec out to be more racist than other parts of Canada, thus adding to the scapegoat echo.

By distracting Canada in a powerful way from the crisis caused by the defeat of Meech Lake and uniting Canadians in a common preoccupation with the crisis and the questions of Canadian identity that it raised, the crisis played a scapegoat function.

Holding Back the Violence

The description of the crisis in Chapter 10 and its mimetic/scapegoat interpretation in the previous sections highlight the near tragic results. The conflict did, indeed, shake Canada to its core. Examining the story closely reveals that there were many redemptive elements—many mimetic structures that seemed to hold the beast of violence at bay. First, there was the peace camp set up at Oka, meant to be a non-violent support effort for the Mohawks. Thousands came from across North America to offer a positive, non-violent show of support.

Second, during the military occupation, no one was shot. Near the end of the crisis, when feelings were running deep and the atmosphere was tense, the Mohawks performed a spiritual ceremony to give them protection from potential danger. The Warriors were told by the spiritual leaders that as soon as one shot was fired, the positive protective medicine would be neutralized. They never fired a shot. Years later, a Canadian soldier, reflecting on the fact that not one shot was fired by the military, attributed this in part to the fact that Canadians, through their peacekeeping training and experience, have learned that their role does not necessarily mean shooting and killing. They have become accustomed to playing this non-combative role. It may have made a difference when the impulse to fire a shot was very overwhelming.

These observations do not minimize the depth of the conflict or the severity of the emotional scars still carried by participants. They are not meant to gloss over the very violent forms of harassment directed at the Mohawks collectively and the beating of individuals. They do point to the fact that the crisis was resolved without the kind of bloodbath for which many were prepared. A mimetic imagination of blessing played a role with both groups. Warriors were looking to their spiritual leaders whose imagination was that of peace. Soldiers were imitating patterns of non-violence that they learned as peacekeepers.

Third, there were countless acts of support for those who were suffering. Many risked their own well-being to bring food to the Mohawks. Clergy volunteered as neutral observers. Many on both sides participated in long and arduous negotiations. Helpful bystanders put significant efforts into expediting peaceful initiatives.[6] All in all, within the Oka/*Kanehsatà:ke* crisis, positive mimetic structures ultimately saved Canada from a contagion of bloodletting violence.

Within the crisis of Oka/*Kanehsatà:ke* of 1990, mimetic structures of violence appeared within many relational systems. These structures interacted with one another, intensifying the whole sense of crisis. It appears that most of those directly involved, along with most Canadians, had a sense of awe that they could be swept along in a chain of events that brought "peaceful" Canada to the very edge of massacre, bloodbath, and rampant violence across the country.

The defensive side of mimetic structures of violence were also in evidence. Mimetic structures of entrenchment involve taking a black and white stand on issues, dividing the world into friends and foes, refusing to be self-critical, and doing everything to save face. It becomes clear that within each of the primary stakeholder groups these same structures were evident. As people exhibited these traits they began to imitate the other side. Within these structures, perceptions are skewed—people from different groups interpret the same event very differently. As I spoke with someone who had been there throughout, he confirmed the presence of these structures. In fact, when he talked with people from different sides who had experienced the same event, the descriptions were so different that it would seem that they had been at different events.

Overall, I have been left with a sense of awe at the power of mimetic structures of violence and entrenchment to take over relational systems. From this sense of awe comes the question: What else could there be? The answer includes mimetic structures of blessing, the next concept to be developed.

Part 3

Blessing

Chapter 12

Structures of Blessing

I developed the concept of mimetic structure of blessing after I had analyzed the Oka/*Kanehsatà:ke* Crisis. I had a sense of awe at the force of something bigger than any one individual that compelled people to assume a violent frame of reference and do things that under any other situation they would find repugnant. It was as though an individual hand pushed them along so that at various stages one could almost hear the actors say, "I had no choice but to...." As I have lived with the concept and watched it in action I have seen it happening to me in some personal conflict situations; after certain exchanges with my wife I have felt upset over some of the things I have said, since they were not consistent with the love I professed to have for her. As I reflected on these structures I realized that there must be something more to life than these mimetic structures of violence. As I searched for a word to express a correspondingly positive impulse to the negative force of violence, I remembered an exhaustive study I had made of the word "land" in the book of Deuteronomy and the association of land with berakah or blessing. In that context, land was the source of sustenance, of necessities, and of prosperity. Land as blessing is the context of living life to the fullest—of a sustainable, creative existence to continue through the generations. I have asked many people for a word that would carry the same meaning and until now I have not found a better word for the concepts I want to convey than "blessing."

Since the concept of mimetic structure of violence was the first concept developed, it functioned heuristically to help discover mimetic structures of blessing. This does not mean that violence is the starting point. Matthew Fox makes an eloquent argument that our world view has to give priority to blessing as the orientation of a world into which violence has been introduced.[1] Violence has become a central issue of our time, especially since it takes significantly more blessing to overcome the strong impression that violence makes upon the world. Within Islam, one good deed counts for ten. A bad deed is counted at par. I have heard that it takes ten positive newspaper articles about a person to balance the effect of one negative story. By penetrating the structures of violence to their depth we can find their vulnerability. The deconstruction of mimetic structures of violence in Chapters 1 to 8 provides the building blocks necessary to not only restore mimetic structures of blessing but also create new structures we might not have imagined before. The result of my study of violence for more than a decade has been to discover paths to blessing in a context of ongoing conflicts and the effects of devastating violence.

The following story, used previously, gives one of the clearest illustrations of the difference between mimetic structures of violence and mimetic structures of blessing:

> Sadhapa died and went on to the other world and asked for a tour of the premises. Hell was the first destination where a group of gaunt, starving, bitter, and miserable people stood surrounding tables of food. The problem was that their forks were longer than their arms so they couldn't get food into their mouths. The next destination was Heaven where a group of well-fed happy people stood around similar tables of food. On close examination, Sadhapa noticed that they had the same long forks as the folks in Hell. The only difference was that they were feeding each other.

In this story the physical space was the same. The difference between the two situations was the thought structures and the value systems of the two populations. Hell had a mimetic structure of violence—*mimetic* in that everyone was imitating the others in not helping others; *structure* in that it was an ongoing pattern and they became gaunt and miserable; *violent* in that they were withholding from each other something essential to the well-being of each.

The people in Heaven illustrate mimetic structures of blessing—*mimetic* in that they imitated each other by feeding one another and each got food; *structure* in that it was an ongoing activity guided by a shared will to help one another; *blessing* in that it contributed to the well-being of each.

Deep-rooted conflicts have a capacity to draw individuals and groups into mimetic structures of violence. Reconciliation has the effect of reducing the grip of mimetic structures of violence and setting people on a trajectory that takes them into mimetic structures of blessing within which they feed one another, to use a metaphor from the story. The image I would like to present is a spectrum.

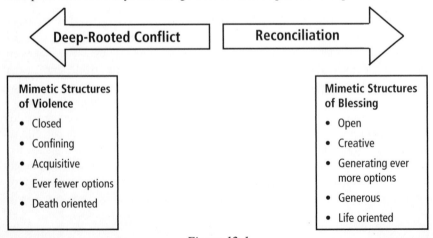

Figure 12-1

On one side, we have mimetic structures of violence. Deep-rooted conflict can push people farther in that direction until the very identities of the people involved are caught up in violence. At the other end of the spectrum are mimetic structures of blessing, in which people are "feeding each other." Reconciliation can be understood as a movement from mimetic structures of violence to mimetic structures of blessing. To understand mimetic structures of blessing we will examine the word "blessing" and then describe the orientation of these structures, explore how they relate to the theoretical notions embodied in mimetic structures of violence, and describe their characteristics.

As I revisited the work that I had done on the Oka/*Kanehsatà:ke* crisis, it became evident to me that there was considerable evidence of blessing in the middle of violence. This shows that mimetic structures of violence and of blessing can be present at the same time. The question is which will become more prominent in a relational system. They are never fixed; there is constant dynamic change as violence increases and decreases and as blessing has its own dynamic. Trends exist, however; a relationship can decline as violence increases and blessing decreases or it can be "on the mend" during a reconciliation process when violence decreases and blessing increases.

Blessing

I chose to designate this positive aspect of mimetic phenomena as blessing, based on the Hebrew word for blessing, *berakah*, which stands as an antithesis to curse. Matthew Fox makes the following observations about blessing:

> As Rabbi Heschel puts it, "Just to be is a blessing; just to live is holy." It is telling that the Hebrew word for blessing, *berakah*, is closely related to the word for create, *bara* (in its noun form, *beriyah*). This suggests that a creation is necessarily a blessing, is wrapped up as a blessing. There is no distrust of creation here. Furthermore, the very word for blessing in Hebrew also means "pool," and with the change of one vowel, to *berakah*, the word means a reservoir where camels kneel as resting place. The images of a pool and a reservoir created by desert people tell us all we need to know about the desirability behind a theology of blessing. The word for covenant, *beriyth,* is also directly related to the words for "create" and for "blessing." A covenant is a blessing agreement, a promise to bless and to return blessing for blessing.[2]

This last phrase, "return blessing for blessing," implies the mimetic character of blessing within a relational system characterized by blessing as opposed to violence.

Like curses, mimetic structures of violence constrict the movement of people, limit life options, and are directed toward death. In contrast, blessings are empowering, lead to creative and ever-expanding options, and are oriented toward life.[3] Blessings are associated with gift, hence with grace (translation of the Greek *charis*, meaning gift) and also love. The root metaphor for *berakah* is the word for knee and the verb to kneel. In the ancient Near East it was customary to kneel down to receive a blessing. Kneeling connoted respect for the Other who was giving the blessing and it also put the recipient in a position of being voluntarily vulnerable. A kneeling position is non-aggressive, a disadvantage in the context of hand to hand combat. The verb *barak* (to bless) has the sense of "empower." Deuteronomy 8:10 gives a picture of eating, being satisfied, and strengthened in the presence of God.

The English word "bless" is derived from an old English word *bledsian*, which means to consecrate with blood. This suggests a connection with blood sacrifice that, according to sacrificial theory of René Girard, is a relatively benign way to accomplish the feeling of reconciliation effected by scapegoating. The pertinent meanings of "bless" in this context are "to wish good to, to feel grateful to, to make happy, prosperous, or fortunate and to praise."[4] Praise corresponds to giving recognition.

Matthew Fox also associates blessing with goodness, relationship, beauty, wisdom, and pleasure. He sees it in the structure of life where living entities are blessed by and are a blessing to their component parts. Likewise, the same entities are life-giving to entities of which they are a part.[5] This fits in with Ken Wilber's concept of holon—an entity that is part of a bigger holon and made up of component holons.

Within mimetic structures of blessing, a dynamic of mutual desire for the well-being of the Other develops, in which both model and imitator become more fully functioning Subjects in the process. The description of this life-opening dynamic in terms of mimetic desire has been developed formally by Rebecca Adams, who was the first to formulate an understanding of mimetic desire as Love.[6] In continuity with Girard, Adams claims that what makes mimetic desire violent and harmful is not the notion of mimesis itself, but the notion of objects and their appropriation; she goes on to clarify that violence really originates even before the scapegoat mechanism—in the conceptual act of turning Subjects, things with unlimited worth and potential, into objects that can be limited and controlled.

Adams also picks up and further develops Girard's observation that the coquette is a Subject who desires herself as an object: men, imitating her desire, begin to desire her as an object of appropriation. However, Adams probes deeper and asks: How did the coquette come to think of herself as an object in the first place? Was it not by adopting or imitating the limiting, objectifying perspective of some other Model prior to this? A person who makes an object of her/himself in order to project that object to others as a Model/Object for their desire is only enacting the logical result of having first been treated as an Object by a previous other Model, who has bequeathed to the coquette an inauthentic, or colonized, Subjectivity.

This same phenomenon can be observed in political terms by looking at the period of colonial expansion when colonial powers treated subjugated peoples, and their lands, as objects to be appropriated. The subjected people internalized this view of themselves and sometimes even aided the colonizers in their own subjugation. In rivalries between colonial countries, lands and their peoples were objects of mimetic desire to be fought over. This process of objectification is one aspect of the way hegemonic structures work. The dominant think of the subjected as objects and the subjected begin to internalize this identity.

In a reverse form of domination structure, leaders can be objectified by the masses they lead; they in turn then think of themselves as objects of desire and try to increase desire of their people for themselves as a way of gaining political power. The examples of Evita Peron or Imelda Marcos, with their adoring crowds and hundreds of shoes, come to mind. Similarly, in a business (as opposed to a political) context, fashion models treat their bodies as an investment—an object to be marketed—to get others to buy. Coquetry, or the desiring of the self to attract the desire of others, thus is actually is a kind of masked colonialism, in which the desire of the colonizer has been so internalized within the Self that it perceives itself in a kind of double-consciousness as an object. This desire for Self as object is then projected outward again as a model for others, as a way to gain power for the self that has been subjugated.[7]

Blessing, in contrast, is oriented toward the development of the Self as a fully functioning, fulfilled Subject, that is, a person with the dignity and inner resources to act directly in the world. Individuals colonized by the desires of others in their capacity for might be called "limited" Subjects. They are persons with a will and point of view, but something limits a full, adequate experience of their personhood. There are many ways a Subject might be limited. As we have just discussed, people might have a split consciousness in which they could partially correctly see (perceive) their oppressive situation in the world, yet have internalized an inability to act upon this knowledge. We might call this kind of person a wounded Subject.

Or someone else might have totally adopted the perspective of another, for instance, and have no trouble acting out the desires of another, even if they were not in the person's best interests. Although this person might not directly experience themselves as split, or alienated from themselves, from a larger perspective we would probably call them an inauthentic, or alienated, Subject. And even though they might seem unified to themselves or others because there is a congruence between their outlook and action, they would probably experience an internal discord and engage in self-defeating behaviours that would point to this alienation in ways of which they are not fully conscious.

Finally, a Subject might be limited, not from any wounding or internalized oppression but simply because they have not yet fully realized some inner capacity to grow, perceive, and act in the world. In this case, limitation should be understood not as a barrier to growth but simply as a yet unrealized potential to grow. No one, no matter how mature or enlightened, has ever become as fully functioning as a Subject as they could possibly be. Therefore, everyone is, in this sense, a limited Subject—what Adams has referred to in her work as a proto-Subject, someone yet unformed who is in potential imitative relation to a model. Taken in this sense, everyone could be thought of throughout life as still like an infant or a child (in a positive way)—ready to perceive and grow into greater maturity. This kind of limitation is open-ended, simply describing as yet unrealized potential. For our purposes here, however, I am interested in unpacking the notion of limitation as a kind of wounding or internalized oppression that actively constricts, leading to violence toward the self and others. I am grateful to Rebecca Adams for telling the story of how she came to the basic insight that led to the concept of Limited Subject.

> The story of how I came to understand René Girard's concept of mimetic desire as Love involves my personal history, as well as a guilty confession. Though I am a person who works on academic problems in philosophy and theology, I am also a *Star Trek* fan. In the Spring of 1994, I was struggling to write a response for a conference dealing with René Girard's work. I had worked with Girard's theory for several years, but I just couldn't solve certain problems I sensed with his concept of mimetic desire. In a recent (Summer 1993) interview I had done with him for the *Journal of Religion and Literature,* Girard had made some remarks about the "goodness" of mimetic desire; this had sparked quite a new line of discussion among those interested in his work. In the interview, he said explicitly that mimetic desire "could" be, or even was "fundamentally," good. Yet almost everything he had said in his work previously seemed to contradict this: he had made a convincing case about the seemingly inevitable relation between mimesis, violence and scapegoating. I was unsatisfied with his answers in the interview, especially his Christian theological claim about the "good mimesis" of the Imitation of Christ being the only alternative to violent mimesis. Just what could this imitation consist of? Did it have to be understood in explicitly, or exclusively, Christian terms? The things he said about mimetic desire just didn't add up logically to me in general. I could see inconsistencies in his statements, but I couldn't figure out exactly where the problem lay.
>
> I was also in a stage in my intellectual and personal journey where these questions really mattered, because I had experienced violence personally. I was stuck, in emotional pain, and I needed answers that really worked. Although I had found help both in therapeutic settings and in spiritual direction, it was critical theory and my knowledge of theology that had radically opened my eyes to the universal nature of my personal problems, by showing how my experience reflected much larger cultural and symbolic systems which reified violence. Feminist and other theory, including the work of René Girard, had helped me powerfully define these problems and come to terms with them. I had especially been helped, as others have been, by Girard's classic analysis of mimetic doubling and

scapegoating: I could see examples in my personal life and all around me. Yet I still could find no adequate positive model for human beings and human relations that worked philosophically. Worse, I was even being told that wanting such a model might be part of the problem; some feminists argue, for example, that all general paradigms are by their very nature violent and oppressive.

In the end, my study of philosophy and academic feminism had actually worsened my feelings of entrapment in victimage patterns. It seemed that although the workings of violence could be described clearly and precisely, a positive alternative to violence could not. This made me feel split between my intellectual and emotional life, and worse, that the world itself might be structured against me, with my need to believe in the reality of love mere wishful thinking. So I was trying to work on a response for the Girard conference, but I was really working on my own internal problems. That's when I "potatoed" out on the couch one evening to watch a rerun of *Star Trek*.

Fiction sometimes knows more than philosophy. As a person whose field is technically literature but who has come to philosophy through the back door, I would be the first to admit this. The great thing about science fiction, especially, is that it can let you imagine things that could never happen. The *Star Trek* episode that day happened to deal with a female alien being called a "metamorph," a woman literally with no mind of her own (*Star Trek*: *The Next Generation*, "The Perfect Mate," Episode 121; first aired May 10, 1992). The story was a thought experiment about a creature entirely determined by mimetic desire, who has no real desire or consciousness of her own, but instead "borrows" these by imitating the desire of the person (in the episode, particularly the males) she is closest to. It seemed unlikely, especially from a feminist perspective, that this premise would lead to anything good for the creature called the metamorph. However, I was hooked into the story line.

The story depicted a situation in which this alien woman was a pawn in a complex political negotiation to be sealed with her arranged marriage. Because her desires would perfectly mirror back the desire of her intended mate, having a metamorph for a mate would be highly desirable, and she was a particularly rare prize in securing an impending political peace alliance. Upon marriage and permanent bonding, her malleable, purely mimetic nature would become fixed upon her mate as the Model, forever perfectly mirroring back his desires, becoming in effect whatever his heart desired at any given time. Unfortunately, she was destined for a petty, uncaring, if not outright corrupt, official.

In the story, the starship *Enterprise* was to deliver the metamorph to her diplomatic destination. As the plot developed, however, an amusing situation unfolded in which this woman wreaked havoc on the ship, because when in proximity to any male of any species, she immediately took on his desires (especially his sexual attraction to her). Since she was in a kind of alien "heat" or highly suggestible state in preparation for her permanent bonding, she began seducing each man according to his own particular tastes and fantasies, which was especially garrulous when encountering a Klingon. Finally, Picard, Captain of the *Enterprise*, agreed to sequester her.

At this point I was beginning to guess where the story might go. Picard comes to visit the metamorph alone to ensure her comfort and in doing so inadvertently becomes the Model whose desire she begins imitating. Picard, as a decent man, recoils at the thought of this gifted, intelligent, articulate being (for him) forever malformed and limited by the petty desires of an unworthy man. Repeated visits by the reluctant but dutiful and concerned Picard have an unintended consequence: she spontaneously bonds with him and therefore permanently imitates or adopts his desire for her. However, because Picard has had no desire to possess her, or even to serve as a Model for her at all, but has only expressed the wish that she could be an independent agent capable of making a free choice and choosing a noble destiny, this is the desire she imitates and, paradoxically, from within the strict confines of her mimetic nature she indeed becomes an independent agent. This was the surprise twist of the story. As I watched, the story demonstrated the possibility that mimetic desire need not entail enslavement, rivalry or violence, but could actually open up into regard for and freedom for another. I had my answer to my theoretical problem with Girardian theory.

This woman's fate was not a happy one, ultimately. The rest of the story is not so important, except to say that because Captain Picard did not actively (but only passively, inadvertently) desire the freedom of the metamorph, she still accepted going through with the arranged marriage, but as, she claimed, a free agent. "From you, I have learned the meaning of duty," she tells the shocked Picard. "I am still empathic. I will still be able to please him." Because Picard's own desires are informed by duty rather than by active, imaginative love for the metamorph's good, they have provided an incomplete mirror; the metamorph never makes it to a fully loving relation with the world and her own well-being. Nevertheless, she gains a freedom of self-awareness and, apparently, of self-chosen action which had been impossible for her before. Unable to desire this freedom for herself or even to understand it until it was made possible by the desire of another, she has been transformed from an object, something which is desired and acted upon by others, into what philosophers call a Subject.

In Continental philosophy, the terms "Subject" and "subjectivity" are important terms of discussion in current debates. When I was in graduate school, this was one of those slippery terms that everyone knew and talked about, but no one ever quite defined. I have since came to my own definition of subjectivity as "a particular point of view from which to view the world and act in it." Everyone obviously has some such point of view. As the *Star Trek* story above illustrates, however, we sense there is something "inauthentic" about having a subjectivity purely derivative of someone else's point of view or will. We all desire to be free. The only alternative has traditionally appeared to be conceiving of human beings as ideally totally free, autonomous agents, an idea central to pure Enlightenment individualism but which I suspect we also know to be untrue, because people are clearly social and inter-dependent beings. The *Star Trek* episode offered a way to think about a third alternative: human beings might be understood as deeply mimetic and thus as profoundly relational (as Girard and many postmodernist thinkers have stressed), yet this would not preclude the possibility of authenticity, defined not as absolute autonomy of action and consciousness, but as the capacity to participate fully in a loving dynamic of giving and receiving in relation to others.

The term "Subject," interestingly, already contains these seemingly contradictory ideas of free agency and independent outlook, but also the notion of dependence on or subjugation to another (as in loyal subjects of the king, or subject to the law). In other words, the word contains right within itself the dual emphases of both acting, yet also being acted upon; of desiring, yet also being receptive to other people's desires. I needed a new kind of model which allowed interchangeability and mutuality of these roles. A whole person or authentic Subject would have to be someone capable of both desiring and acting, and also capable of being acted upon, yet in life-enhancing, rather than violent, ways for both self and others. Although I had experienced this kind of loving, creative relation with the world and other people and at times, the theological and philosophical descriptions of love, I had seen seemed inadequate to describe it. Some of them even seemed just plain wrong.

Of course, life is not as stark as these old sci-fi shows on TV, which is what makes them seem hokey, yet also strangely capable of clarifying certain abstract philosophical concepts. These tales cannot give us a direct model for what life is really like. Even were we to grant that human beings are mimetic, none of us is totally, utterly mimetic like the metamorph—a blank slate while yet conscious and adult. Likewise, few people are entirely negatively enslaved by the will of another, and probably no one has experienced a completely positive mimetic relationship of perfectly-mirrored goodwill. Nevertheless, the *Star Trek* story throws the basic dynamics of mimetic desire and subjectivity into stark relief. The "purely" mimetic metamorph in the *Star Trek* episode was an imaginative abstraction which suggested to me a kind of fundamental story about the nature of subjectivity itself, a new paradigm about consciousness, where it comes from, and how it works. Freud has such a story: He claimed that subjectivity is formed through the infant's imitation of the Father's desire for the Mother, and this desire, along with its sublimation in the Unconscious upon the internalization of the Incest Taboo, is what forms the basis of subjectivity. This triangular model of desire and subjectivity, however, is tragic: Freud built the story around the scaffolding of the Oedipus myth, which ends of self-hatred and mutilation.

Girard critiques Freud's account and offers his own triangle in terms of mimetic desire which, in contrast to Freud's, is ungendered (*Violence and the Sacred*, p.169 ff). At first, this had seemed promising to me because women are not simply portrayed as passive objects of desire in Girard's thought. They could also be Subjects, those desiring, and Models whose desires others could imitate. But in Girard's account, I still had a problem: mimetic desire seemed always to lead to envy, rivalry with the model, violence or scapegoating. Girard's suggestion that we should take God as an object of desire, or imitate only God's desire (that is, non-violent Love) as a Model as a way to get out of this problem, really didn't work, at least as he stated it. Girard never seemed to have examined how some of the traditional Christian notions about "love" still worked out problematically in regard to mimetic desire and scapegoating. In Freud, the mimetic double-bind which leads inevitably to violence toward either self or other is easy to see: If the infant imitates the Father, he automatically becomes the Father's rival for possession for the Mother as object of sexual desire, and then he must either "kill" the father, or sublimate his desire for the Mother and submit to the Law of the Father. In Freud, killing one's original desires and accepting this split, permanently alienated subjectivity is what actually makes civilization possible. In Girard's proposed solution, human beings are still caught in a similar double-bind, through it is harder to see, because it has been so commonplace in Christian theology to say things such as that we must submit our own selfish wills to God's perfect one, or in common sense fashion to say that real love means giving up our own desires for those of others. But these types of ideas about love end up forcing us into rivalry with God or others for "possession" of own wills, subjectivity and very selves as the object. We are then supposed to relinquish our wills and desires and "submit" to the higher good of love; the only alternative is competition with the other, and not to do so is "pride" or "selfishness." So even if we say that God is "love," or loving others is the highest good, this way of looking at things ends up involving doing violence to oneself, and then accepting a kind of doublethink that this is a necessary part of love. For someone who has experienced violence, this type of reasoning has a very ominous ring.

It should be noted that neither Freud nor Girard has a very satisfactory model of what the formation of authentic subjectivity might look like, especially from the point of view of the person doing the imitating. Why is this important? Freud's and Girard's assumptions that imitation of the Model's desire must always lead to some form to violence toward self or others were especially problematic for me as a woman who had actually experienced psychological deformation. While I no longer wanted to be a slave of others' desires, neither did I want to become one who could now wield power over others, or a Model whom others would envy and violently imitate. Neither did I think I should have to give up my own legitimate desires to be an agent or a Subject in my own right, because that was exactly what I had been denied in an unjust situation. These paradigms failed to model how I could become a whole, empowered person in the world without assuming the kind of violence which had victimized me in the first place! Since I was a philosopher, this really bothered me logically. But my struggle with this was also very personal and devastating. I knew too much to simply go back to the naive belief that I could just become "independent," not mimetically related to others, as a way to be empowered as an agent who could really think and act. Yet I didn't know how not to be a victim, because I didn't have an adequate conceptual model to tell me how to change.

The *Star Trek* story, however, illuminated new intellectual possibilities for me. In my development of the new model of mimetic desire as Love, I called the one to be formed, the one imitating the desire of the Model, the "Proto-Subject." The Proto-subject, like the metamorph in the story or the infant in Freud's triangle, is somehow still "incomplete" as a human person with an internalized point of view and capacity to act. Within the context of the paradigm, the term "Proto-Subject" indicates the nature of this hypothetical not-yet-but-potential Subject doing the imitating, and the paradigm is designed to show how this Subjectivity that isn't there yet somehow comes to be. In the *Star Trek* example, the Proto- or incomplete Subject was the metamorph, whose consciousness and will were completely defined by mimetic desire. The Models she looked to at first were the various men on the ship, and she perfectly imitated and mirrored back to each the projected content of his own desire for "the perfect mate." But when the Model became Captain Picard, he avoided her attempts to imitate his desire for her as a mate; he actually renounced possessing her as an object of emotional and sexual satisfaction for himself. Instead, all he wanted, he said, was for her to be independent and free. This is what would satisfy him. Naturally, but also strangely, since this was his truest desire, it was the one she imitated. Because Picard had taken as his "object" of desire the freedom and well-being of the other, the metamorph was able suddenly to acquire this own desire for herself. Stated in terms of Girard's triangle, my insight was that

when Picard as the Model desired the subjectivity of the
metamorph (the Proto-Subject), and the Proto-Subject then
imitated that desire, then the Proto-Subject ended up desiring
her own Subjectivity! More generally, it would then follow that
if the Model were reciprocally to imitate the desire of the Proto-
Subject, the Model would begin to desire his or her own
subjectivity, too. Then both might start desiring not only their
own and each other's subjectivity, but the subjectivity of others
as well. Once begun, there was no telling where this positively
contagious chain-reaction of mimetic desire might lead. New
and expanded Subjects, a new relationship of mutual desire for
the good of each, entire new creative realities with other people
and external objects in the world could come to be! The new
paradigm described an open system of intersubjectivity with its
own creative, generative dynamic which potentially could
expand eventually to include everyone and everything. There
was nothing wrong with mimetic desire. Violence lay not in
mimetic desire, but in the temptation to turn things into mere
objects which could be controlled or possessed, just as I had
once experienced in my own past.

This new formulation of mimetic desire gave me the tools to
challenge some inadequate theological, philosophical, and even
common sense ideas I had been taught about love. I could now
see that real love automatically confers autonomy and dignity,
in the sense of precluding mere imitation of the Model's desire
in any small, diminishing sense. So it became easier now to
clarify that anything which diminishes others or turns them into
mere copies of the Model cannot be real love (even if the
Model is God). And I realized that although Girard advocated
taking God as a Model, Girard had never asked what God
desired! The *Star Trek* episode suggested the answer to this
question: God desired my Subjectivity! God did not desire that
I negate my will, my own desires, or myself, even for my "own
good," as I had been taught. Although so simple at first it
seemed self-evident, I perceived I was onto a radical idea. This
solution released me from a position of victimage which would
diminish me or cast me permanently into a merely receptive
role (even in relation to God or others I might be trying to
love). Rather, I could now learn to give and receive
authentically, defined as making those choices which were life-
enhancing for both myself and others. I could become a whole
person with dignity, resources and the capacity to will and act
without demeaning others; in fact, contrary to what I had been

taught, loving myself would be loving others, because making loving choices would expand, enrich and challenge us both, as well as keep us in right relation. Finally, I could stand up against violence, and I could Model this kind of love for others, empowering them too. Working out the philosophy had enabled me to critique my theology and had become my therapy as well.

As a person who had experienced very real diminishment and even abuse, this theoretical breakthrough was important to me. It was not merely intellectually vindicating but emotionally and spiritually empowering, both for myself and others. I had found a way to stop acting out a personal story of victimage, and to show how a victimage story was not the only human story possible. By working out the rigorous philosophy underlying the ideas, I could finally check my experience against some external template, by looking at all the different logical permutations of mimetic desire and seeing how my perceptions and actions fit into them. This gave me a permanently altered perspective from which to check the nature of my own perceptions and actions, as well as those of others, a perspective which has since proved capable of generating tremendous personal insight and new theoretical models for others to use.

I also saw, however, that I had stumbled onto something much bigger than just a personal way to heal and describe a healthy self-esteem. This simple paradigm implied a much bigger, cosmic story about desire, human meaning and history, of the kind usually associated with religious traditions and philosophical systems. The paradigm could be described using two different languages: a theological language which I valued and with which I was comfortable, but also a philosophical language which could be understood entirely on its own terms, logically and symbolically, without dependence on explicitly theological concepts and language. Theologically, I saw that mimetic desire could now be understood as the desire of God for the subjectivity of everything. And if God desired the Subjectivity of everything, and this desire was creative and contagious, it meant that Love was the engine at the heart of the universe. Not love as powerless, passive or sentimental, but as creative, dangerous and new; not as tame, but as wild and even frightening. This model put God's love back together with God's beauty, creativity, justice and power. I finally understood what it meant to say not just that God loves, but that "God is love."

Philosophically, I saw that when I combined what I had learned with the work of others, I could now describe love and human relations in a way which was both a logically and emotionally powerful. And this paradigm of Love had real power: It could confront and overcome political and social injustice informed by projection and scapegoating, because it could not only describe and unmask the mechanisms of violence, but show what their alternative looked like. It was imaginatively stronger than the soul murder of internalized oppression. For me, and for many others who come from religious traditions, this ultimate creative reality which liberates, underlies and sustains everything is what we would call God. As a Christian, I would say that I believe Christ is the unique revelation of this divine Love. But for practical purposes, it isn't essential that others use this particular religious language to describe this Reality. What is important is that they can participate in it. The new model simply says that human beings can enter into this ongoing, unfolding creation of a loving universe by desiring the subjectivity of others, and ultimately, of everything that is, because someone else has first desired that for us.

And it all began with a *Star Trek* episode!

– Rebecca Adams (Star Date 45761.3)

The violence of trauma or strong threats to identity needs, or lack of adequate models, can immobilize people into the position of victims. In Adams' terms, these kinds of limited or wounded Subjects[8] are forced to inhabit a false system of representation that creates "falsely-constructed subjectivity, abject will, and captive agency."[9] They have imitated a Model whose mediation has actually encouraged them to engage in false perception, self-destructive acts, and self-hatred. Perpetrators of violence, likewise, may lose a sense of the fullness of their humanity through guilt brought on by their violent actions.

Part 1 included a story told by a Croatian woman whose pacifist friends had joined the military and participated in atrocities. Years later they couldn't sleep at night (a well-recognized phrase for guilt) and had become pitiful, immobilized, and needy individuals. Clearly, even though they were perpetrators of violent acts, they were also victims since they had been caught up in a violent system to which they, for some reason, had assented. And even if they thought they had "freely" consented to participate in this system and carry out the violent desire for retribution of some of their nationalist comrades, this "choice" was obviously false for who they were. They felt deep internal discord and trauma (guilt) for having violated their own principles. They had been diminished into inauthentic, alienated Subjects.

Consider, however, a situation in which a person, serving as a mimetic model for another, desired that Limited Subject's fullness of being. That Limited or Proto-Subject, imitating the desire of the Model, would then begin to desire his or her own subjectivity, thereby becoming less limited and beginning to move along an open path characteristic of blessing. Adams' insight opens the possibility of a whole new set of mimetic phenomena, all oriented toward creativity and blessing. For instance, the Limited Subject might imitate the Model in desiring the subjectivity of other people, including third parties, or the model her/himself. This would lead to greater subjectivity, understanding and capacity for action for all. If the Model were, in turn, to imitate the Limited Subject's desire in a kind of feedback loop, instead of leading to violence and rivalry, these reciprocal acts of mimetic desire would only lead to even greater subjectivity of the Model and the person who has been the Limited Subject. As this happens, a sense of mutuality of mediation—of giving and receiving—develops. The result is not only enriched individual subjects but an enriched relationship between them and the potentiality of even more relationships with others. What some have called gift or grace emerges as the dynamic that begins with the desire for the well-being of the other.[10] Adams refers to the mutual, open-ended expression of desire described in this process as "the intersubjective creative love of self and other."[11] This is in contrast to definitions of love that assume that the self must be expelled or suppressed in favour of the other.

In more recent discussions, Adams has noted that modeling the desire for the well-being of *both* the other *and* oneself is, in fact, essential. Not only is this the only way the Model can avoid doing violence to his or her own subjectivity in the process of modeling, especially if the Model is someone who previously has experienced oppression, but it is also necessary for the other, the Limited Subject, on the receiving end. By modeling the desire for his or her own well-being, the Model's desire becomes a positive example of healthy self-esteem, teaching the Limited Subject how to love oneself in correct, appropriate ways.

Ken Wilber's distinction between the interior and exterior aspects of existence help in understanding the concept of inter-subjective creative love. Wilber argues that the brain can be understood through observing the neurobiological physiology of the brain. Although we can measure brain waves, examine electrical currents, and trace the existence of minute neurotransmitters, no information derived from even the best scientific procedures reveals what that brain is thinking about. To get to the interior of the mind, one has to engage in dialogue.

Inter-subjective love has two aspects. The exterior aspect is the action dimension. The subject engages in actions that contribute to the well-being of the other. These actions and their effects can be observed. The interior aspect involves intention—a desire to attend to the well-being of the Other. Sometimes this desire can be inferred from the actions and context or it may come out through dialogue. The well-intended action may be, however, counterproductive and actually diminish the well-being of the other. On the other hand, an empowering action may be motivated by self-interest alone. If the actions, intentions, and effects align themselves with one another there is congruence and love as a mimetic phenomenon approaches its fullness.

Mimetic Structures of Blessing and Theories of Deep-Rooted Conflict

Mimetic structures of blessing can be understood by using various theories in the same way that theories help explain mimetic structures of violence.

Human needs theory helps illuminate mimetic structures of blessing at three levels. At the first level, human needs theory helps builds on Adams' paradigm of mimetic desire as love by helping the model to see what desiring the well-being of another really consists of. For a person to experience well-being means that person has appropriate satisfiers for the human identity needs of meaning, connectedness, action, security, recognition, and the like, and that these are all well-integrated around a high level of Selfness. Human needs theory can also help a person who is a Limited Subject clarify their areas of greatest need. Also, at this first level, we can see that mimetic structures of blessing involve a new way of satisfying identity needs through a positive opening up to the Other. When a person begins to experience a satisfaction of these needs through dialogue, solidarity, and intersubjective connectedness in a mimetic structure of blessing, a new set of satisfiers takes over. One's own identity needs begin to be satisfied through processes that also enhance the well-being of the Other. As the Other flourishes, this new Self feels satisfied.

When our family was living in Thompson, in northern Manitoba, I had the wonderful experience of entering into the world of Canada's First Peoples. I went to Native Awareness training sessions and absorbed the traditional teachings. I worked beside Aboriginal people on issues of criminal and social justice. I loved and respected those whose stories I heard and whose teachings I integrated into my own world view. One problem area niggled away in my unrefined consciousness regarding native people: my negative stereotypes around "drunk Indians." One day my wife, Gloria, called me from the store in the local mall where she worked part time. A First Nations person significantly under the influence of alcohol was in the store and she was nervous and asked for my help. I went to the mall and offered to take the man out for coffee. We sat across from one another in the coffee shop for a good length of time. He talked openly about life on the trapline—how he was separated from his children and thought about them often when he was alone in the woods. He talked of his love of the trees, almost as though they were people. By the time we finished, I could truly say that I loved this man. Through dialogue I had opened myself to him and could sympathetically enter his world. He was no longer a "drunk Indian" but a fellow human being with dignity and worth.

At a second level, human needs theory used to illuminate mimetic structures of blessing can clarify how in some instances the very formulation of needs satisfiers induces violence. In some cases the satisfiers themselves are violent (for instance, when people get recognition for killing or terrorizing others). But positive satisfiers, neutral in themselves, can also become violent if used in a way that deprives others of the satisfaction of their own significant identity needs. For example, the land called the Pines at Oka/*Kanehsata:ke* functioned as a needs satisfier for the Mohawks and the municipal council/golf club, which caused them to fight violently over it. But when people on both sides of such a conflict find it possible to raise the question of changing their identity needs by reframing their satisfiers, people can begin contributing to each other's needs satisfaction. This can only happen through an open dialogue which changes the question from How can I get or maintain everything I feel I need to be satisfied? to How can my Other and I use our passionate desire for the same thing in order to understand our identities at a deeper level?

At a third level, we can conceptualize how mimetic structures of blessing become institutionalized in a way that allows people to create ongoing need satisfiers. One way of understanding what is involved is to look at the opposite. A totalitarian regime, such as the one that dominated the Soviet Union for 70 years, made it difficult for many to find identity needs satisfiers. The regime forced people to adhere to a Communist meaning system and those who found meaning in their Christian faith were repressed. The use of informants and political terror (arrests at night, lack of due process, and Siberian work camps) made it difficult for people to trust one another and to satisfy needs for connection. Limits on individual freedoms curtailed action and ongoing fear of state terror made people feel insecure. For a limited number of people, who were part of the Communist Party elite, the system satisfied their identity needs. We can ask the question of political, social, and economic institutions: Do they provide a context and culture of blessing for the people within them and affected by them? In other words, do they help people find meaning, connectedness, security, and recognition, and enable them to take meaningful action?

Let us now turn our attention to mimetic theory. Using the mimetic family of concepts we have developed—mimetic desire, mimetic rivalry, mimetic doubling, and mimetic selfness—we can now unpack new dimensions of mimetic structures of blessing. I see at least seven different possibilities, and there are probably more variations.[12] To see how mimetic structures of blessing open up new creative possibilities, let us start with the basic situation of a Model desiring the well-being of a Limited Subject, as we have discussed before. Now suppose that this Limited Subject, imitating the Model's desire, comes to desire her own well-being. This will, in turn, lead to an increase of her self-esteem and self-respect, strengthen her self-confidence, and lead to self-recognizance. As a second possibility, suppose the Limited Subject also imitates the Model's desire for the Model's own well-being. This will lead to a back-and-forth mutual and reciprocal valuation, increasing the well-being of both parties in the relational system. Take a third possibility: having known what it feels like to be in need and also be cared for, a person who has been a Limited Subject can become a Model for a second Limited Subject, desiring that person's well-being, as his own well-being was once desired. Meanwhile, in a fourth possibility, the original Model may find other Limited Subjects to care about. Then, in a fifth possibility, other people, observing the positive interaction between this Model and Limited Subjects, imitate the pattern of relating to other people in a way that shows their care for the well-being of the other. In a sixth possibility, something then begins to happen collectively: groups of people begin to desire the well-being of individuals, or other groups of people, who are suffering. Finally, in an seventh possibility, imagine that formal institutional structures and educational teachings develop that reinforce this practice of desiring the well-being of the Other, within given cultural contexts.

All these new tools can help us further understand ideas we have encountered before, such as victimization. As we saw earlier, a person who has been a victim can lose all sense of Self at a profound level, losing a realistic outlook on reality, their agency (ability to act), and their sense of worth. As one woman victim put it, she felt like "a piece of shit." Our new human needs knowledge about how trauma freezes the human psyche illuminates the process by which some victims internalize a view of themselves as worthless or helpless and become frozen in that mindset. Adams points out that while we often talk about those with power needing to let go of an ever-increasing need for power over others, people who have been powerless victims need a different emphasis: they need, in contrast, to let go of the view of reality in which their own worth and power to act have been extinguished. Stories of people who have walked a similar path can be a key factor in helping both kinds of people, by giving them models to imitate. For perpetrators, exposing the overall pattern of the violence can be helpful, particularly if stories of perpetrators who have changed their relation to their victims can be included. Victims also need to see models, such as examples of different kinds of concrete expression of care offered by a Model who desires the well-being of their Other. This allows both perpetrators and victims to imagine change.

If we return now to what we learned about scapegoat theory and mimetic structures of violence, we can see parallels in how mimetic structures of blessing work. In scapegoating, people are united in violence. Imagine, however, a situation in which people are united instead in working for the well-being of others. To do so, their identity needs must be collectively satisfied by this positive action. When people are united around a positive-centred practice, they can experience the same exhilaration around the shared experience as in the violent scenario.

Looking at these mimetic phenomena more abstractly, we notice that Girard refers to mimetic rivalry and doubling as a violence of undifferentiation; people lose their identity in that of the other. Likewise, scapegoating is a violence of differentiation in which the scapegoat is totally differentiated, to the extent that they are excluded from the community. We can hypothesize from this that there should be the possibility for a blessing of differentiation and a blessing of undifferentiation as an antidote to each of these types of violence.

In a mimetic doubling situation, the relational system is closed and the people identify strongly with each other. Two things can help bring a corrective sense of differentiation. The relational system can be opened up—they can develop new relationships—and they can start finding points of identification with others. A good example of turning a mimetic rivalry into a blessing of differentiation comes in the book of Genesis of the Hebrew Bible. In this story, Abraham and Sarah were travelling with Abraham's nephew Lot, and his wife and family, to the promised land. Each was very prosperous and their cattle and sheep were competing for food and water. The servant shepherds got into regular conflicts over livestock and resources. At one point Abraham realized that they were experiencing a mimetic structure of violence that would only get worse. He spoke with Lot and suggested they needed some differentiation—they needed to go their separate ways. Abraham gave Lot first choice of a place to settle. Lot chose the lower Jordan valley and made friends with the people of Sodom and Gomorrah. Abraham chose the hill country. The mimetic structure of undifferentiated violence was transformed into a mimetic structure of differentiated blessing.

It can work the other way as well: sometimes a structure of differentiation, as opposed to one of undifferentiation, is needed to change a system from violence to blessing. A mimetic structure of differentiated violence occurs when the Other is dehumanized and demonized. The scapegoat effect projects the problems onto the differentiated scapegoat. What is needed is a mimetic structure of undifferentiated blessing, meaning that the humanity of the scapegoat other is seen; to the group the scapegoat becomes a human being as they are. Miroslav Volf talks about this using the image of embrace.[13]

Jesus' story of the Good Samaritan is an example. In this story, a Judean walking from Jerusalem to Jericho is attacked, beaten up, and robbed. Religious leaders, noted for their goodness, walk by their fellow co-religionist and ignore him. He is now the differentiated Other because he is wounded and penniless. Finally, a Samaritan, another member of a differentiated Other group, comes by. He attends to the wounds of the victim, takes him to an inn, and offers to pay the expenses of convalescence. This story has multiple mimetic structures of undifferentiated blessing. At a primary level, the one wounded and penniless is embraced by the Samaritan as a suffering human being. The ethno-group difference is transcended. At another level, the Jewish Jesus is telling a story that makes the differentiated Samaritan a hero, making the point that no group has a monopoly on goodness.

A mimetic structure of differentiated blessing occurs as children grow up and move away from their parents. At a certain point they feel that the family unit hems them in. The internal family rivalries develop into mimetic structures of violence of undifferentiation—the family system is closed and people identify closely with one another. As children move out on their own it can become a blessing of differentiation. They establish their own identity; they get some distance. And it can happen with parents and child each wishing the well-being of the other.

A number of years ago, a friend taught me that to have a good open fire you need to place the logs on the fire at the right distance apart. One log doesn't burn well alone, but if two logs are too close not enough air flows between them for proper combustion and the fire dies down. If they are too far apart they do not warm each other sufficiently and the flame dies out. While burning the logs, the distance needs to be occasionally adjusted. Likewise, in a mimetic structure of blessing the differentiation/undifferentiation distance needs to be adjusted so both Self and Other can live fully.

At another level, a mimetic structure of blessing can be highly undifferentiated. This occurs when a profound sense of oneness with an Other takes one to a higher level of consciousness. This is described by Ken Wilber as a "nondual" experience in which the Self is open to and enfolds otherness within itself and is enfolded by otherness. Fritjof Capra, a scientist, and David Steindl-Rast, a Benedictine monk, describe this idea in terms of a profound sense of belonging to the universe. Paul Pearsall, a psychoneuroimmunologist, expresses this in terms of transpersonal exchanges of heart energy.[14] Psychiatrists Thomas Lewis, Fari Amini, and Richard Lannon, in their book *A General Theory of Love,* talk about how our limbic systems can be so filled with love that we connect with one another profoundly in a way that transcends language.[15] This experience may change, but by entering into this level of consciousness we create an openness to Others that turns into an ongoing attitude as exemplified for example, by Mother Teresa. This attitude nourishes mimetic structures of blessing. It is highly mimetic in that mutuality is involved. At a non-verbal level there is a mutual opening up and enfolding of the being of one within the other. On the physical level this can be expressed in an embrace in which both people benefit from a mutual exchange of positive energy.

Turning to hegemonic structures, we note that they can be framed as mimetic structures of violence in that they limit the opportunities and capacities for action on the part of the Subjected. As these structures become entrenched, the Subjected could be enframed as limited, wounded, or alienated Subjects. These oppressive structures have deprived them of the ability to move, perceive, and act freely. To work toward mimetic structures of blessing means more than simply wishing for the personal well-being of the Subjected; it means working strenuously to remove the cultural and social impediments to their flourishing. This means to address the physical limitations imposed on them: the political discrimination, the economic levers that systematically benefit the Dominant, and the identity and language elements that constantly frame them in an inferior light. By confronting these structural injustices, the strength of the dominating presence can be reduced. Hegemonic structures also dehumanize the Dominant, who are cut off from full human relationships with those they dominate by the power they wield. As their power is reduced through structural change, the Dominant are also allowed to find new identities and develop more complex relationships with people, which can become new satisfiers for their identity needs.

When we consider ethnonationalism as the driving force behind certain mimetic structures of violence, we note a strong sense of differentiation based on ancestry, ethnicity, religion, land, and politics. Mythologies around chosen traumas and glories reinforce the sense of being special. Identity-need satisfiers are framed to exclude key groups of outsiders, and economic life and practice are geared to enhance one identity group at the expense of others. In a situation in which two ethnonational groups are enframed within a relational system, imagining a mimetic structure of blessing means opening up new identity categories in which each can begin to include the other in empowering ways. To make this happen, new transcendent categories of identity definition may need to take place. A sense of civil rights not based on ethnic connections may be the medium for establishing a mimetic structure of blessing.

To illustrate, let me tell the story of a man who was once the most wanted man in Great Britain—let's call him Tim. I heard his story in the 1980s when he was visiting Ottawa. His pre-teen childhood crimes started him on a path that led to murder and the hardening of attitudes of hate toward anyone associated with civic authority. In desperation about how to handle people like him, the correctional service of Scotland put Tim into a small, experimental, and democratic prison in which prisoners and guards together would make the rules. His turning point from violence to blessing occurred when he, for the first time, held a fellow prisoner accountable for breaking the rules. Antagonism between guards and prisoners is as intense as many ethno-driven conflicts. In the individual identity all that matters is belonging to one group or the other and there is unquestioning support for someone of your own group. For Tim to hold a fellow prisoner accountable meant that he had a sense of belonging to a transcendent entity that included both prisoners and guards. This is equivalent to someone in an ethnically divided place, like the former Yugoslavia, holding a member of their own group accountable for violence done to someone from the other side.

Having examined how mimetic structures of blessing might appear in contrast to particular aspects of theoretical sides of mimetic structures of violence, let us now look more closely at some of the positive characteristics of these structures.

Characteristics of Mimetic Structures of Blessing

In general, mimetic structures of blessing are open and life-oriented, involving creativity and generosity. Mimetic structures of blessing result in trust, love, and joy, which are their driving dynamic.

First, mimetic structures of blessing tend to be *open* and expanding. They make room for newness—for new people, new paradigms, and new ways of doing things. Openness does not mean discarding or disdaining what is old; rather, it means not to be locked into what was before. Likewise they are open in allowing freedom from arbitrary constraints. At times, this openness is to traditions from the past.

Second, mimetic structures of blessing are *life-oriented*. A life-orientation respects the moving spirit of life. It is the flow of energy manifest in biological life but it also is manifest in the fullness of life-energy of people and beings. It respects "living life to the fullest." Within a relational system characterized by a mimetic structure of blessing, a fullness not only of biological, but imaginative, cultural, and spiritual life for each individual becomes important.

Third, mimetic structures of blessing involve *creativity*, putting elements of life together in new ways that will contribute to life. (The opposite of this is a subverted sense of creativity that can be involved in mimetic structures of violence as people create new ways of hurting one another.) Creativity expands options, creating a bigger pie rather than just fighting over the size of a piece of a given pie. It is associated with openness, in that creativity demands the space for new things to be developed. Creativity mimics the natural biological order that tends to multiply species and different types of individual living beings through new combinations of genes. The creative side of mimetic structures of violence includes stimulation; although it might involve conflict, the conflict is used to produce positive, life-oriented results. New options for living are generated within structures of creativity.

Mimetic structures of blessing also include an attitude of *generosity*. Generosity of spirit leads to constantly giving one to another. The impulse toward blessing means that gifts are intended to contribute to the well-being of the Other.

The spirit of generosity generates a framework of abundance where it becomes evident that mutual generosity produces more. By letting go, as opposed to grasping and clinging, more and more is generated and everyone benefits in the collective generation of more.

The other side of generosity is thankfulness, which acknowledges that what has been received has been a gift.

Within the structure of giving and receiving is a receptive orientation to life. As was pointed out at the beginning, one of the root metaphors of blessing is kneeling, which puts one in a position of respect and vulnerability.

Being open and receptive demands trust; as one experiences mutual giving and receiving, trust is strengthened. The attitude of caring for the well-being of the other comes out of love; love in turn grows within a mimetic structure of blessing. Finally, one can experience great joy as a result of mutual exchanges within a mimetic structure of blessing.

Mimetic structures of blessing occur within a values framework where mutual well-being takes precedence over a "survival of the fittest, fight to the death" mentality. Rivalry and conflict can play a role within mimetic structures of blessing but this role overall should be one that enhances well-being. By definition, mimetic structures of blessing cannot be forced upon people; the force would turn even the best-intentioned situation into violence.

The values framework can operate at either an explicit level or a tacit level. Some people, by living out a value system that honours the dignity of everyone, can teach this value system non-verbally. Our mimetic instincts are so strong that we can pick up on these values at a tacit level and pass them on in the same way. On the other hand, there are times when values associated with a mimetic structure of blessing need to be spelled out, digested, talked about, and even debated.

A key ethical dimension within a mimetic structure of blessing relates to justice. There are many approaches to justice, including restorative justice, distributive justice, and historical justice. All of these contribute to better relationships among people.

I have had my own sense of historic justice coming from my own historically based identity. In each case, my sense of justice has meant respecting and embracing the Other and being open to what I could do that might be empowering. Four groups have stood out for me: Jews, Slavs, First Nations, and Women. In each case I had the sense that an identity group to which I belonged—Christian, Mennonite, Euro-Canadian, male—has contributed to historic injustices. In the case of Jews, it has been systematic persecution by Christians over the centuries. In the case of Slavs, it was the mistreatment of peasants in the southern part of the Russian Empire by Mennonite farmers. In the case of First Nations, it was Mennonite acceptance of land taken by the Canadian Government and given freely to Mennonite immigrants. In the case of women, it has been the exclusion of women and their concerns from so much of society. These instances of historical karma have led me to take long-term actions involving learning, embracing, and acting.

In high school I read some histories of the Jews and made a speech about them in a public speaking contest in the '60s. Eventually, I had the chance to develop close relationships with Jewish people, particularly through a Jewish-Christian dialogue. Regarding Slavs, I studied Russian for two years in university and developed a proposal for a university exchange program. I ended up befriending a number of Ukrainians and worked actively on conflict resolution programs for Ukraine. My path with Aboriginal people led to developing personal relationships as well as working on issues of economic development, self-government, criminal justice, and conflict resolution with First Nations organizations. My own sense of justice with regard to women made a feminist out of me, prompted an egalitarian approach to marriage, and saw me working on issues of patriarchy in relation to violence against women.

In each of these cases my actions have led to rewarding relationships, personal growth, and new understandings. The personal cost has involved additional work and a willingness to reshape my identity. The hardest part has been giving up my own "right" answers to questions of life.

Enframing

Mimetic structures of blessing occur within relational systems that can be enframed just as in mimetic structures of violence. In fact, enframing becomes crucial in the overall evaluation of these structures. For example, within a hegemonic structure, a relational system including only the dominant group might seem to have within it a mimetic structure of blessing; however, the well-being of the people involved is at the expense of those dominated. During the slavery era of the eighteenth and nineteenth centuries, for example, one could imagine communities in which relational systems of white people were very civil to one another. People might be concerned about their neighbours' illness and do what they could to help their white neighbours. Meanwhile, they would be participating in another relational system involving "Negro" slaves; this relational system would exemplify a mimetic structure of violence. Within that world, a distinction in terms of relative violence or blessing could also be made between household relational systems. In some cases, slaves would be lashed and raped; in others slaves would be treated with respect and become almost like family members.

Similarly, in ethnonationalism a relational system enframed within the group might show signs of mutual empowerment. As soon as another ethnic group is considered, however, there are signs of violence. Take the situation in Rwanda. I am told that in many villages several decades ago Hutu and Tutsi youth participated in the same initiation rituals by which they were recognized as adults. Their separate ethnocultural differences were not considered a problem. Later, as violence erupted between the groups, their differences became important to the point that everyone had an identity pass specifying if the person was Hutu or Tutsi. Those identity cards do not exist today and open discourse around who belongs to which group is discouraged, but everyone is constantly aware of these groupings. This awareness is a major factor in interpersonal relationships. What we see is, first, a situation where the relational enframing included everyone without major distinctions; secondly, a situation in which the enframing included people as belonging to an identity group; and, last, a situation in which there is a tacit awareness of groupings.

Within a mimetic structure of violence, enframing in everyone's mind becomes increasingly fixed; boundaries are strictly maintained and those not qualifying for membership are excluded. Mimetic structures of blessing tend to open the door to one's Others—to those not belonging. Where there has been a rift, the process of reconciliation involves the sense of opening up to the other.

The evolution of democratic systems of governance can be viewed as an evolution of greater openness to people previously disenfranchised. In the English tradition, under the divine right of kings, kings had all the power. In this context, for lords to be acknowledged within the system as having a role in decision making opened things up; eventually common people played a role in electing their own representatives to a House of Commons. The evolution continued in Canada as women got the vote, and then First Nations people and non-European immigrants such as the Chinese. Eventually, citizenship took on a civic, as opposed to an ethnic, character. This shows that one key feature of mimetic structures of blessing is that the enframing becomes open.

In this regard, it is important not to erase all distinctions among people. Cultures need to be valued and there is much about the various languages and cultures of our world that need to be remembered and carried on. Open relational systems mean that various ethnocultural distinctions are respected and valued.

Emplotting

Just as mimetic structures of violence can be enframed to include either small or large groups, they can be emplotted in terms of duration. Some mimetic structures of blessing are short-lived, but recur again and again. For example, in some communities it is natural to bring food to bereaved families when they experience a death. The gifts of food might occur over a few weeks and then stop. This pattern occurs with the next significant loss to another member of the community.

Some mimetic structures of blessing take years to develop. I have described the growth of democracy as an ever larger enframing of the voting population. The same example shows how mimetic structures of blessing can assume a life of their own. The development of a long-lasting, trusting friendship or a good marriage can be considered an ongoing mimetic structure of blessing.

Structures within Structures

Adapting Ken Wilber's concept of holon, we can observe that every structure is made up of substructures and is itself a part of a larger structure. In some cases, the relationship between the larger structures and the smaller structures is like a hologram where each part is a microcosm of the whole. In other cases, structures resemble the body with its parts and subsystems, each playing a different but complementary role. Within a well-functioning democracy characterized by mutual empowerment of the whole population, there is a combination of the hologram and body aspects of mimetic structures of blessing within a larger mimetic structure of blessing. The hologram metaphor clarifies the fact that every institution within the country operates on similar democratic principles following similar rules. My father tells the story of a time when he was on the board of Mennonite Brethren Bible School in Herbert, Saskatchewan. A number of board members, recent arrivals from Russia, were accustomed to running all of their internal affairs on their own. They were about to take action to close the school on their own when my father, who had been born and raised in Saskatchewan, informed them that in Canada there is a different way of doing things. The school had a provincial charter and the school would have to be closed in a manner that met the legal requirements of the Province of Saskatchewan. The relational system between a church-run school and the government was structured differently in Canada than in south Russia. The point is that a relational system, such as a province, has laws, norms, and customs that affect the day-to-day life of its citizens and the way institutions are run. Where living under these laws, norms, and customs is fair, transparent, and just, they can be an empowering factor for mimetic structures of blessing. Where they are unjust, unfair, heavy-handed, and corrupt, they constitute mimetic structures of violence.

The body metaphor applies to the interconnected functioning of legislative, executive, and judicial branches of a democratic government. Just as we need cardio-vascular, digestive, and endocrine systems operating in an interconnected way within our body, so we need interconnected relational systems functioning in society.

A culture can evolve in such a way that it becomes a mimetic structure of blessing for those dwelling in it. A culture can also stagnate or deteriorate into a mindless legalism so that many members of the culture experience it as a mimetic structure of violence. Emplotment involves historical analysis to tell the story of the development of mimetic structures of blessing. It also points to times of both gradual and sudden structural change. This leads us to transformation of structures.

Transformation of Structures

As René Girard observed that there can be a kaleidoscopic change in structures of violence from mimetic doubling to scapegoating, so we can observe that the structures within a relational system can be transformed from violence to blessing or from blessing to violence. Sometimes this takes place almost instantly and at other times it takes place through a thousand hurtful comments and actions, each of which might seem innocuous at the time but add up cumulatively to a change in the orientation of the relationship from blessing to violence. When I was working in the area of crime prevention, I remember reading in a report that throughout the twelve years of schooling in North America, students receive an average of 22,000 put-downs from fellow students, teachers, and others. If this is true, we can see that the school culture has the potential to diminish self-esteem. It would be interesting to have an estimate on the number of compliments each receives during a dozen years of schooling. The transformation from violence to blessing may also happen through a thousand acts of respect and kindness or some dramatic event.

The transformation of structures takes place mimetically. This mimetic transformation can take place when two parties imitate one another through a feedback loop so that when one starts on a violent path the violence is returned with interest. Similarly, a good turn can be subject to the mimetic effect where kindness is returned with kindness that leads to a mimetic structure of blessing.

Another way transformation happens is when everyone acts in concert through a virtually simultaneous mimetic effect in which there is a crescendo of activity. This is evident after a disaster when everyone donates money, food, and clothing to victims. The efforts of everyone are subject to imitation by everyone.

A third way in which transformation happens is when a leader takes an initiative that resonates with people within a relational system and inspires people to mimetically follow the lead. This happened in South Africa when Nelson Mandela and De Klerk developed a black-white relationship that opened the way to dismantle apartheid.

When mimetic structures of violence have within them mimetic structures of entrenchment, creating a black-and-white approach, mimetic structures of transcendence are needed. These structures are made up of creative acts that transcend the entrenched boundaries. A key example was the trip of President Anwar Sadat of Egypt to Israel when these two countries were formally at war. His action set in motion a process that led to peace between the two countries. He literally transcended the borders that defined their warring nations. Transcendence is about opening oneself to new, previously unimagined, realities—about opening one's Self to the Other. It is an openness to new meaning systems, relationships, and actions. It means letting go of control over the means of security. With this concept we can now picture a structural map with two axes as follows:

Mimetic Structures

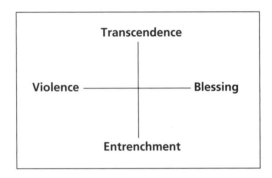

Figure 12-2

When we put this scheme together with the key concepts of Miroslav Volf, we see that violence and entrenchment together contribute to his theme of exclusion; transcendence and blessing contribute to embrace, a metaphor for positive human interactions. In his analysis of the components of embrace we can detect transcendence (opening to the Other) and blessing (the mutual benefit of closeness as well as the freedom to let go).

> The four structural elements in the movement of embrace are opening the arms, waiting, closing the arms, and opening them again. For embrace to happen, all four must be there and they must follow one another on an unbroken timeline; stopping with the first two (opening the arms and waiting) would abort the embrace, and stopping with the third (closing the arms) would pervert it from an act of love to an act of oppression and, paradoxically, exclusion. The four elements are then the four essential steps of an integrated movement.[16]

What we have done in this chapter is to establish an overall conceptualization and vocabulary for understanding mimetic structures of blessing. This has included looking at the analogies to the various aspects of mimetic structures of violence, exploring what it means to desire the well-being of the Other, linking blessing with enframing and emplotting, and, finally, taking a high altitude look at transformations of structures. This more theoretical and abstract look at structures has overlooked the emotional pain caused by violence, the ongoing effects of traumatization, and the huge ontological rift caused by deep-rooted conflict with its walls of distrust and hatred. It has not dealt with the powerful impulse toward revenge and the longing to see enemies suffer. These are the challenges for reconciliation, and these challenges make the sense of transformation from violence to blessing very real.

Chapter 13

Reconciliation

Reconciliation means
    to stop imitating
        the entrenched patterns
            of past violence,
    and to imagine,
        imitate and create
            life patterns
                of well-being
meeting the identity needs of Self and Other.

When I used to give a two-day seminar on reconciliation, I would tell participants that we didn't know much about this complex phenomenon but that it would be worthwhile to spend two days exploring it. Without exception, each seminar was tremendously enriching for everyone involved. Likewise, I write this chapter with a sense of delight.

People from around the world have attended my seminars and I asked them to explain the words for reconciliation in their languages. From the root metaphors came interesting ways of conceptualizing what is involved in reconciliation. I have also found it insightful to focus on the role that emotions play in both deep-rooted conflict and reconciliation, and we explore this dimension. As participants in my workshop have brainstormed elements of reconciliation, they have produced many items that I have synthesized into a number of key elements. The chapter concludes with a framework for reconciliation that integrates understandings of mimetic structures of violence and mimetic structures of blessing.

Root Metaphors and Cognates

The word "reconciliation" is derived from the Latin words *re* (again), *com* (together), and *calare* (call) meaning call together again or make friendly again. The word "council" comes from the same roots. This root metaphor suggests that gathering and interaction are at the root of Latin-based words for reconciliation.

Rabbi Arnie Fine suggests *peshera* as the closest Hebrew equivalent to reconciliation. It means "to make an agreement." Related words involve going between two parties to find a solution or offering a solution.[1] Root metaphors of *peshera* include to melt, or to be lukewarm; these suggest that the cold-heartedness of those in a conflict situation needs to be melted, and that the mutually beneficial solution is somewhere between hot and cold.

From the root metaphors we get the idea that violence has caused an emotional hurt and a payment or ritual is needed to restore the emotional equilibrium. There is also the sense that true reconciliation should show on a person's face.

The Greek word *katallasso* comes from root words *kata,* a preposition meaning "towards," and *allasso,* meaning "change." The sense is that there is significant change within oneself to make appeasement or create a positive disposition toward the other.

Abdi Hersi from Somalia provided this explanation:

Reconciliation (*heshiis, nabad raadin*) in Somali means "let us talk," and "let us talk" means let us reconcile. This is manifest in their most important prayer, which runs as: "God, give us peace and milk and protect us from the adversaries of war and drought." Peace is precious and as sweet as milk. Some Somali proverbs are the following:

Somali language	English translation
• *Nabadi waa naas irmaan*	Peace is like a feeding breast.
• *Walaalo is jecelway xoolo badiyaan, walaalo is necebina way xabaalo badiyaan*	Brothers who love each other gain wealth, brothers who hate each other gain the grave.
• *Nabad baa caano macaan*	At times of peace, milk is sweet.

Jai Jai Jang offers the following account from a Chinese perspective:

Reconciliation means to live in harmony with people, making concessions, and mediating. The Chinese people like to live in harmony, and always avoid direct conflicts with one another. The Chinese believe that if the harmony is broken, any bridge to make peace becomes more difficult. Therefore, concessions usually are made before any confrontation is launched. If ever a conflict takes place, there are still middle men who would be willing to mediate the situation from escalating. In short, reconciliation in Chinese is a synonym for prevention of conflicts.

Inuuqatigiikkannilirniq is the Inuktitut word for reconciliation used among the Inuit of Canada's north. Janet McGrath explains it this way:

inuuqatigiingniq roughly means "harmonious relations," although literally it is "people living together." The Inuit way was to rely on this core value, as the Inuit view is one of complete interdependence, with each other and nature. The word *inuuqatigiikkannilirniq* means to restore *inuuqatigiingniq* once again. The Nunavut Government's department of Education has a central document which was researched by Inuit, defining core values for curriculum development; it is called Inuuqatigiit, as all other values and principles flow from this core value. Think about it: Inuit have no history of war. Characteristically, on April 1, 1999 a new boundary was created in Canada, creating a new territory which is over 1/5th of Canada's entire land mass (2 million square km). It was all done through peaceful negotiations and *inuuqatigiingniq*, the Inuit way. The 85% Inuit living in the area simply wanted the flexibility to do things differently.

Richard Batsinduka has explained that in Kenyarwanda the concept of reconciliation is rooted in a metaphor that means to straighten crooked sticks so that there is a clear flow of energy between them.

Exploration of these root metaphors creates a field of meaning, a repository of concepts, that can be used as tools to clear the path toward reconciliation at key times. In addition to these are cognate terms such as healing, including trauma healing, remorse and forgiveness, and embrace.

Reconciliation: Inside and Out

As I pointed out earlier, Ken Wilber develops the idea that the same phenomena can be experienced from both the inside and outside. When someone is sick and recovers, they have their own inner experience of being sick—they feel sick—and of feeling better. Those around them can see that they are sick. They notice the lethargy, the tired eyes, and other effects of illness, and it becomes evident when they feel better. Health professionals can observe the effects of the sickness and recovery. In the same way, reconciliation is something that can be experienced from the inside and observed from the outside. In fact, as one seminar participant noted, reconciliation with others involves a reconciliation within. These two aspects of reconciliation feed one another in a circular motion—as one is reconciled within one's Self, it contributes to reconciliation with one's Other, and as reconciliation begins with one's Other it helps one be reconciled within.

The starting point for reconciliation is deep-rooted conflict, which likewise has its inner and outer aspects. Deep-rooted conflict is a pulsating dynamic. On the outside it can be seen in overtly violent acts. One does something to harm the Other who in turn retaliates in kind and with interest. Experienced within, the conflict pulsates between feeling hurt, maybe to the point of being traumatized, feeling like a victim, and feeling such hostility that one's energy is mobilized to hurt the perpetrator.

Reconciliation has two significant moments. The first is an escape from the mimetic structure of violence brought about by the deep-rooted conflict. The second is the creative construction of mimetic structures of blessing. Each of these has a dynamic, back-and-forth quality. The first moment of escape from mimetic structures of violence involves healing and forgiveness as internal phenomena that release some of the hold violence has on us. A dance of trust is building that includes expressions of remorse and forgiveness between Self and Other and takes both parties further out of a violent mode. Actions of restitution or restoration, on real or symbolic levels, help muffle the cries for violence in the name of justice. The *transition* to the second moment of reconciliation includes reconnecting the parties and reframing past and present reality. The second moment itself involves creating new, and mutually empowering, relational structures. These two moments need not happen in this sequence. Experiencing something new and creative may prepare someone for healing and forgiveness or vice versa. All of these actions can be examined internally through the experience of those in the reconciliation process; and they can be described externally. To provide a framework that describes what is happening internally, we need to understand the inner life of emotions.

Emotions

Emotions have everything to do with interpretation. The story is told of a boy who was dared to pound a stake into the ground in a cemetery at midnight near the grave of a recently deceased person. In the dark, as he crouched to pound in the stake, the bottom of his coat got caught between the stake and the ground and was secured to the ground by the stake. As he went to leave he felt a tugging on his coat. He was terrified and passed out because he interpreted the tugging as being related to spirits in the cemetery. From the outside, it is apparent that the tugging he felt on his coat was benign; as he experienced this internally, he interpreted it as a dark force and was terrified.

Within the brain, when a sense perception comes in through the spinal cord, the amygdala receives the message first. It is an almond-shaped part of the brain that serves as traffic director for incoming sensory data. The amygdala makes an immediate cursory interpretation of the data and sends the perception to the appropriate part of the mind-body. If there is immediate danger, the amygdala might cause a muscle to move involuntarily, as when the hand touches something hot. The hand is removed before there is any sensation of pain within the brain. If the sensation resembles something associated with trauma in the past, the signal is directed to the limbic system, the emotional part of the brain, which engages all of the physiological coping mechanisms associated with the previous trauma. The limbic brain gets the endocrine system to pump out hormones to raise the heart rate and dilate blood vessels in the nose (to get more oxygen), the hands (for a potential fight), and the legs (for potential flight). This immediate reaction takes place involuntarily—we do not decide that we want to have an emotional reaction, it just happens.

This emotional reaction involves the heart, which has a special thinking, regulating, and energy-generating side. The heart is the centre of a whole system of neuro-emotional activity involving cells throughout the body, including all vital organs. The body memories are rekindled as the body energy pulsates with a realization of real or potential hurt and the possibility of hostile or other toxic survival mechanisms. The limbic system of the brain cannot make temporal distinctions, so the wounds of the past are brought back with an immediacy as though they have just happened. The emotions pulsating within the body take control of the mind, which begins racing to think about what to do in response. The mind, as a slave to emotions, works in a logical way with the terms of the logic dictated by the emotions. If flight is called for, the mind races to think of a place to go. If fighting is called for, the mind will size up the situation and marshal the tools of conflict available. If submission has been the pattern of the past, then the mind thinks how to communicate this submission. Meanwhile the brain is pumping out this hurt and hostile energy.

When we put temporality into the equation, the structure may appear to have short, almost instantaneous, wave cycles or it may be spread out over a period of time. Terrorists, for example, come under the influence of powerful negative emotions based on victimization of themselves or their people and are driven by these emotions to use their brains to plan and contrive violent ways of retaliating over a long period of months or years. The logic of their actions makes sense when we plug in the emotional-heart energy pulsations of hurt, anger, fear, and hostility.

Reconciliation is a complete inner transformation that involves the brain and heart working in time to reverse a default setting containing a combination of trauma, victimization, and violence. This default setting corresponds to mimetic structures of entrenchment. The first step is to put the default setting on hold through awareness of one's emotional reality and use self-discipline to suspend disbelief about a new and different reality. This new reality is informed by imagining what might be possible and the imagination is informed by teachings involving story and stipulation.

Putting the default setting of hurt and hostility on hold is the very beginning of the reconciliation process. What it does is to create some inner space for something new to happen. It introduces a degree of openness and receptivity to something new from the Other. If there is immediate re-victimization, it opens up all the old emotions. If the Other, who is experiencing something similar, internally pauses at the same time, a space is created for a forward movement in the reconciliation process.

At this point, the hermeneutical tuner is hyper-sensitized to threatening signals. The smallest indicator of a message of antagonism is immediately perceived and amplified by the brain with a commensurate emotional physiological reaction. To sustain the first moment of reconciliation, there have to be clear and unambiguous signals that will increase a sense of security. This can then buy time to come to terms with the emotions of anger, hurt, and depression that prompt either immobilization or a return to hostility. In cases of enormous hurt, the signals of reassurance must be pronounced and sustained. In case of post-traumatic stress disorders, ongoing efforts are needed to simply quiet emotional and heart energy pulsations that course through the body in a perpetual cycle.

When I left the Canadian Institute for Conflict Resolution (CICR), I was traumatized. Dreams of programs that I had nurtured with a number of people for years were suddenly snuffed out. It was like experiencing a death of someone close to me. I was in a debilitating mimetic structure of violence.

Inner reconciliation came in several ways. First, "angels," people with positive, encouraging energy, came into my life almost daily. Second, hugs from people who brought their hearts into close proximity and whose bodies stimulated the outpouring of positive neuropeptides within me replaced my negative emotions. Likewise, massage and acupressure undid some of the physiological tightness. Third, prayer and meditation helped to quiet my anxious spirit. Finally, the use of my theories helped to make sense of what was happening around and within me. These all helped me to prepare for a new life, which in turn prepared me for an eventual, positive relationship with CICR.

There are degrees of trauma. In some instances babies get hatred with their mother's milk, an image someone gave me. Group memories of violence, injustice, and hurt are built up through generations. In some cases, battles are allowed to run their course. It is only through war weariness that people reach the first moment of reconciliation in which their default settings of hostility and violent revenge are put on hold to allow for a peace process. We must enter an exploration of the elements of reconciliation with a deep and profound respect for the feelings of people involved in a deep-rooted conflict that grasps them in mimetic structures of violence and entrenchment.

Key Elements of Reconciliation

In one of the many brainstorming sessions I led on elements of reconciliation, one of the participants piped up, "Balls, it takes balls to reconcile." I put "balls" up on the flip chart thinking that we had a new root metaphor for the courage it takes to embark on a process of reconciliation with one's adversary. Immediately, a woman in the group called out "ovaries," and another word was added to the list. The latter generated the notion that reconciliation is akin to reproduction, to the creation of new life. The two metaphors, in juxtaposition, compare to the power-receptivity dialectic of Chinese thought. The male-female dialectic represents the wholeness of humanity, the "both... and..." mentality of the mediator; and the Self-Other dialectic indicates that it takes both parties within a relational system to reconcile and change that relational system from one dominated by mimetic structures of violence to mimetic structures of blessing. The following key elements evolved over time with suggestions from many persons. These intertwined processes can be repetitive and cyclical.

1. Deal with the Pain

It is difficult, if not impossible, to start a process of reconciliation when the pain of violence is visceral, recent, and overwhelming. When people are traumatized through the loss of loved ones, through having observed many deaths, or having been terrified to the core of their being, they are not ready to start a discourse or any process that involves their relationship with an enemy. I remember a Bosnian Muslim (now called Bosniac) of Albanian ethnic origin, married to a Bosnian Serb, who attended one of my seminars. In the course of the seminar I learned that his wife's parents had been killed by fellow Serbs because they would not participate in ethnic cleansing. The emotions associated with that were still so fresh that he was not comfortable going to additional seminars on the theme of deep-rooted conflict and reconciliation. Pain must be dealt with through a combination of healing processes, support from empathetic others, and time.

2. Create a Safe Space

Reconciliation demands a space and time in which the fear of additional violence is diminished. Violence can be physical, emotional, symbolic, or sexual. It can involve threats, intimidation, or usurpation of the future. Violence can conjure up past hurts and use them to sabotage the present. Creating a safe space means finding a neutral place, since places can bring back memories; a neutral time, since some times are symbolic—such as anniversary dates for battles, attacks, or victories; and a neutral process. Part of creating a safe space is to ensure that nothing in the process can be subverted for harm to either party through future legal action or because either has become vulnerable to future mischief. In some instances, safety can come through ground rules or a legal framework that safeguards the process.

Another aspect of a safe space is the involvement of a third party who is trusted by each party and able to provide reassurances of safety. John Paul Lederach suggests that the following aspects of reconciliation practice say something about the character of the third party: reconciliation is relationship-centred, involving accompaniment and humility; it restores the fabric of community; and it can be thought of as wandering in a desert.[2] These images suggest an ongoing commitment to people through a very open-ended process.

A safe space can never be guaranteed simply because of the complexity of human beings. Events, reactions, and behaviours cannot be fully controlled in matters of the human heart. Risk must be diminished enough for the parties to move ahead; if risk is not totally eliminated, participation in a process of reconciliation demands courage on the part of protagonists.

When we look at safety from the perspective of trauma and mimetic structures of entrenchment in which the core of the Self is overtaken with fear, our sensitivity to matters of security is intensified. There is a need for a safe process but also a need for security over the long term. There is something paradoxical about this: some parties need the promise of security to engage in a reconciliation process but it is in reconciliation that true security can be found.

3. Break the Trance

At one of my seminars, a participant blurted out that for a reconciliation process to begin, something had to happen to break the trance of the participants. This raises the question of what "trance" means in the context of a deep-rooted conflict. The word can mean "a dazed or stunned condition"; it comes from an old French word meaning a fear of coming evil and a verb meaning to be numb with fear.[3] In this context it has the sense of being immobilized by the image of the Other as a dehumanized, demonized Monster. It is an illogical state dominated by conflicting and paralyzing emotions, including a fear of the Other and an opposite fear of not dealing with the Other. Breaking the trance can involve seeing the human face of the Other, a paradigmatic change of how one sees the Other, and a recognition that the Other is also suffering.

Seeing the human face of the Other allows for respect for the identity need satisfiers of the Other. It means that the story of the Other is accepted as at least worth listening to. Breaking the trance involves a softening of the heart,[4] a change in attitude toward the Other. On one occasion Sylvère Kabwa organized a dialogue of Burundian Hutus and Tutsis in Canada. Wounds of the past had created deep distrust between the groups. The turning point in the dialogue came when one of the participants exclaimed, "I know how my people have suffered through the conflict but I had not realized how much your group suffered as well." That kind of "aha" moment can break the trance.

In some cases, starting with a positively-centred process can have the effect of bringing people into close enough proximity to break the trance. Humour, children, and food have a role to play. It was reported in one of my seminars that "in the Somali culture there is the role of Khat, a stimulant plant that is usually used in the reconciliation meeting; it has the ability of easing the conversation by making the communication more relaxed."[5]

I have sometimes thought that a massage or acupressure treatment before a reconciliation process might be good preparation.

4. Introduce or Recall Teachings

Where does the impulse for reconciliation come from? Why do people want to reconcile rather than go with the default setting of their emotions that prompts continued retaliation and violence or a total withdrawal from the Other? Why are people in some contexts relatively quick to pursue a reconciliation process while in others the impulse to escalate conflict is dominant? The answer is, in part, that certain teachings have the effect of inspiring the imagination so that people can see the possibility of reconciliation and of prompting the conscience so that attempting reconciliation is seen as at least morally desirable and potentially morally imperative.

I use the term "teaching" in a special technical sense. It is based on the Hebrew word *torah* that is derived from *yarah*, the verb to teach. *Torah* in the Hebrew Bible has the sense of setting out the direction of the path and enabling one to live a good life.[6]

It includes the customs, moral imperatives, and stories that together develop a moral outlook that enables one to make good decisions while walking the path of life. It defines what is central and most important with the idea that one not stray too far to the right or to the left. This word is often misleadingly translated as "law," which in the Roman Law tradition has the idea of defining the outer limits of what behaviour is acceptable—we must be "within the law" and to go outside the law is to "break the law." Teachings within every religious and cultural tradition are designed to help people get along with one another. Some of these teachings are "reconciliation readiness" teachings, fostering attitudes that prepare for a favourable disposition to a reconciliation process or to at least see reconciliation as an end worth pursuing. This includes the generosity of spirit that enables one to go beyond the default settings of violence and vengeance. Some of these teachings directly advocate reconciliation and actually propel one in that direction.

When Abdi Hersi, a Somali friend, returned to Somalia from Canada to use his training as a Third Party Neutral, he got the local people in a semi-literate rural setting to engage in sloganeering. They made banners with traditional teachings that would help the reconciliation process and displayed these publicly.

Stories of Reconciliation

Stories about reconciliation can be included under the rubric of teaching. They have the advantage of including both a context and a temporal unfolding of events and make reconciliation come alive. One of the most helpful stories in this regard is the story of Joseph recorded in both the Hebrew Bible and the Qur'an. I will present the story in some analytical detail because it provides one of the best examples of the narrative structure of reconciliation.

The story of Joseph illustrates various components of reconciliation. His reconciliation with his brothers takes place within a personal narrative that begins with young Joseph observing a reconciling meeting between his father Jacob and his uncle Esau. To understand the significance of that reconciliation we start with the conflict between these two twin brothers.

René Girard sees the rivalry between Jacob and Esau as an example of rivalry between brothers, the type of rivalry that has been evident in many times and places.[7] In this case, the rivalry is over the birthright, the privilege due the eldest son. Younger brother Jacob, whose name means "supplanter," tricked his father into giving him the birthright and blessing. Esau was furious and intent on killing Jacob, who went to live with his mother's brother Laban. While working for his uncle, he acquired two wives and two concubines and had eleven sons and one daughter. After more than two decades away he decided to return to the place he came from, which meant confronting Esau.

The night before the meeting, Jacob wrestled with a being. Because the two were perfectly matched, the struggle went on all night. At the beginning, the being was described as a man. At the end, when Jacob was winning, in Girard's words,

> he becomes a God from whom Jacob demands and obtains a blessing. In other words, the combat of *doubles* results in the expulsion of one of the pair, and this is identified directly with the return to peace and order.[8]

The pattern is a relationship of doubles, a period of indecision, and a resolution through violent expulsion.[9]

This interesting variation on the theme of doubles shows a fusion of scapegoating with a mimetic conflict. In other words, Girard establishes a category for one's double becoming an enemy and possibly a scapegoat. It is as though the scapegoat action of fighting with the being, demanding a blessing, and letting the being escape, cleared up something within Jacob that paved the way toward reconciliation. As far as he was concerned, he had encountered a divine Being face-to-face.[10]

When Jacob met Esau he said, "…for to see your face is like seeing the face of God, and you have received me favourably."[11]

In wrestling with the being, Jacob could transfer all the violence he felt for Esau onto his Other.[12] This wrestling shows an inner spiritual struggle resulting in a change of identity and involving a new name that reflected a new way of being and acting. Israel means "God persisted,"[13] implying that Jacob was subject to the persistence of God. The way out of the struggle, that is, receiving a blessing while being marked physically through a hip displacement, is interpreted by James Williams as being victorious without scapegoating or becoming a scapegoat.[14]

Both brothers underwent a change of name, which implied a change of identity. Earlier, Esau's name, which was derived from his hairy skin,[15] had been changed to Edom, meaning "red" or "ruddy" referring to the red lentil soup for which he sold his birthright. This selling of the birthright initiated the deep-rooted conflict between the brothers; it was the beginning of a process of Jacob acquiring what was rightfully Esau's based on birth order. At the end of the night encounter with a divine being, Jacob's name was changed to Israel—the name given to a people and a country. It is ironic that *Edom* refers to the genesis of the mimetic structure of violence and *Israel* harks back to the beginning of a reconciliation that would allow each brother to be a founder of a people. The reconciliation was not lasting. Israel, according to the biblical story, was a people with whom God persisted and the Edomites were a people and country considered arch enemies of Israel and subject to genocide and subjugation by Israel during much of the monarchy.[16]

How This Reconciliation Happened

The process of reconciliation between Jacob and Esau started with Jacob sending a large number of animals to Esau as a peace offering. The gift acknowledged that there was an ongoing conflict and that Jacob had wronged Esau. It was a way of making things up to his brother. When they met in dramatic fashion, they embraced, and Esau offered to protect Jacob's family for the rest of their trip back to southern Israel. Young Joseph witnessed this coming together of brothers who had had such a deep-rooted conflict that Esau had wanted to kill Jacob. After more than twenty years, Jacob was still afraid that he might do it and politely declined the offer of protection.

Joseph, as the favoured son, stood out among his brothers, who had mimetic desire for him. He got a special coat from his father and had dreams of his family bowing down before him. Eventually, he became a scapegoat in classical fashion. He was sold into slavery by his brothers and ended up in Egypt. When he became powerful and prosperous in Egypt, his family was subject to famine and came to Egypt for food. Joseph, the victim, was now in power, unknown to his brothers. He tested them by giving them food, but demanded that his younger brother Benjamin return the next time. Benjamin was now the favoured son of the father Jacob, who could not trust his other sons with the second son of his favourite wife, Rachel. The famine persisted and Judah promised his father that if Benjamin got into trouble, he would put himself in Benjamin's place for the sake of preserving his younger brother. Isaac's sons returned to Joseph, who set up a situation where Benjamin was implicated in the "theft" of his goblet. As Judah promised, he offered to take Benjamin's place and all the brothers showed remorse for what they had done to Joseph. Joseph then disclosed his identity and embraced his brothers. He then reframed the situation, saying that God had directed events so that he could be in a position to look after them. He had the whole family moved to Egypt so that they could be cared for throughout the famine.

Earlier in this story, the young Joseph had witnessed a process of reconciliation involving his father and uncle. This allowed him to imagine that reconciliation between brothers in conflict was possible. He eventually imitated reconciliation, and started a process that initiated a mimetic structure of blessing. It was mimetic in three senses: it was patterned after the previous reconciliation, it was triggered by Judah's offer to take Benjamin's place,[17] and it was received mimetically by Joseph's brothers who trusted him enough to actually move to Egypt. It was blessing in that it was life-giving and creative—introducing new options and reframing the situation to absolve the brothers of guilt. Time had passed since his victimization, during which Joseph changed from being a victim to becoming an actor. His identity was transformed, enabling him to move from being acted upon to taking responsible action. Had he been totally caught in the grasp of a mimetic structure of violence he could not have changed the situation to one of blessing— looking out for the well-being of his brothers. We also note that his brothers expressed remorse to him, and Judah especially showed that his attitude toward Benjamin, the favoured son, was different than it had been toward Joseph. Throughout the lifetime of the protagonists, the process of reconciliation appears to have continued.

There is a need to collect, disseminate, and study contemporary stories about reconciliation. Noteworthy among these are the works of Moral Re-armament and the European Platform.[18]

5. Embark on Gradual Reciprocated Initiatives
in Tension-Reduction (GRIT)

At some point in the process, there is a need for a mimetic dance called GRIT. The idea is that one of the parties makes a positive gesture toward the Other. This positive gesture is a signal of openness to a reconciliation process. It may be all that they are able to do within the risk allocation that they consider safe. If this positive gesture is met with a positive response by the Other, the initial party is then prepared to risk another positive step toward the Other. The idea is that as each party takes a step toward the other in this mimetic dance, they eventually get close enough to embrace, which, as Miroslav Volf points out, is more a long-term end than an immediate reality.

The GRIT concept was developed by Charles E. Osgood during the Cold War.[19] After the Cuban Missile Crisis, President John F. Kennedy was so shaken by what had almost happened that he went to Osgood, the head of the American Psychological Association, for advice on how to proceed in a way that would diffuse the tensions that could lead to a nuclear conflagration. He was told about the GRIT concept, and, in short order, Kennedy made a speech in which he reflected sympathetically about the experience of the peoples of the Soviet Union. Within days Khrushchev, head of the USSR, responded similarly with some positive comments about the United States in one of his speeches; Kennedy then added more constructive observations in his next speech. This GRIT process was still in its early, but effective, stages when Kennedy was assassinated.[20]

What happens during the GRIT process is a gradual opening up of the Self to the Other. First, this opening of the Self involves a willingness to see the world through the eyes of the Other. Second, one's inner self is opened to the Other, enabling the Other to see the world through one's own eyes. This kind of exchange occurs in a true dialogue.

Several things can skew the process. First is asymmetrical disclosure, in which one side does most of the talking. This can take two forms: the more verbal party can overwhelm the other with information and dominate the situation. On the other hand, one side can disclose sensitive information, through questioning, making them too vulnerable too soon. Periodic reflection about the process itself can help to determine the comfort level with what is happening. The process can also be skewed if one of the parties does not participate in good faith or if pressure tactics are used.

In theoretical terms, the parties are together breaking free of mimetic structures of violence and entrenchment. It is natural that there will be setbacks and moments of self-doubt, especially if these structures have taken over one's identity.

Several things can happen during the GRIT process, things that are important in and of themselves: truth-telling, and signals of remorse and forgiveness. These elements demand separate treatment.

6. Truth-telling

As was previously pointed out, a distinction can be made between table truth and public truth. Table truth represents the private truth that is discussed only with family and trusted friends. It is wired to emotions and includes stereotypes and attitudes that, if uttered in public, would be classified as "politically incorrect." Table truth is a primary motivator in deep-rooted conflict. Public truth may be another angle, a small portion of the table truth, a distortion, or a fabrication for the sake of expediency or safety. In the case of people of great integrity or who have nothing to lose, public truth can be very close to the table truth.

Truth has different levels. As was pointed out in Chapter 9, our reconstruction of the past involves memory, story, and interpretation, following Paul Ricoeur's *mimesis$_1$*, *mimesis$_2$*, and *mimesis$_3$*. Truth is concerned about all three levels: What happened? What is the context of what happened? and What was the meaning of what happened? In each case there is a tendency to skew the truth at every level. First, at the level of what happened, people have a greater tendency to forget what they did that might have hurt the other person or group. Second, in terms of the narrative sequence, people will emphasize all of the contributing factors that led or even "forced" them to take the action they did. The overarching message in the narrative is that they did what they did for good reason; they were justified in taking the action that they did. Third, at the level of interpretation, people will judge themselves on the basis of their intention and judge the Other on the basis of action. They will see the action of the Other as a real threat to a core identity needs satisfier or value. They will frame their actions as something done for well-thought-out reasons as opposed to something done in imitation of the violence of the Other or something driven by a vengeful attitude. Truth-seeking involves bringing into the open the truth of each party at all three levels.

Ken Wilber approaches truth from the perspectives of internal and external truth. External truth is based on what can be observed, on empirical truth. Internal truth is based on how people experienced something within themselves. Somebody can say something that is externally true but may be internally false, as in the case when someone, trying to say something they believe is false, inadvertently tells the truth. Both aspects must be revealed. Similarly, again following Wilber, individual truth needs to be compared to collective notions of what is true.

7. Signalling Remorse and Forgiveness

As the truth comes out and people listen to one another at all three levels of truth, paradigms begin to change. Suddenly, people begin to see their own actions in the light of the Other's experience. This is, of course, a best-case scenario. Parties may also retreat into a defensive shell and stonewall around their position. There are a number of different structural realities. Both parties may be more or less equal in strength, and the hurt and violence each suffered may be more or less equal. Or the situation may be asymmetrical, as in a violent hegemonic structure in which, for example, a marriage partner routinely abuses the other or a genocide in which the proportion of hurt is overwhelmingly skewed.

In the case of the Rwandan genocide, for instance, as the stories of what happened are told, it is revealed that there was a counterattack. Throughout the genocide an estimated 800,000 Tutsis were killed. The counterattack on Hutus resulted in an estimated 10,000 deaths. For Hutus, it is important that this counter-attack be part of the story. For Tutsis, the relatively small number of Hutu deaths—both in proportion to the Tutsis killed and as a percentage of the Hutu population—means that this aspect of the story demands little attention and could be misleading if it is framed as somehow balancing or diminishing the genocidal action against Tutsis.

Keeping proportionality in mind, in the course of sharing stories in a GRIT process, signals of remorse, understanding, and forgiveness are sent. Dave Worth of the Mennonite Central Committee tells the story of a community justice initiative that involved separate support groups among rape victims and rapists. At one point the rape victims showed an interest in meeting rapists who were not the perpetrators in their particular situation. As rapists and rape victims met and told their stories, at one point a rape victim said to one of the rapists, "I can start to understand you and your situation... but the man who attacked me, *he* was an animal." At that point everything was silent for a moment, and the rapist responded, "*I* was an animal." The expression of understanding communicated the rape victim's view of the rapist as a person; that signal of understanding gave him the space to send a signal of remorse through his response that his actions were not right. He did it by using the same root metaphor—animal—to stand for an inhuman action.

Forgiveness is giving up the right to retribution. It involves a conscious decision to block the emotional default setting that prompts us to mimic violence and desire harm for our adversary. Signals of forgiveness can indicate that, at a minimum, no further harm is intended although distance, both physical and spiritual, may be needed. At a maximum, it results in an enthusiastic, from-the-heart desire for the well-being and prosperity of the adversary. At a minimum, signals of forgiveness are a will and resolve to stop the escalating cycle of violence and revenge.[21]

Throughout the process of reconciliation, forgiveness becomes ever more a part of the living reality of the people involved; it can be expressed in words, actions, and rituals. Eventually, it is woven into the reality of daily life. Complete forgiveness is best captured in the concept of a forgiveness tense, as described by Daryold Corbiere Winkler:

> Rupert Ross...tells of a Mi'kmaq community who, in the effort to revitalize their language, learned that it once had an ancient verb tense that had fallen into disuse and was remembered only by a few of the elders. The tense was specifically designed to indicate to all that "this event has been concluded to the satisfaction of all." In English it has been called the forgiveness tense; it allows people to speak about a conflict for the lessons it contains, while making it clear that the victims have been appeased and healed, and the wrongdoers restored to full honours within the community.[22]

8. Identity Transformation

Chapter 8 pointed out that within mimetic structures of violence owing to a deep-rooted conflict, identities are formed in such a way that to meet the identity needs satisfiers of one party the identity needs satisfiers of the other would, of necessity, be threatened. The path of reconciliation in this situation means that people have to rethink their identities. GRIT, truth telling at all levels, and signals of mutual understanding provide a basis to begin to rethink identity needs satisfiers. The brain develops thought patterns along neurological pathways. The more they are used, the stronger they become. Certain identity needs satisfiers function as truisms, expressed as ideas and stories so often they are not subject to question. For instance, the story of a chosen trauma of one's identity group may have been told over and over again. To reformulate the story or reflect critically on it, or to view it from the "other side," can be very threatening. Rethinking identity might mean a critical review of past narratives in which glories are tempered by the realization that one group's (or individual's) glories might have caused others to suffer. Likewise, chosen traumas could be tempered by the context and could be reframed in terms of positive outcomes in the face of tragedy.

Realizing that hegemonic structures limit mutual identification opens the possibility for sharing sources of meaning and power. Donna Hicks develops the concept of reconciliation as identity reconstruction in the context of what she calls the high and the low power groups. One step is "to create the conditions so that the two former enemies could develop a 'mutually tolerable' interpretation of events."[23] This "co-construction of reality" would "enable them to leave the past and envision the possibility of a shared future." She describes the implications for the high and low power group as follows:

> For the high power group, exposing oneself to the not-so-righteous aspects of one's identity can be extremely difficult and embarrassing. The first phase is to break one's denial that one is capable of inflicting injury upon the other. This would require the safest of environments, with the support of a nonjudgmental third party, who could create the conditions for such self-analysis. Perpetrators would have to engage in a slow process of exposure before they could be able to expose themselves to those whom they have injured.[24]

In the case of the low power group, the emphasis would be to "articulate what happened to them and to have it acknowledged by the other that what happened to them was wrong and that no human being should have to suffer the way they did."[25] Both identities need to be unfrozen. However, she suggests more emphasis should be put on breaking the denial of high power groups so that they can come to terms with what they have done in a way that protects their human dignity "as they take responsibility for their actions and still maintain their psychological integrity."[26]

Honestly listening to the full perspective of an Other is truly a humbling experience, since it takes us off our pedestal, which gives exclusive pride of place to our self-justifying perspectives.

In my own case, dialogues with others have expanded my sense of identity to include both new types of satisfiers (such as desiring the well-being of the Other) as well as a sense of identification with other groups.

Change of identity might mean reframing our identity group to either expand the group or include other overlapping circles of identity.

9. Creating Rituals

So much of what takes place during the process of reconciliation takes place within our interior universe. What we experience as our internal life is a composite of brain-body-heart-gut interaction. It involves pulsating energy, a flow of neurotransmitters that determine what we experience as emotions, hormones that energize particular body parts, physiological blockers that keep these stimuli from going out of control, and raging thoughts that run through mazes until they mentally hit a brick wall or find a new path. Appropriate rituals can provide a visual and experiential replication of what is going on within. These rituals not only express an inner reality, they also allow for a symbolic exchange with the Other that can, in turn, affect the interiority of each. Rituals can show in schematized fashion what the conflict was all about, show how the process of reconciliation has helped to shrink the mimetic structures of violence, and open the way to mimetic structures of blessing.

In a reconciliation ritual developed by Rebecca Adams, each party pours salt into water to symbolize the pain of their experience. This pain is described as the salt is poured into the water. At another stage in the ritual the salt water is thrown over the feet of the Other symbolizing releasing the past hurt. Different religious and cultural traditions have rich resources to offer in the development of rituals; new rituals need to be created.

10. Healing

Paul Pearsall develops a cardio-energetic approach to healing that he defines as follows:

> Healing is making whole, reconnecting, recovering molecular memories that promote healing, and being alert to risks to our well-being from being out of balance with the energy of all systems around us.... Healing with the heart is not "trying to heal" but allowing the heart's natural healing energy and all the memories of healings that have ever occurred to resonate within you, and being still and "thoughtless" enough to allow one's own heart to fall into a shared coherence with other hearts in a form of compassionate prayer beyond words.[27]

Deep-rooted conflict, through severe threats to our identity need satisfiers and through a mimetic trap that can make us obsessed with a competition with our Other, can traumatize us, shake us to the core, and deprive us of sleep. We can be out of sync with ourselves, cut off from a former friend, hurting with grief from loss of loved ones, and agonizing over broken relationships. All of this cries for healing, for a recovery of internal balance, and a sense of inner peace and well-being.

Several years ago I gave a workshop on deep-rooted conflict and reconciliation in Salzburg. Two women from Croatia came for the event. After it was over, I went for a long walk back to the country place where we were staying with one of these women. As we talked, she shared with me the story of the genesis of the ethnic conflicts in Croatia that touched off waves of conflict throughout the former Yugoslavia resulting in ethnic cleansing, command rape, and a host of other atrocities. Among the stories she told were those of several young men who had been pacifists. Against their better judgment, they joined the army in the hope of doing some good. When the fighting was over they came to her and confessed that they too had committed atrocities. They were tormented with guilt that left them sleepless, anxious, and feeling terrible about themselves. My friend said her efforts to help them get their lives back together hardly made a dent in their overwhelming need for healing. Just as victims have great need for healing, so do perpetrators.

11. Reframing

In the Joseph story told previously, we notice that part of the process of Joseph's reconciliation with his brothers was reframing the situation. He told his brothers that this situation had happened for a reason. His reframing, which came after they had shown a profound remorse, was a way of setting their hearts at peace to erase their guilt. Reframing changes the meaning of an event or action. It can transform suffering from that which is interpreted as victimization to a source of wisdom, insight, or a new direction. Reframing allows us to take emotional memories that have no temporal distinction and bring them into a narrative in which the element of time figures predominantly. It takes away the power of the hurt to perpetually enslave.

12. Structural Change

Ultimately, reconciliation has to involve structural change. The first aspect is, in general, to reconfigure the relationship so that all parties can be empowered to live full lives. Some of this involves an attitude and value change. These attitudes and values have to be expressed in new teachings that include customs, behaviours, manners of interacting, and laws. Where governance has been oppressive, some institutions need to be deconstructed and new ones built in their place. Anatol Rapoport develops the idea that war, like slavery, is an institution and that we could imagine banishing this institution.[28]

Where there are hegemonic structures contributing to the mimetic structures of violence, these structures have to be changed as part of the process of reconciliation. This means changing all five aspects of hegemonic structures: 1. physical relationships; 2. definition of political rights; 3. economic rules that favour one group; 4. discursive structures in which languages diminishes one group; and 5. the spirit, presence, energy, or heart. Each group must be mutually opened up since each holds the key to the other's liberation. The process of transformation from a hegemonic structure to a post-hegemonic structure can be a long and painful process. Along the way those who were subjected might become dominant in a new hegemonic structure. Those who were oppressed often end up oppressing others when they are liberated. To prevent this from happening, there needs to be an open discussion about these structures and ethical standards must be developed to prevent another round of oppression.[29]

13. Celebration

Reconciliation needs to be celebrated. Celebration can involve eating, drinking, singing, joy, and laughter. It is a way of consolidating and recognizing the progress that has been made. Celebration is a way of reframing the story of the relationship among peoples.

These elements are given in an order that might occur in some situations. The elements may not occur in this order, however, nor are they usually dealt with in a once-for-all kind of way. Rather, they may work in a cyclical fashion. One may have to return to any one of them repeatedly. The new structures that are developed will have to be refined and the celebration may only be the beginning of a dynamic new life in which there may be relapses into conflict.

Dialectical Nature of Reconciliation

Throughout this discourse I have referred to reconciliation as a process. This emphasizes the dynamic nature of reconciliation and the sense that it is continuing. One can also look at reconciliation as an atemporal "thing," just as light can be thought of as both a wave (including temporality) and a photon particle (thing). Reconciliation may happen in a process where all of the elements come together simultaneously in a way that defies temporal explanation. The story of Joseph and his brothers effectively frames reconciliation as a process. However, one can focus on the instant when Joseph saw his brothers in their humanity and vulnerability in a new way—when he disclosed himself, saying, "I am Joseph." At that instance their reality changed. In an instant, violence was transformed into blessing. Something happened in Joseph's heart that was profoundly moving. His brain, heart, and body were all involved.

The mystery of reconciliation is that at some times there is truly a surprise of the spirit in which an entire situation is changed profoundly. One can say, "But it was the process and all the factors that led up to the reconciliation that are part of it." One can also answer that another person experiencing all the things that Joseph experienced could have hard-heartedly said to his brothers, "Okay, now I am going to teach you what suffering is really all about. I will show you what it means to be separated from family: each of you is going to be exiled to a different city. You will not see your father or children again." Instead, Joseph said, "Move here together where you will be looked after." Reconciliation cannot be programmed. As John Paul Lederach has observed, there is no technique that will make reconciliation happen.[30] We can, however, envision a framework for a process that would make room for all of these elements.

Framework for Reconciliation

At the beginning, it is important to bring to consciousness what we are up against in a deep-rooted conflict. There is a Self and there is an Other who is a Self and for whom the initial Self is an Other. Feelings of anger, hostility, envy, resentment, and hurt overtake the parties involved. These feelings commandeer the brain, which develops its own powerful logic within which there is a rationale for the conflict and a justification for seeking to hurt the Other. The body is either smashed and partially immobilized or every sinew and fibre is poised to act defensively or to take the appropriate counter-actions for the sake of "justice."

The deep-rooted conflict has a primary enframing around a relational system involving Self and Other. Self and Other may be individuals who define their identities in large measure by the conflict, in which the previous description works in a literal way. Self and Other may also be collectives in which the previous words function metaphorically to describe the dynamics of the collective. If collectives are involved they might have internal deep-rooted conflicts within their groups and a decision could be made to drop the reconciliation to a smaller level and focus on these conflicts. However, it is assumed that the primary conflict overshadows these internal conflicts and, for the moment, sufficiently unites each Self and Other in a common cause against one another.

The following framework is based on the assumption that parties are in a dialogical mode. What do I mean? Dialogue comes from the Greek words *dia* and *logos* meaning through and word. The image is of a free flow of meaning. Physicist David Bohm has developed the idea of dialogue to mean allowing the hidden assumptions, the vast tacit dimension of one's life, to somehow find expression.[31]

When people are truly in dialogue they end up "thinking together." Dialogue can be distinguished from discussion and debate, each of which has some degree of wanting to make a point, advance a position, or win.

Dialogue involves brain, heart, and body—*brain* in that creative ideas can be generated in thoughtful discourse; *heart* in that the profound emotional memories, deeply held values, and core attitudes need to be brought into play; and *body* because traumatic and ecstatic memories can be stored throughout the body at the cell level. Reconciliation, to be complete, has to have a positive effect at all of these levels.

To get into a dialogical mode means to suspend disbelief within the brain. If there is an inner logic at play that justifies hurt to the Other, this inner logic has to be put on hold. There has to be an openness to understanding the inner logic of the Other and a willingness to share with the Other all the reasons why one might want to hurt the Other. At this level, dialogue becomes the flow of logic as Self and Other disclose the kinds of logic driving each party. At the level of the heart there must be an openness to eventually embrace the Other: as Miroslav Volf distinguishes between being ready to embrace and being open to embrace eventually. The suspension of disbelief is also a suspension of hard- and cold-heartedness, an insight from Bob Birt. This does not mean that the heart is immediately warm and soft but rather that it does not insist on remaining hard and cold. The dialogical mode is initially an in-between mode; it is not fully trusting but is open to trust. It is partially vulnerable without giving up "weapons"; it is at the turning point where the current inertia is slowed to the point that may allow change of direction.

Chapter 15 will discuss processes and approaches that might foster a dialogical mode of being in which there is some openness to the possibility of reconciliation. The first challenge is to limit the hold, power, and devastation of mimetic structures of violence. One must remember that deep-rooted conflicts may serve the short-term interests of some parties. Some people make money from these conflicts, leaders use these conflicts to become popular, and as they define the identities of people the conflicts become a cherished part of who they are: "I will live and I will die a patriot (or whatever identity signifier fits)." Hence, the path to reconciliation is never straightforward.

Phase 1 – Deliverance from Mimetic Structures of Violence

The goal of phase 1 is to first understand and name the ways in which a deep-rooted conflict has marred the lives of Self and Other. This will involve a continuous back and forth rhythm between teaching the concepts and vocabulary of deep-rooted conflict and exploring through dialogue what these concepts mean in a given situation. All of the concepts for phase 1 are developed in detail in Part 1 of this book, and I will move fairly quickly through the framework. My comments can be taken as meta-theory, explaining why each theoretical concept is useful at the point where it is introduced. The different parts of the framework involve questions with an implied shared task for Self and Other to answer the questions as comprehensively as possible together.

One way of looking at what will be happening comes from the realization that there is something chaotic about deep-rooted conflict. At one level it includes much of what political psychologists call illogical. Looking at it from within the human person we can invoke Konrad Lohrenz's metaphor of a "parliament of instincts"—a host of different voices, impulses, and drives within the human person and within the human community.[32] As chaos theory points out, there is within chaos a hidden order. The theoretical perspectives used here help us to "see" and name the order within deep-rooted conflicts.

The meta-theoretical observation for the organization of Phase 1 is that it follows the sequence of memory, story, and coherence developed in Chapter 2 and modeled after Ricoeur's *mimesis*$_1$, *mimesis*$_2$, and *mimesis*$_3$. We first need to get the "bits" of information about the conflict—who, what, where, and when. Then we will introduce the temporal and causal dimension and look at what all of this means.

Step 1 – Basic Information about the Conflict – Enframing

First, it is important to ensure that Self and Other are talking about the same conflict and have a shared understanding of who is involved and what happened. Together they can enframe the conflict and even map out the parties, including persons involved in a primary way, a secondary way, and a tertiary way. They can identify groups and subgroups, stakeholders, and interest groups. In the process, it might be necessary to identify subconflicts that are a part of the larger conflict.

It would also be good to assess the current situation of the conflict, paying attention to its effects, impact, and costs.

Step 2 – Conflict as Narrative – Emplotting

When did the conflict start and what key events and actions were taken in the course of the conflict? These questions form the basis for a dialogical process meant to develop a shared story of the conflict. Each side's chosen traumas and chosen glories will be included. It should also be possible to go back to a time before the deep-rooted conflict. The process of identifying key events from the past will begin to create a shared understanding of what happened. This might itself raise some controversies, since what one side sees as a relevant event might not appear to matter to the other side. These controversies can be embraced and welcomed because they start to clarify fundamental assumptions, perspectives, and starting points.

Step 3- Looking at the Conflict Theoretically

As the conflict is examined dialogically using the following theoretical perspectives it should become clearer to all how the conflict escalated and what has been its impact on the human persons involved. For each theoretical perspective, information from Part 1 can be used as the basis for dialogue. The following theoretical concepts can be used to try to understand the conflict.

Human Identity Needs

Which needs satisfiers are affected? Which need categories were most affected as the conflict was beginning? Which need categories are most significant to the parties now? What would it take to satisfy identity needs for both sides?

Mimetic Phenomena

Are there patterns of mimesis going on? What forms of violence are imitated? What about mimetic desires? Who are the models? To what degree are identities formed mimetically? Who are the scapegoats?

Hegemonic Structures

Are hegemonic structures present within the conflict? How does each side experience these structures?

Ethno-Religious-Cultural Issues

How are ethnicity, religion, ancestry, land, and politics implicated in the conflict? What are the economic implications of these ethnonational distinctions? Who is benefiting from the conflict?

Gender

How do men and women experience the conflict? Are there similarities for genders across "enemy" lines?

Intensifiers

Which of the following intensifiers of conflict are present: rhetoric of us-versus-them, difficult life circumstances, bystanders encouraging the conflict, loss of face, dehumanization, or demonization?

Step 4 – Acknowledgement of Harm Done

Parties are encouraged to talk about their own participation in mimetic structures of violence and the results of that participation.

Step 5 – Choosing a Future Path

When it is clear what mimetic structures of violence are really all about, the parties can make a decision with a more complete awareness of the implications of their choice. They can decide to go back to a path of violence and justify this on the basis of their own logic of "justice," which is about punishment, retribution, and revenge. Or they can decide on a path of reconciliation, realizing that reconciliation does not necessarily imply closeness.

Step 6 – Dealing with the Past

In dealing with the past, the following are important actions to consider.

Check for Truth

Participants need to be given the opportunity to add any aspect of the truth that hasn't been told or ask questions of the Other that still haven't been answered.

Express Remorse

Participants should be given the chance to respond to the experience of the Other. This could range from acknowledging that they have suffered to taking responsibility for causing that suffering and apologizing. Sometimes in the case of historical injustices, people will have to acknowledge harm done by their ancestors. For example, when the Mennonite Brethren Church was formed in the southern Russian Empire in the 1860s, other Russian Mennonites persecuted this new movement. In the 1960s, 100 years later, the General Conference Mennonite Church, made up of descendants of the persecutors, wrote a letter of apology to the Mennonite Brethren.

Make Restoration

In acknowledging the loss of the Other, particularly if there has been asymmetric loss or confiscation of land or property, it is important to make restitution. If there is hurt, loss of life, or intangible damage, symbolic restitution can be made.

Offer Forgiveness

To forgive is to agree that no further punishment or retaliatory violence is needed or called for. Where the price of restitution that has been agreed upon is higher than can reasonably be borne by the Other, and this is worked out in good faith, forgiveness may be extended to part of the debt acknowledged to be owed by the Other. Throughout, the dignity of each party needs to be maintained. The dignity principle can help to pace the process of forgiveness.

Reframe the Story of the Relationship

Just as Joseph reframed the story of his arrival in Egypt in the light of a higher goal, participants might wish to reframe the story of their conflictual relationship in the light of the reconciliation. This reframed story would include positive highlights of their shared past, acknowledgment of hurt and trauma, and what they have learned about each other through the process.

Participate in a Ritual of Reconciliation

A ritual of reconciliation could be prepared to tell the story in a schematized and symbolic way offering symbolic actions to let go of past traumas and injustices. Reconciliation not only involves dealing with the past, it includes co-creating mimetic structures of blessing.

Phase 2 – Freedom to Co-create Mimetic Structures of Blessing

Mihaly Csikszentmihalyi, in his book *Creativity*, observes that the structure of creativity involves indwelling a domain, making the creative contribution, and finally having the field validate the fact that the creative act was sound and significant.[33]

In the case of a deep-rooted conflict, the dialogical work previously described would have the effect of getting each person involved to indwell the conflict and to indwell the world of the Other. The creative act is to produce a framework for a mimetic structure of blessing. The validation will first come from selling the framework to other parties and, ultimately, from the ongoing interaction between the parties.

One of the first things to determine is whether the mimetic structure of blessing needs to be oriented toward differentiation or toward undifferentiation. If there is a clear hegemonic structure or the parties have been highly differentiated to the point of each seeing the other as a thing, then it becomes important to have a mimetic structure of blessing based on undifferentiation. One needs to build bridges of understanding so that each starts to see the humanity of the Other. If there has been a mimetic rivalry between people who have become undifferentiated and highly dependent on one another for identity in a closed relational system, then a mimetic structure of blessing based on differentiation could be called for. This could involve bringing more people into the relational system, finding more physical space to create some distance, or agreeing on distinct goals or objects of desire.

Creating a mimetic structure of blessing involves examining all of the theoretical perspectives from the point of view of mutual empowerment. If identity needs have been defined so that for one to be satisfied the Other has to suffer, then the question becomes, How can identity needs be satisfied in a way that both can flourish? Finding positive satisfiers in one need category can strengthen the Self and open the possibility for finding satisfiers in need categories where the satisfiers of Self and Other butt up against one another. Mimetic theory can function heuristically as it asks these questions: Who are positive Models to emulate? What is their view of the Other that bears imitation in a non-conflictual way? What of the Other does one admire? and What are objects of mimetic desire that are not zero-sum? In the case of symbolic places that are not zero-sum, meaning that if one party owns the property the other cannot, understanding more deeply why certain sites are important can help to respect the Other.

Awareness of hegemonic structures leads both parties to start looking at the implications of changing such structures. The Dominant may be carrying many responsibilities of which the Subjected are unaware. Freedom from domination may look easy but might necessitate learning new skills, acquiring an inner ability to take initiative and action, and assuming responsibility for more things. The change in structure may involve a major redistribution of wealth to equalize the playing field. A new approach to language will need to root out those aspects of everyday speech that give prominence to one group over the other.

The categories of ethnonationalism can likewise be used to create new mimetic structures of blessing. The use of perceived shared ancestry of each separate group as a divisive tool may be deconstructed to allow for the historical reality that if you go back farther both groups share a common ancestry. The reality is that through intermarriage ancestry is generally more shared than groups tend to realize. Identifying those who have a mixed ancestry and giving them a special role in the relational system moves the centre of attention from that which creates difference to that which creates interconnections. Ethnic distinctions can be copied, where appropriate, and simply respected as culturally enriching aspects of reality. Celebrations of past accomplishments can be shared. Regarding religion, people can be invited to share in each other's religious celebrations, as was suggested in a recent meeting of our Muslim-Christian Dialogue.

Gender, too, can be the basis for blessing. Sometimes women can work together across the Self-Other split and men can likewise develop links. It is also possible that mixed groups including both genders from both sides of an identity group conflict can meet together and can mutually enhance each other's understandings of the role of gender in everyday life and how everyone can be empowered to live life to the fullest.

There is a place for people to simply wish out loud, to let their minds go in terms of their dreams for mimetic structures of blessing. To fulfill the dreams, hard work needs to be done to re-orient the customs, laws, decision-making, governance, and other aspects of everyday life. There is a need to think of supraordinate, or overarching, goals and to look at how rules, patterns, and values can be adjusted to meet these goals in an ongoing way. Ongoing processes will need to be built into the calendar for a reality check on how things are going and to resolve the inevitable conflicts that will come up. New policies and programs may need to be created and implemented to ensure that there is ongoing, positive interaction among groups.

Inevitably the effect of reconciliation is relief, joy, and well-being.

Until now, I have attempted to stay clear of theological discourse, although I have made reference to words and stories from the Hebrew Bible where these have been crucial for conceptual development. I have refrained from theological language for the sake of developing a discursive framework that is inclusive; that can be used by people not accustomed to thinking in theological categories. The following chapter introduces a conceptual dialogue between some of the concepts developed so far and theological ideas.

Chapter 14

Theological Reflections

It is a special gift to be liberated from the violent structures
of mimetic rivalry and scapegoating, it happens by being
truly open to a transcendent reality, it does not come
about by way of accomplishment, otherwise it would
prompt another round of rivalry.[1]

One aspect of current theological thought involves the practice of using theology in a particular context. What if the context is deep-rooted conflicts, and these conflicts are seen to be fuelled by some form of Christian belief? What if the theological discourse becomes a trigger for negative reservoirs of emotion that intensify intrapersonal, interpersonal, and inter-group conflicts? Contextual theology demands that one enter into the kind of discourse that makes sense within a deep-rooted conflict situation without preventing the participation of some protagonists.

Robert Schreiter believes contextual theology consists of two approaches: ethnographic and liberation.[2] The first emphasizes the characteristics and values of a particular identity group; the second emphasizes social change based on analysis of oppressive structures. Within the context of *conflict*, a theological framework picks up on both of Schreiter's categories and introduces additional factors. A study of identity-based conflict pays attention to distinctives of particular identity groups. In this regard, it is like ethnographic-based theology, except that it must consider what is important to both sides in the conflict. Like liberation-based theology, it is interested in social change as it looks for factors and processes to promote reconciliation and the well-being of both oppressed and oppressors. A third aspect of the theology related to deep-rooted conflict is the discourse of conflict studies theorists, many of whom are not theologically inclined, as may be the case for a good number of the participants in the conflict.

There is the danger of creating a meta-conflict between those who identify with theological discourse and those who do not. This latter point creates a paradox for the theologian, whose work is meant to have a peaceful effect, in that using in-house theological concepts could add another level of conflict to an already difficult situation. What is needed is a dialogical methodology, that is, a free flowing exchange of meaning including the tacit presuppositional base underlying the discourse. For dialogue to take place, a conceptual structure is needed to serve as an interface of ideas between non-theological and theological discourse.

I believe that the concepts of mimetic structures of violence and mimetic structures of blessing are a framework for reconciliation. They can provide an interface of ideas for a mutually productive dialogue among theological and non-theological theorists interested in addressing deep-rooted conflict. These same concepts can be understood theologically and the interaction of the theological and non-theological can produce mutually stimulating discoveries.[3] Some of the concepts already introduced have their origin in the Hebrew Bible.

Theological Concepts of Deep-Rooted Conflict

The concept of mimetic structures of violence and various Biblical representations of evil are quite similar. The link can be seen in the relationship between Saul and David, as described in the first book of Samuel in the Bible. Saul had just heard the people glorifying David by singing that while Saul had killed thousands, David had killed ten thousands. A feeling of mimetic desire, rivalry, and doubling overwhelmed him as he attempted to kill David, whom he had loved and whose presence he had enjoyed. After several unsuccessful attempts, Saul became obsessed with murdering David. Clearly, Saul's needs for meaning, recognition, and connectedness were unsatisfied because of his mimetic comparison with David. Had David not been praised, Saul would have been content. Since Saul and David represented the tribes of Benjamin and Judah, respectively, and, hence, the offspring of Rachel and Leah, the social identity and ultimate pre-eminence of one of these identity groups was at stake.[4] It is sadly ironic that their greatness was based on how many each had killed.

We know that deep-rooted conflicts, based on a mimetically defined threat to identity needs, are very real. But where do they come from? In the stories of Saul and David, a name was given to the impulse at the root of the conflict. The Biblical writer, aware of the power of this impulse, described it as "an evil spirit from God."[5] Similarly, when David wanted to conduct a census, possibly motivated by a mimetic rivalry with other kingdoms and a desire to prove his own power, he was said to be motivated by "the anger of the Lord."[6]

The impulse was seen to represent sacred violence. It is interesting that when the same story is told by the Chronicler, the spirit prompting the action that resulted in suffering and death was attributed to a spirit from Satan.[7] In the New Testament, Satan is the name given to the tempter. In doing so, the Gospel writers bring the Hebrew-Aramaic word for "adversary" into the Greek lexicon. Satan as adversary can be seen as mimetic rival, the instigator of acquisitive mimetic desire, and as persecutor. In Paul's Epistle to the Romans, the impulse toward destructive tendencies is defined as the power of sin and death or the lust of the flesh. The precursors and symptoms of deep-rooted conflict are frequently referred to as sin.

Some insights about mimetic structures of violence come from the symbols of demons and the devil. There is a clear association between the devil and deception. In the words of Jesus,

> You are of your father the devil, and your will is to do your father's desires.
> He was a murderer from the beginning, and has nothing to do with the truth,

because there is no truth in him. When he lies, he speaks according to his own nature, for he is a liar and the father of lies.[8]

Associating the devil with lies, emphasizes, for Girard and the theologians who followed him, the ability of mimetic desire to trick people into thinking that they will be satisfied when they acquire what the other has or wants. In truth, they will always be disappointed. "Father" is used in New Testament writings to talk about the person who inspires or generates a general set of characteristics. Children of Abraham are thought to have the characteristics of Abraham, but children of the devil pick up the murderous tendency shown in the scapegoat phenomenon. To be children of the devil is to be caught up in mimetic structures of violence.

The power orientation of evil is developed in Ephesians when the writer admonishes the reader to put on the whole armour of God "to be able to resist the devil's tactics. For it is not against human enemies that we have to struggle, but against the Sovereignties and the Powers who originate the darkness in this world, the spiritual army of evil in the heavens."[9] Walter Wink equates the "Powers" with structures of domination.[10] Girard develops the notion of Satan as the accuser who rallies both the elite and mobs to scapegoat a victim they deem illegitimate. The concept of accuser, coupled with a passion for power, provides the impetus and rationalization for those who would dominate others. In a particular conflict, accusations play a significant role; antagonists become mini-Satans as they embody the Accuser *par excellence*.

Etymologically, "devil" is a translation of diabolis from dia *(dia)* and bolis *(bolis)*. Bolis is derived from the verb "to throw" and the meanings for dia, include between, across, or through. Each adds a different meaning. If the etymology is to throw *about* or *across*, as Gil Bailie prefers, the root metaphor suggests that a devil-like person "sows discord and division" and "breeds animosity."[11] Taking "between" as the meaning for dia, the devil is one who throws something *between* two parties. This "throwing between" resembles an object of mimetic desire that comes between two people or groups who become Model-Obstacles for one another.

The *diabolos* produces all the psychosocial complications for which Girard's mimetic theory so ably accounts. The fundamental tool of the *diabolos* is what the author of the book of Wisdom called "the devil's envy," the mimetic incentives that generate the delusions and distractions of the social melodrama. At the critical moment, when these passions have sown enough frenzy and reduced a society to pandemonium, the *diabolos* changes its modus operandi. The *diabolos* becomes the *Satan*. Suddenly, the accusing finger points, and a violent avalanche is set in motion, the end result of which is a pile of stones, a glorious memory, and the rudiments of yet another of the kingdoms of "this world." What the *diabolos* divides, *satan* unites, minus the victim that makes the union possible.[12]

Bailie argues that the snares of *diabolos/satan* were broken by Jesus, not through "superior understanding" but through "God-centeredness."[13] "Sin" also needs to be considered when dealing with deep-rooted conflict as a movement into mimetic structures of violence.

Robert Hamerton-Kelly sees in Paul's concept of the "failed mind" (ἀδόκιμος νοῦς) a corruption of desire from which

> comes the deeply destructive forces of disorder, the vices that destroy human community: "wickedness, evil, covetousness, malice…envy, murder, strife, deceit, malignity…gossips, slanderers, haters of God, insolent, haughty, boastful, inventors of evil, disobedient to parents, foolish, faithless, heartless, ruthless" (Rom. 1:29-31). It is not difficult to see how all of these vices stem from mimetic rivalry.[14]

By means of Adam, "Paul is able to communicate the nature of sin as something that is both an act of individual irresponsibility and an imprisonment within a system of irresponsibility, both the individuality and the universality of sin."[15] Hence, Hamerton-Kelly writes that desire is deformed through mimetic desire, with contributions from original sin and an external force.

This same sense of being overwhelmed by a power beyond oneself is compared by Paul to the power of sin and death. It is a power that subverts the Torah—which is clearly right, good, and a gift of grace—by making adherence to the Torah a matter of mimetic rivalry, thus upsetting the very purpose of the Torah.[16] Paul equates the power of sin and death to being caught up with unbridled envy, greed, and lust—manifestations of an uncontrolled mimetic desire.

Mimetic structures of violence are oriented toward death, legalism, rivalry, and restricted options. They may move alternately from the appearance of a strict order, which may be covertly oppressive, to a kind of chaos as when "all hell breaks loose." As people get caught up in these structures, their very identity is centred on violence either as victims or as perpetrators.

In Girard's analysis of Dostoevsky's writings, the personal struggle of individuals caught in the clutches of obsessive mimetic doubling comes through with incredible poignancy. He expresses the hold that mimetic desire can have on an individual or group. With Dostoevsky he takes us along a path that leads to the unmasking of social messianism, doubt, and pride—words associated with the temptations of Jesus. Of these, pride is seen as particularly powerful:

> At the heart of everything there is always human pride or God, that is, the two forms of freedom. It is pride that maintains troubling memories deeply concealed; it is pride that separates us from ourselves and others. Individual neuroses and oppressive social structures stem essentially from pride hardened and petrified.[17]

Girard sees Dostoevsky first regarding himself as a sinner and, through a structure similar to Augustine's *Confessions*, opening himself to spiritual healing—a theme of death and resurrection.[18] Defining resurrection in terms of release from the forces of evil captures only half of the meaning of salvation. Reconciliation includes a deliverance *from* the structures of violence and a freedom *to* live a creative life of blessing.[19]

Theological Understandings of Mimetic Structures of Blessing

The designation blessing is based on the Hebrew [בְּרָךְ], which stands as an antithesis to curse. Like curses, mimetic structures of violence constrict the movement of people, limit life options, and are directed toward death. Blessings, in contrast, are empowering, lead to creative and expanding options, and are oriented towards life.[20]

Blessings are associated with gift, hence with grace and also love.

Rebecca Adams is the primary contributor to an understanding of love in mimetic terms.[21] As one desires the well-being of the Other, the Other imitates this love and desires her or his own well-being. Adams refers to this expression of love as the "intersubjective creative love of self and other."[22] She makes the link to Jesus through 1 John:

> The words of first John are the religious formulation of this same idea of the simple unity of familial, social and metaphysical realism, and our intimate, even commonsensical, human access to creative desire: "Beloved, let us love one another. For love is of God, and he who loves is born of God, and knows God. He who does not love does not know God for God is love." (1 John 4:7-8) From a reassessed Girardian point of view, the implication is that to imitate (follow in the way of love) in the way I have described is to "imitate Christ." To participate in an intersubjective gaze of loving creativity with others through mimetic desire is to imitate, image or reflect God.[23]

How is such love made real? At a theoretical level, using human needs theory, if subjectivity is about meeting human identity needs, then love is to enable the subject to find satisfiers to those needs. At a practical level, intersubjective love through mimetic structures of blessing becomes apparent in stories.

Two Prostitutes and Solomon

The story of two women prostitutes fighting over a baby (1 Kings 3) illustrates a conflict resolved with the help of a neutral third party—Solomon. Key to the resolution is an act of life-giving love by the real mother. Girard sees this as one of the closest actions to that of Christ.

In this story, two women, each with a baby, fall asleep at the same place. In the morning one of the women realizes that her child has died during the night. Before the other woman awakes, she switches the babies. When the other mother awakens, she recognizes that the dead child beside her is not hers. The dispute over who owns the living child is taken to Solomon, who decides that the living child should be cut in half with each mother getting one half. The real mother promptly states that the child should live and should be left with the other woman. Solomon recognizes the truth and returns the child to the rightful mother.

Girard suggests that the fact that both women were harlots is indicative of a "lack of differentiation" with a symmetry representing "the very essence of human conflict."[24] Solomon, asked to decide who should get the baby, suggested that the child literally be divided between the two women. Girard observes that the "Latin word *decidere* means etymologically to divide by the sacrificial knife, to cut the throat of a victim."[25] The dominance of mimesis over genuine love is revealed within the woman who switched the babies: the "only thing that counts for her is possessing what the other one possesses. In the last resort, she is ready to accept being deprived of the child as long as her opponent is deprived of it in the same way."[26]

Girard argues against using sacrificial language to describe the action of the real mother. He notes that it plays down the difference in action and attitude, relegating "to the secondary level what is most important for the real mother 'that her child should live.'"[27] He stresses that the "sacrificial definition always emphasizes renunciation, death and split subjectivity; that is to say, it emphasizes the values that belong to the bad mother, including the element of mimetic desire, which is identical with what Freud calls the death instinct."[28] The real mother's action speaks to an awful dilemma:

> Like Judah at the end of the Joseph story, the good harlot agrees to substitute herself for the sacrificial victim, not because she feels a morbid attraction to the role but because she has an answer to the tragic alternative: kill or be killed. The answer is: be killed, not as a result of masochism, or the "death instinct," but so that the child will live.[29]

Girard compares the role of Solomon to that of God who wants neither child nor mother to die. Girard observes that God

> is not on earth to put an end to the conflicts between doubles; on earth, there is no King Solomon who can bring about the rule of true justice. The human situation, at its most basic level, depends on there being no Fathers and all-wise kings to ensure the rule of justice for a humanity that continues in a state of eternal infancy…. So the only way of doing the will of the Father, on earth as it is in heaven, is by behaving like the good harlot, by taking the same risks as she did, which should be done not in a spirit of sacrificial gloom or morbid preoccupation with death but in a spirit of love for true life, so that life may triumph.[30]

As a story of reconciliation, it demonstrates love as the driving force to effect a change. The mother's desire for the well-being of the child is what determined the outcome. Solomon also desired the well-being of both biological mother and child.

The other key feature was the importance of truth. Solomon's articulation and discernment of the truth made it possible for the mother and child to be reunited. The movement went from being a structure of violence in which a child was stolen from its mother to becoming a structure of blessing. Furthermore, the reconciliation was just—for the wrong mother to get the baby or for the baby to be killed would have been unjust. A key aspect of the reconciliation process was that it was directed by a wise person whom both parties respected.

Solomon took a creative and dramatic step to discover the truth. He exposed the objectifying nature of the conflict by treating the child as a material object, an object that could have been cut in half. He also exposed the objectifying nature of the mimetic rivalry. Killing the baby would have equalized the rivalry—both women would have been equally childless but it would have murdered the child. The resolution was a mimetic structure of blessing in that it took place in a context of a violent structure of undifferentiation (doubling) and introduced a life-giving structure of differentiation in that the true mother decided not to imitate the action and attitude of her rival.

Girard's observation that it is important to take risks for the life of the Other is important. However, although there may be no wise kings, I would argue that there is a role for people who can introduce structures of blessing for those caught in mimetic structures of violence.[31] James Williams uses Psalm 72, the psalm about the righteous king, to make the point that it is incumbent on people in leadership to play such a role.

Jesus

As we use Biblical and theological concepts to show the process of reconciliation, we must acknowledge that for many caught up in deep-rooted conflicts the theological world lacks credibility.[32] This is especially true of Christology, the study of the role and person of Jesus Christ, and it is largely the result of violence that was perpetrated in the name of Christ and Christian complicity in developing colonial hegemonic structures. Christian theologians also tend either to be preoccupied with a spiritualized message or to adopt a gospel that has lost its transcendence.[33] It is true that much violence has been perpetrated in the name of Christ. Christianity itself has not escaped being taken over by structures of mimetic violence and scapegoating.

Endless rivalries and deep-rooted conflicts within Christendom should not distract us from the insights available from the life, teachings, death, and resurrection of Jesus. In fact, as these insights reach the inner reaches of our individual psyches and the hidden recesses of ecclesiastical structures, something may change. We may begin to live so that those around us will say, as the Canaanites were reported to have said of a Torah-living people: "Surely, that great nation is a wise and discerning people."[34]

As we look at the story of Jesus, we must keep this question in mind: What did Jesus do and say to address deep-rooted conflict?

Jesus entered a world rife with deep-rooted conflict. Judaism was divided into two factions: Hellenistic and Palestinian Judaism centred in Alexandria and Jerusalem, respectively. Palestinian Judaism was deeply divided among the High Priest, Sadducees, Pharisees, Zealots, and Essenes, each of which had internal rivalries. For example, the Pharisees were torn between the school of Hillel and the school of Shammai. Most of these Jewish groups were pitted against the Roman authorities politically and Hellenism culturally. Status was based on citizenship and rank within hierarchies. Tribal differences were kept alive, with the tribe of Judah predominating. Antagonism between Jews and their Samaritan cousins was intense. Conflicts among all of these groups included stereotypes and ethnomyths of differentiation. Many issues that Jesus addressed centred on these conflicts.

We pick up the story as Jesus approaches the beginning of his public ministry. His first experience is the temptation in the wilderness. The three temptations are all about mimetic desire: the Tempter tries to raise within him a desire for the power to produce food (social messianism); the prestige attached to safely jumping from the temple; and the power associated with hegemony over political kingdoms. The temptations themselves tell a great deal about mimetic desire. That Jesus was tempted meant that he was not immune from mimetic desire. In each case, he places the mimetic temptation into a broader, transcendent frame of reference; in doing this he robbed it of its power to entice. This was the first time Jesus stood up to powers that were associated with mimetic structures of violence.

One of his first actions, as Jesus began his ministry, was to gather together a group of disciples. This group addressed identity-based conflict because he chose people from a variety of identities: Galilean fishers, an urban tax collector, a Zealot, and an Israelite "in whom there was no guile"—a pious upholder of the Torah. There were rivalries among the disciples, including who would be the greatest in the final kingdom.[35] By announcing and demonstrating the primacy of servanthood, he showed the vanity of mimetic rivalries over prestigious positions and the desirability of working for the well-being of the Other. For him to bring this disparate group together shows his power to set up structures that transcend identity-based rivalries.

As Jesus walked through the towns and villages of Judah, Samaria, and Galilee he encountered many people who were possessed by an "evil spirit." The most dramatic story, told in chapter 8 of the book of Luke, involved casting out a legion of demons from a man who had become the perpetual scapegoat of his village. By releasing the demons, which had legitimized the scapegoating, Jesus dismantled the mimetic structure of violence. The demons then possessed a herd of pigs and the action of this herd of pigs, when they ran over a cliff, demonstrated the contagious nature of mimetic violence. Time after time, Jesus released people from the forces of evil that restricted their life options, opening up new possibilities for them.

Repeatedly, Jesus encountered situations where it was considered natural that someone be excluded because of their identity. In one case, a woman who was a "sinner" entered a Pharisaic dinner party and displayed her love for Jesus.[36] When he was criticized for accepting her in that situation, he insisted on opening the doors to her.[37] In other cases, he ate with "publicans and sinners" who were considered "unclean."[38] One of these was Zacchaeus, who, after his encounter with Jesus, repaid those whom he had cheated.[39] When Jesus delivered the daughter of the outsider Syrophoenician woman from an "unclean spirit," he called attention to her status but accepted her on her show of faith.[40] In his encounter with the Samaritan woman, Jesus transcended cultural boundaries by talking respectfully with her. The type of blessing exemplified in these cases where he reached out to ones violently differentiated is a blessing of undifferentiation.

Jesus revealed a God who was totally loving and non-violent. The Hebrew Bible contains many indications that God is essentially loving. Moses reminds God on two occasions that God's character is slow to anger and great in mercy.[41] On both these occasions the people had violated the covenant, prompting a crisis in which Moses himself was the intended scapegoat. While there is much in the Hebrew Bible that reveals a God who stands with victims and one whose חֶסֶד (hesed - merciful love) endures for ever, Jesus reveals something starkly unequivocal about the loving nature of God that can take the form of opening communities to outsiders.

> The image of God which [Jesus] proposes to us in the parable of the lost sheep (Luke 15:3-7) is exactly the inverse of the god we've seen. According to this parable the mercy of God is shown *not* to the group, but to the lost member, to the outsider. I ask you to consider quite how extraordinary this change of perception with respect to who God is turns out to be: mercy has been changed from something which covers up violence to something which unmasks it completely. For God there are no "outsiders," which means that any mechanism for the creation of "outsiders" is automatically and simply a mechanism of human violence, and that's that.[42]

The act of opening up communities and pointing out the violence in keeping them closed was very threatening to those who wanted to keep a closed community.

The challenging questions put to Jesus turned on identity distinctions. He was asked about paying taxes to Caesar, a question that was really about differentiation between Jews and Romans. He replied, "Render to God the things that are God's and to Caesar the things that are Caesar's."[43] When he was asked who was the neighbour, his story featured the Other, the Samaritan, as the one who showed what it meant to be a good neighbour.

Where Jesus was pushed towards a violence of differentiation, of making a group ontologically different and a potential scapegoat, his replies transcended difference, reframing the discourse to include new reference points. He took people out of a closed system of discourse, a system that violently turned in on itself and the people within it,[44] and brought them to a new awareness with a understanding of differentiation and undifferentiation. Where the Samaritans and Romans were the scapegoat Other, he developed a blessing of undifferentiation showing how, at a human level, people could be connected. Repeatedly he urged them to love one another as he had loved them, showing love to be a matter of mimesis.

Jesus' command that we love one another is deemed by Alison to be an "open definition" or "flexible paradigm." He paraphrases John 14:23 as follows:

> It is allowing their imagination and practice to be expanded beyond the culture sunk in death in which they were born, by means of what I have taught and carried out, that people love me. Your loving me consists exactly in this. By doing this, the entirely living and creative self-giving of my Father will come to possess you, and the Father and I will make of you someone who is an active, visible, historical participant in our creation a story of a diversity which knows not death.[45]

He goes on to paraphrase the love commandment as follows:

I am going to my death to make possible for you a model of creative practice which is not governed by death. From now on this is the only commandment which counts: that you should live your lives as a creative overcoming of death, showing that you are prepared to die because you are not moved by death, and you are doing this to make possible a similar living out for your friends.[46]

Jesus encountered people who were both victims and perpetrators of violence and he urged a movement towards the Other in a context that values the transcendence of differences. Where the Self was a victim, Jesus encouraged victims to continue to take the initiative; even being slapped should not lead to inaction but to turning the other cheek. He cautioned the vulnerable to remove the grounds for antagonism by potential perpetrators of violence. Where the Self is a potential perpetrator of violence, Jesus urged mercy.[47]

His relationship with God is ultimately what saved Jesus from participating in structures of violence. Throughout his ministry he was tempted to assume the mantle of political Messiah; he resisted the temptation. The only context in which he urged the word to go out that he was a Messiah was in Samaria,[48] where the concept of Messiah was that of a teacher.[49] Finally, he was tempted not to take his teaching to its logical conclusion when Peter urged him not to follow the path to the cross. When Jesus said to Peter, "Get behind me, Satan!" he was essentially saying, "Peter, you are getting sucked in by the mimetic structures of violence that surround you. You are operating on deceitful and murderous assumptions that a political Messiah put in place by force will bring life and goodness to your people." Later, when Jesus asked in prayer to God that his cup be taken from him, he concluded: "Not my will but yours be done."

Ultimately, what it took for Jesus to be the way, truth, and life was to simply allow the force of mimetic structures of violence to expend itself on him without allowing himself to imitate the pattern. In this way, he exposed these structures for what they were. His overwhelming conviction that it was the will of God that he make himself vulnerable to the violent forces erupting around him was the factor that prompted him to take that path.

Here [in 1 John 4:8-10] we have the element of the discovery of the absolutely vivacious and effervescent nature of God leading to the realization that behind the death of Jesus there was no violent God, but a loving God who was planning a way to get us out of our violent and sinful life. Not a human sacrifice to God, but God's sacrifice to humans.[50]

Schwager presents this love of God as tied to God's revelation of what is dark and evil as follows:

Therefore let us now turn our attention once again to the figure of Jesus. The prophet from Nazareth announced a God of loving kindness and uncovered the evil which lurks as a dark volition and mysterious passion deep in the hearts of human beings. These inclinations—as the judgement discourses of the New Testament, in contrast to the Greek tragedies, show—lead one not simply to kill but even to Hell. Therefore murder is here no longer the last dark point of reference. Murder becomes itself a parable of an even darker world and of an even deeper suffering, and allows a world which is eternally closed-in-on-itself to show through.[51]

Schwager's sense of a world "closed-in-on-itself" shows the tendency of mimetic structures of violence to become constrictive and restrictive.[52] Schwager's connection between the revelation of a God of love and the exposure of violent structures creates a radical break between God and the force of violence. If a key function of violence is to be "closed-in-on-itself," it means that the force of love is always opening up the system in creative ways.

Jesus was himself a victim of violence and Schwager shows how he identifies with victims:

It is precisely as victim that he intercedes for his enemies, and he identifies himself with them insofar as they are harmed by evil. As a result, people find themselves simultaneously in two camps. As *sinners* they turn against the crucified one, as *victims* of their own and others' misdeeds, they are accepted into a new community of prayer and hope before God, by him whom they have hurt. The cross effects a division within persons.[53]

Schwager argues that Jesus on the cross identified with people as victims, not sinners. However, key leaders in the early Christian church, such as the apostles Peter and Paul, are shown to be people with whom sinners can identify. Theologically, then, as we view any deep-rooted conflict, we can see people as both perpetrators and victims of violence. In specific instances some people are clearly only victims. In other cases, the roles swing back and forth or form mimetic chains. This sense of people playing two different roles is illustrated in the parable of the victim who was deeply in debt. After he was forgiven his debt, he proceeded to oppress the person who owed him a much smaller amount.[54] Only with an acknowledgment of being both victim and perpetrator can one concentrate on healing the victimization; this healing should prevent the victim from becoming a perpetrator of violence.

Jesus made himself voluntarily vulnerable[55] to victimization:

Jesus did not react with violence in turn against the violence which threatened him. He in fact commanded a disciple, who wanted to defend him with a sword, to desist from doing so. Jesus also did not—in contrast to the prophet Jeremiah—curse his enemies before God, but instead prayed for them. Consequently, he remained absolutely true to his message about the God of enemy-love and of nonviolence even in extreme mortal anguish.[56]

Jesus never suggested that he was acting on his own; instead, he constantly pointed toward the one whom he called Father. He believed that his sojourn on earth made it possible for everyone to have a relationship with God that was similar to his own.

His resurrection, as James Alison asserts, meant that the forces of violence had no power in the ultimate scheme of things.[57] According to Alison, Jesus kindled an imagination within his followers that involved a new, non-sacrificial way of being; in fact, Jesus himself had a new imagination. We will look at the significance and characteristics of this imagination.

> We have seen that Jesus knew from the beginning what he was doing, completely possessed as he was by his quickened imagination of the ever-living God. It was this which enabled him to stage a solemn mime in the midst of this death-based culture, so that he might be killed as a way of leading people out of that culture based on death, allowing us to come to be what God always wanted us to be, that is, utterly and absolutely alive with him.[58]

Jesus acted in accordance with his imagination. As such, he becomes a Model whose imagination and the actions associated with it can be subject to mimesis.

Alison gives us an idea of what it means to have a new imagination. He tells the story of a motorcycle instructor who demonstrated a jump through a ring of fire over fifteen cars, landing on a ramp on the other side:

> His novice bikers had previously considered this impossible: fear of gravity and of fire had definitively held them back from trying it. Their instructor has produced in them a belief in him, in a way that they can imitate, and then they do the same as he.[59]

Alison argues that Jesus likewise, "was producing in his disciples a belief in the non-importance of death by passing through it himself in the first place to show that it is possible."[60] In Jesus' case, he told them in advance what was going to happen (John 14:29) so that they would believe that it was possible to die and yet live.

This new imagination, kindled by Jesus, was eschatological. It was an imagination fixed on a living God: eschatological in that it offered an understanding of "a mode of time which has no end,"[61] not meant for some future time, but rooted in the present. Alison argues that when Jesus says, "I go to prepare a place for you," he was not referring to the afterlife, but a place to begin living in the present time. The implication of the eschatological imagination is that the Heideggerian ontology of humankind as "beings toward death" is transposed into "beings toward life."

What is the meaning of this eschatological imagination? It is based on transcendence, relationship, and love. Living out the eschatological imagination involved God and Jesus as actors, as Models to follow. Alison describes the work of God at the crucifixion as follows:

> When we speak, then, of God as love, it is not as if God loved us by throwing Jesus to us as if we were a pack of hungry crocodiles. No, God's love for us is the love by which Jesus was empowered as a human being to create for us—which means to understand and imagine and invent for us—

a way out of our violence and death.... The Father was present at the cross not as a spectator, but as the source of the loving self-giving which was bringing into existence the possibility that we humans might overcome death and its domination in our lives: God was not attending our show, but was busy in making of a typical show of ours a revelation of himself to us.[62]

Jesus, in turn, had his "extraordinary imagination, utterly fixed on God, in such a way that as a human being he could produce the final touch of divine creation, which consists in creatively imagining a way in which we—the rest of the human race—might be set free from what seems to be our very nature: mortality, and the way in which death runs our lives."[63] The eschatological imagination is based on an understanding that a transcendent God has been actively working with us at inventing a way out of violence and death.

This way out of violence and death is founded on the possibility of relationships. As David Burrell points out, this means imitating the relationship between Jesus and God:

What proves remarkable, for Schwager, is the way in which Jesus' call to erstwhile disciples to follow him is carefully crafted to circumvent the conflict potential to all *mimesis*. As the gospel of John articulates so clearly, the call to follow him is in fact an invitation to enter into the same relationship which obtains between Jesus and the Father. And since the object is not to gain the Father's approval, but rather to receive Jesus' own gift of friendship, and thereby enjoy intimacy with God, desire is transformed from striving to an "active receptivity." Discipleship, then, is a far cry from "imitating Jesus," but rather an invitation to enter into something entirely gratuitous and hence quite unanticipatable: friendship with God. This new mode of life expresses itself in service: "anyone who wants to be great among you must be your servant, and anyone who wants to be first among you must be your slave" (Mt 20:26-27).[64]

Burrell's comments highlight two important components: active receptivity and a willingness to serve. He also makes it clear that the relationship is with God but the expression is in the actions taken toward others. Jesus' words about servanthood are striking in the context of coming to terms with conflictual mimetic desire—the one who wants to be first will become the servant. It is the one engaged in mimetic rivalry who can look to humble service as the way out of the structure. In fact, the simple acknowledgment of the desire to be first already begins to dissipate the power of the structure. Some people who have had a tendency to serve too much do not need to hear this; rather they need to hear a message about their own dignity—to celebrate themselves as loved by God and worthy of good things.

Eschatological imagination must be rooted in love. As Jesus pointed out, the priority in the Torah is to love God with all one's heart, soul, strength, and might (mind is the New Testament formulation). The second commandment is to love one's neighbour as oneself. Jesus took the love commandments one step further, when he prayed that the relationship between God and those who came after him would be like the relationship he had with his eternal Parent and commanded his followers to love one another as he had loved them. This brings us back to the challenge to love, which is a challenge to participate in mimetic structures of blessing. The most demanding aspect of this is to love one's enemies. This means to work toward the transformation of those who are angry and violent[65] create a world without scapegoats,[66] and do so without self-destructing.[67]

We have shown that the theological idea of mimetic structures of blessing is centred on love within a similar field that includes grace and mercy. It demands justice rooted in truth, as shown in the story of the two prostitutes. Within a mimetic structure of blessing there is joy and delight in opening up communities to those excluded. It becomes important to resist the temptation of mimetic structures that lead to violence; this takes keen self-awareness. We also see an openness to transcendence, an insistence on being an actor even if that action involves making oneself vulnerable, and a strong sense of duty that precludes violence.

Creating a Theological Framework for Reconciliation

For myself as a theologian, the dialogue between the literature in the theoretical fields about deep-rooted conflict and theological concepts has had the creative effect of producing the concepts of mimetic structures of violence and mimetic structures of blessing. These can be described in non-theological terms in their own right. Particular concepts associated with mimetic structures of blessing, such as grace and love, can be understood in another way when developed theologically. Presenting these terms in non-theological ways in a secular context can contribute understandings that are helpful to people in the context of conflict. By offering clues to theological connections, I can reveal an openness to questions that might introduce theological discourse. A respectful dialogical space within which the secular, non-theist can be embraced on their own terms must be developed; then the unconditional love associated with mimetic structures of blessing in a theological sense can be expressed in a non-theological way.

Now, to speak in theological terms, let me synthesize what I have developed, expressing it in what Ken Wilber would describe as the Ascending approach to life. I begin with an awareness of a Transcendent Spiritual Other, a Creator associated with the evolution and development of life in all its wonderful forms. This Transcendent Self is in constant spiritual dialogue with humanity so that there is room for humans to grow, develop, and act on their own; at the same time there are significant influences from the realm of the Spirit. Some people can be acutely aware of these influences and flow with them. Others cut off their spiritual sensitivity or let it atrophy. People can become enmeshed in mimetic structures of violence that divert them from the best path they could follow and detract from the possibility of blessing.

This Creator arranged for Jesus to live on earth in a way that could demonstrate new possibilities for mimetic structures of blessing. These were expressed through teachings about the kingdom of God, through healing and reconciling ministries, and through a willingness to submit to the power of mimetic structures of violence without becoming violent. In doing this, he provided a new imagination of what was possible and the tools to make it happen. One of the most important of these tools was a forgiveness of people caught within these mimetic structures of violence. This profound forgiveness is shown in Jesus' words: "Father, forgive them, for they know not what they do." Through his teachings and example Jesus demonstrated creative love.

As we become aware of our own involvement with mimetic structures of violence, we have an assurance that through forgiveness of ourselves and others we can be released from these structures. We also have assurances that the energy to build mimetic structures of blessing—even in the face of violent challenges—is available through the Creator who has energy on tap. Theologically, this energy is named as the Holy Spirit, who either defends or empowers, as is needed. Evidence that this Spirit of Blessing is present is an awareness of love, joy, peace, patience, voluntary vulnerability, hope, and boldness.

Because humans have the freedom to constantly create new mimetic structures of violence, it can be difficult at times to see the potential and presence of mimetic structures of blessing. That is why special awareness is necessary.

The path of reconciliation involves: acknowledgment of participation in these mimetic structures of violence and of what happened to people as a result; an openness to change course; a release of the hold of violence, retaliation, and revenge through a profound letting go of violence at all levels; and a willingness to learn, create, and develop understandings of what blessing might mean in your context. The final step is to act upon this information.

Within a Catholic context, these generic steps could be followed specifically through the Sacraments, especially that of Reconciliation. Within the Mennonite tradition these would be expressed through personal salvation and a life of Christian discipleship (as shown in the German word *nachfolge*—following after Jesus). The language of the Biblical prophets emphasizes *shuv shuvut*—two Hebrew forms of the word for turning around, giving a powerful emphasis to the dynamic of inner change from violent attitudes to those of salvation and blessing. Whatever particular form the transformation takes, there is a profound turning around of one's situation that takes the combined energy of the Self and the Transcendent Other. It can also involve the collective community.

The world of theology and the world of humanistic and social sciences have provided questions and insights that have helped each world discover new things in this path to developing a framework for reconciliation. Awareness of human needs, ethnonationalism, and other concepts associated with deep-rooted conflict provide a new awareness of the context in which Jesus lived and moved. This helps to see, in a new way, the significance of his responses in particular situations. Going the other way, an awareness of the theological roots of blessing have led to the discovery of new insights about creativity and open systems within the non-theological domain.

Within the context of deep-rooted conflict, theology involves creating a respectful space for non-theological discourse. It means being open to a dialogue that plumbs the depth of being, that opens the Self to the World of the Other, and an opening of the Self to the Other. When this happens, always be open to the surprises of the Spirit.

Chapter 15

From Violence to Blessing

In the afterlife story, where people were starving for lack of collaboration in hell and people fed one another with their long forks in heaven, the question of violence to blessing can be expressed simply: How can we get people to start feeding one another? In Rebecca Adams' definition of love as desiring the well-being and subjectivity of the Other, the question is: How do we introduce mutually imitated caring into a relationship of mimetic hate, hostility, and violence?

Human identity needs theory challenges antagonists to re-define their identity, the very core of their being, so that leading a satisfying life does not hurt others in the process. Scapegoat theory offers the challenge to reconcile groups and communities without creating scapegoats. In hegemonic structural analysis, the goal is to transform these structures into something that "works" for everyone without creating new inverse hegemonic structures.

We must remember that human beings are capable of hurting each other in horrific ways. The torture chambers re-created in any wax museum graphically illustrate this violence. I spoke recently with Mike Baxendale, who told the story of the highway to hell in Iraq during the Gulf War of 1991. Several kilometres on this highway were strewn with bombed out vehicles and body parts, with the stench of burning flesh in the air. The mass graves and individual stories of the brutality of murder and rape that are on the news daily drive home the reality of violence.

More subtle forms of violence, such as playing psychological games, leave no scars—at least not on the outside. These include telling prisoners in solitary confinement every day that their food is poisoned or releasing prisoners one minute before midnight on the last day of their sentence. Human beings have a tremendous capacity to justify violence and to nurture violent thoughts and deeds by dwelling on hurt, perceived injustice, and comparison with others. Mimetic structures of violence can so seize the minds and hearts of people that they look for every opportunity to harm their Other.

Blessing. Now that is a different story—many stories, in fact. The language of blessing is the language of gift, of receiving or giving something. At the very least we have been given the language, culture, and stories of our ancestors. We have been given the insight, ideas, and institutions of those who have been creative in the past. We are constantly constructing what we say and what we do with the tools of the past. Within many cultures, mimetic structures of blessing are structures that allow people to collaborate and work together for good. In cultures around the world hospitality is shown to strangers—another form of blessing. Many people participate in random acts of kindness and a substantial number of people actually devote their entire lives to serving others out of a sense of care for their well-being. Some people risk their lives to save others—people such as firefighters, physicians and nurses in war zones, and politicians who put their careers at risk to do the right thing. Signs of blessing are all over the world.

Many deep-rooted conflicts occur between individuals and peoples who were once friends. In fact, closeness and intimacy set up a relational system where mimetic conflicts become most intense. This means that there must be many unconscious memories of blessing—memories of a time before the conflict or before it was so intense. One of the challenges of transforming violence to blessing is to recover these lost memories of blessing. Tearing something down is much harder than building it up. Moving from violence to blessing takes an immense amount of positive energy—the good news is that positive energy increases when resources are combined.

The Origins of Community-Based Conflict Resolution

I began a doctoral program at Saint Paul University in 1991 to do my homework on the subject of deep-rooted conflict between identity groups. The Canadian Institute for Conflict Resolution (CICR) is located at Saint Paul University and Bob Birt had just returned to Ottawa to head the Institute. I began to drop by for coffee with Bob and this allowed me to observe the beginnings of the community-based conflict resolution methodology that he developed and to help implement the principles.

Bob drew significantly on ancient Chinese thought for the principles he first announced in a 1994 speech. A key principle is the idea that everyone in a community should have access to the same conflict resolution training principles and skills. Known as the principle of union, it is based on the Taoist observation that all streams run into the same river. A second principle is that gathering, itself, is a conflict resolving activity. Gathering, in this context, is the process of getting the right people into a conflict resolving process or training activity. The third is the principle that community-based conflict resolution should be inclusive and barrier free. A fourth principle is that you start out with an activity that is positively centred, or non-issue based. Fifth, it is important to welcome everyone who might come to this activity. The sixth principle is that dignity and respect foster trust, and where trust is present the truth will come out. And last is the question, Who else should be here?

In the following years, Bob developed the idea that Third Party Neutral training could serve as a positively centred activity, and that this training in the context of the above principles could itself resolve conflicts.

In September 1994, I began a one-year residency at CICR that eventually led to my assuming presidency of CICR in 1996. In the early years of my involvement, I did most of the gathering for the training courses, trying to use the gathering process to bring together people who needed to talk. For a long time we tried, as a matter of principle, to include at least one police officer in each training group. Together with Gary Nelson of the Ottawa Police, we began a Cops and Kids program for police recruits in which they took two days of conflict resolution training with young people. For a number of years every new recruit with the Ottawa Police took this kind of training. The gathering process involved people from almost every sector of society and immigrants from every part of the world. As the president of the *Canadian* Institute for Conflict Resolution, I made a point of including First Nations, French, English, and New Canadians—the four sets of voices I knew to be essential in bringing a sense of national reconciliation to Canada.

In 1996, Richard Batsinduka came to see me. He had been personally devastated by the genocide in Rwanda. After taking initial training at CICR, he, too, decided to do a residency. As he learned more about community-based conflict resolution, he became convinced that this could work in Rwanda. In the summer of 1997, he went to Kigali, Rwanda, and gave two Third Party Neutral training sessions, using training as an intervention to bring people together. In each case, Hutus and Tutsis were involved in the training. This balance of Hutus and Tutsis was important in his initial training. He also needed representation from the right government departments, non-governmental organizations, and churches. Because of the overwhelming majority of women in Rwanda after the genocide, it was also important to have many women present in the initial process.

When he came back we worked on a longer-term strategy to bring a group of eight Hutus and Tutsis to Canada for a full training program with Richard coaching some of them to become trainers. Through the process, a thousand Rwandans received Third Party Neutral training; the ripple effects are still continuing. On one occasion when Richard was in Rwanda, he heard about a change of heart in the man who had killed his brother. Here is an account of his reconciling encounter with this man.

> ...Batsinduka went to the prison...[to] meet the murderer..."When he came in, I stood up, but I could not speak. I was sweating and he was shaking, avoiding my eyes."

> The murderer, Diogène, told Batsinduka how he had decided to repent, after some Christians had visited the prison. "Most of the prisoners think I am an idiot, but if I can have your forgiveness, nothing else matters," he said.

> Batsinduka asked Diogène if he understood how, in killing these people, he had not only destroyed them, but the whole community. Would he be ready to meet the community and ask for their forgiveness?

> "He did not reply, just burst into tears. After about 10 minutes, I asked again and he said yes, he would meet the community and do whatever they wanted. And if they wanted him to die, he would die happily, as long as they forgave him.

"I said, 'As far as I am concerned I am forgiving you from the bottom of my heart.' I felt warm in my heart: that I had done something Vincent would have wanted me to do."

Batsinduka went back to his in-laws and explained what had happened. "I am convinced he wants to repent," he said. "Now it's up to you." Diogène's future will depend on the relatives of his other victims. "But after I talked to him, he had hope."

And what hope does Batsinduka have for forgiveness in Rwanda? "It requires moral values many don't have or surrendered because of what happened in the country." He puts his hope in education, which could free Rwandans from the prison of their own personal suffering, and help them to understand that others have suffered too.[1]

Another person with whom I had the privilege to work was Vesna Dasović Marković, who was recruited to take training by Brian McQuinn, a young Resident working on international applications of community-based conflict resolution. When I initially suggested that Vesna give training in her native Bosnia, she resolutely replied in the negative. More than a year later she came to see me and stated that she was ready to train in Bosnia and Herzegovina. Her initial pilot training in the summer of 1998 involved gathering Serbs, Croats, and Muslims together for training in Banja Luka, a Serb-dominated province, and in Mostar where Muslims lived on one side of the river and Croats on the other.

When she began this program in Bosnia, it was absolutely imperative that Serbs, Croats, and Bosniacs all be present. Finding a neutral place for the program was a challenge. In Vesna's case, organizing the program in the city of Mostar was difficult. The most neutral place she could find was a community centre in a sliver of Bosniac territory on the Croat side of the river. Contacting people was difficult because phones did not connect from one side of the river to the other. Getting Serbs to participate was extremely difficult since they were afraid to enter the city. Because of her commitment to the methodology, she spared no effort until she succeeded in getting two Serbs to come into the city of Mostar for training along with Croats and Bosnians.

In both Rwanda and Bosnia, where the effects of mimetic structures of violence are some of the worst in the world, the efforts of Richard and Vesna and the teams they created helped to introduce mimetic structures of blessing using the methodology of community-based conflict resolution.

An Intervention Strategy

Using the experience of those working in community-based conflict resolution and the framework developed in Chapter 13, we can now develop intervention scenarios that enable people in a deep-rooted conflict to begin a path of reconciliation. Reconciliation is not, however, a function of technique, though certain techniques might help, and it is not about programming people to be different. Reconciliation starts with Levinas' observation that the interiority of each person is infinite and cannot be boxed in. Nonetheless, teachings and processes can expedite reconciliation; there are conditions under which reconciliation is more likely to occur. Physicians and midwives cannot guarantee the birth of a healthy child but can make it more likely that certain complications will not harm the new baby. In the same way, Third Party Neutral interveners cannot guarantee that reconciliation will happen. But they can create conditions under which it is more likely to happen.

A third party intervener is someone who is conscious of a deep-rooted conflict and wants to initiate change. Such an intervener needs to be specially prepared in terms of skill-development, background knowledge, and, above all, internal preparation. The intervener must have a vision for transformation and yet be completely open to ideas and events that don't fit that vision. There must be a willingness to embrace every party in the conflict, treating each with dignity, valuing them as human beings, and showing respect for them. There must be both transparency of vision and a poker-faced ability not to disclose confidential information. The intervener must be willing, even predisposed, to give others credit if they verbalize ideas sprouted from seeds planted by the intervener. An intervener must be able to flow with the energy of the moment and, at the same time, keep a firm hand on process and a strong commitment to enforce process principles.

A third party intervener may be motivated by an ethic of caring directed to the parties involved. Interveners may see this role as a lifelong calling or may be specially positioned to deal with one particular conflict because of a history of past relationships. An intervener may also be a professional, motivated by the particular challenges of some conflicts and the prospect of making a living working to resolve deep-rooted conflicts.

Working on the assumption that a deliberate attempt to challenge and transform mimetic structures of violence demands an interactive process, the first question to be asked is: Who should be there? This question raises the issue of gathering, which is itself an important initial conflict-resolving process. The gathering process is meant to bring the right people to the right place at the right time. In the process of gathering, each participant must be briefed about the process. This entails explaining the point of the process, introducing the other parties to the process, and explaining what is expected of them. The gathering process involves many one-on-one conversations. Inevitably, one conversation opens up new possibilities for others who can be invited.

A group of 16 or 20 people is an optimal size for an initial process. The initial intervention in a conflict between identity groups must involve a balanced group representing the most important stakeholder groups. The conflict has to be enframed asking the question: Who are all the persons or groups involved in this conflict?

As the key subgroups are identified, it is important to find representatives who are open to a process and will continue to hold the respect of their constituency. If they move too far ahead of their own group in any process, they may be perceived as selling out to the Other. Getting a balanced group involves attending to gender, class, position, sector, and any other distinguishing feature that is significant to the dynamics. Sometimes a power behind the scenes needs to be considered.

As already mentioned in Chapter 13, the people who come into a reconciliation process need to be in a dialogical mode; that is, they must have an attitude to discuss openly with other people to bring out everyone's truth. They should be prepared to treat everyone involved with dignity and respect. The question then becomes: How do people prepare for this?

Where there are post-traumatic stress disorders, people will need counselling from professionals or peers who can help them articulate for themselves what they are experiencing. Sometimes a process skill development course should be first offered to a group on each side to lay a foundation. Then alumni from each group can join to begin the process of understanding the dynamics of the conflict.

Where possible, it is desirable for a balanced group from each side to join in process skill development training. This training could be Third Party Neutral training, training in dialogue process, circle process, or some other form of conflict resolution training. Whatever type of training, it should be experiential, it should put people into smaller groups, it should be interactive, it should be positively centred and non-issue-based, and it should train people in the principles that expedite conflict resolution. Examples of such principles are

> Listen with your ears, your eyes, and your heart.
> Think through what you say and do.
> Be aware of your emotions; don't let them undermine the process.
> Treat each person as though they had infinite worth.
> Respect the views of each person even though you don't agree with them.

Additionally, it is worthwhile to explore teachings from participants' culture that help people live in harmony and to learn about processes that they have seen used to resolve conflicts. Through one-on-one meetings with potential participants, interveners can determine if they are ready for the dialogical process.

At this point, I can imagine how the process could unfold as I remember a Middle East case study that I conducted in 1999. With the help of Heyam Qirbi, an Arab Muslim friend, I gathered a group of five Arabs, several informed people who didn't have a particular bias, and Yitzak, a Jewish friend who had known a number of founders of the State of Israel and who had visited there often. (I tried very hard to balance the number of Jews and Arabs, but could not do that; Yitzak was a very strong spokesperson for the Jewish Israeli perspective and held his own quite nicely.) We started by identifying conflicts in the Middle East. (This activity was positively centred and non-issue-based; we could all work together to identify conflicts.)

Of the conflicts we identified we chose the Persian Gulf War and the Arab-Israeli conflict to analyze, and we spent a day on each. After the enframing and emplotting, in which we asked who was involved and what happened, we did an analysis together using the theories of deep-rooted conflict presented above. The third day we devoted to developing scenarios for reconciliation. That day, Yitzak came a little late. The group had developed such a close bond by this time that on his arrival everyone spontaneously broke into a round of welcoming applause. Some of the ideas for reconciliation identified by that group were truly amazing.

In October 1999, I delivered a seminar on deep-rooted conflict and reconciliation in Mostar. The week before, Vesna had offered a Third Party Neutral training workshop. In my seminar were Serbs, Croats, and Bosniacs, all of whom had taken TPN training—some the week before and others in previous sessions. After looking at deep-rooted conflict together in that context, we moved into a reconciliation mode. The group brainstormed over 60 elements of reconciliation. The process itself was reconciling. At the end of the session, an Imam from a Mosque on the other side of the river eagerly gathered all the flip-chart sheets so he could type them up for distribution to the group, which he did. Up until the previous week, when he came for the TPN training, he had not had any contact with a non-Muslim for the four years since the end of the ethnic cleansing and civil war.

In both the Middle East case study and the Mostar seminar we created together a mimetic structure of blessing in that we were all feeding each other. But we did not address systematically all of the personal pain and the structural issues that needed to be addressed. With the framework developed in Chapter 13, it is possible to imagine a two-week process that would look first at deep-rooted conflict and mimetic structures of violence and then systematically work at imagining and creating new possibilities for reconciliation and mimetic structures of blessing.

Synchronicity and Surprises

My son, Quinn, works in the fraud department of a major credit card company. He told me recently that he does his job with compassion. What this means to him is that he empathizes with the people whose lives fall apart, who experience tragedy, or who lack the personal life skills—any of which might lead them to use their or another's credit card irresponsibly. Does this mean that he lets them off the hook lightly? Absolutely not. If they have run up an account and are legally responsible for what is owing, they are held to what they owe. In the process, however, rather than being harangued, confronted in a menacing manner, or lectured in a way that would make them feel worse about a situation, they encounter someone who shows some feeling and understanding for their plight.

The fraud department of a multinational banking institution hardly seems the first place to look for examples of mimetic structures of blessing. This very incongruity makes it striking—a surprise. The story is illustrative of the way in which, when we look carefully, we can find people who make a positive difference in the lives of people even though the bigger relational structures are hardly defined in terms of looking out for the well-being of the Other.

When my daughter Natasha went to Taiwan to give swimming lessons to children with disabilities, she was surprised to find the pool not yet completed. She developed her own job description: to simply love the children.

I have had the good fortune to know Tim Maindonald, Chaplain General for the Canadian armed forces. He has told me stories of soldiers on peacekeeping duty who came across humanitarian disasters and worked hard to get shoes for barefoot children and food for starving people. It was certainly not their job to embark on these humanitarian initiatives, but the fact that they, as individuals trained for combat, opened their hearts to suffering people reveals the potential for mimetic structures of blessing to emerge in surprising contexts.

I believe that people of goodwill can find a way of making a positive difference in the lives of others in any situation. My friend Wilf, an ex-con who had killed his best friend while under the influence of alcohol, used to make a point of giving money (out of the little he had) to panhandlers because he knew what a hard life on the street was like. My Aboriginal friend Louise, who had tasted life's sorrows, once won a few hundred dollars in a lottery. She immediately changed it to $5 bills and distributed the money on the streets to Ottawa's poor. A few years ago I caught a glimpse of Oprah's show when she had people telling stories of random acts of kindness.

As compared to a broad strategy for reconciliation involving a concerted effort over a long period of time, as developed in the Chapter 14, I am talking about developing ad hoc mimetic structures of blessing by individuals who simply wish to make a difference in their own way. Sometimes it is a one-time occurrence and sometimes it is a long-term commitment to, for example, work as a volunteer for a cause that makes the lives of people better.

Sometimes what starts as a small ad hoc initiative ends up having a major impact on the lives of many. More than 50 years ago, a woman accompanied her husband who was working for Mennonite Central Committee to a poor Southern country. As a gesture to help struggling local artisans she brought a suitcase full of their wares to sell back in North America. This spontaneous gesture was the genesis of what has become Ten Thousand Villages, a multi-million-dollar fair trade enterprise using the services of thousands of volunteers to market products made in underdeveloped countries in North America in a way that helps numerous artisans sustain themselves.

Similarly, in 1974, Dave Worth and Mark Jantzi were probation officers in Kitchener-Waterloo. In their charge were some adolescent boys who had vandalized more than twenty homes. When they met with the judge before sentencing they suggested that it would be nice if these young offenders would meet the victims. "Impossible!" replied the judge. However, when they went into the court he sentenced the youth to meet with their victims under the supervision of Worth and Jantzi and to make appropriate reparation. This event started a Victim-Offender Reconciliation Program (VORP) that mimetically inspired a host of such programs across North America and in Europe.

In the 1980s I was part of a team that evaluated mediation services in Winnipeg, one of these programs. I heard how a staff member would go to the police station every morning and read the new files. Staff members followed up, appropriately, those that looked like they held the potential for mediation. If both parties would agree, volunteer mediators would lead them through a process. For those who go to mediation there is generally an 80 per cent success rate. Correctional Services Canada now has a division dealing with restorative justice. This practical work had the theoretical spin-off of introducing a restorative justice paradigm into the criminal justice world. One of the primary theoreticians is Howard Zehr, whose book *Changing Lens*[2] has been used around the world. This theoretical development in turn inspired and provided legitimacy to a host of other programs designed to humanize the process and to allow victims, offenders, and communities to generate positive, constructive, and creative responses to the violence of crime.

One person who heard of the VORP program in Kitchener-Waterloo was Sheriff Douglas Call of Genesee County in New York. He developed a vision to bring victims and offenders together in the case of serious crimes like rape and homicide. He developed a victim-centred approach that led to some very creative sentences that actually helped victims and the community. One example involved a businessman who had killed a man in an accident while driving drunk. Part of the sentence was for this man to purchase for the city a "Jaws of Life" machine designed to help removed injured people from cars wrecked in accidents. Doug Call inspired Dave Gustafson in British Columbia to embark on similar programs dealing with some of the most severe types of crimes.

Gloria Neufeld Redekop, in her social history of Mennonite women's societies, showed how these societies provided a place for women to both flourish and provide a substantial service to others:

> Mennonite women's societies became a context where Mennonite women could be full participants in every aspect of worship and, at the same time, become involved in missions and service in their own way.[3]

Within a hegemonic structure these women, as those dominated, created a separate structure of blessing. As greater opportunities opened up within the broader church, personal gifts nurtured in these societies were used in another relational system.

These stories, while important in and of themselves, become metaphors to show how acts of blessing that combine a desire for the well-being of others with creativity and openness have a mimetic ripple effect far beyond what was intended.

One of the things that I have observed in many instances has been the role of synchronicity. This word comes from the Greek words *syn* and *chronos* meaning "together" and "time" respectively. The root metaphor means that things come together at the same time. In his book on synchronicity, Joseph Jaworski develops the concept that people on trajectories that are not causally linked encounter one another at a critical time to make a positive difference to one another.[4]

There was synchronicity in my starting a doctoral program at Saint Paul University in 1991, the very year that Bob Birt came back to Ottawa to work at CICR. Here is a more recent example. As I was writing this chapter, I received a call about a used stove we had for sale. The call turned out to be from someone deeply concerned about the violent conflicts I was writing about.

Just as there is something illogical about what drives deep-rooted conflicts, there is something that transcends logic and rationality involved in the evolution of reconciliation and mimetic structures of blessing. This something includes the energy we project; body, brain, and heart memories of past reconciliations; positive emotions; teachings that make a difference; and synchronicity.

Several years ago, I spent some time with former General Joseph Lagu, then roving ambassador for peace from Sudan. He had led the Southern army of rebels in fighting Northern Sudan in the 1960s and '70s. He told me that he was selected as a bright young man to go to officer training school in the North. When the southern rebellion was started he was called upon to lead the military initiative. He talked Israel into providing military assistance so that they could keep the Sudanese army distracted from fighting Israel at the time of the Six Day War. In the context of a mimetic structure of violence where hostile feelings were high, a planeload of northerners crash-landed in territory controlled by Lagu's army. Fortunately, no one was killed in the crash; however, Lagu's advisors urged him to massacre the lot of them in the same way southerners had just been massacred by the North. Lagu decided to sleep on it; at night what came to him was the story of the feeding of the five thousand from the New Testament, a story that had been taught to him at the Anglican residential school he had attended. He decided to feed the prisoners and let them go. This act had a number of positive ripple effects within the country. It was interesting that the plane landed where it did, and that teachings given by teachers who never dreamed that one of their students would be a military commander had such a surprising impact.

I have learned that children can play a significant role in the transition from violence to blessing. My daughter Lisa, whose perpetual smile has warmed the hearts of many, guided me into a unique opportunity in an unexpected way. One night in the early 1990s, I went to "Parents' Night" at her dance class. Also in attendance was Ovide Mercredi, National Chief of the Assembly of First Nations (AFN), whose daughter was also in the class. He invited me to do some work on economic development at AFN. A few weeks later, the resident Elder asked to see me. When he asked me how I had ended up there, I told him about Lisa and the dance class. He responded, "The children have called you… what you do here will be good and pure." His blessing was a blessing within a blessing, and it reminded me to honour the well-being of children.

Over the years, as I have offered seminars on reconciliation, an important part of each seminar has been for people to tell their own stories of reconciliation. Time and again they have told stories in which the most unexpected events, actions, or comments triggered what appeared to be a spontaneous process of reconciliation. Here is an example from Somalia contributed by Abdi Hersi:

The Roots of Reconciliation

In the period of turmoil and uncertainty, and in the absence of legitimate state institutions, clans and sub-clans have reverted to their own traditional structures. Particular emphasis has been given to the appointment of sultans—a secular political office, sanctioned by religion. Other important traditional elements have been the mediating authority of Akils, or heads of Dia-paying lineage groups, and the elders and religious leaders whose roles have been expanded in the recent years due to the vacuum left by the collapse of the Barre administration.

All clans in Somalia and some of the larger sub-clans now have their own Supreme Council of Elders, known as Guurti. These fulfill a dual role as legislature and executive, with responsibility for everyday questions arising within the clan and also for arbitration between different clans.

Progress to Peace

The mechanisms for establishing peace depend on joint community committees formed at the local level that are empowered to implement agreements reached by Councils of Elders. Another local authority, known as "the committee, which uproots unwanted weeds from the field," is responsible for dealing with banditry and minor disturbances. This localized approach to peacekeeping began with a series of inter-clan reconciliation conferences in the 1990s and gradually advanced to district, regional, and national levels. The authorization of agreements at peace conferences is given by clan elders, but other traditional leaders—politicians, military officers and particularly religious men and poets—have also played a crucial role in any peace process.

Religious figures, such as sheikhs or Islamic scholars, take their duties as peacemakers seriously. Their authority is based on the esteem in which they are held as spiritual leaders, as distinct from Akils and sultans, whose status is more secular. Spiritual leaders are seen as ideal and neutral arbiters with allegiance to universal Islamic values that transcend clan loyalties. They do not settle disputes themselves or sit in judgment. This is the work of elders in council. Instead, their task is to encourage rivals to make peace. To this end, independent delegations of renowned holy men have taken part in all the major peace initiatives between previously hostile clans in Somalia.

Poetry, which is the most celebrated and respected art form in Somalia, has also been marshalled to the cause of peacemaking. Through metaphor and allusion, oral poetry can tap the richest reserves of Somali discourse; it is widely understood and enjoyed and, like the mass media in the west, it has the power to influence opinion.

Women have played a significant part in peacemaking. After marriage, a woman retains her kinship ties with her father's group, even though they are often denied the property rights that these entail. The dual kinship role conferred by marriage has often existed across two neighboring, but warring, clans with the result that women have suffered unduly in Somalia's upheaval. It has also meant that women have taken on a new and active function as ambassadors between rival groups—the group that they married into and the group they were born into. This is a function of their traditional role in systems of exchange.

Modern technology has also been instrumental in the reconciliation process. In the past, radio communication was the monopoly of the government and international organizations. Recently, however, the elders of several bitterly embattled clans in Somalia have remained in constant radio contact during periods of tension, and radio links have provided vital channels for negotiation.

— Abdi Hersi

Visions of Blessing: From Heart to Globe

One of the biggest challenges for me is to continue to find my own paths of reconciliation. Knowing all the theories of deep-rooted conflict does not prevent me from having my own such conflicts. The path from violence to blessing always starts at home. I have also come to realize that the principle of subversion has tremendous validity; it informs us that anything intended for good can be subverted for evil purposes. Hence, a second challenge is to first discern how something that camouflages for blessing is really intended for violence. What appears to be assistance to people can easily become the means of controlling them or, in another instance, the means of getting another kind of benefit. On the other hand, there are circumstances that might appear at the beginning as structures of violence but because they are moving things toward reconciliation and blessing are really positively oriented. So much depends on where people are coming from.

Tilman Martin was at one time chaplain at a medium security penitentiary. I worked with him on a number of programs. One of the programs he developed was a Christian Action Group that became a community within the penitentiary. A Christian Action Committee made up of prisoners ran it. Many on the Committee were not Christian; at one time it was headed by a Jew. A key aspect of the programming was bringing volunteers into the Chapel to meet with prisoners. After each meeting, Tilman would debrief the event with his Committee. If a volunteer had been harassed or not treated respectfully, Tilman would gently make this observation to the Committee and they would deal with it. It never happened again. I remember Tilman observing to me that his Committee used means of discipline that he and I would never dream of using. In this case, in a context where violent people were held in a mimetic structure of violence (physically and relationally), what might look like violence through a camera could in fact be closer to blessing since it established the possibility for good and mutually beneficial relationships.

Having headed an organization devoted to conflict resolution that developed deep internal divisions, I have a great deal of humility when it comes to formal efforts to bring about reconciliation. Not that I think that we should avoid these: by all means, we must develop institutions that effectively address the structures of violence that threaten the lives of people and life in the biosphere generally. But part of the vision that I have for structural transformations is to have congruence at every step of the way. People working for changes that imply long-term blessing, especially for those victimized in ways they themselves do not even comprehend, must be careful not to introduce structures of violence into the relational systems within their organizations and close to whatever home might mean for them.

I have helped develop a paradigm of cooperative approaches to crowd dynamics. The idea is to bring protesters, their targets, police, and bystanders together to find a way in which public dissent can be registered without the violence associated with dissenters at international summit gatherings. In the process, I have seen activists who espouse causes close to my heart treat police with disrespect, and I have heard of police violence directed towards peaceful protesters. We each have our Others who become the depersonalized enemies whom it is very difficult to love.

This is at the heart of the transformation, to let the power of love work its magic in healing relationships and in driving us to devise new institutions of governance, new policies, and new programs that make blessings flow. How can we equalize wealth where the inequalities are the result of centuries of violence and exploitation? How do we allow the powerless a voice in the mega projects that potentially affect the health and well-being of many persons? How do we change the mimetic rivalries of the super-rich who acquire more and more to beat their rivals without thinking about what they are doing or even asking why they are doing it?

If the powerful could really understand mimetic structures of blessing and begin to work within their realms of action to make these structures come into place, the world would be a different place. The problem is that people who live and work in the world of the warrior, to use a phrase from Freeman Dyson,[5] put their professional energies into mimetic structures of violence. On the side, in their personal life, they might make contributions to what would be closer to blessing. A crass example could be a Nazi officer in charge of a concentration camp that was systematically killing people who might volunteer to help starving German widows and orphans.

So many people are caught up in similar structures; their primary energy through their jobs in some way contributes on a grand scale to violence even though their personal values and preferences are inclined toward blessing. North American consumers support sweat shop factories by buying cheap merchandise. The poor single mother who can barely afford to feed her children could well be the one buying the less expensive merchandise manufactured by child labourers on the other side of the globe. For her, the bargain is a blessing because it enables her to buy something new for her children that she might not otherwise afford; on a larger scale, she is participating in a relational system with violent dimensions.

These dynamic mimetic structures of violence are all around us. Unless we totally withdraw from life in the world and live as hermits, we are caught up in them in some way or another. They are like huge webs of oppressive energy pulsating around the globe. They help define our identities so that we think we absolutely must acquire something at the expense of the Other for our own well-being. Gandhi disrupted the British economic hegemonic structure by telling people they could make their own salt and their own cloth. The best way to change these structures of violence is for sensitive people, who understand what is happening, to let people know how they can do things differently in their own spheres of influence. Identity-based conflict can lead to genocide in places like Rwanda and Bosnia, but it can also product more diffuse, but equally real, suffering through policies like the sanctions against Iraq that have resulted in untold suffering and death.

To turn the situation around will take a willingness to open ourselves to embracing and listening to everyone who is involved. It will take creative thinking and synchronicity. It will take sustained additional research and development. In the end, we may have to become like children who forgive easily and find delight in the most surprising situations.

Epilogue

Reflections on September 11, 2001

September 11 and its aftermath conjure up deep and conflicting emotions within the human family. These emotions could easily fuel additional mimetic structures of violence. We could, however, make a choice to put our interpretive, imaginative, and behavioural power into generating mimetic structures of blessing. To this end I wish to start with an old story.

The story about Cain and Abel is told in chapter 4 of the book of Genesis in the Bible. Cain, the farmer, presented some of his vegetables as a sacrifice to the Lord but the sacrifice was not favourably accepted. Abel presented an animal from his flock as a sacrifice and the Lord accepted this sacrifice. Cain, filled with anger and resentment, killed Abel when no one was looking. To punish Cain, the Lord decreed that he had to wander the earth without settling down, but the Lord also put a mark on Cain to protect him from revenge.

We can ask ourselves, how could Cain's violence have been prevented? As we look at Cain's situation, we realize that his identity needs were threatened when his sacrifice was not accepted. First, his meaning system was threatened. Why was Cain's offering not accepted but Abel's was? It seemed unjust to him. The sacrifice took place within a meaning context of emerging religion and culture. That whole meaning system was undermined if the sacrifice was not accepted. The sacrificial action was woven into the agriculture cycle; it came after he had raised the vegetables. Being thwarted at this point threatened the ongoing action of farming.

His need for connectedness, with the Divine and with Abel, was threatened. If the sacrifice was considered a kind of fertility rite, its failure could call into question future crops, so Cain's security was also threatened. Finally, not receiving recognition resulted in a deep sense of shame that fuelled the resentment toward Abel. In addition to his identity needs, there was a mimetic rivalry — Cain identified with his brother and having his sacrifice accepted became the object of intense mimetic desire.

Suppose Abel$_2$ had read earlier portions of this book and became aware of how deeply his brother, who was older and more powerful than he was, had been hurt. What could he do? First, he would develop an attitude of desiring the subjectivity of Cain, really longing for Cain's well-being. His first impulse might be to pray for Cain; specifically he might even entreat the Lord to accept Cain's next vegetarian sacrifice.

He could approach Cain in a helpful kind of way. This would be tricky, because if he were too helpful and empathetic, Cain would feel that he was the object of pity and lose face. If he was too ambiguous in his approach, Cain would become suspicious about what was going on. If he started by pointing out what happened, Cain might think he came to show him up or to rub his face in this humiliation.

Abel$_2$ could start out with the observation, "Say, Cain, I heard that the Lord doesn't seem to take too well to vegetable sacrifices." This puts the focus on the Lord, rather than on blaming Cain, who already feels like a victim and is doubtless in an entrenchment mentality.

Cain would say sullenly, "Isn't that the truth. I just don't know what's happening."

Abel$_2$ could then say, "Look, Cain, I don't know what's behind this but I would really like to help you find a way to have a good experience of sacrifice. I don't have to get involved, but if you like I will do what I can."

Cain could reply, "I tried my best. They really were the best veggies I had. I don't know what to do."

Abel$_2$: "I feel kind of awkward about the situation. Without you having an acceptable sacrifice, the approval of mine feels a little hollow—not that I don't appreciate Divine favour, I really do, but I care so much about you that it seems incomplete."

Cain: (*sarcastically*) "Start the violins... I'm really not a charity case."

Abel$_2$: "I know. You are a great farmer. It's just this religious side of life that needs to be worked out."

Cain: "Have you got any ideas?"

Abel$_2$: "We could try some experiments. I could give you an animal from my flock; you could try that."

Cain: "I'd feel better about buying it; then at least I've given something. Do you know how to cook with veggies?"

Abel$_2$: "As a matter of fact, I just mentioned to the family that eating veal, lamb, or goat meat every day is kind of a drag. I could do with some new foods in my diet."

The dialogue would go on and eventually Cain would get an acceptable sacrifice, Abel would not get murdered, and they would continue an ongoing trading relationship in which each would literally help feed the other. The next time Abel$_2$ was in a pinch, Cain would, in imitation of Abel$_2$, sensitively approach his brother with an offer to help. This mutual attending to the needs of one another would develop into and exemplify a mimetic structure of blessing.

The Cain Complex

In the original story recorded in Genesis, we find that when the Lord did not recognize Cain's sacrifice, Cain "burned with anger very much" and "his face fell." In the Hebrew root metaphors of burning and a falling face, we have the expression of compound emotions related to a threat to human needs. The burning anger is related to a threat to his meaning system—it did not seem fair and just that his sacrifice was ignored by the Divine Spirit. It was also a threat to his security as related to the continuity of the culture he was founding. In that context, to be ignored by God did not augur well for sustained blessing. The fallen face expresses the depression of not being able to act in the way he was accustomed, a sadness in the lack of connectedness to the Spirit of the universe, and a deep shame that somehow he was not recognized as being acceptable. All of these threats occurred in the context of a mimetic rivalry with his brother. Had the Lord not received his brother's sacrifice with favour, Cain would have had none of these feelings.

Cain becomes an archetype of a powerful entity that feels wrongly victimized and, as a result, experiences the emotions of anger, fear, depression, disappointment, and shame. These combined emotions lead to a Manichean interpretation of reality that can be expressed this way: "My problems are entirely the fault of my Other's meaning system, action, connectedness, confidence, and recognition." This in turn leads to the violent impulse to kill one's Other.

What does Cain need? As a victim, Cain needs to be understood at the level of identity needs. As a potential perpetrator, Cain needs a framework within which his actions can be understood, and he also needs alternate satisfiers to his identity needs that do not involve violence. Cain needs to see the humanity of his Other and the potential to participate in the development of new mimetic structures of blessing. Without these he will resort to killing his Other. In the revised story of Cain and Abel just told, Abel$_2$ tried to address these needs.

I will now look at two different parties from the perspective of the Cain syndrome and provide a response from Abel$_2$.

Cain Complex 1 – The United States of America

September 11 brought on a "fiercely burning anger and a fallen face" within the United States. The fallen face was seen in the sadness, the lamentation for the victims, the inability of many to go to work, the memorial services, and the cancellation of airline flights. The burning anger, which is still very much present, comes from both the fear of another attack and the sense of injustice. Many Americans feel that the people behind September 11 are totally evil, have no redeeming value, and simply need to be snuffed out. Any attempt to explain why this happened or to look at root causes is interpreted as compromising an unequivocal denunciation of this evil action.

The United States, acting out of this Cain complex, took swift action by declaring a war on terrorism—terrorists are the American Other—and acting to kill or capture Osama bin Laden and members of the Al Qaeda network. Nothing—

laws, rules of international combat, or custom—would stand in the way of this objective. Abel had succeeded, through a single act of sacrifice, in shaking Cain to the core of his being, and Cain had to kill Abel.

First Reflection

A week after September 11, I was asked to speak at a public prayer meeting at Ottawa City Hall. This is what I said:

BISMALLAH ALRAHMAN ALRAHEEM
BARUCH ATTAH ADONAI ELOHENU

The first of the phrases, "In the name of God, most merciful and compassionate," uses Arabic words related to the Hebrew word *rachamin*, a word for compassion that is derived from the word for womb. It is a deep feeling for someone that goes right down to our abdomen; it is like the care of a mother for the child in her womb.

The second is Hebrew for "Blessed are you, Lord, our God." It is a return to transcendence. "Baruch," the word for "blessed," means to be empowered. It speaks of expanding life options, creativity, sustenance, growth, and vitality.

When our mind's eye zooms in on September 11, we focus on a picture of victimization: victimization that includes violent loss of life, injury, and destruction. At the human level it means that thousands and thousands of people are wailing the loss of wives, husbands, fathers, mothers, children, and friends. In one of the e-mails forwarded to me is an account of seven people who perished on September 11—people who worked for the high-tech company where my daughter works. Some who perished were from overseas, including India. Most gripping was the realization that one young father, on the plane that crashed in Pennsylvania, doubtless helped to divert the plane from its target of destruction.

The God portrayed in the Bible and the Qur'an is a God with a special feeling for victims; a God who hears the cries of the poor, oppressed, and bereaved; a God who is present with them; and a God who responds to their needs, even though this response is not always in the form that people might demand.

Victimization can be seen as an attack on the identity of the persons involved. It is an attack on the sense of security, resulting in overwhelming fear. We saw this fear on September 11 and we continue to hear of it being present among the people of New York in a particular way. Children who were once free to explore their neighbourhoods on their own must now be accompanied by older siblings or adults. Those who watched the tragedy play out across their television screens likewise felt a threat to security and additional fear.

The violence is also an attack on one's connectedness, the circle of people with whom one belongs. Relationships with those who perished were severed forever. When we think of our own circles of friends and acquaintances, we can think of hundreds of people who know us and whom we know. All would be affected if we were snatched away. For each victim who died in the attack, many people are directly affected.

The events of September 11 attacked our capacity for action. The resulting security measures will slow down our travel for years to come, sometimes to the point where the trips we wish to take will not be taken. It immobilized millions of people who could not go to work or do any of the things they had planned to do.

The violence of September 11 was, for many, an attack on their meaning system. Their sense of justice was deeply violated, resulting in an awesome, seething anger. The self-understanding that the United States had of being a relatively safe place was replaced with a great sense of vulnerability. The paradigm of the nation shifted in a matter of hours.

Finally, this violence meant that there are people out there who do not recognize the United States as the force for good in this world that has been woven into the American self-understanding. This produces a lack of well-being, a sense that there is something fundamentally wrong with the world.

Victimization so intense in all areas of identity is traumatizing. It cuts an emotional channel through our bodies, mixing together pain, anger, sorrow, depression, and fear. These emotions start to define the points of necessary healing. It is this pain that we call upon the Spirit of the Creator to address. At the same time, we are all called upon to be agents of healing and hope for healing.

Though we are now focusing on the tragic victimization of thousands of people through a human act—one of the most horrible scenarios that we could imagine short of all-out war, nuclear bombs, or chemical attacks—let us not lose sight of the tremendous victimization occurring daily through human-made structures of violence. As this event reminds us of the awful pain and anger inflicted by violence, let it teach us to empathize more deeply with those experiencing deep loss around the globe. Let it teach us to reflect on the violent dimensions of our own thoughts and actions. The events of September 11 show us how profoundly this world is interconnected. What we do affects the whole.

As a result of the September 11 attacks, we have also been subject to the language of war, retaliation, and vengeance and to the prospect of violent attacks at the hour the Americans choose. The emotional impulse toward violence is understandable. Structures of violence are subject to imitation; violence is more contagious than AIDS. It takes on a life of its own. Like the devil, though, it is deceptive and murderous. (The word "devil" comes from *diabolis*, which is made up of *dia* [between] and *bolis* [to throw]. The image of diabolic violence is that it throws something between us to create a rift, a separation that results in dehumanization and demonization.) It suggests that all will be made better with only a few more offerings to the Emperor (god) of violence. And violence is so often the winner.

Our prayer must now be that the structures of violence that brought us to September 11, 2001, will be supplanted with structures of blessing, of mutual empowerment, of us feeding one another, of us creating new ways of attending to the hurts of the earth as biosphere, and of the world as an interconnected web of vulnerable living beings.

Rather than swords being beaten into ploughshares, ploughshares were made into swords as airplanes, the instruments of peaceful travel, were made into living bombs of destruction. Let us now hope and pray that, just as dramatically, the impulses toward violence will be transformed into an energy of redress of global inequality, and that there will be a will to start on a path where justice is seen as making things right.

The culture of the United States is being imitated around the world. It is a leader, setting the standard in so many areas of human life. Now it has undergone suffering that has hurt it to the core. Our hope is that it will set a new standard for the world to follow, a standard of transforming violence to blessing, war to peace.

For this to happen, healing needs to occur. We return our focus to where we started: on the hurting, crying individuals who have lost loved ones along with their hope, security, meaning, and joy.

Cain Complex 2 – The Community of Osama bin Laden

On September 11, Cain killed Abel. This time it was people within the orb of Osama bin Laden who took the violent action. The action bears all the marks of someone "burning fiercely with anger and having a fallen face."

What constitutes the equivalent of God not having recognized the sacrifice of Cain? Since the Enlightenment, the West has been in a state of ascendancy culturally, politically, and militarily. This is epitomized by cultural, technological, and military hegemonic structures, with the United States emerging as the most dominant. As Peter Bergen puts it:

> Since Napoleon's armies invaded Egypt in 1798, the story of Muslim relations with the Western powers has been one of the inexorable decline of Muslim military power and the rise of the West, culminating in the British and French defeat of the Ottomans and colonization of much of the last Islamic empire after World War I.[1]

In the post-colonial era, many in the Middle East were left in countries that did not conform to historical boundaries with leaders they had not chosen. Though oil wealth was evident, many Muslims lagged in personal development for a number of complex reasons, many having to do with the lack of democratic institutions and domination by autocratic leaders. (Ironically, in past decades Iraq had achieved an exemplary literacy rate through a network of women organized by the Bath party. Society changed as Saddam Hussein took more firm control.)

The result was that in the Muslim world there was a self-perception of decline in relation to the West and, with that, a lack of initiative. This is captured by Wahida Chishti Valiante, Vice-President of the Canadian Islamic Congress:

> The Qur'anic message of peace, justice, and the middle way —
> what the Qur'an identifies as "a balanced Umma"—has been
> brought home most tellingly in the light of recent events....
> Today, more than ever, Muslims should focus on global
> renewal, a genuine resolve to emerge from the cocoon of their
> long, self-induced intellectual and spiritual paralysis, self-pity

and inaction, and meet head-on the challenges facing them in the so-called "new world order."

There are many historical and political reasons for the current state of the worldwide Umma, but its plight is rooted mainly in having ignored or denied certain facts for far too long. First and foremost, the present "backwardness" of many Muslim communities and societies stems from a sense of powerlessness induced by defeatist attitudes and the inability to free themselves from an oppressive, bloody and divisive colonial past. Many Muslim countries are abundantly blessed in natural and human resources, yet are inept at utilizing these riches for the betterment of their citizens. Every conceivable element is present for growth and progress, but they are instead exploited by others, and by the selfish motives of those who seek power only for themselves.

Today, those people who are most heavily burdened by abject poverty and ignorance have so little say in their own, or their nations' affairs. Apathy and lack of awareness have only contributed that much more to their misery and suffering and in most cases, their fate is ultimately in the hands of autocratic rulers. The principle of consultation and consent—or Al-Shura, the normative Islamic principle of polity—has become bent and twisted to suit the interests of the few.

Intellectual discourse on issues of import, or Ijtihad, has been another casualty of Muslim apathy. Its absence among the Umma has suppressed the spirit of enlightenment, reflection, and action, allowing instead for a mediocre status quo to continue. Those leaders and intellectuals who disregard the Qur'anic edict that the people's condition will not change unless they change their own thinking and behaviour, do so at their peril. If they do not rise, even now, to fulfill their dual role as a dynamic force for renewing the Qur'anic vision of justice and equality and motivation of the Muslim masses, to change the existing order, they will share in the blame and the world tragedy that is unfolding before us. The Qur'an admonishes us to uphold our prime responsibility as Allah's viceregents on earth; that is, to struggle (engage in Jihad) against oneself, and against social ills such as world poverty, oppression, war, ignorance, violence, injustice, racism, and religious hatred.[2]

— Walida Chishti Valiante

The picture presented by Wahida Chishti Valiante is one of a people that has been acted upon, that has been dominated and that is struggling to regain a capacity to act. Picking up on Rebecca Adams' idea of desiring the fullness of being for people who are wounded or limited subjects, this picture suggests to us that those in the Western world do what we can to support and encourage the coming into being of a full subjectivity on the part of the Muslim world; that is, to become actors along the lines suggested by Valiante at the end of her piece. The reality is that those who feel threatened and vulnerable gravitate towards mimetic structures of entrenchment with their legalistic directives; their stark "good versus evil" framing of reality, and their "us versus them" discourse.

Osama bin Laden's view of the world was influenced by Abdullah Azzam, born near Jenin, Palestine, in 1941. Azzam helped recruit and inspire fighters in the Afghan war against the Soviets within a framework that included the restoration of the

> Khalifa, the dream that Muslims around the world could be united under one ruler. His motto was "Jihad and the rifle alone: no negotiations, no conferences and no dialogues." He put that belief into practice, often joining the mujahideen battling the Soviets in Afghanistan. And it was not simply from Afghanistan that the infidels had to be expelled. Azzam wrote: "This duty will not end with victory in Afghanistan; jihad will remain an individual obligation until all other lands that were Muslim are returned to us so that Islam will reign again: before us lie Palestine, Bokhara, Lebanon, Chad, Eritrea, Somalia, the Philippines, Burma, Southern Yemen, Taskent and Adalusia [southern Spain].[3]

We see in this statement a wish to break free from hegemonic structures and the espousal of an ethnoreligious nationalism that integrates an ancestral vision, religion, peoplehood, land, and political control. Within this framework, acute irritants were American support of the State of Israel and American military troops on the Saudi Peninsula. Wahida Valiante suggests that bin Laden adopted a more militant position towards the United States as a result of his own experience:

> I believe that in order to describe Ossama's world-view more accurately would be to also include his personal experiences with America, who trained him, used him, abused him, and then discarded him. Rejection is a very powerful emotion – from love and admiration to hate and anger – and this must have found expression in the ideology [expressed above].[4]

There was doubtless wounded pride after bin Laden's offer to fight Saddam Hussein after the occupation of Kuwait was rejected by the Americans. This in no way justifies any of bin Laden's violent actions, but it might help to understand his motivation.

To understand why bin Laden makes the leap from opposition to American policies to killing thousands of U.S. civilians, one must grasp that in his mind the United States has been equally violent in its treatment of Muslim civilians. On the al-Qaeda videotape circulating around the Middle East during the summer of 2001, bin Laden repeatedly returns to the theme of Muslim civilians under attack in countries from Israel to Iraq, for which he blames the United States. He rages over pictures of dying children in Iraq, saying, "More than a million [Iraqis] die because they are Muslims," and refers to [former U.S.] President Clinton as a "slaughterer." For bin Laden it's quite simple: attacks against American citizens are necessary so that they can "taste the bitter fruit" that Muslim civilians have long tasted.[5]

Bin Laden acted within this framework, engaging in a war against the United States in a manner not to be restrained by any laws, customs, or rules of international combat.

The bin Laden community is made up of teachers, fighters, and ordinary people for whom bin Laden is a hero (in the 1990s, Osama was a very popular name for babies in one Muslim country.)[6] The bin Laden community does not include those large blocs of Muslims for whom Islam is a religion of peace or the feminist Muslim women taking courageous action in the fields of medicine and education. The bin Laden community also does not include those Muslims working for democracy, nor those who live pious lives of blessing within their family and work contexts.

I asked a Canadian Muslim scholar about where to place bin Laden within the world of Islam. He pointed out that one of the teachings of the Prophet was to be aware of excessiveness or extremes. He transliterated the Arabic word as *ghloww*. Bin Laden, he suggested, was in a mode of thought and action that went contrary to this Islamic teaching.

This bin Laden community—for whom the economic, military, and political power of the United States is the Abel that shows up the fact that the Lord does not appear to look favourably upon the sacrifice of Cain—does still exist. Abel, in their eyes, must then be murdered.

Second Reflection

A skilled stonemason swings a hammer to hit a stone at just the right point to split it open, revealing the inner structure of the rock. The September 11 planes of destruction broke into the consciousness of the global community to reveal a multiplicity of mimetic structures of violence, each with its own bloody history. Implicated first is an anti-Jewish sentiment, which can be traced back to vitriolic anti-Semitic rhetoric of the fifth century and is now finding renewed expression in the desecration and bombing of synagogues. The anti-Muslim sentiment is so strong that Muslims in North America feel pressured to change their names and to give their children non-Muslim names to avoid harassment, arrest, and persecution. There is a foreboding resentment among many Muslims in the grand Umma stretching from North Africa east to Indonesia, a resentment toward leaders who seek first personal aggrandizement. The West and Israel, who are the scapegoats, are perceived as illegitimate because of the plight of Palestinians, a "decadent lifestyle," military positions on the Arabian Peninsula, and general cultural dominance. There are the violent structures associated with rivalries over oil, structures that make non-persons of the unfortunate indigenous peoples from Colombia, to Sudan, to Uzbekistan who happen to live on top of the oil reserves.

The many other structures include the huge mimetic structures of violence associated with the drug trade that contain substructures of rivalries over territory and money; implicated among these are Afghanistan and the covert interests of intelligence organizations. (Ironically, Afghanistan was occupied by the United States and its allies just in time to plant opium poppies.) Then there are violent structures of arms dealings, including the cascading of arms, where people upgrade their guns and sell their old weapons to those poorer than themselves. Superimposed are gender-based structures, from the debilitating policies toward women used by the Taliban to the brutal rape of Muslim women in India. Concerns over nuclear weapons have resurfaced; worry over chemical and biological weapons has intensified. We begin to see within the split-open rock of global consciousness these massive, intertwined structures of violence that have an impact on most inhabitants of the planet. We can also mention the suicide bombers, the Israeli attacks on Palestinian communities, the bombing of Afghanistan, and the many Afghanis and four Canadians killed by "friendly fire."

Few people realize how far-reaching the hegemony of American language, culture, and power really are. When I was in Frankfurt, Germany, a few years ago, I wanted to buy souvenirs for my family. I walked into a huge music store, looking for a distinctively German CD. Rows upon rows of CDs were filled with American artists. I finally had to ask for assistance and was directed to a tiny shelf of popular German music. When I was in Austria in 1999, a business person from Germany remarked that 80 per cent of business in Germany is conducted in English. Whether his figure is precise or not is beside the point; English has become the lingua franca of business and culture. Americans have become accustomed to the world bending to accommodate them. They are used to acting as though they have a right to do what they want to do, even if it means invading a country for any reason the United States holds to be just. It has established such a commanding presence in the world that if the United States declares something to be in its interests, people get out of the way or help along, if they know what is good for them. Anyone accustomed to the dominant position in a hegemonic structure is indignant, offended, and angry if that position is threatened.

It is very difficult to talk to someone (an individual or collective entity) under the following conditions:

1. When you have an insight about that person or community and you feel they are unreceptive to that insight.

2. When someone in a mimetic structure of entrenchment regards you as an enemy if you say anything that disagrees with the dogma they have defined to be true for themselves.

3. When someone has been victimized and feels like a victim.

4. When someone is more powerful than you, particularly if this power has been translated into an ongoing hegemonic structure and your well-being depends on their goodwill.

5. When someone comes across as being totally authoritative.

As human beings, talk at the level of dialogue is one of the greatest gifts we have to sort out our basic problems. However, difficulties like the five just listed make it difficult to start a dialogue, and the structures that would enable us to overcome these difficulties (along the lines of what is developed in Chapters 13 and 15) are not in place.

When I first started giving two-day seminars on reconciliation, I began each seminar by saying that we know very little about reconciliation but that it is good to spend two days trying to discover what it is all about. Without exception, the reconciliation seminars were a good experience for everyone involved. In like manner, I would say now that we know very little about what mimetic structures of blessing might look like and how they could be achieved in the post-September 11 world. But wouldn't it be nice if people around the world would set aside two days for a dialogue with a mixture of people about what it would mean for mimetic structures of blessing to be introduced to their relational systems? Wouldn't it be empowering if these ended with people deciding to take some action—to show consideration, to start additional dialogues, to write letters with ideas, or to pick up on any of the elements of reconciliation described in Chapter 13?

Having lived in the United States for four years and having visited the 48 states south of Canada, I have learned to love that country dearly. I have a feeling for the sense of loss Americans feel. The United States is a mimetic model for the world. It has set many trends in culture, commerce, and military development. Though Americans have rich and deep spiritual traditions, they have played a role in the commercialization of culture so that people in many parts of the world have joined with them in defining identity and culture through various aspects of economic life.

I would like to invite Americans to begin a thorough examination of commercial activity from the perspective of mimetic structures of violence and of blessing. Who is blessed and are they really blessed? Who suffers from the structures that are in place, keeping in mind not only the peoples of the world but the environment and natural order? What would it take to introduce mimetic structures of blessing into many relational systems, including peoples from around the world? I would challenge them to invite individuals from many of the world's peoples to engage in this critical reflection with them. I challenge them to initiate open-ended dialogues with the people who feel least acknowledged by their policy makers. I challenge them to desire the well-being of those limited in their subjectivity around the world. I challenge them to embrace the Muslim world.

I also have well-established relationships with people from Israeli and Palestinian communities. I know that there are many good, peace-loving people among them. I am also convinced that those who are taking strong, hard-line militant positions are doing so for reasons that are understandable in the light of ideas I developed in Chapters 1 to 8. I also sense that there are hegemonic structures that are substructures of the mimetic structures of violence that grip relational systems between and within their communities. All of the five reasons that make talk difficult apply to so many people.

Most of them trace their ancestral and spiritual roots back to Hagar and Sarah through their sons Ishmael and Isaac. Perhaps their imaginations could be stimulated so that they could imagine their foremothers being reconciled; perhaps imagining reconciliation might stimulate a new path of action. There is much within their different cultures that lends itself to blessing—from the caring family relationships of Palestinians to the Days of Atonement that structure into Jewish consciousness the possibility of leaving violence behind and imagining a new year of blessing. I encourage them, too, to begin creative dialogues on mimetic structures of blessing—dialogues that include those who identify with those responsible for violent acts and policies.

The community of Osama bin Laden and Al Qaeda has demonstrated that they have the power to be supremely disruptive to the West in general and the United States in particular. They keep alive the prospect of being destructive in the future. They may think that in some way they are doing something that might eventually benefit their people. My fear is that their actions will only serve to intensify mimetic structures of violence and that the ripple effects will only cause more suffering. I challenge them to rethink their approach to influence the world, to transform their orientation from violence to blessing.

September 11 exposed many conflicts, stereotypes, and hegemonic structures around the world. Oil interests, drug trade, intelligence operations, and substantial loss of life through "collateral damage" are all part of the equation. A full and careful analysis using the theoretical framework of mimetic structures of violence and mimetic structures of blessing would take several books. I have tried to show how knowledge of this framework can expand our imagination of the kind of world that it is possible for us to create together. Among human beings, change and creativity start with imagination. That is how an understanding of deep-rooted conflict can open paths to reconciliation with the help of the Spirit of a Creator who empowers us to love when our inclination is to hate.

Notes

Chapter 1
Deep-Rooted Conflict

1   Walker Connor, *Ethnonationalism: The Quest for Understanding* (Princeton: Princeton University Press, 1994), 44.

2   Vamik D. Volkan, "An Overview of Psychological Concepts Pertinent to Interethnic and/or International Relationships," in *The Psychodynamics of International Relationships*, ed. Vamik D. Volkan, Demetrios A. Julius, and Joseph V. Montville (Lexington & Toronto: Lexington Books, 1990), 38. Michael Ignatieff makes the same point in *Blood and Belonging: Journeys into the New Nationalism* (Toronto: Penguin Books, 1993).

3   Pierre L. van den Berghe, in "The Biology of Nepotism," *Bigotry, Prejudice and Hatred: Definitions, Causes & Solutions*, ed. Robert M. Baird and Stuart E. Rosenbaum (Buffalo: Prometheus Books, 1992), 133-134.

4   Ibid.

5   Statement and translation from Vesna Dasović Marković.

6   See Paul Ricoeur, "L'idéologie et l'utopie: deux expressions de l'imaginaire sociale," *Autres Temps*, No. 2 (Été 1984):53-64, for a definition of utopia as the imagined future of a group, in contrast to the pejorative connotation of utopia as something unrealistic and unattainable.

7   See Peter A. Olsson, "The Terrorist and the Terrorised: Some Psychoanalytic Considerations," in *The Psychodynamics of International Relationships*, 185, for a description of a particular case of this happening among Palestinians.

8   Brice R. Wachterhauser, "Prejudice and Reason," in *Bigotry, Prejudice and Hatred*, 143. For a description of the tacit dimension in which the unarticulated prejudices reside see Michael Polanyi, *Personal Knowledge: Towards a Post-Critical Philosophy* (New York: Harper and Row, 1958; Harper Torchbook edition, 1964), 69-245.

9   Rita R. Rogers, "Intergenerational Transmission of Historical Enmity," in *The Psychodynamics of International Relationships*, 91-96.

10 Miroslav Volf, "Exclusion and Embrace: Theological Reflections in the Wake of 'Ethnic Cleansing,'" presented at a joint conference of the Gesellschaft für evangelische Theologie and Arbeitskreis für Evangelische theologie in Potsdam, Germany, February 15-17, 1993, 10.

11 Vern Redekop, *Scapegoats, the Bible and Criminal Justice: Interacting with René Girard* (Akron, PA: Mennonite Central Committee, 1993), 9.

12   For a collection of essays describing violence against women in the context of war, see Anne Llewellyn Barstow, ed. *War's Dirty Secrets: Rape, Prostitution, and Other Crimes Against Women* (Cleveland: Pilgrim Press, 2000).

13   Catharine MacKinnon, "Crimes of War, Crimes of Peace," in *On Human Rights: The Oxford Amnesty Lectures*, ed. Stephen Shute and Susan Hurley (New York: Harper Collins Basic Books, 1993), 89.

14   Ibid., 90. As well, even U.N. peacekeeping troops have been reported to engage in rape. (91) See also Chung Hyun-Kyung, "Your Comfort Versus My Death: Korean Comfort Women," in *War's Dirty Secrets: Rape, Prostitution and Other Crimes Against Humanity* (Cleveland: Pilgrim Press, 2000), 13-25.

15   John W. Burton used this phrase to define "provention," a word he coined in contrast to the term *prevention*, which "has the connotation of containment." See his *Conflict: Resolution and Provention* (New York: St. Martin's Press, 1990), v.

16   Paul Sites, *Control: The Basis of Social Order* (New York: Dunellen, 1973).

17   John W. Burton, *Resolving Deep-Rooted Conflicts* (Lanham: University Press of America, 1987), 15. Note that Sites himself was heavily influenced by Maslow.

18   John W. Burton, *Deviance, Terrorism and War* (Oxford: Martin Robertson, 1979).

19   Ibid., 36.

20   Ibid.

21   Ibid.

22   Ibid., 33.

23   Joseph V. Montville, "Epilogue: The Human Factor Revisited," in *Conflict and Peacemaking in Multiethnic Societies*, ed. Joseph V. Montville (Lexington: Lexington Books, 1990), 536-37.

24   Ibid., 537.

25   Burton states in *Resolving Deep-Rooted Conflicts* that an assumption of his approach is that "the identity group, not the state and its institutions, is both the appropriate unit of analysis and the explanation of conflict. In other words, the assertion is that effective political power rests finally with identity groups (ethnic, cultural, language, class and other) and not with authorities." (23)

26   Ibid., 2.

27   Ibid.

28   Ibid., 15.

29   Roger Fisher, William Ury with Bruce Patton, ed., *Getting to YES: Negotiating Agreement Without Giving In* (New York: Penguin Books, 1991).

30   Burton, *Resolving Deep-Rooted Conflicts*, 15.

31   Ibid.

32   Donald L. Horowitz, *Ethnic Groups in Conflict* (Berkeley: University of California Press, 1985), quoted in ibid., 8.

33   Stephen Ryan, *Ethnic Conflict and International Relations* (Brookfield: Dartmouth, 1990), xxii.

34   Note the following examples: "In his analysis of ethnic and religious conflict in 25 countries during 1987, Don Podestra tells us that 'These simmering conflicts [are] rooted in the most basic forms of human identity,' reflecting 'the need to assert group identity,' and originating in one particular emotion: a fear of group extinction.... Barbara Harff and Ted Robert Gurr [1988] have examined instances of massive state repression leading precisely to group extinction: forty-four episodes of genocide and policide that have occurred in all world regions since 1945, with estimated casualties ranging from seven to sixteen million people: 'at least as many who died in all international and civil wars in the period.' ...Gurr and James Scarritt [1989] have estimated that there are 246 minority groups at risk in ninety-five countries." (Dennis Sandole, "Biological Basis of Needs," in *Conflict: Human Needs Theory,* ed. John W. Burton [New York: St. Martin's Press, 1990], 62-63.) Besides these examples, the amount of published material on various "ethnic conflicts" grew rapidly during the 1990s.

35   Burton, *Resolving Deep-Rooted Conflicts,* 17.

36   Johan Galtung, "International Development in Human Perspective," in *Conflict: Human Needs Theory,* ed. John Burton (New York: St. Martin's Press, 1990), 301-335.

37   Burton, *Resolving Deep-Rooted Conflicts,* 16.

38   Ibid., 21.

39   Stephen Cohen and Herbert Kelman, "The Problem-Solving Workshop: A Social Psychological Contribution to the Resolution of International Conflicts," *Journal of Peace Research* XIII-2 (1976):79-90.

40   Joseph V. Montville, "Transnationalism and the Role of Track-Two Diplomacy," in *Approaches to Peace: An Intellectual Map,* ed. W. Scott Thompson and Kenneth M. Jensen (Washington, D.C.: United States Institute of Peace, 1991).

41   See Joseph V. Montville, "The Psychological Roots of Ethnic and Sectarian Terrorism," in *The Psychodynamics of International Relationships,* 172-173, for a description of the activities of the Group for the Advancement of Psychiatry involving three hundred American psychiatrists who pioneered an "application of self-psychology theory to the Israeli-Palestinian conflict."

42   For a description of this concept developed by Charles Osgood in the 1960s, see Charles W. Kegley, "Neo-Idealism: A Practical Matter," *Ethics and International Affairs* 2 (1988):183 and Charles E. Osgood, *Perspective in Foreign Policy* (Palo Alto: Pacific Books, 1966).

43   Ronald Fisher, "Prenegotiation Problem-Solving Discussions: Enhancing the Potential for Successful Negotiation," *International Journal* XLIV (1989):467.

44   For a definition of action research, see Frank Dukes, "Action Research," in *Conflict: Readings in Management and Resolution,* ed. John W. Burton and Frank Dukes (New York: St. Martin's Press, 1990), 288-298.

45   Burton, in *Resolving Deep-Rooted Conflicts*, 15, observes that "[s]ome explanation was still required as to why parties were unwilling to meet within existing institutions, and what kind of institutions would be acceptable and helpful. This *proved not to be possible until there had been further developments by sociologists and other theorists in the general field of conflict and behavior*." (Italics mine.)

46   Ibid., 25.

47   Ted Robert Gurr, "Communal Conflicts and Global Security," *Current History* Vol. 94 (May 1995):212.

Chapter 2
Human Identity Needs

1   These include Dennis Sandole, "The Biological Basis of Needs in World Society," in *Conflict: Human Needs Theory* (New York: St. Martin's Press, 1990), 61, and Ronald Fisher, "Needs Theory, Social Identity and Eclectic Model of Conflict," in *Conflict: Human Needs Theory*, 91-93, who, besides giving his own critique of Maslow's hierarchy, summarizes criticisms Lederer and Galtung make of the concept of a needs hierarchy and provides alternate formulations developed by Klenberg, McClelland and Cantril. Herbert Kelman also takes a position that needs are not hierarchically arranged in "Applying a Human Needs Perspective to the Practice of Conflict Resolution: The Israeli Palestinian Case," in *Conflict: Human Needs Theory*, 283. Also, Johan Galtung, in "International Development in Human Perspective," in *Conflict: Human Needs Theory*, 332, n.7, suggests that "any vertical ordering of needs is likely to be reflected in social stratification one way or the other, and a theory of needs hierarchy may therefore easily become a justification of social hierarchy."

2   This resulted in a book edited by John W. Burton, *Conflict: Human Needs Theory* (New York: St. Martin's Press, 1990).

3   Vern Neufeld Redekop, "The Role of Deep-rooted Conflict and Its Resolution in Regional Economic Development," Unpublished, 1992.

4   Katrin Gillwald, "Conflict and Needs Research," in *Conflict: Human Needs Theory*, 118. (To avoid confusion in tracking down Gillwald's publications, note that her earlier work is listed under her maiden name, which is Lederer.)

5   Ibid., 121.

6   William R. Potapchuk, "Processes of Governance: Can Governments Truly Respond to Human Needs?" in *Conflict: Human Needs Theory*, 265.

7   Oscar Nudler, "On Conflicts and Metaphors: Toward an Extended Rationality," in *Conflict: Human Needs Theory*, 177.

8   Ibid.

9   Ibid., 177-178, quoting A. Heelan, *Space Perception and the Philosophy of Sciences* (Berkeley: University of California Press, 1983), 10.

10   Ibid., 179.

11   Ibid.

12   Ibid., 187.

13   Ibid., 187-188.

14   Ibid., 190.

15   Ibid., 191.

16   For a detailed analysis of the role of root metaphors in how we conceptualize reality see George Lakoff and Mark Johnson, *Metaphors We Live By* (Chicago: University of Chicago Press, 1981).

17   This was recounted by Morton Kelsey at an Anglican Church day of prayer and renewal in Montreal in the 1970s.

18   Yona Friedman, "The Role of Knowledge in Conflict Resolution," in *Conflict: Human Needs Theory*, 259.

19   Ibid., 260.

20   Ibid., 261.

21   Mary Clark, "Meaningful Social Bonding as a Universal Need," in *Conflict: Human Needs Theory*.

22   Ibid., 39.

23   Ibid., 41.

24   Ibid., 43.

25   Ibid., 47.

26   Ibid., 46.

27   Edward Azar, "Protracted International Conflicts: Ten Propositions," in *International Conflict Resolution: Theory and Practice*, ed. Edward E. Azar and John W. Burton (Boulder: Lynne Rienner Publishers, 1986).

28   Clark, "Meaningful Social Bonding as a Universal Need," in *Conflict: Human Needs Theory,* 49-50.

29   For a collection of essays on attachment theory see Colin Murray Parkes and Joan Stevenson-Hinde, eds., *The Place of Attachment in Human Behavior* (New York: Basic Books, 1982), especially Robert Hinde, "Attachment: Some Conceptual and Biological Issues," Robert S. Weiss, "Attachment in Adult Life," Peter Marris, "Attachment and Society," and Scott Henderson, "The Significance of Social Relationships in the Etiology of Neurosis."

30   Peter Marris, "Attachment and Society," in *The Place of Attachment in Human Behavior,* 191.

31   Michael Ignatieff, *Blood & Belonging: Journeys into the New Nationalism* (Toronto: Penguin Books, 1993), 10.

32   Peg Neuhauser, *Tribal Warfare in Organizations* (Cambridge: Ballinger Publishing Company, 1988).

33   Ibid., 5.

34   Ibid., 44-47, 64-67.

35 Ibid., 5, citing Edward T. Hall, *Beyond Culture* (New York: Doubleday/Anchor, 1976), 43.

36 Ibid., 88.

37 Ibid., 89.

38 Burton, "Conflict Resolution as a Function of Human Needs," in *Conflict: Human Needs Theory,* 192-3.

39 Terrell A. Northrup, "The Dynamic of Identity in Personal and Social Conflict," in *Intractable Conflicts and Their Transformation*, ed. Louis Kriesberg, Terrell A. Northrup and Stuart J. Thorson, with a foreword by Elise Boulding (Syracuse: Syracuse University Press, 1989), 73. For material on group identity formation in a context of power imbalance see David Steele, "Theological Assessment of Principled Negotiation as a Role Model for Church Involvement in the Mediation of International Conflict" (Unpublished, 1990), 13-15.

40 Coming from a different perspective, the reality of this dynamic is reinforced by Steven Box, who argues that the crimes of the powerful are minimized even though in actual fact they may be more devastating than the crimes of the powerless which are widely publicized in crime stats. See Steven Box, *Power, Crime, and Mystification* (New York: Tavistock Publications, 1983), passim.

41 Walter Brueggemann, *The Land: Place as Gift, Promise and Challenge in Biblical Faith* (Philadelphia: Fortress Press, 1977).

42 Fritjof Capra, David Steindel-Rast and Thomas Matus, *Belonging to the Universe: Explorations on the Frontiers of Science and Spirituality* (San Francisco: HarperSanFrancisco, 1992).

43 Ramashray Roy, "Social Conflicts and Needs Theories," in *Conflict: Human Needs Theory*, ed. John W. Burton, 135.

44 Paul Sites, *Control*.

45 Emmanuel Levinas, *Totality and Infinity: An Essay on Exteriority*, trans. Alphonso Lingis (Pittsburgh: Duquesne University Press, 1969), 21.

46 See Nathaniel Branden, *Pillars of Self Esteem* (New York: Bantam, 1995).

47 Paul Sites, *Control,* 10.

48 Ibid., 37.

49 Ibid., 73.

50 Lawrence Haworth, *Autonomy: An Essay in Philosophical Psychology and Ethics* (New Haven: Yale University Press, 1986).

51 Ibid., 55.

52 Ibid., 207.

53 Francis Fukuyama, *The End of History and the Last Man* (New York: Avon Books, 1993).

54 Ibid., 163.

55 Ibid., 165.

56   Ibid.

57   Ibid., 171-2.

58   Ibid., 172-3.

59   Roy F. Baumeister, "Violent Pride: Do People Turn Violent Because of Self-Hate or Self-Love?" *Scientific American,* April 2001, 96-101.

60   For the full story see Kristin Metz, "Passionate Differences: A Working Model for Cross-cultural Communication," *Journal of Feminist Studies in Religion* (6-1, Spring, 1990, 131-151).

61   For examples see Mihaly Csikszentmihalyi, *Creativity: Flow and the Psychology of Discovery and Invention* (New York: HarperCollins, 1996).

62   Paul Ricoeur, *Oneself as Another* (Chicago: University of Chicago Press, 1992).

63   Debra Niehoff, *The Biology of Violence* (New York: The Free Press, 1999).

64   James Gustafson, *Can Ethics Be Christian?* (Chicago: University of Chicago Press, 1975).

65   Chris Mercogliano and Kim Debus, "The Heart's Intelligence: An Interview with Joseph Chilton Pearce," *In Touch,* Autumn 2001, 11.

66   Ricoeur, *Oneself as Another,* 317-355.

67 Paul Sites, "Needs as Analogues of Emotions," in *Conflict: Human Needs Theory.*

68   Ricoeur, *Oneself as Another.* Ricoeur's concept of dialectic refers to two different aspects of an entity that are both needed to understand the whole and cannot be dissolved into one another.

69   These are inspired by Paul Ricoeur's concepts of $mimesis_1$, $mimesis_2$, $mimesis_3$, developed in *Time and Narrative,* Vol. 1, trans. Kathleen McLaughlin and David Pellauer (Chicago: University of Chicago Press, 1984).

70   Bob Birt stressed the importance of validation as a need category in private conversations.

71   Desmond M. Tutu, *No Future Without Forgiveness* (Toronto: Doubleday, 1999), 29-30.

72   I am indebted to Paul Sites, "Needs as Analogues of Emotions," in *Conflict: Human Needs Theory,* for making the connection between needs and emotions. Recent work by neurobiologists makes the connection even stronger: Debra Niehoff, *The Biology of Violence,* and Candace Pert, *Molecules of Emotion* (New York: Touchstone, 1997).

73   See Ken Wilber, *A Theory of Everything* (Boston: Shambhala, 2001).

74   Niehoff, *The Biology of Violence.*

75   "[F]ear is associated with the autonomic processes indicating the action of epinephrine(E) and anger with the action of norepinephrene (NE). Both of these neurochemicals activate the sympathetic nervous system (SNS), although in different ways. Satisfaction and depression, which appear to depend on variable activation of the parasympatheic nervous system (PNS) have been associated with the action of acetylcholine (ACh) which is the neurotransmitter of the PNS." Sites, "Needs as Analogues of Emotions," in *Conflict: Human Needs Theory,* 8, quoting David Funkenstein, "The Physiology of Fear and Anger," *Scientific American,* 192 (1955):78-80.

76 Ibid., 22.

77 cf. Branden, *Pillars of Self Esteem*.

78 Jean Vanier has a very poignant chapter on loneliness in his *Becoming Human* (Toronto: Anansi, 1998); it is based on his work with mentally challenged individuals who suffer grave threats to their need for connectedness.

79 Sites, "Needs as Analogues of Emotions," in *Conflict: Human Needs Theory*.

80 Victoria Rader, "Human Needs and the Modernization of Poverty," in *Conflict: Human Needs Theory*, 228.

81 Steven Box, *Deviance, Reality and Society* (Toronto: Holt, Rinehart and Winston, 1981), *Power, Crime and Mystification* (London: Tavistock, 1983), and *Recession, Crime and Punishment* (London: MacMillan Education, 1987).

82 Potapchuk, "Processes of Governance," in *Conflict: Human Needs Theory*, 270.

83 Ibid., 271.

84 Ibid.

85 Fisher, "Needs Theory, Social Identity and Conflict," in *Conflict: Human Needs Theory,* 104-105.

86 Ibid.

87 Galtung, "International Development," in *Conflict: Human Needs Theory,* 318-19.

88 Ibid., 267. Richard Rubenstein, "Basic Human Needs Theory: Beyond Natural Law," in *Conflict: Human Needs Theory,* also refers to false and partial satisfiers. His examples are the Ku Klux Klan 'Klaverns' which are close in subjective terms. "Just as tribal identity, say, satisfies a genuine identity need partially (and, to the extent that it represents a stopping point, creates a 'false need'), jobs satisfy a genuine need for creative associated work partially. The latter creates a false need for what bourgeois and state managed societies define as "work" (i.e., toil). The 'ethic of work,' which vainly attempts to make a virtue of necessity, and unmistakable signs of disintegration in the workplace—for example, massive use of narcotic drugs by workers attempting to make intolerable jobs tolerable—reveal how false this need is." 351.

89 Ibid. Kelman also makes a distinction between legitimate and illegitimate satisfiers of needs in "The Israeli-Palestinian Case," 291.

90 Richard E. Rubenstein, "Basic Human Needs Theory: Beyond Natural Law," in *Conflict: Human Needs Theory* (336-355), 345.

91 Ibid., 346.

92 Laura Stover, private correspondence.

93 Rubenstein, "Basic Human Needs Theory: Beyond Natural Law," in *Conflict: Human Needs Theory,* 347.

94 Ibid., 349.

95 Capra, Steindal-Rast and Matus, *Belonging to the Universe*.

Chapter 3
Imitation and Identity

1   See "desire" in the World Book Dictionary.

2   René Girard, *The Girard Reader*, ed. James Williams (New York: Crossroad, 2000), 286.

3   Ricoeur, *Oneself as Another*.

4   This evidence can be found in the extensive work of Girard (see bibliography) and the secondary literature around his thought. For a comprehensive bibliography see the *Bulletin of the Colloquium on Violence and Religion*. Also note the articles in *Contagion: Journal of Violence, Mimesis, and Culture*.

5   There are a number of biblical allusions to the connection between heart (interiority) and action or fruit. For example, "What comes out of the mouth proceeds from the heart, and this is what defiles. For out of the heart come evil intentions, murder, adultery, fornication, theft, false witness, slander." Matthew 15:18, 19, NRSV.

6   Girard points out in *"To Double Business Bound"* (Baltimore: John Hopkins University Press, 1992), 201, that a pre-mimetic desire stage is identified as mimetic interference: "When any gesture of appropriation is imitated, it simply means that two hands will reach for the same object simultaneously: conflict cannot fail to result.... There must be a mimetic element in the intraspecific fighting of many animals, since the absence of an object—the flight of the disputed female, for instance—does not always put an immediate end to the fighting. Eventually, however, the fighting comes to an end with a kind of submission of the vanquished to the victor. The dominated animal always yields to the dominant animal, who then turns into a model and guide of all behavior, *except appropriation*. Unlike animals, men engaged in rivalry may go on fighting *to the finish*." (Italics mine.)

7   This is consistent with Mary Clark's observations in "Meaningful Social Bonding as a Universal Human Need," in *Conflict: Human Needs Theory, 34-59*, about the development of a larger brain as necessary for the evolution of culture. She emphasizes the role of community in passing on the culture a child needs to survive; Girard's work emphasizes that much of what is passed on is passed on mimetically.

8   Girard, in *Deceit, Desire, and the Novel* (Baltimore: John Hopkins University Press, 1990), 17, distinguishes between a "romantic" understanding of desire which holds that desire springs up spontaneously within people and a "romanesque" understanding which holds that desire is mediated through others. More precisely, he states that "we shall use the term *romantic* for the works which reflect the presence of a mediator without ever revealing it and the term *novelistic [romanesque]* for the works which reveal this presence." Evidence of the latter in literary masterpieces led him to the initial insights of his theory. See ibid., 38-39.

9   Girard, *Things Hidden Since the Foundation of the World* (Stanford: Stanford University Press, 1987), 283-291; see also Roel Kaptein, *On the Way to Freedom* (Dublin: The Columba Press, 1993), 14-21. Note also Girard, *A Theater of Envy*, 116: "Our perspicacity in such matters is always rooted in self-criticism: mimetic desire is the same in all human beings, regardless of such circumstances as age, gender, race, and culture."

10   Girard, *Deceit, Desire, and the Novel*, 17.

11   Ibid., 41-44.

12   Ibid., 9.

13   See ibid., 6: "everything about the desire which is copied, including its intensity, depends upon the desire which serves as the model."

14   For a description of feedback as resulting in a runaway chain of events, see *Things Hidden*, 292.

15   Girard, *"To Double Business Bound,"* 48.

16   Girard, *Things Hidden*, 296.

17   Interestingly enough, the same illustration is used in both *Violence and the Sacred*, 146-147, and *Things Hidden*, 290.

18   Girard, *Deceit, Desire and the Novel*, 11.

19   Ibid.

20   Ibid., 44.

21   Girard, *Things Hidden*, 286.

22   Girard, *"To Double Business Bound,"* 39.

23   Ibid., 41.

24   Ibid., 299.

25   Ibid., 305.

26   Girard, *Things Hidden*, 305.

27   Girard, *"To Double Business Bound,"* 63-64.

28   e.g., ibid. 48: "Everywhere we repeatedly uncover the delirious exchange with the same monstrous idol…"

29   Girard, *Things Hidden*, 296.

30   Ibid., 289.

31   Ibid.

32   Ibid., 307.

33   Ibid.

34   Ibid.

35   Girard, *Deceit, Desire and the Novel*, 54.

36   Ricoeur, *Oneself as Another*; see pages 180-194 for a discussion around the dialogical and dialectical nature of self-esteem.

37   Note that mimetic desire is portrayed negatively in its association with these passions. Girard has stated that mimetic desire may also be very positive but that he has spent his writing career looking at its dark side. In Chapter 12 we will use a conceptualization developed by Rebecca Adams to look at the positive side of mimetic desire.

38   Girard, *"To Double Business Bound,"* 62.

39 An observation made by Jean-Pierre Dupuy at the Colloquium on Violence and Religion, June 1994.

40 In this regard, a comparison can be made to Macintyre's concepts of basic actions, many of which are action chains which in turn can be joined to constitute practices. In the same way, there can be basic objects, chains of objects, and the ongoing generation of objects such that anything the Model has or does can be the object of desire. See Alasdair Macintyre, *After Virtue: A Study in Moral Theory* (Notre Dame: University of Notre Dame Press, 1981).

41 Girard, *Things Hidden*, 295.

42 Ibid.

43 Polanyi, *Personal Knowledge*.

44 For examples, see*"To Double Business Bound,"* 96: "Delirium is nothing but the obligatory outcome of a desire that imbeds itself in the impasse of the obstacle model.... When effects of the universal double bind become too extreme to stay hidden, we speak of psychosis." *Things Hidden*, 332: "'primary masochism' is in fact none other than conflictual mimesis.... The subject has repeatedly observed the disillusionment that he experiences when he defeats his own rival and remains the unchallenged and secure possessor of the object. To counteract such disillusionment, this subject will henceforth place all his faith in an impenetrable obstacle. The only type of model that can still generate excitement is the one who cannot be defeated, the one who will always defeat his disciple.... In sadism, he plays the role of the model and persecutor. Here, the subject imitates not the desire of the model, but the model himself, in what now forms the major criterion for selecting this model: his violent opposition to all conceivable aspirations of a normal human being."

45 Girard, *Things Hidden*, 378.

46 Ibid., 300.

47 "Interdividual" is a word coined by Girard to describe the blurring of distinctions between Self and Other.

48 Girard, *Things Hidden*, 314. This is the same as "violence of indifferentiation." cf. Robert North, "Violence and the Bible: The Girard Connection," *Catholic Biblical Quarterly*, 47-1 (1985):7.

49 Ricoeur, *Oneself as Another*, 190ff.

50 Girard, *The Scapegoat* (Baltimore: John Hopkins University Press, 1989), 13.

51 Girard, *Things Hidden*, 93.

52 Ibid., 92.

53 Ibid., 93.

54 Ibid., 9.

55 Girard, *Deceit, Desire and the Novel,* 157.

56 Ibid., 158; cf. the observation of former hostage Terry Waite on *Morningside,* a national radio program of the Canadian Broadcasting Corporation (April 24, 1995), that every group which is open to violence for political ends attracts psychopaths who are only interested in violence and who do not wish to stop being violent when there is a peace accord.

57   Ibid., 121-122.

58   bid., 123.

59   Girard, *Things Hidden*, 391.

60   Ibid.

61   William Shakespeare, *A Midsummer Night's Dream,* Act One, Scene I, 80.

62   Girard, *A Theater of Envy: William Shakespeare* (Leominster and New Malden, UK: Gracewing and Inigo Enterprises, 2000), 46.

63   Ibid., 47.

64   Ibid.

65   Ibid.

66   Girard, *Things Hidden*, 11.

67   Ibid., 12.

68   bid., 26.

69   Ibid., 25.

70   Ibid., 26.

71   Ibid., 413.

72   Ibid.

73   Ibid., 378.

74   Ibid.

75   Ibid.

76   Ibid., 379.

77   Ibid., 370.

78   Ibid., 37. This point resonates with the analyses of the relationship between leader and community made by social psychologists.

79   William Shakespeare, *Troilus and Cressida,* Act Four, Scene IV, 281. The rest of the dialogue quoted is from the same scene.

80   Girard, *A Theater of Envy*, 130.

81   Ibid., 121-128.

82   Girard, *Things Hidden,* 300.

83   Observation of Jean-Michel Oughourlian, ibid., 300.

84   For examples, see Girard, *A Theater of Envy*, 35, 48, 62.

85   Ibid., 19.

86   Ibid., 117.

87   Ibid.

88   Ibid., 145.

89   Ibid., 86.

Chapter 4
The Scapegoat Function

1   Girard, *The Girard Reader*, 12.

2   This was Girard's emphasis at the June 1994 gathering of the Colloquium on Violence and Religion in which he argued by analogy that the court records of the Dreyfus Affair pointed to an actual incident.

3   For an examination of some of the issues related to this concept within the Christian tradition see Raymund Schwager SJ, "The Theology of the Wrath of God," in *Violence and Truth*, ed. Paul Dumouchel (Stanford: Stanford University Press, 1988), 44-52.

4   Vern Neufeld Redekop, *Scapegoats, the Bible and Criminal Justice.*

5   Girard, *The Scapegoat,* 49.

6   Ibid., 51.

7   Girard, *Violence and the Sacred*, 74.

8   Ibid., 49.

9   Ibid.

10   Ibid., 67.

11   Ibid., 49.

12   Ibid., 14.

13   Ibid., 15.

14   Ibid.

15   Ibid., 46.

16   Ibid., 47.

17   Ibid., 79.

18   Girard, *The Scapegoat*, 21.

19   Girard, *Violence and the Sacred*, 68.

20   Raymund Schwager SJ, *Must There Be Scapegoats? Violence and Redemption in the Bible* (Leominster and New York: Gracewing and Crossroad, 2000), 16-17.

21   Ibid., 23.

22   Ibid., 100, 106, 119.

23   Ibid., 161.

24   Ibid., 83.

25   Girard, *Violence and the Sacred*, 83.

26   Vern Neufeld Redekop, *Scapegoats, the Bible, and Criminal Justice*, 12-13.

27   Girard, *The Scapegoat*, 12.

28   Ibid.

29 William Shakespeare, *Julius Caesar,* Act One, Scene III, 73-82.

30 Girard, *A Theater of Envy,* 205.

31 Girard does a full analysis of a medieval text about Jews and the plague in *The Scapegoat,* 1-17.

32 Girard, *The Scapegoat,* 13.

33 Girard, *Violence and the Sacred,* 13.

34 Ibid., 86.

35 Ibid., 95.

36 Ibid., 78.

37 Girard, *The Scapegoat,* 15.

38 Ibid., 22.

39 Ibid., 104.

40 Ibid., 106.

41 I will use "scapegoat" generically for surrogate victims of generative scapegoating as well as sacrificial victims who are part of an ongoing ritual.

42 cf. Job 29:2-25, in which it becomes clear that Job had formerly been the first among equals, commanding respect wherever he went. This observation comes from René Girard, *Job: The Victim of His People* (Stanford: Stanford University Press, 1987).

43 Girard, *The Scapegoat,* 18-19.

44 Girard, *Violence and the Sacred,* 77.

45 See ibid., 8, for a development of this tension between being within yet outside the community and the types of difference which would set a victim apart from the community.

46 Ibid., 95.

47 Robin Morgan, *The Demon Lover: The Roots of Terrorism* (Toronto: Penguin, 1989).

48 For a well-developed description of what is entailed in exclusion see Miroslav Volf, *Exclusion or Embrace: A Theological Exploration of Identity, Otherness, and Reconciliation* (Nashville: Abingdon Press, 1996).

49 Girard, *Violence and the Sacred,* 28.

50 Ibid., 35-36.

51 Ibid., 35.

52 Ibid.

53 Ibid.

54 Ibid., 35-36.

55 Ibid., 33.

56 Ibid., 31.

57 Ibid.

58   Ibid.

59   Ibid., 79.

60   Ibid.

61   Ibid.

62   Ibid., 78.

63   Ibid., 94.

64   Ibid., 159.

65   Girard, *A Theater of Envy*, 203.

66   Girard, *Things Hidden*, 105-6.

67   Ibid., 106.

68   Ibid., 90-91.

69   Ibid., 94-95.

70   Girard, *Violence and the Sacred*, 3, drawing on Joseph De Maistre, "Éclaircissement sur les sacrifices," *Les Soirées de Saint-Pétersbourg* (Lyons, 1890), 2:341-42.

71   Ibid., 3.

72   Ibid., 104. The example is described in detail in pages 104-110. The additional detail about the harvest festival comes from Richard Batsinduka.

73   Ibid., 105.

74   For a discussion of the factors in choosing ritual victims, see ibid., 269-273.

75   Ibid.

76   Ibid., 101-102.

77   Ibid., 102.

78   Ibid., 8.

79   Ibid., 99.

80   Ibid., 98.

81   Ibid., 100.

82   Girard, *"To Double Business Bound,"* 207.

83   Girard, *Things Hidden*, 386.

84   Girard, *Violence and the Sacred*, 16.

85   Ibid., 84.

86   Ibid., 85.

87   Ibid., 31.

88   Girard, *A Theater of Envy*, 211.

89   Ibid., 213.

90   Ibid., 214.

91   Ibid.

92 Ibid.

93 Ibid., 214-15.

94 Ibid., 216.

95 Ibid.

96 Ibid., 253.

97 Ibid.

98 Ibid., 255.

99 Ibid., 255.

100 Ibid., 273.

101 Girard, *The Scapegoat*, 175.

102 Ibid., 166.

103 Matthew 7:6 quoted in Girard, *The Scapegoat*, 182.

104 Ibid., 183.

105 See Girard, *Job: The Victim of His People* and *Things Hidden*, Part II.

Chapter 5
Hegemonic Structures

1 George C.L. Cummings, "Black Theology and Latin American Theology," in *New Visions for the Americas: Religious Engagement and Social Transformation*, ed. David Batstone (Minneapolis: Fortress, 1993), 215-229.

2 For a detailed account see William Manchester, *The Arms of Krupp, 1587–1968* (Boston: Little, Brown and Co., 1968).

3 Antonio Gramsci, *The Modern Prince and Other Writings* (New York: International Publishers, 1968), 66.

4 Ibid., 66-67.

5 Cornel West, *Prophesy Deliverance! An Afro-American Revolutionary Christianity* (Philadelphia: Westminster Press, 1983), 49-50, quoted in George C.L. Cummings, "Black Theology and Latin American Theology," 217-18.

6 Daniel T. Linger, "The Hegemony of Discontent," *American Ethnologist* 20(1):3-24, 4.

7 Ibid.

8 Stephanie Y. Mitchem, "Womanists and (Unfinished) Constructions of Salvation," *Journal of Feminist Studies in Religion*, 17-1, Spring 2001.

9 Ibid, 89.

10 Ibid.

11 Vern Neufeld Redekop, *Scapegoats, The Bible and Criminal Justice*.

12 Cummings, "Black Theology and Latin American Theology," in *New Visions for the Americas*, 220-225. Note as well the formation of pre-hegemonic, neo-hegemonic and counter-hegemonic structures.

13 Hermann Rebel, "Cultural Hegemony and Class Experience: A Critical Reading of Recent Ethnological-Historical Approaches," *American Ethnologist* 16-1 (Feb. 1989), 122.

14 Rafael Moses, "Shame and Entitlement: Their Relation to Political Process," in *The Psychodynamics of International Relationships*, 131.

15 Vern Neufeld Redekop, "The Centrality of Torah as Ethical Projection for the Exodus," *Contagion: Journal of Violence, Mimesis, and Culture* 2 (Spring, 1995).

16 Cummings, "Black Theology and Latin American Theology," in *New Visions for the Americas*, 218.

Chapter 6
Ethnonationalism

1 Walker Connor's *Ethnonationalism: The Quest for Understanding* includes a collection of his writings from the late 1960s to 1994.

2 Ibid., 1. Note that "nation" can also be defined in civic terms where citizenship has nothing to do with ancestry. For the time being we will work with Connor's concept because this is still a powerful motivator in many conflicts.

3 Ibid., 42.

4 Ibid.

5 Ibid., 48. cf. Patrick Macklem, "Ethnonationalism, Aboriginal Issues, and the Law," in *Ethnicity and Aboriginality*, 9, where he points out that the "sense of being different requires a referent, a 'them,' being different, in other words, requires the construction of an other."

6 Connor, *Ethnonationalism*, 81-82.

7 Michael D. Levin ed., *Ethnicity and Aboriginality: Case Studies in Ethnonationalism*, (Toronto: University of Toronto Press, 1993), 5. The idea of ethnodrama links the theory of ethnonationalism to the work done of victimization described below.

8 Connor, *Ethnonationalism*, 145. cf. John E. Mack, "The Enemy System," *The Psychodynamics of International Relationships*, 62: "Each nation, no matter how bloody and cruel its beginnings, depicts to itself its origins as a glorious time of splendid heroes who vanquished less worthy foes or enemies. Although the idea of the *chosen* people is classically associated with Israel, each nation connects its mission with a sacred purpose, sanctified by its version of God."

9 Manning Nash, *The Cauldron of Ethnicity in the Modern World* (Chicago: University of Chicago Press, 1988), 10-11.

10 Connor, *Ethnonationalism*, 156.

11 Ibid., 198.

12 Gurutz Jáuregui Bereciartu, *Decline of the Nation-State*, tr. William A. Douglas (Reno: University of Nevada Press, 1994), 144.

13 Gurr, "Communal Conflicts and Global Security," 213.

14   Levin, *Ethnicity and Aboriginality*, 3.

15   Ibid., 4.

16   Ibid.

17   Ibid., 3.

18   Ibid.

19   Ibid., 4-5.

20   Michael Asch, "Aboriginal Self-Government and Canadian Constitutional Identity: Building Reconciliation," *Ethnicity and Aboriginality*, 29-30.

21   Ibid.

22   Ibid., 30.

23   Ryan, *Ethnic Conflict and International Relations*, 18.

24   Niehoff, *The Biology of Violence*, 33-38.

25   Vamik Volkan, *Blood Lines: From Ethnic Pride to Ethnic Terrorism* (Boulder: Westview, 1998), 44.

26   Andrew Bell-Fialkoff, *Ethnic Cleansing* (New York: St. Martin's Griffin, 1999), 83.

27   Volkan, *Blood Lines*, 111.

28   Ibid., 204.

29   Volkan, *Blood Lines*.

30   Bell-Fialkoff, *Ethnic Cleansing*.

31   Begley, "Religion and the Brain," *Newsweek*, May 7, 2001, 50-57.

32   Bell-Fialkoff, *Ethnic Cleaning*, 11-18, 60.

33   Samuel P. Huntington, *The Clash of Civilizations and the Remaking of World Order* (New York: Touchstone, 1996).

34   For a full development of this paradox, see R. Scott Appleby, *The Ambivalence of the Sacred: Religion, Violence, and Reconciliation,* with a foreword by Theodore M. Hesburgh (Lanham: Rowan & Littlefield, 2000).

35   This distinction is developed by Walter Brueggeman, *The Land.*

36   Ellen Shenk, *Outdoor Careers: Exploring Occupations in Outdoor Fields*, 2nd ed. (Mechanicsburg, PA: Stackpole Books, 2000), 20.

37   Demetrios A. Julius, Joseph V. Montville and Vamik D. Volkan, eds. "Introduction," *The Psychodynamics of International Relationships*, ix.

38   Steven Forde, "Classical Realism," in *Traditions of International Ethics*, ed. Terry Nardin and David R. Mapel (Cambridge: Cambridge University Press, 1992), 62.

39   Ibid., 63. See also Janine Chanteur, *From War to Peace* (Boulder: Westview Press, 1992) in which she analyzes the Western philosophical tradition, which accepts that the normative state of being between nation-states is that of war and that peace is defined as a temporary break in hostilities.

40   Ibid., 76.

41   Ibid., 78-79.

42   By way of a mapping of individuals around Morgenthau, he was influenced by E.H. Carr and Christian realist Reinhold Niebuhr, and was succeeded by his student Kenneth Thompson, who was given the mantle to revise Morgenthau's influential *Politics Among Nations: The Struggle for Power and Peace*. Other outstanding individuals in the realist school include Dean Acheson, George F. Kennan, Walter Lippman, and Henry Kissinger.

43   Hans Morgenthau and Kenneth W. Thompson, *Politics Among Nations: The Struggle for Power and Peace* (New York: Alfred A. Knopf, 1985), parts five and six.

44   Ibid., 330.

45   Jack Donnelly, "Twentieth-Century Realism," in *Traditions of International Ethics*, 85.

46   Ibid., 99. Note that Kissinger is using the word "nation" synonymously with "state."

47   Walker Connor in *Ethnonationalism: The Quest for Understanding*, 155. See also Gurutz Jáuregui Bereciartu, *Decline of the Nation-State*, tr. William A. Douglas (Reno: University of Nevada Press, 1994), 123ff., for a description of the identity crisis facing European states. Also Clifford Young, "The Dialectics of Cultural Pluralism: Concept and Reality," in *The Rising Tide of Cultural Pluralism*, ed. Crawford Young (Madison: University of Wisconsin Press, 1993), 4-19.

48   R.B.J. Walker, "The Concept of Culture in the Theory of International Relations," *Culture and International Relations*, ed. Jongsuk Chay (New York: Praeger, 1990), 12-13.

49   Thomas Hylland Eriksen, in "Ethnicity and Nationalism: Definitions and Critical Reflections," *Bulletin of Peace Proposals* Vol. 23-2 (1992):222, points out that ours is a world in which the present number of states could easily double and could conceivably grow to 10,000 if every ethnic group got its own territory.

50   Ignatieff, *Blood and Belonging*.

51   See Horowitz, *Ethnic Groups in Conflict*, 169, for a table of stereotypes.

52   Ibid., 102.

53   Ibid., 65.

54   Bereciartu, *Decline of the Nation-State*, 159, referring to Roland Breton, *Les Ethnies* (Paris: Presses Universitaires de France, 1981). John Rawls, "The Law of Peoples," *On Human Rights*, 55, lists seven principles reflecting the rights and duties of peoples including freedom and independence, equality, self-defence but not a right to war, nonintervention, observation of treaties, observation of restrictions in wars of self-defence, and honouring human rights.

55   For an assessment of issues pertaining to self-determination see Nihal Jayawickrama, *The Right of Self-Determination*, The Report of the Martin Ennals Symposium of Self-Determination, a Satellite Conference for the 1992 World Conference on Human Rights, co-sponsored by the College of Law, University of Saskatchewan and International Alert.

56   Levin, *Ethnicity and Aboriginality*, 4.

57   Ryan, *Ethnic Conflict and International Relations*, citing L. Kuper, "The Prevention of Genocide: Cultural and Structural Indicators of Genocidal Threat," *Ethnic and Racial Studies*, 12-2 (1989).

58   Macklen, "Ethnonationalism, Aboriginal Identities, and the Law," in *Ethnicity and Aboriginality*, 11.

59   Ibid., 12.

60   For an excellent study of the phenomenon see Mark Juergensmeyer, *Terror in the Mind of God: The Global Rise of Religious Violence* (Berkeley: University of California Press, 2001).

61   Montville, "The Psychological Roots of Ethnic and Sectarian Terrorism," in *The Psychodynamics of International Relationships*.

62   Kaptein, *On the Way to Freedom*, 70-71.

Chapter 7
Self–Other Dynamics

1   Levinas, *Totality and Infinity*, 21.

2   Ibid., 22-23.

3   Ibid., 46-47.

4   Ibid., 23.

5   Ricoeur, *Oneself as Another;* the concept is developed on pages 169-202.

6   Chanteur, *From War to Peace*.

7   Gloria Neufeld Redekop, "Survival in War and Famine: The Experience of Mennonite Children and Women in the Ukraine (1917–1925)." Presented at "The Quiet in the Land? Women of Anabaptist Traditions in Historical Perspective," June 8-11, 1995, Millersville University, Millersville, Pennsylvania.

8   Levinas, *Totality and Infinity*, 155.

9   Chanteur, *From War to Peace*, 204.

10   Contribution by Shirley Paré, CD, MPA, retired military officer, and trained third party neutral. She served in the Canadian Forces as Staff Officer to the Ministers' Advisory Board on Gender Integration in the Canadian Forces from 1994 to 1996, Department of National Defence, Canada.

11   Paul Ricoeur, *Oneself as Another*, 4-11.

12   Horowitz, *Ethnic Groups in Conflict*, 140.

13   Demetrios A. Julius, "The Genesis and Perpetuation of Aggression in International Conflicts," *The Psychodynamics of International Relationships*, 97.

14   Ibid., 99.

15   Ibid.

16   Ibid., 101-102.

17   John E. Mack, "The Enemy System," *The Psychodynamics of International Relationships,* 57-69.

18   Ibid., 61. The "tendency to hold an outside people or another country responsible for one's own misfortunes is, in this sense, built into the psychology of national history. National leaders, knowing this, may become adept at maintaining power through keeping their people's attention focused on the threat of an outside enemy."

19   Ibid., 62.

20   Ervin Staub, *Roots of Evil: The Origins of Genocide and Other Group Violence* (Cambridge: Cambridge University Press, [1989], 1992).

21   Ibid. See Part I for a development of the framework and Parts II and III for an application of the framework to the Nazi Holocaust, the Turkish genocide of the Armenians, Cambodian genocide and mass killing in Argentina.

22   John E. Mack, "The Psychodynamics of Victimization Among National Groups in Conflict," in *The Psychodynamics of International Relationships,* 119-129.

23   Ibid., 123.

24   Ibid.

25   Ibid., 125.

26   Joseph V. Montville, "The Psychological Roots of Ethnic and Sectarian Terrorism," in *The Psychodynamics of International Relationships*, 163-180.

27   Ibid., 163. He points out that "the ethnic group continues to feel threatened because the authors of the historic hurt," an ethnically different tribe or nation, "have neither accepted responsibility for their acts nor apologized for them. The victim group, therefore, feels a conscious or unconscious threat to its present and future well-being or even to its very survival."

28   Ibid., 169. See also Joseph Montville, "Epilogue," in *Conflict and Peacemaking in Multiethnic Societies,* Joseph V. Montville, ed. (Lexington: Lexington Books, 1990), 538.

29   Ibid., 165.

30   Ibid., drawing on Jean Knutson, "Victimization and Political Violence: The Spectre of Our Times," uncompleted book ms, 1981.

31   Ibid., 169-70.

32   Ibid., 174.

33   Volkan, "An Overview of Psychological Concepts Pertinent to Interethnic and/or International Relationships," in *The Psychodynamics of International Relationships*, 31-46.

34   Ibid., 33.

35   Ibid.

36   Ibid., 31.

37   Ibid, 38.

38   Rogers, "Intergenerational Transmission of Historical Enmity," in *The Psychodynamics of International Relationships,* 91-96.

39   Ibid., 92.

40   Ibid.

41   Ibid., 92-93.

42   Rafael Moses, "Self, Self-view, and Identity," in *The Psychodynamics of International Relationships*, 50.

43   Ibid.

44   Ibid., 51

45   Ibid., 52.

46   Ibid., 53.

47   Moses, "The Leader and the Led: A Dyadic Relationship," in *The Psychodynamics of International Relationships*, 205-217.

48   Rogers, "Intergenerational Transmission of Historical Enmity," in *The Psychodynamics of International Relationships*, 93.

49   Moses, "On Dehumanizing the Enemy," 111.

50   Ibid., 114.

51   Ibid., 115.

52   Willard Gaylin, *Caring* (New York: Knopf), 162-163, quoted in Montville, "The Psychological Roots of Ethnic and Sectarian Terrorism," in *The Psychodynamics of International Relationships*, 168-169.

Chapter 8
Structures of Violence

1   For a good analysis of the use of mimesis by different philosophers see William Schweiker, "Religion and the Philosophers of Mimesis," in *Curing Violence*, ed. Mark I. Wallace and Theophus H. Smith (Sonoma: Polebridge Press, 1994), 25-42.

2   Joseph Montville, "The Psychological Roots of Ethnic and Sectarian Terrorism,"in *The Psychodynamics of International Relationships, Volume I: Concepts and Theories*, 119-129.

3   Walter Wink, *Naming the Powers* (1984), *Unmasking the Powers* (1986) and *Engaging the Powers* (1992), all Philadelphia: Fortress Press.

4   Recounted by a Bosnian friend.

Chapter 9
Understanding Through Interpreting

1   Ricoeur, *Time and Narrative, Vol. 1*, ix.

2   Ibid., 52-76. Note that I will be adapting these levels in my own way but the framework I am using comes directly from Ricoeur.

3   Wilber, *A Theory of Everything*.

4   Polanyi, *Personal Knowledge*, 135-202.

5   Volf, *Exclusion or Embrace*, 9.

6   This corresponds to Paul Ricoeur's concept of mimesis$_1$ described in *Time and Narrative Vol. I*, 55.

7   Ibid., 65-66. This second phase corresponds to Ricoeur's mimesis$_2$.

8   Ricoeur, *Oneself as Another*, 341-355.

9   Gerald Alfred, *Heeding the Voices of Our Ancestors: Kahnawake Mohawk Politics and the Rise of Native Nationalism* (Toronto: Oxford University Press, 1995), 18-19.

10   Wilber, *A Brief History of Everything* (Boston: Shambala, 2001).

11   Ricoeur, *Time and Narrative, Vol. I*, 65.

12   This connection was made in a personal conversation.

13   Compare with Ricoeur's mimesis$_3$, *Time and Narrative, Vol. 1*, 70-71.

Chapter 10
The Oka/*Kanehsatà:ke* Crisis of 1990

1   Since there are many spellings of names of Mohawk places, groups and concepts, for the sake of consistency I will be using the Mohawk spellings as found in Brenda Katlatont Gabriel-Doxtater and Arlette Kawanatatie Van Den Hende, *At the Woods' Edge* (Kanesatake Education Center, 1995), an historical anthology written by the Mohawks of *Kanehsatà:ke*. Within quotes from other sources, I will use the spelling as found in those quotes.

2   Among the Mohawks, frequent comparison is made between themselves and the Jewish people; reclaiming the land of Israel has inspired the Mohawk imagination.

3   *At the Woods' Edge*, 381; Ronald Cross and Hélène Sévigny, *Lasagna: The Man Behind the Mask* (Vancouver: Talonbooks, 1994), 33.

4   *Basic Call to Consciousness* (Mohawk Nation via Rooseveltown, NY: Akwesasne Notes, 1978), 8-9. For a full development of these concepts see Taiaiake Alfred, *Peace, Power, Righteousness: An Indigenous Manifesto* (Don Mills: Oxford University Press, 1999).

5   Gabriel-Doxtater and Van Den Hende, *At the Woods' Edge*, 33.

6   Ibid., 23.

7   The Peacemaker is associated with *Kaianere'kó:wa*— the Great Good, Great Peace, Great Law which is the foundational teaching expressing the values, organization and desired relationships among the *Rotinonhseshá:ka* (Longhouse People including all the peoples of the Iroquois Confederacy). He made his appearance after a long period of wars among these peoples. See ibid., 9, n. 6 for a discussion of the possible dates ranging from 800 to 1500 CE.

8   *At the Woods' Edge*, 16. Note, 6, that the *Rotinonhseshá:ka* formed a Great League of Peace, the *Kaianere'kó:wa*, which, in addition to the *Kanien'kehá:ka*, included the

O'nientehá:ka (People of the Standing Stone—Oneidas), *Onont'keháka* (People of the Hill—Onondagas), *Kaionkeháka* (People of the Great Pipe—Cayugas) and the *Shenekeháka* (People of the Great Mountain—Senecas).

9   Ibid., 23.

10   Ibid., 26. The French preferred "Mission du Lac des Deux Montagnes" as a place name and in 1868 changed the name to Oka.

11   Ibid., 27.

12   Ibid., 31.

13   Ibid., 33.

14   Ibid., 57, drawing on Brian Young, *In Its Corporate Capacity: The Seminary of Montreal as a Business Institution* (Montreal: McGill–Queen's Press, 1816-17), 39.

15   *At the Woods' Edge*, 51.

16   Ibid., 53, n. 7, drawing on *Sir William Johnson Papers*, Volume X, Seven Years War, 302-305.

17   Ibid., 54, quoting speech delivered by Daniel Clause, May 6, 1762, *Sir William Johnson Papers*, Vol. X, the Seven Years War, 445-449.

18   Ibid., 72.

19   Ibid., 62.

20   Ibid., 62.

21   After 1847 a significant number of Mohawks joined the Methodists, but the Sulpicians accelerated the sale of land to Catholic colonists. See Pierre Trudel, "Le térritoire d'Oka, une véritable pomme de discorde," *La Presse* (July 14, 1990), B-3.

22   *At the Woods' Edge*, 82-83, drawing on "Crisis in the Canadas: 1838–1839," *The Grey Journals and Letters*, Edited by William Ormsby (Toronto: MacMillan, 1964), 20 and Herbert Bauch, "Quebec's Memory," *Montreal Gazette*, March 25, 1995, B-2.

23   Ibid., 170.

24   Ibid., 185.

25   Christina Coraggio, "Historian offers solution to Oka dispute," *Montreal Gazette*, July 19, 1990, A-4. She refers to the work of historian Michel Girard, who researched the history of the Oka forest for his doctorate at University of Ottawa.

26   *At the Woods' Edge*, 228, drawing on In the Superior Court, Justice Hutchinson present, no. 2001, Judgement, N.A.C., RG13, Vol. 2432, File A 500.

27   *Ibid.*, quoting Notes of Judge Carrol, December 29, 1911, N.A.C., RG13, Vol. 2432, File A500, Trans, B.G.

28   *Ibid.*, 230.

29   Ibid., 233, drawing on J.R. Millar, "Great White Father Knows Best: Oka and the Land Claims Process," *Native Studies Review*, Vol. 7, No. 1, 36.

30   André Picard, "A question of nationhood," *The Globe and Mail*, July 21, 1990, D-1.

31   Matthew Fraser, *Quebec Inc.: French-Canadian Entrepreneurs and the New Business Elite* (Toronto: Key Porter Books, 1987), 4.

32   Gerald R. Alfred, *Heeding the Voices of Our Ancestors*, 18-19.

33   Ibid., 58.

34   Ibid., 59.

35   "Warrior's Words Call for Execution," *Indian Time Akwesasne*, July 6, 1990, 1.

36   Ibid.

37   Richard Wagamese, "Oka leader 'perverting' Great Law" Warriors ideas blasted but barricade backed," *Calgary Herald,* July 20, 1990, 1. It is noted that "in his visits with supporters of the Warriors Society, Porter says he has noticed a disturbing tendency for rhetoric and the absence of free thought. Any arguments supporters make is based on the same set of ideas and those ideas originate from Hall, he says."

38   Gerald R. Alfred, *Heeding the Voices of Our Ancestors,* 186.

39   Ibid., 184.

40   Ibid., 76.

41   *At the Woods' Edge,* 239 quoting Joint Committee, Appendix XVI, 318.

42   The Canadian Press, "Battle lines were drawn thirty years ago," *Ottawa Citizen,* July 13, 1990, A-3.

43   Geoffrey York and Loreen Pindera, *People of the Pines: The Warriors and the Legacy of Oka*. Toronto: Little, Brown and Company (Canada), 1991, 44-45.

44   Carrie Buchanan, "Residents oppose golf development," *Ottawa Citizen*, July 13, 1990, A-3.

45   York and Pindera, *People of the Pines*, 48.

46   Ibid., 50.

47   Within *Kanehsatà:ké* are various groups with different mixtures of religious affiliation and commitment to traditional ways. This group was a Christian group committed to a traditional Iroquois system of governance.

48   York and Pindera, *People of the Pines*, 51.

49   Ibid., 53.

50   Ibid., 59.

51   Ibid., 66.

52   Ibid., 75.

53   Ibid., 62-63.

54   Don McGillvray, "Natives want more than Ottawa's trinkets," *Montreal Gazette,* July 19, 1990, B-3.

55   York and Pindera, *People of the Pines*, 76.

56   Ibid., 77.

57   John Ciaccia, *The Oka Crisis: A Mirror of the Soul* (Dorval: Maren Publications, 2000), 59-60. He points out in his reflections on the letter that it was Charles Dickens who first wrote that the law is an ass and that he deliberately quoted Dickens through a Québec premier.

58 Ibid., 79.

59 John Davidson, *Canadian Press Release*, July 9, 1990.

60 York and Pindera, *People of the Pines*, 81.

61 Mark Richardson and Francine Dubé, "Oka standoff continues," *Ottawa Citizen*, July 14, 1990, A-1.

62 York and Pindera, *People of the Pines*, 37-38.

63 Ibid., 192.

64 Patricia Poirier, "Police jam church to mourn slain officer," *Globe and Mail*, A-4.

65 John Davidson, Canadian Press Release, July 13, 1990.

66 Elizabeth Thompson, "Army troops at the ready," *Montreal Gazette*, July 17, 1990, A-6.

67 "Mohawks boast they can match police firepower," *Montreal Gazette*, July 13, 1990.

68 Mike King, "Mercier Bridge destruction easy: explosives expert," *Montreal Gazette*, July 13, 1990. Also referred to in "La population blanche excédée s'en prend aux Mohawks de Kahnawake," *Le Devoir*, July 14, 1990.

69 Pierre Bellemare, "La guerre des nerfs s'intensifie à Kahnawake," *La Presse*, July 13, 1990, A3.

70 Francine Dubé, "Fallout from Oka: bitter residents, business losses," *Ottawa Citizen*, July 15, 1990, A-2.

71 York and Pindera, *People of the Pines*, 228.

72 Ibid., 229.

73 Peter Stockland, "Native effigy burned," *Ottawa Sun*, July 16, 1990, 4.

74 Christina Coraggio, "Chanting mob curses Mohawks," *Montreal Gazette*, July 16, 1990, A-1.

75 Ibid.

76 Ibid.

77 Jack Branswell, *Canadian Press Release*, July 19, 1990.

78 Carrie Buchanan, "Getting mad: Commuters want their bridge back," *Ottawa Citizen*, July 17, 1990, A-4.

79 The text of his letter was published under the headline "Oka: les enjeux vont au delà de la stricte légalité," *Le Devoir*, July 12, 1990.

80 Patricia Poirier, "Châteauguay mayor defends community," *The Globe and Mail*, July 20, 1990, A-4.

81 Ibid.

82 Bob Cox, *Canadian Press Release*, July 18, 1990.

83 Ibid.

84 "Trois évêques pressent les gouvernements de négocier," *La Presse*, July 13, 1990. Note also that Gilles Lesage writing in *Le Devoir* concluded that "[o]utre la légalité, la justice et l'équité sont en cause," under the headline "Des barricades sentenaire: les

enjeux d'Oka dépassent la stricte légalité," July 13, 1990, 12. See also Michel Roy, "Négocier avec les autochtones," *Le Droit*, July 14, 1990, 19.

85 Patricia Poirier, "Châteauguay mayor defends community," *The Globe and Mail*, July 20, 1990, A-4.

86 Ibid.

87 Ibid.

88 York and Pindera, *People of the Pines*, 227. Lopez also suggested that Canadian Indians be shipped to Labrador if they wanted their own country.

89 Francine Dubé, " Mayor's friends urge use of force," *Ottawa Citizen*, July 16, 1990, A-3.

90 André Picard and Patricia Poirier, "Peaceful end to Oka standoff possible," *The Globe and Mail*, July 16, 1990, A-1.

91 Jane Armstrong, "More talks needed in standoff," *Toronto Star*, July 16, 1990, A-10.

92 Ibid., 219.

93 "Keep security," *Canadian Press Release*, July 16, 1990.

94 "Neighbors smuggle supplies to Mohawks," *Toronto Star*, July 17, 1990, A-6.

95 Ibid.

96 York and Pindera, *People of the Pines*, 198.

97 Ibid.

98 Ibid.

99 Ibid., 211.

100 Aaron Derfel, Police trying to starve out Indians, critics charge," *Montreal Gazette*, July 17, 1990, A-6.

101 Ibid.

102 *Canadian Press Release*, July 17, 1990, 2.

103 *Canadian Press Release*, July 17, 1990.

104 Patrick Doyle, "Make plans to defend native lands chiefs told," *Toronto Star*, July 21, 1990, A-1.

105 Ibid.

106 Patrick Doyle, "Ottawa accused of retaliating for Meech defeat," *Toronto Star*, July 20, 1990, A-10.

107 Ibid.

108 Janis Hass, "Discontent will spread, Indians say," *Ottawa Citizen*, July 15, 1990, A-2.

109 Brian Maracle, "Wake up," *Ottawa Citizen*, July 20, 1990, A-14.

110 "B.C., Manitoba roads blocked in sympathy," *Ottawa Citizen*, July 19, 1990, A-5.

111 Picard and Poirier, "Peaceful end."

112 Robert Fife, "No fed deals during siege," *Ottawa Sun*, July 20, 1990, 4.

113 John Davidson, *Canadian Press Release*, July 18, 1990, 2.

114 *Canada AM* Transcript, CTV, M.T.T. [Media Tapes and Transcripts] Ltd., July 18, 1990, 4.

115 Tim Harper, "Days of rage: The new face of the Indian movement," *Toronto Star,* July 14, 1990, 1.

116 York and Pindera, *People of the Pines*, 278-279.

117 Ibid., 274.

118 Ibid., 214-215.

119 Ibid., 271.

120 Alexander Norris, "Portrait of a Mohawk fighter," *Montreal Gazette*, July 15, 1990, A-6.

121 Francine Dubé, "Oka residents divided on police presence," *Ottawa Citizen*, July 17, 1990, A-3.

122 Rob Bull, *Canadian Press Release*, July 17, 1990.

123 *Canadian Press Release*, July 16, 1990. Note that early on some of the Mohawks poured bottle after bottle of liquor down the drain to remove it from temptation's reach (York and Pindera, *People of the Pines*, 193).

124 Doyle, "Make plans."

125 Ingrid Peritz, "Native chiefs call on PM to recall Parliament," *Montreal Gazette*, July 21, 1990, A-6.

126 Peggy Curran, "Siddon holds firm on federal course," *Ottawa Citizen*, July 21, 1990, A-5.

127 Ray Di Gregorio, "Chiefs seek international sanctions to settle native land disputes," *Ottawa Citizen*, July 21, 1990.

128 Tom Siddon in an interview on *Canada AM,* July 20, 1990. Transcript, 2.

129 Charlie Fidelman and Aaron Derfel, "Police hold back jeering mob at boundary of Kahnawà:ke," Montreal Gazette, July 15, 1990, A-6.

130 Patrick Doyle, "Blockade to be lifted at bridge to Montreal," *Toronto Star*, July 15, 1990, A-1 and *People of the Pines*, 227.

131 Ibid.

132 York and Pindera, *People of the Pines*, 227.

133 Peter Stockland, "Native effigy burned," *Ottawa Sun*, July 16, 1990, 4.

134 Patrick Doyle, "Police ban Canadian flag at barricade," *Toronto Star*, July 16, 1990, A-1.

135 Christina Coraggio, "Chanting mob curses Mohawks," *Montreal Gazette*, July 16, 1990, A-1.

136 York and Pindera, *People of the Pines*, 218.

137 Ibid., 216-217.

138 Jeff Heinrich, Peter Kuitenbrouwer and Charlie Fidelman, "Ciacca: We can hope," *Montreal Gazette*, July 13, 1990, A-1.

139 *Canadian Press Release,* July 18, 1990.

140 York and Pindera, *People of the Pines*, 249.

141 Ibid., 250.

142 Ibid., 250-51.

143 Ibid., 203-205.

144 Ibid., 206.

145 Ibid., 222-23.

146 Ibid., 223.

147 Ibid., 219.

148 Ibid., 218-19.

149 Ibid., 293.

150 Ibid., 294-95.

151 Ibid., 295.

152 Ibid., 295-96.

153 Ibid., 296-97.

154 John Ciaccia, *The Oka Crisis*, 256.

155 York and Pindera, *People of the Pines*, 298.

156 Ibid., 304.

157 Ibid., 307.

158 Ibid., 306.

159 Ibid., 308

160 Ibid., 316.

161 Ibid., 320.

162 Ibid., 321.

163 Ibid., 335.

164 Craig MacLaine and Michael S. Baxendale, *This Land Is Our Land: The Mohawk Revolt at Oka* (Montreal: Optimum, 1990), 62.

165 York and Pindera, *People of the Pines*, 336.

166 Ibid., 344-46.

167 Cross and Sévigny, *Lasagna* (Vancouver: Talon Books, 1994), 96.

168 David Johnston, "The stare: Private becomes unofficial hero of Oka standoff," *Montreal Gazette*, September 15, 1990, A-8.

169 York and Pindera, *People of the Pines*, 271. Additional information about Brad Larocque can be found on 269-271.

170 Ibid., 358.

171 Ibid., 361.

172 Ibid., 364.

173 Ibid., 367-68.

174 Ian MacLeod, "Mohawks claim European support," *Ottawa Citizen*, September 17, 1990, A-3.

175 Ibid.

176 March Henton, "'We're sitting on a powder keg': Chiefs fear increased violence by natives," *Toronto Star*, September 17, 1990, A-15.

177 Ibid.

178 York and Pindera, *People of the Pines*, 383.

179 Lynn Moore, "'We won't ever forgive,' Mohawk teenagers warn: Army raid united community, they say," *Montreal Gazette*, September 21, 1990, A-5.

180 "We oppose terrorism," *Edmonton Journal*, September 19, 1990.

181 Marina Jimenez, "Police call Mohawks 'terrorists' in national ad," *Edmonton Journal*, September 19, 1990.

182 Ibid.

183 Eloise Morin, "Surete's image takes beating: Force's chief issues apology for first time," *Toronto Star*, September 21, 1990, A-23.

184 Ibid.

185 John Yorkton, "Native issue is becoming a linguistic war," *Montreal Gazette*, September 11, 1990, B-3.

186 Ian MacLeod, "New Oka deal sought: Middle-ground solution possible, says negotiator," *Ottawa Citizen*, September 13, 1990, A-3.

187 York and Pindera, *People of the Pines*, 392.

188 Cross & Sévigny, *Lasagna*, 105.

189 Karen O'Brien, "Outrage still simmers among Oka participants," *The Spectator*, October 29, 1990, C-3.

190 Ibid.

191 Cross and Sévigny, *Lasagna*, 50.

192 Ibid., 79.

193 Ibid.

194 Ibid., 169-70.

195 André Picard, "Standoff at Oka increases tension over language," *The Globe and Mail*, September 14, 1990.

196 Robin Philpot, *Oka: dernier alibi du Canada anglais* (Montreal: VLB éditeur, 1991), 26-33.

Chapter 11
Interpreting the Oka/*Kanehsatàke* Crisis

1   York and Pindera, *People of the Pines*, 410.

2   Furthermore, these divisions were reinforced by religious divisions with Catholics and Anglicans supporting an open vote for the Band Council. See Pierre Trudel, "Les revendications des Mohawks de Kahnesatake," *Le Devoir*, July 14, 1990, A-5.

3   François Forest, "Il ya un temps pour la négociation et un temps pour réagir...," *La Presse*, July 13, 1990.

4   York and Pindera, *People of the Pines*, 286; see also 284.

5   See Robert Hull, "Kanienkehaka Chronology: The Mohawk Crisis in Quebec and its Aftermath, July to December 1990," *The Conrad Grebel Review*, 9-2 (Spring 1991): 103-114 for a description of many such behind-the-scenes undertakings.

Chapter 12
Structures of Blessing

1   Matthew Fox, *Original Blessing* (New York: Jeremy P. Tarcher/Putnam, 2000).

2   Ibid., 46.

3   See Francis Brown et al., *The New Brown-Driver-Briggs-Gesenius Hebrew and English Lexicon* (Lafayette: Associate Publishers and Authors, Inc., 1980), s.v. בָּרַךְ See also Vern Redekop, "Moses' Perspective on War and Peace Based on the Book of Deuteronomy," unpublished Senior Seminar Paper, 1982, 22, n.12.

4   s.v. blessing, *World Book Dictionary*.

5   Fox, *Original Blessing*, 7, 44.

6   Rebecca Adams, "Mothers, Metamorphs, Myth and Mimesis: A Creative Reassessment of Mimetic Desire," unpublished paper presented at the COV&R Conference on "Violence and the Subject of Responsibility," Loyola University, June 2, 1995, later published as "Loving Mimesis and Girard's 'Scapegoat of the Text': A Creative Reassessment of Mimetic Desire" in *Violence Renounced: René Girard, Biblical Studies, and Peacemaking*, ed. Willard M. Swartley (Telford: Pandora Press, 2000), 277-307.

7   I am indebted to Rebecca Adams for the clarification and development of this section. Some of the ideas in this and the next three paragraphs, and the way they are expressed, are her original contribution. The term "double-consciousness" was first coined by W.E.B. Du Bois in his book *The Souls of Black Folk* (1903) to describe the splitting of Self experienced by African-Americans under racism.

8   Adams' formal notion of the "Proto-Subject" should be distinguished from the way I am discussing the cases of actual people, or groups of people, who are not fully functioning Subjects because of the experience of colonization, trauma or wounding. First, the term "Proto-Subject" has certain technical meanings within Adams' argument. In Adams' work, the term "Proto-Subject" simply emphasizes incompleteness as the

potential for Subjectivity, especially within her abstract paradigm of mimetic desire. In the sense that every person is always potentially an even more fully-realized Subject than at present, everyone is always, at all times, a "Proto-" or potential Subject. So while it would not be incorrect to use the term "Proto-Subject" in a more general way to describe any person who imitates the desire of a Model, it may not the most useful term in describing the specific experience of persons who have experienced colonization, trauma or wounding, for several reasons.

First, the type of "incompleteness" I am focusing on primarily concerns the practical limitation of real peoples' already existing wills and   consciousness because of harmful or inadequate Models. Second, as Adams has pointed out to me, not every Proto- or potential Subject is limited in the sense of being colonized, traumatized or wounded (at least in theory). Third, I need to keep in mind that there are historically and socially specific differences between the ways that individuals, or groups of individuals, can be limited in their subjective outlook (i.e., not everyone who has been victimized has been victimized in the same way; being colonized may not function quite the same way as being victimized or wounded, etc.).

For all these reasons, therefore, Adams has helped me work out the alternative general term "Limited Subject," which is still somewhat similar to her term but more appropriate to my argument. I define a Limited Subject as a person (or a group) who does not have a fully functioning Subjectivity because of having had past inadequate or harmful Models. Like Adams' original term "Proto-Subject," this term still stresses the ideas of incompleteness and the future potential for fuller subjectivity. This new term, however, allows me to focus on my analysis of limitation, while allowing room to remember that there may be specific differences between wounded Subjects, traumatized Subjects, or colonized Subjects. Yet as a frequently used, general term, it can still encompass all these (and perhaps other) examples.

9   Adams, "Loving Mimesis," 288.

10   There is a fine line between truly giving something to enhance the subjectivity of the other or giving a gift in order to draw attention to oneself through what Girard observes to be a reverse mimetic desire: i.e., competition over who can give the biggest gift.

11   Adams, "Mothers, Metamorphs, Myth and Mimesis," 15.

12   The Seminar on "Understanding Reconciliation" led by Vern Neufeld Redekop and Rebecca Adams, St. Paul's Episcopal Church, Harrisburg, PA, April 24, 1999, was an important generative event for working out these ideas.

13   Volf, *Exclusion or Embrace*.

14   Paul Pearsall, *The Heart's Code: Tapping the Wisdom and Power of Our Heart Energy* (New York: Broadway Books, 1998).

15   Thomas Lewis, Fari Amini and Richard Lannon, *A General Theory of Love* (New York: Random House, 2000).

16   Volf, *Exclusion or Embrace*, 141.

Chapter 13
Reconciliation

1   Francis Brown et al., *The New Brown-Driver-Briggs-Gesenius Hebrew and English Lexicon* (Lafayette: Associate Publishers and Authors, Inc., 1980), s.v. פֶּשַׁר.

2   John Paul Lederach, "Five Qualities of Practice in Support of Reconciliation Processes," in *Forgiveness and Reconciliation: Religion, Public Policy and Conflict Transformation*, ed. Raymond G. Helmick, S.J. and Rodney L. Petersen (Philadelphia: Templeton Foundation Press, 2001), 183-194.

3   *World Book Dictionary*.

4   Bob Birt sees the softening of the heart as the central concept behind reconciliation.

5   Quoted from unpublished seminar notes.

6   Vern Redekop, "The Centrality of Torah as Ethical Projection to the Exodus," *Contagion: Journal of Violence, Mimesis, and Culture*, Vol. 2, 1995, 119-144.

7   Girard, *Things Hidden*, 142.

8   Ibid., 142.

9   Ibid.

10 So Jacob named the place Peniel, meaning, "I have seen a divine being face to face, yet my life has been preserved." Genesis 32:31, *Tanakh*.

11 Genesis 33:10b, *Tanakh*.

12 James Williams, *The Bible, Violence and the Sacred: Liberation from the Myth of Sanctioned Violence* (New York: HarperCollins, 1991), 48.

13 *The New Brown-Driver-Briggs-Gesenius Hebrew and English Lexicon*, s.v. יִשְׂרָאֵל, 975.

14 Williams, *The Bible, Violence and the Sacred*, 49.

15 *Tanakh*, Genesis 25:25, note "c."

16 Frank Crüsemann, "Dominion, Guilt, and Reconciliation: The Contribution of the Jacob Narrative in Genesis to Political Ethics," trans. Carl S. Ehrlich, *Semeia*, 66 (1994): 67-77. Note also that Israel had twelve landed tribes plus the Levites and Edom a similar number; cf. Genesis 36:15-19 in which thirteen grandsons of Esau are listed with one being differentiated and Genesis 36:40-43 in which eleven landed tribes are listed.

17 The structure was very similar to when Joseph was sold; it was an all-against-one situation. The story was changed from the first round of dealing with the Rachel son by Judah's offer. This time Benjamin was the only Rachel son left. Judah, a son of Leah, instead of using this opportunity to get rid of the favourite, actually offers to stay in his place.

18 See *People Building Peace: 35 Inspiring Stories from Around the World*, a publication of the European Centre for Conflict Prevention, in co-operation with the International Fellowship of Reconciliation (IFOR) and the Coexistence Initiative of the State of the

World Forum, 1999; see also *For a Change*, the magazine of Initiatives of Change, the new name for what was known as Moral Re-Armament. Another good resource is Douglas Johnston and Cynthia Sampson, eds., *Religion: The Missing Dimension of Statecraft* (New York: Oxford Univesity Press, 1994).

19　Charles E. Osgood, *Perspective in Foreign Policy* (Palo Alto: Pacific Books, 1966).

20　This story was told to me by Professor John Sigler, who heard it from Charles Osgood himself.

21　For a clear discussion of forgiveness in relation to justice see Miroslav Volf, "Forgiveness, Reconciliation, and Justice: A Christian Contribution to a More Peaceful Social Environment," *Forgiveness and Reconciliation*, ed. Raymond G. Helmick, S.J. and Rodney L. Peterson, 27-50.

22　Daryold Corbiere Winkler, "Forgiveness and Reconciliation: Lessons from Canada's First Nations," in *The Challenge of Forgiveness*, ed. Augustine Meier and Peter VanKatwyk (Ottawa: Novalis, 2001), 51. Quote is from Rupert Ross, *Returning to the Teachings* (Toronto: Penguin Books, 1996), 188-9.

23　Donna Hicks, "Identity Reconstruction in Reconciliation," *Forgiveness and Reconciliation*, ed. Raymond G. Helmick, S.J. and Rodney L. Peterson, 146.

24　Ibid., 147.

25　Ibid.

26　Ibid., 148.

27　Paul Pearsall, *The Heart's Code*, 210.

28　Anatol Rapoport, *Peace: An Idea Whose Time Has Come* (Ann Arbor, MI: The University of Michigan Press, 1992).

29　See my "The Centrality of Torah" article for a sustained argument about this subject.

30　"Five Qualities in Support of Reconciliation Processes," in *Forgiveness and Reconciliation*, ed. Raymond G. Helmick, S.J. and Rodney L. Petersen, 183-194.

31　David Bohm, *On Dialogue*, edited by Lee Nichol (New York: Routledge, 1997).

32　Konrad Lohrenz, *On Aggression*. Marjorie Kerr Wilson, trans. (New York: Harcourt, Brace and World, 1966). Original *Das Sogenannte Böse: Zur aturgeschichte der Aggression*, 1963.

33　Mihaly Csikszentmihalyi, *Creativity*.

Chapter 14
Theological Reflections

1　Inspired by Ephesians 2:8.

2　Robert J. Schreiter, *Constructing Local Theologies* (Maryknoll: Orbis, 1986), 13.

3　For an example of how such a dialogue can be structured more formally as discourse see Fritjof Capra, David Steindl-Rast and Thomas Matus, *Belonging to the Universe: Explorations on the Frontiers of Science and Spirituality* (San Francisco:

HarperSanFrancisco, 1992). Note as well that the mimetic hypotheses of René Girard were first published in totally non-theological discourse; it took 20 years after his discovery of mimetic desire for the publication of *Des choses cachées dupuis la fondation du monde* (Paris: Éditions Grasset & Fasqueslle, 1978) in which he linked mimetic and scapegoat theory with Biblical and theological concepts. His work serves as a natural source in the development of a discursive framework in this context.

4   Donald M. Taylor and Lise Dubé, "Two Faces of Identity: The 'I' and the 'We'," *Journal of Social Issues*, 42-2 (1986): 81-82; note that the personal and social identities are intertwined.

5   1 Samuel 18:10; 19:9.

6   2 Samuel 24:1.

7   1 Chronicles 21:1.

8   John 8:44.

9   Ephesians 6:11-12 (Jerusalem Bible).

10   Walter Wink, *Engaging the Powers: Discernment and Resistance in a World of Domination* (Minneapolis: Fortress Press, 1992).

11   Gil Bailie, *Violence Unveiled* (New York: Crossroad, 1995), 204.

12   Ibid.

13   Ibid., 207.

14   Robert G. Hamerton-Kelley, *Sacred Violence: Paul's Hermeneutic of the Cross* (Minneapolis: Fortress, 1992), 98-99.

15   Ibid., 90.

16   I am indebted to John E. Toews for this reading of the Epistle of Paul to the Romans; see his commentary on Romans (forthcoming) for a complete development.

17   René Girard, *Resurrection from the Underground:Feodor Dostoevsky,* ed. and trans. by James G. Williams (New York: Crossroad, 2000), 139-140.

18   Ibid., 140-41.

19   These two dimensions of reconciliation correspond to what Elmer Martens describes as "two kinds of divine activity. Deliverance is that work of rescue from evil which God brings about through his intervention. Blessing is the continuous work of God by means of which he sustains life, empowers persons and ensures a state of well-being." See his *God's Design: A Focus on Old Testament Theology* (Grand Rapids: Baker Book House, 1986 [1981]), 39.

20   See Francis Brown et al., *The New Brown-Driver-Briggs-Gesenius Hebrew and English Lexicon* (Lafayette: Associate Publishers and Authors, Inc., 1980), s.v. בָּרַךְ. See also Vern Redekop, "Moses' Perspective on War and Peace Based on the Book of Deuteronomy," unpublished Senior Seminar Paper, 1982, 22, n.12: "The word *barak* (to bless) has the sense of 'empower'.... There is in the three-verb sequence [of Deut. 8:10] a picture of eating, being satisfied, and strengthed in the presence of God."

21   Rebecca Adams, "Loving Mimesis," *Violence Renounced,* Willard M. Swartley, ed. (Pandora Press, 2000). See also her vignette in Chapter 12 of this book.

22   Ibid.

23   Ibid.

24   Girard, *Things Hidden*, 237-39.

25   Ibid., 238.

26   Ibid., 238-39.

27   Ibid., 241.

28   Ibid.

29   Ibid., 242.

30   Ibid., 242-43.

31   Williams, *The Bible, Violence and the Sacred*, 142.

32   See Schwager et al., "Dramatic Theology as a Research Program," unpublished paper presented at the Colloquium on Violence and Religion at Stanford University, June, 1996, 1.

33   James Alison, in *Raising Abel: The Recovery of Eschatological Imagination* (New York: Crossroad, 1996), 30-33, equates the first with many in the reformation tradition and the second with a Roman Catholic natural law tradition. Within the second, one finds many historical-critical Biblical scholars and social gospel advocates.

34   Deuteronomy 4:6, *Tanakh: A New Translation of the Holy Scriptures According to the Traditional Hebrew Text* (Jerusalem: The Jewish Publication Society, 1985).

35   Matthew 20:20-28.

36   Luke 7:36-50.

37   I am indebted for this insight to Thomas Wieser, "Community: Its Unity, Diversity and Universality," *Semeia*, 33 (1985) 88, where he argues that Jesus aims at abolishing the distinction between insiders and outsiders.

38   Mark 2:15-17; Matthew 9:9; Luke 5:29-32.

39   Luke 19:1-10.

40   Mark 7:24-30; Matthew 15:21-28.

41   Exodus 34:6-7 and Numbers 14:15; see Vern Redekop, *A Life for a Life? The Death Penalty on Trial* (Scottdale: Herald Press, 1990), 38, for my translation and commentary.

42   Alison, *Raising Abel*, 35.

43   Matthew 22:21; Mark 12:17; Luke 20:25.

44   Linda Munk, "The Design of Violence," *Journal of Literature & Theology*, 4-3 (November 1990): 259-60.

45   Alison, *Raising Abel*, 70-71.

46   Ibid., p. 71.

47   Redekop, *A Life for a Life?*, 44-47.

48   John 4:25-26.

49   I am indebted to John E. Toews for this insight.

50   Alison, *Raising Abel*, 46.

51   Raymund Schwager, "Suffering, Victims, and Poetic Inspiration," *Contagion: Journal of Violence, Mimesis, and Culture*, Vol. 1, 1994, 66.

52   For a discussion on both violent mimetic structures and the sense of a closed system see Munk, "The Design of Violence," esp. 259-260.

53   Raymond Schwager, S.J., "Christ's Death and the Prophetic Critique of Sacrifice," *Semeia*, 33 (1985):118.

54   Matthew 18:28-35.

55   For a development of the concept of vulnerability in the context of violent conflict see my "Response to *The Challenge of Peace: God's Promise and our Response*," an unpublished paper prepared for Mr. Geoffrey Pearson, Executive Director, Canadian Institute for International Peace and Security, August 20, 1985, 8-10.

56   Schwager, "Suffering, Victims, and Poetic Inspiration," *Contagion: Journal of Violence, Mimesis, and Culture*, 67.

57   Alison, *Raising Abel*, 25-30.

58   Ibid., 54-55.

59   Ibid., 61.

60   Ibid.

61   Ibid., 110.

62   Ibid., 60.

63   Ibid., 74.

64   David B. Burrell, "René Girard: Violence and Sacrifice," *Cross Currents*, 28 (Winter 1988-89): 447. Note that there is an apparent contradiction between Alison's point that Jesus' imagination is to be subject to mimesis and Burrell's observation that we must go beyond "imitating Jesus" to a relationship with God. Burrell's use of quotation marks signals a reference to the traditional notions of imitation of Christ; however, his point anticipates a formulation of love defined in terms of mimetic desire by Rebecca Adams as developed above.

65   Raymund Schwager, S.J., *Jesus im Heilsdrama: Entwurf einer biblischen Erlosüngslehre*. Innsbruck: Tyrolia-Verlag, 1990, 220-42; note that Schwager emphasizes Jesus' role as an actor through the crucifixion. Even his last word_"Father, into your hands I commend my Spirit"_was an action on his part. In this respect he did not have a victim mentality, even though he was identifying with all who had been victimized.

66   Schwager et al, "Dramatic Theology as a Research Program," 11-12, provides the following hypothesis: "A deep, true and lasting peace among people which is not based on sacrificing third persons and can exist without polarization onto enemies is very difficult or even exceeds human strength. If it nevertheless becomes reality, this is a clear sign that God Himself (the Holy Spirit) is acting in the people. The logic of incarnation is shown in the Biblical message as well as numerous 'signs of the times' in human history."

67   Schwager, *Jesus im Heilsdrama*, 243, talks about how love can be perverted into a kind of masochism; this is to be avoided.

Chapter 15
From Violence to Blessing

1   Richard Batsinduka, "Meeting Vincent's murderer," *For a Change*, October/November 2001.

2   Howard Zehr, *Changing Lenses: A New Focus for Crime and Justice* (Scottdale: Herald Press, 1990).

3   Gloria Neufeld Redekop, *The Work of Their Hands: Mennonite Women's Societies in Canada*. Studies in Women and Religion / Études sur les femmes et la religion, Vol. 2. (Waterloo, ON: Wilfrid Laurier University Press, 1996).

4   Joseph Jaworski, *Synchronicity: The Inner Path of Leadership* (San Francisco: Berrett-Koehler, 1998).

5   Freeman Dyson, *Weapons and Hope* (Toronto: Harper & Row, 1984), 4-5.

Epilogue
Reflections on September 11, 2001

1   Peter L. Bergen, *Holy War, Inc.: Inside the Secret World of Osama bin Laden* (New York: The Free Press, 2001), 75.

2   *Canadian Islamic Congress Electronic Bulletin*

3   Bergen, *Holy War, Inc.*, 52-53.

4   From Wahida Valiante's correspondence in response to this section.

5   Bergen, *Holy War, Inc.*, 99.

6   Ibid., 125.

Selected Bibliography

Adams, Rebecca. "Mothers, Metamorphs, Myth and Mimesis: A Creative Reassessment of Mimetic Desire." Unpublished paper presented at the COV&R Conference on "Violence and the Subject of Responsibility," Loyola University, June 2, 1995, later published as "Loving Mimesis and Girard's 'Scapegoat of the Text': A Creative Reassessment of Mimetic Desire." In Willard M. Swartley, ed., *Violence Renounced: René Girard, Biblical Studies, and Peacemaking*. Telford: Pandora Press, 2000, 277-307.

Alfred, Gerald. *Heeding the Voices of Our Ancestors: Kahnawake Mohawk Politics and the Rise of Native Nationalism*. Toronto: Oxford University Press, 1995. (To avoid confusion in tracking down Alfred's publications, note that his later work is listed under his original name, which is Taiaiake Alfred.)

Alfred, Taiaiake. *Peace, Power, Righteousness: An Indigenous Manifesto*. Don Mills: Oxford University Press, 1999.

Alison, James. *Raising Abel: The Recovery of Eschatological Imagination*. New York: Crossroad, 1996.

Appleby, R. Scott. *The Ambivalence of the Sacred: Religion, Violence, and Reconciliation*. Lanham: Rowan & Littlefield, 2000.

Asch, Michael. "Aboriginal Self-Government and Canadian Constitutional Identity: Building Reconciliation." *Ethnicity and Aboriginality*, 29-30.

Azar, Edward E. and John W. Burton, eds. *International Conflict Resolution: Theory and Practice*. Boulder: Lynne Rienner Publishers, 1986.

Bailie, Gil. *Violence Unveiled*. New York: Crossroad, 1995.

Baird, Robert M. and Stuart E. Rosenbaum, eds. *Bigotry, Prejudice and Hatred: Definitions, Causes and Solutions*. Buffalo: Prometheus Books, 1992.

Barstow, Anne Llewellyn, ed. *War's Dirty Secrets: Rape, Prostitution, and Other Crimes Against Women*. Cleveland: Pilgrim Press, 2000.

Basic Call to Consciousness. Mohawk Nation via Rooseveltown, NY: Akwesasne Notes, 1978.

Batsinduka, Richard. "Meeting Vincent's Murderer." In *For a Change*, October/November 2001.

Baumeister, Roy F. "Violent Pride: Do People Turn Violent Because of Self-Hate or Self-Love?" *Scientific American*, April 2001, 96-101.

Begley, Sharon. "Religion and the Brain." *Newsweek*, May 7, 2001, 50-57.

Bell-Fialkoff, Andrew. *Ethnic Cleansing*. New York: St. Martin's Griffin, 1999.

Bereciartu, Gurutz Jáuregui. *Decline of the Nation-State*, tr. William A. Douglas. Reno: University of Nevada Press, 1994.

Bergen, Peter L. *Holy War, Inc.: Inside the Secret World of Osama bin Laden*. New York: The Free Press, 2001.

Bohm, David. *On Dialogue*, edited by Lee Nichol. New York: Routledge, 1997.

Box, Steven. *Deviance, Reality and Society*. Toronto: Holt, Rinehart and Winston, 1981.

———. *Power, Crime and Mystification*. New York: Tavistock, 1983.

———. *Recession, Crime and Punishment*. London: MacMillan Education, 1987.

Branden, Nathaniel. *Pillars of Self Esteem*. New York: Bantam, 1995.

Brueggeman, Walter. *The Land: Place as Gift, Promise and Challenge in Biblical Faith*. Philadelphia: Fortress Press, 1977.

Burrell, David B. "René Girard: Violence and Sacrifice." *Cross Currents*, 28. Winter 1988-89: 447.

Burton, John W., ed. *Conflict: Human Needs Theory*. New York: St. Martin's Press, 1990.

———. *Conflict: Resolution and Provention*. New York: St. Martin's Press, 1990.

———. *Deviance, Terrorism and War*. Oxford: Martin Robertson, 1979.

———. *Resolving Deep-Rooted Conflicts*. Lanham: University Press of America, 1987.

Burton, John W. and Frank Dukes, eds. *Conflict: Readings in Management and Resolution*. New York: St. Martin's Press, 1990.

Capra, Fritjof, David Steindl-Rast and Thomas Matus. *Belonging to the Universe: Explorations on the Frontiers of Science and Spirituality*. San Francisco: HarperSanFrancisco, 1992.

Chanteur, Janine. *From War to Peace*, trans. Shirley Ann Weisz. Boulder: Westview Press, 1992.

Chay, Jongsuk. *Culture and International Relations*. New York: Praeger, 1990.

Ciaccia, John. *The Oka Crisis: A Mirror of the Soul*. Dorval: Maren Publications, 2000.

Cohen, Stephen and Herbert Kelman, "The Problem-Solving Workshop: A Social Psychological Contribution to the Resolution of International Conflicts." *Journal of Peace Research* XIII-2. 1976): 79-90.

Connor, Walker. *Ethnonationalism: The Quest for Understanding*. Princeton: Princeton University Press, 1994.

Cross, Ronald and Hélène Sévigny, *Lasagna: The Man Behind the Mask*. Vancouver: Talonbooks, 1994.

Crüsemann, Frank. "Dominion, Guilt, and Reconciliation: The Contribution of the Jacob Narrative in Genesis to Political Ethics," trans. Carl S. Ehrlich. *Semeia*, 66. 1994):67-77.

Csikszentmihalyi, Mihaly. *Creativity: Flow and the Psychology of Discovery and Invention*. New York: Harper Collins, 1996.

Cummings, George C.L. "Black Theology and Latin American Theology." In *New Visions for the Americas: Religious Engagement and Social Transformation*, ed. David Batstone. Minneapolis: Fortress, 1993, 215-229.

Dozier, Rush W., Jr. *Why We Hate: Understanding, Curbing, and Eliminating Hate in Ourselves and Our World*. New York: McGraw-Hill, 2002.

Dyson, Freeman. *Weapons and Hope*. Toronto: Harper & Row, 1984.

Eriksen, Thomas Hylland. "Ethnicity and Nationalism: Definitions and Critical Reflections." *Bulletin of Peace Proposals* Vol. 23-2, 1992.

Fisher, Roger, William Ury with Bruce Patton, ed., *Getting to YES: Negotiating Agreement Without Giving In*. New York: Penguin Books, 1991.

———. "Prenegotiation Problem-Solving Discussions: Enhancing the Potential for Successful Negotiation." *International Journal* XLIV. 1989): 467.

Fox, Matthew. *Original Blessing*. New York: Jeremy P. Tarcher/Putnam, 2000.

Fraser, Matthew. *Quebec Inc.: French-Canadian Entrepreneurs and the New Business Elite*. Toronto: Key Porter Books, 1987.

Fukuyama, Francis. *The End of History and the Last Man*. New York: Avon Books, 1993.

Funkenstein, David "The Physiology of Fear and Anger." *Scientific American*, 192. 1955, 78-80.

Gabriel-Doxtater, Brenda Katlatont and Arlette Kawanatatie Van Den Hende. *At the Woods' Edge*. Kanesatake Education Center, 1995.

Galtung, Johan. "International Development in Human Perspective." In *Conflict: Human Needs Theory*, ed. John Burton. New York: St. Martin's Press, 1990, 301-335

Girard, René. *Deceit, Desire, and the Novel: Self and Other in Literary Structure*. Baltimore: John Hopkins University Press, 1990. Originally published in French as *Mensonge romantique et vérité romanesque*.

———. *The Girard Reader*, James Williams, ed. New York: Crossroad, 2000.

———. *I See Satan Fall Like Lightning*. Maryknoll, NY/Ottawa: Orbis/Novalis, 2001. Originally published in French as *Je vois Satan tomber comme l'éclair*.

———. *Job: The Victim of His People*. Stanford: Stanford University Press, 1987. Originally published in French as *La route antique des hommes pervers*.

———. *Resurrection from the Underground: Feodor Dostoevsky*, ed. and trans. by James G. Williams. New York: Crossroad, 2000. Originally published in French as *Dostoievski: du double à l'unité*.

———. *The Scapegoat*. Baltimore: John Hopkins University Press, 1989. Originally published in French as *Le bouc émissaire*.

———. *A Theater of Envy: William Shakespeare*. Leominster (Herefordshire) and New Malden, U.K.: Gracewing and Inigo Enterprises: 2000. Originally published in French as *Shakespeare: Les feux de l'envie*.

———. *Things Hidden Since the Foundation of the World*. Stanford: Stanford University Press, 1987. Originally published in French as *Des choses cachées dupuis la fondation du monde*.

———. *"To Double Business Bound": Essays on Literature, Mimesis, and Anthropology*. Baltimore: John Hopkins University Press, 1992.

———. *Violence and the Sacred*. Baltimore: John Hopkins University Press, 1988. Originally published in French as *La violence et le sacré*.

Gramsci, Antonio. *The Modern Prince and Other Writings*. New York: International Publishers, 1968.

Gurr, Ted Robert. "Communal Conflicts and Global Security." *Current History* Vol. 94. (May 1995):212.

Gustafson, James. *Can Ethics Be Christian?* Chicago: University of Chicago Press, 1975.

Hamerton-Kelley, Robert G. *Sacred Violence: Paul's Hermeneutic of the Cross*. Minneapolis: Fortress, 1992.

Haworth, Lawrence. *Autonomy: An Essay in Philosophical Psychology and Ethics*. New Haven: Yale University Press, 1986.

Helmick, Raymond G., S.J., and Rodney L. Petersen, eds. *Forgiveness and Reconciliation: Religion, Public Policy and Conflict Transformation*. Philadelphia: Templeton Foundation Press, 2001.

Horowitz, Donald L. *Ethnic Groups in Conflict*. Berkeley: University of California Press, 1985.

Hull, Robert. "Kanienkehaka Chronology: The Mohawk Crisis in Quebec and its Aftermath, July to December 1990." *The Conrad Grebel Review*, 9-2 (Spring 1991): 103-114

Huntington, Samuel P. *The Clash of Civilizations and the Remaking of World Order*. New York: Touchstone, 1996.

Hyun-Kyung, Chung. "Your Comfort Versus My Death: Korean Comfort Women." In *War's Dirty Secrets: Rape, Prostitution and Other Crimes Against Humanity*. Cleveland: Pilgrim Press, 2000, 13-25.

Ignatieff, Michael. *Blood and Belonging: Journeys into the New Nationalism*. Toronto: Penguin Books, 1994.

Jaworski, Joseph. *Synchronicity: The Inner Path of Leadership*. San Francisco: Berrett-Koehler, 1998.

Jayawickrama, Nihal. *The Right of Self-Determination*, The Report of the Martin Ennals Symposium of Self-Determination, a Satellite Conference for the 1992 World Conference on Human Rights, co-sponsored by the College of Law, University of Saskatchewan and International Alert.

Johnston, Douglas and Cynthia Sampson, eds. *Religion: The Missing Dimension of Statecraft*. New York: Oxford Univesity Press, 1994.

Juergensmeyer, Mark. *Terror in the Mind of God: The Global Rise of Religious Violence*. Berkeley: University of California Press, 2001.

Julius, Demetrios A., Joseph V. Montville and Vamik D. Volkan, eds. *The Psychodynamics of International Relationships*. Lexington & Toronto: Lexington Books, 1990.

Kaptein, Roel, with the co-operation of Duncan Morrow. *On the Way to Freedom*. Dublin: The Columba Press, 1993.

Kegley, Charles W. "Neo-Idealism: A Practical Matter." *Ethics and International Affairs* 2 (1988):183

Kriesberg, Louis, Terrell A. Northrup and Stuart J. Thorson, eds. *Intractable Conflicts and Their Transformation*. Syracuse: Syracuse University Press, 1989.

Kuper, L. "The Prevention of Genocide: Cultural and Structural Indicators of Genocidal Threat." *Ethnic and Racial Studies*, 12-2, 1989.

Lakoff, George and Mark Johnson, *Metaphors We Live By*. Chicago: University of Chicago Press, 1981.

Lederach, John Paul. "Five Qualities of Practice in Support of Reconciliation Processes." In Raymond G. Helmick, S.J. and Rodney L. Petersen, eds. *Forgiveness and Reconciliation: Religion, Public Policy and Conflict Transformation*. Philadelphia: Templeton Foundation Press, 2001, 183-194.

Levin, Michael D. ed. *Ethnicity and Aboriginality: Case Studies in Ethnonationalism*. Toronto: University of Toronto Press, 1993.

Levinas, Emmanuel. *Totality and Infinity: An Essay on Exteriority*, trans. Alphonso Lingis. Pittsburgh: Duquesne University Press, 1969.

Lewis, Thomas, Fari Amini and Richard Lannon, *A General Theory of Love*. New York: Random House, 2000.

Linger, Daniel T. "The Hegemony of Discontent." *American Ethnologist* 20(1):3-24, 4.

Lohrenz, Konrad. *On Aggression*. Marjorie Kerr Wilson, trans.. New York: Harcourt, Brace and World, 1966. Original *Das Sogenannte Böse: Zur aturgeschichte der Aggression*, 1963.

Macintyre, Alasdair. *After Virtue: A Study in Moral Theory*. Notre Dame: University of Notre Dame Press, 1981.

MacKinnon, Catharine. "Crimes of War, Crimes of Peace." In *On Human Rights: The Oxford Amnesty Lectures*, ed. Stephen Shute and Susan Hurley. New York: Harper Collins Basic Books, 1993, 89.

MacLaine, Craig and Michael S. Baxendale. *This Land Is Our Land: The Mohawk Revolt at Oka*. Montreal: Optimum, 1990.

Manchester, William. *The Arms of Krupp, 1587–1968*. Boston: Little, Brown and Co., 1968.

Martens, Elmer. *God's Design: A Focus on Old Testament Theology*. Grand Rapids: Baker Book House, 1986 [1981].

Mercogliano, Chris and Kim Debus, "The Heart's Intelligence: An Interview with Joseph Chilton Pearce." *In Touch*, Autumn, 2001, 11.

Metz, Kristin. "Passionate Differences: A Working Model for Cross-cultural Communication." *Journal of Feminist Studies in Religion*. 6-1, Spring, 1990, 131-151.

Millar, J.R. "Great White Father Knows Best: Oka and the Land Claims Process." *Native Studies Review*, Vol. 7, No. 1, 36.

Mitchem, Stephanie Y. "Womanists and (Unfinished) Constructions of Salvation." *Journal of Feminist Studies in Religion,* 17-1, Spring 2001.

Montville, Joseph V., ed. *Conflict and Peacemaking in Multiethnic Societies*. Lexington: Lexington Books, 1990.

Morgan, Robin. *The Demon Lover: The Roots of Terrorism*. Toronto: Penguin, 1989.

Morgenthau, Hans and Kenneth W. Thompson, *Politics Among Nations: The Struggle for Power and Peace*. New York: Alfred A. Knopf, 1985.

Munk, Linda. "The Design of Violence." *Journal of Literature & Theology*, 4-3. November 1990): 259-60.

Nardin, Terry and David R. Mapel, eds. *Traditions of International Ethics*. Cambridge: Cambridge University Press, 1992, 62.

Nash, Manning. *The Cauldron of Ethnicity in the Modern World*. Chicago: University of Chicago Press, 1988.

Neuhauser, Peg. *Tribal Warfare in Organizations*. Cambridge: Ballinger Publishing Company, 1988.

Niehoff, Debra. *The Biology of Violence*. New York: The Free Press, 1999.

North, Robert. "Violence and the Bible: The Girard Connection." *Catholic Biblical Quarterly*, 47-1. 1985, 7.

Osgood, Charles E. *Perspective in Foreign Policy*. Palo Alto: Pacific Books, 1966.

Parkes, Colin Murray and Joan Stevenson-Hinde, eds., *The Place of Attachment in Human Behavior*. New York: Basic Books, 1982.

Pearsall, Paul. *The Heart's Code: Tapping the Wisdom and Power of Our Heart Energy*. New York: Broadway Books, 1998.

People Building Peace: 35 Inspiring Stories from Around the World, A publication of the European Centre for Conflict Prevention, in co-operation with the International Fellowship of Reconciliation. IFOR) and the Coexistence Initiative of the State of the World Forum, 1999.

Pert, Candace. *Molecules of Emotion*. New York: Touchstone, 1997.

Philpot, Robin. *Oka: dernier alibi du Canada anglais*. Montreal: VLB éditeur, 1991.

Polanyi, Michael. *Personal Knowledge: Towards a Post-Critical Philosophy*. New York: Harper and Row, 1958; Harper Torchbook edition, 1964.

Rapoport, Anatol. *Peace: An Idea Whose Time Has Come*. Ann Arbor, MI: The University of Michigan Press, 1992.

Rebel, Hermann. "Cultural Hegemony and Class Experience: A Critical Reading of Recent Ethnological-Historical Approaches." *American Ethnologist* 16-1, Feb. 1989, 122.

Redekop, Gloria Neufeld. "Survival in War and Famine: The Experience of Mennonite Children and Women in the Ukraine. 1917–1925." Presented at "The Quiet in the Land? Women of Anabaptist Traditions in Historical Perspective." June 8-11, 1995, Millersville University, Millersville, Pennsylvania.

–– ––. *The Work of Their Hands: Mennonite Women's Societies in Canada*. Studies in Women and Religion / Études sur les femmes et la religion, Vol. 2.. Waterloo, ON: Wilfrid Laurier University Press, 1996.

Redekop, Vern Neufeld. "The Centrality of Torah as Ethical Projection for the Exodus." *Contagion: Journal of Violence, Mimesis, and Culture* 2, Spring, 1995.

———. *A Life for a Life? The Death Penalty on Trial*. Scottdale: Herald Press, 1990.

———. "Moses' Perspective on War and Peace Based on the Book of Deuteronomy." Unpublished Senior Seminar Paper, 1982, 22, n.12.

———. "Response to *The Challenge of Peace: God's Promise and Our Response*." Unpublished paper prepared for Mr. Geoffrey Pearson, Executive Director, Canadian Institute for International Peace and Security, August 20, 1985.

———. "The Role of Deep-rooted Conflict and Its Resolution in Regional Economic Development." Unpublished, 1992.

———. *Scapegoats, the Bible and Criminal Justice: Interacting with René Girard*. Akron, PA: Mennonite Central Committee, 1993.

Ricoeur, Paul. "L'idéologie et l'utopie: deux expressions de l'imaginaire sociale." *Autres Temps*, No. 2, Été 1984.

———. *Oneself as Another*. Chicago: University of Chicago Press, 1992.

———. *Time and Narrative*, Vol. 1, trans. Kathleen McLaughlin and David Pellauer. Chicago: University of Chicago Press, 1984.

Rogers, Rita R. "Intergenerational Transmission of Historical Enmity." In *The Psychodynamics of International Relationships*, ed. Vamik D. Volkan, Demetrios A. Julius, and Joseph V. Montville. Lexington & Toronto: Lexington Books, 1990, 91-96.

Ross, Rupert. *Returning to the Teachings*. Toronto: Penguin Books, 1996.

Ryan, Stephen. *Ethnic Conflict and International Relations*. Brookfield: Dartmouth, 1990.

Schreiter, Robert J. *Constructing Local Theologies*. Maryknoll: Orbis, 1986.

Schwager, Raymund, S.J., "Christ's Death and the Prophetic Critique of Sacrifice." *Semeia*, 33, (1985): 118.

———. *Must There Be Scapegoats? Violence and Redemption in the Bible*. Leominster and New York: Gracewing and Crossroad, 2000.

———. "Suffering, Victims, and Poetic Inspiration." *Contagion: Journal of Violence, Mimesis, and Culture*, Volume 1, 1994, 66.

———. "The Theology of the Wrath of God." In *Violence and Truth*, ed. Paul Dumouchel. Stanford: Stanford University Press, 1988, 44-52.

———. *Jesus im Heilsdrama: Entwurf einer biblischen Erlosüngslehre*. Innsbruck: Tyrolia-Verlag, 1990. Published in English under the title *Jesus in the Drama of Salvation: Toward a Biblical Doctrine of Redemption* (New York: Crossroad, 1999).

——— et al., "Dramatic Theology as a Research Program." Unpublished paper presented at the Colloquium on Violence and Religion at Stanford University, June, 1996, 1.

Shenk, Ellen. *Outdoor Careers: Exploring Occupations in Outdoor Fields*, 2nd ed.. Mechanicsburg, PA: Stackpole Books, 2000, 20.

Sites, Paul. *Control: The Basis of Social Order*. New York: Dunellen, 1973.

Staub, Ervin. *Roots of Evil: The Origins of Genocide and Other Group Violence*. Cambridge: Cambridge University Press, [1989], 1992.

Steele, David. "Theological Assessment of Principled Negotiation as a Role Model for Church Involvement in the Mediation of International Conflict." Unpublished, 1990.

Swartley, Willard M., ed. *Violence Renounced: René Girard, Biblical Studies, and Peacemaking*. Telford: Pandora Press, 2000.

Taylor, Donald M. and Lise Dubé. "Two Faces of Identity: The 'I' and the 'We'." *Journal of Social Issues*, 42-2. (1986): 81-82

Tutu, Desmond M. *No Future Without Forgiveness*. Toronto: Doubleday, 1999.

van den Berghe, Pierre L. "The Biology of Nepotism." In *Bigotry, Prejudice and Hatred: Definitions, Causes & Solutions*, ed. Robert M. Baird and Stuart E. Rosenbaum. Buffalo: Prometheus Books, 1992, 133-134.

Vanier, Jean. *Becoming Human*. Toronto: Anansi, 1998.

Volf, Miroslav. "Exclusion and Embrace: Theological Reflections in the Wake of 'Ethnic Cleansing,'" presented at a joint conference of the Gesellschaft für evangelische Theologie and Arbeitskreis für Evangelische theologie in Potsdam, Germany, February 15-17, 1993, 10.

— — —. *Exclusion or Embrace: A Theological Exploration of Identity, Otherness, and Reconciliation*. Nashville: Abingdon Press, 1996.

Volkan, Vamik D. *Blood Lines: From Ethnic Pride to Ethnic Terrorism*. Boulder: Westview, 1998.

Wallace, Mark I. and Theophus H. Smith, eds. *Curing Violence*. Sonoma: Polebridge Press, 1994.

West, Cornel. *Prophesy Deliverance! An Afro-American Revolutionary Christianity*. Philadelphia: Westminster Press, 1983.

Wieser, Thomas. "Community: Its Unity, Diversity and Universality." *Semeia*, 33 (1985) 88

Wilber, Ken. *A Brief History of Everything*. Boston: Shambhala, 2000.

Wilber, Ken. *A Theory of Everything: An Integral Vision for Business, Politics, Science and Spirituality*. Boston: Shambhala, 2001.

Williams, James. *The Bible, Violence and the Sacred: Liberation from the Myth of Sanctioned Violence*. New York: HarperCollins, 1991.

Wink, Walter. *Engaging the Powers: Discernment and Resistance in a World of Domination*. Minneapolis: Fortress Press, 1992.

Winkler, Daryold Corbiere. "Forgiveness and Reconciliation: Lessons from Canada's First Nations." In *The Challenge of Forgiveness*, eds. Augustine Meier and Peter VanKatwyk. Ottawa: Novalis, 2001, 51.

York, Geoffrey and Loreen Pindera. *People of the Pines: The Warriors and the Legacy of Oka*. Toronto: Little, Brown and Company (Canada), 1991.

Young, Clifford. "The Dialectics of Cultural Pluralism: Concept and Reality." In *The Rising Tide of Cultural Pluralism*, ed. Crawford Young. Madison: University of Wisconsin Press, 1993. 4-19.

Zehr, Howard. *Changing Lenses: A New Focus for Crime and Justice*. Scottdale: Herald Press, 1990.

Index

A

B